Disruptive Innovation and Emerging Technologies for Business Excellence in the Service Sector

Vipin Nadda
University of Sunderland, London, UK

Pankaj Tyagi
Chandigarh University, India

Malini Singh
Amity University, India

Priyanka Tyagi
Chandigarh University, India

A volume in the Advances in Marketing, Customer Relationship Management, and E-Services (AMCRMES) Book Series

IGI Global
PUBLISHER of TIMELY KNOWLEDGE

Published in the United States of America by
IGI Global
Business Science Reference (an imprint of IGI Global)
701 E. Chocolate Avenue
Hershey PA, USA 17033
Tel: 717-533-8845
Fax: 717-533-8661
E-mail: cust@igi-global.com
Web site: http://www.igi-global.com

Library of Congress Cataloging-in-Publication Data

Names: Nadda, Vipin, 1970- editor. | Tyagi, Pankaj Kumar, 1979- editor. | Singh, Malini, 1976- editor. | Tyagi, Priyanka, 1981- editor.
Title: Disruptive innovation and emerging technologies for business excellence in the service sector / Vipin Nadda, Pankaj Kumar Tyagi, Malini Singh, and Priyanka Tyagi, editors.
Description: Hershey, PA : Business Science Reference, 2021. | Includes bibliographical references and index. | Summary: "The book provides an in-depth understanding of various dimensions of scope of disruptive business innovation, to help readers understand the contributions and implications of disruptive technology, and aid in trend forecasting, design thinking and its applications, and the role of data mining & predictive analysis in today's business world"-- Provided by publisher.
Identifiers: LCCN 2021030092 | ISBN 9781799891949 (hardcover) | ISBN 9781799891956 (paperback) | ISBN 9781799891963 (ebook)
Subjects: LCSH: Service industries. | Information technology--Management. | Organizational effectiveness.
Classification: LCC HD9980.5 .D527 2021 | DDC 658--dc23
LC record available at https://lccn.loc.gov/2021030092

This book is published in the IGI Global book series Advances in Marketing, Customer Relationship Management, and E-Services (AMCRMES) (ISSN: 2327-5502; eISSN: 2327-5529)

British Cataloguing in Publication Data
A Cataloguing in Publication record for this book is available from the British Library.

Advances in Marketing, Customer Relationship Management, and E-Services (AMCRMES) Book Series

ISSN:2327-5502
EISSN:2327-5529

MISSION

Business processes, services, and communications are important factors in the management of good customer relationship, which is the foundation of any well organized business. Technology continues to play a vital role in the organization and automation of business processes for marketing, sales, and customer service. These features aid in the attraction of new clients and maintaining existing relationships

The Advances in Marketing, Customer Relationship Management, and E-Services (AMCRMES) Book Series

addresses success factors for customer relationship management, marketing, and electronic services and its performance outcomes. This collection of reference source covers aspects of consumer behavior and marketing business strategies aiming towards researchers, scholars, and practitioners in the fields of marketing management.

COVERAGE

- Mobile CRM
- B2B marketing
- Database marketing
- Mobile Services
- CRM in financial services
- Relationship Marketing
- Text Mining and Marketing
- Cases on Electronic Services
- Legal Considerations in E-Marketing
- E-Service Innovation

The Advances in Marketing, Customer Relationship Management, and E-Services (AMCRMES) Book Series (ISSN 2327-5502) is published by IGI Global, 701 E. Chocolate Avenue, Hershey, PA 17033-1240, USA, www.igi-global.com. This series is composed of titles available for purchase individually; each title is edited to be contextually exclusive from any other title within the series. For pricing and ordering information please visit http://www.igi-global.com/book-series/advances-marketing-customer-relationship-management/37150. Postmaster: Send all address changes to above address.

Titles in this Series

For a list of additional titles in this series, please visit:
www.igi-global.com/book-series/advances-marketing-customer-relationship-management/37150

Cases on Academic Program Redesign for Greater Racial and Social Justice
Ebony Cain-Sanschagrin (Pepperdine University, USA) Robert A. Filback (University of Southern California, USA) and Jenifer Crawford (University of Southern California, USA)
Information Science Reference • © 2022 • 361pp • H/C (ISBN: 9781799884637) • US $195.00

Adoption and Implementation of AI in Customer Relationship Management
Surabhi Singh (IMS Ghaziabad, India)
Business Science Reference • © 2022 • 272pp • H/C (ISBN: 9781799879596) • US $215.00

Handbook of Research on IoT, Digital Transformation, and the Future of Global Marketing
Hatem El-Gohary (College of Business and Economics, Qatar University, Qatar) David Edwards (Birmingham City University, UK) and Mohamed Slim Ben Mimoun (Qatar University, Qatar)
Business Science Reference • © 2021 • 471pp • H/C (ISBN: 9781799871927) • US $295.00

Management and Marketing for Improved Competitiveness and Performance in the Healthcare Sector
José Duarte Santos (Polytechnic Institute of Gaya, Portugal) and Inês Veiga Pereira (ISCAP, Polytechnic Institute of Porto, Portugal)
Business Science Reference • © 2021 • 355pp • H/C (ISBN: 9781799872634) • US $225.00

Advanced Digital Marketing Strategies in a Data-Driven Era
Jose Ramon Saura (Rey Juan Carlos University, Spain)
Business Science Reference • © 2021 • 342pp • H/C (ISBN: 9781799880035) • US $225.00

Blockchain Technology and Applications for Digital Marketing
Rohit Bansal (Department of Management Studies, Vaish College of Engineering, Rohtak, India) Pacha Malyadri (ICSSR, Center for Economic and Social Studies, India) Amandeep Singh (Chitkara Business School, Chitkara University, Punjab, India) and Asif Pervez (Jamia Millia Islamia University, India)
Business Science Reference • © 2021 • 329pp • H/C (ISBN: 9781799880813) • US $225.00

IGI Global
PUBLISHER of TIMELY KNOWLEDGE

701 East Chocolate Avenue, Hershey, PA 17033, USA
Tel: 717-533-8845 x100 • Fax: 717-533-8661
E-Mail: cust@igi-global.com • www.igi-global.com

Table of Contents

Detailed Table of Contents

recent findings from this field show that the hospitality sector has already begun to adopt innovations gradually to respond to consumer behavior transition driven by on-demand services. Finally, the author concludes with the assertion that disruptive innovations are pivotal in the survival and sustenance of the hospitality businesses.

Firms can be seen as value facilitators, offering various types of services for consumer consumption, as well as value-generating methods, while following a service viewpoint. It has been proposed that a company's relationships with consumers are used to influence value generation processes. Different experiences influence the form and kinds of meaning that consumers interpret in terms of interactive, relativistic, preferential, or perception beliefs, as well as self- and other-oriented values, in these systems. The aim is to make the procedure easier by grouping alternative options into three main explanatory stages of means. Furthermore, the classification's aim was to include an exhaustive classification when none existed in the marketing literature. The three levels are paradoxically both connected to and independent of each other, according to a general observation made here. They can appear concurrently or independently of one another, but they can also be defined separately.

Online travel agencies (OTAs) are online travel platforms like Expedia.Com, Make My Trip, Booking.com, and Travelzoo, etc., which sell travel-related products and services such as hotels, flights, travel packages, rentals, amenities, and activities to customers. OTAs work as an intermediary between suppliers and customers and help both in selling and buying the products and services. Over the period, due to technological advancement, OTAs have captured an average of 40% to 50% of the total global travel market. Users of online travel agencies are also increasing significantly as they are getting numerous benefits like saving of time and money, cheapest fares, best travel options and deals, customize packages, and superior value propositions. The present study is empirical in nature and has measured the perception and satisfaction level of uses towards various products and services of online travel agencies (OTAs).

Geospatial technology refers to data and information that identifies the location of specific features on the Earth's surface. The term refers to collective data in which the technologies involved have geographic or locational dimensions. Geospatial information is attached to any information related to space (i.e., locational component [latitude and longitude]). When location information is added to any dataset, it is transformed into geospatial data. For example, if the population of a region's various districts is stored in a spreadsheet, it is not spatial. If a population map is created for this region, it becomes geospatial data. Geospatial technology is widely used in tourism and has changed the travel landscape. Tourism and hospitality brands use technology to identify the geospatial context and improve customer engagement and help Tourists to plan holiday trips.

We are using technology for e-learning platforms, blended platforms, and formal education platforms. Formal education is a structured and systematic form of learning. For formal education, we can say face-to-face or on-campus education. Formal education is classroom based, meaning everything a student learns comes from books and other educational materials with the sole purpose of educating students. Internet gives us the option to meet around the world. Internet distance education is a natural consequence of industrial transformations from a manufacturing economy, in which standard educational practices are based, to an information economy, in which greater autonomy, collaboration, flexibility, and a project orientation to work are the norm. The internet did not cause changes in education, but rather enabled educators to meet new demands for instructional practices and outcomes and adapt to a rapidly changing economic and social environment that was beginning to outpace the academy.

This study aims to analyze the impact of business sophistication on marketing knowledge. The research combines bibliometric literature review, preferred reporting items for systematic and meta-analyses (PRISMA), and empirical approach to collect extensive sample data GII (Global Innovation Index) of 50 countries' business sophistication technologic input-output framework. Furthermore, the research uses multiple linear regression analysis to test the proposed hypotheses. Business sophistication impacts positively on marketing knowledge. However, each technological input pillar behaves differently. This study derives managerial strategies and policies from marketing knowledge.

The purpose of this study is to determine the effect of organizational innovation capabilities of hotel businesses on mobile applications. In line with this purpose, data were collected with a survey technique in March 2021 with 225 managers working in hotels with tourism operation licenses in the Cappadocia region. In the research, Pearson correlation analysis was used to determine the relationship between organizational innovation capabilities of hotel businesses and mobile applications use. Simple regression analysis was performed to determine the impact of organizational innovation on mobile applications. In this study conducted in the Cappadocia region, it was determined that the organizational innovation capabilities of hotel businesses affect the use of mobile applications. Therefore, these results show that the use of mobile applications by hotel businesses varies depending on their organizational innovation capabilities.

Performance management is a valuable tool for any organization to achieve its strategic objectives and align its resources. It is identified to lead a productive workforce and improves employee engagement. However, due to the disruption of technology in the various dimensions of the environment, HRM systems have undergone many changes. Organizations have adapted to the technological outburst and synchronized their activity around it. Present times observe a heavy use of technology in the day-to-day HR functions. Performance management has also been hugely impacted by the manifestation of technology, where many organizations have adopted the use of technology for the same. The stance of the management on the

Preface

Emerging technologies are innovative technologies that have been recently developed, are under development or will be developed within the next few years. Disruptive technologies, however, are innovations that drastically change the way organizations and industries function. They force businesses to alter the way they manage operations, so they do not lose market shares or fall into irrelevancy.

Innovation is a human-centered perspective and process. Innovation can be intangible, as opposed to technology, which is tangible. You can even apply the innovation process to your everyday life. Technology can be used to implement innovation, but the technology itself doesn't produce innovation.

The book *Disruptive Innovation and Emerging Technologies for Business Excellence in the Service Sector* is an attempt to understand the role of innovation and technology in service sector. The book discusses different aspects of innovation and technology being used or are expected to be used in coming future which will help service sector to excel in business

The key areas discussed in the books are:

- **Impact of Mobile Technology to Enhance the Customer Service Experience in SME Hotels**

This chapter has analysed the impact of mobile technology to enhance the customer service experience in the SME hotel sector. Most of the hotels nowadays use their mobile enabled website, and third-party mobile platforms for supporting customers' activities including booking and payment. They offer Wi-Fi services to their customers during their stay. Mobile technology enabled applications has helped their customers to make online hotel bookings easier and more convenient as it helps customers to book hotel rooms from any geographical location with no hassle by eliminating tradition communication needs and reducing time needed for booking and check in.

- **Disruptive Innovations: A Mechanism for Achieving Business Distinction in the Hospitality Industry**

The significant competitive environment around the hospitality industry triggers the exploration of novel ways and elements of coherent performance. Although disruptive innovations in the hospitality industry are complex, it provides compelling opportunities. Moreover, its emergence cannot be bestowed upon the current pandemic, since it is as old as business itself. The aim of the current chapter is to capture the role of disruptive innovation in enabling the hospitality industry to engineer business excellence. Also, the chapter attempts to provide insights into the potential disruptions that will rule the hospitality industry in the future. The recent findings from this field show that the hospitality sector has already begun to adopt innovations gradually to respond to consumer behavior transition driven by on-demand services. Finally, the author concludes with the assertion that disruptive innovations are pivotal in the survival and sustenance of the hospitality businesses.

- **Customer Perception and Brand Image Through Sensory Marketing**

Firms can be seen as value facilitators, offering various types of services for consumer consumption, as well as value-generating methods, while following a service viewpoint. It has been proposed that a company's relationships with consumers are used to influence value generation processes. Different experiences influence the form and kinds of meaning that consumers interpret in terms of interactive, relativistic, preferential, or perception beliefs, as well as self- and other-oriented values, in these systems. The aim is to make the procedure easier by grouping alternative options into three main explanatory stages of means. Furthermore, the classification's aim was to include an exhaustive classification when none existed in the marketing literature. The three levels are paradoxically both connected to and independent of each other, according to a general observation made here. They can appear concurrently or independently of one another, but they can also be defined separately.

- **Evaluation of E-Service Satisfaction Among Online Travel Agency (OTA) Users**

Online travel agencies (OTAs) are online travel platforms like Expedia.Com, Make My Trip, Booking.com, and Travelzoo, etc., which sells travel related products and services such as hotels, flights, travel packages, rentals, amenities, and activities to customers. OTAs work as an intermediary between suppliers and customers and help both in selling and buying the products and services. Over the period, due to technological advancement, OTAs have captured on an average 40% to 50% of the total global travel market. Users of online travel agencies are also increasing significantly as they are getting numerous benefits like saving of time and money, cheapest fares, best travel options and deals, customize packages and superior value propositions etc. The present study is empirical in nature and has measured the perception and satisfaction level of uses towards various products and services of online travel agencies (OTAs).

- **Geospatial Application in Tourism Study on Geoportal as Expedient Tool for Holiday Trip Planning**

Geospatial Technology refers to data and information that identifies the location of specific features on the earth's surface. The term refers to collective data in which the technologies involved have geographic or locational dimensions. Geospatial information is attached to any information related to space, i.e., locational component (latitude and longitude). When location information is added to any dataset, it is transformed into geospatial data. For example, if the population of a region's various districts is stored in a spreadsheet, it is not spatial. If a population map is created for this region, it becomes geospatial data. Geospatial technology is widely used in tourism and has changed the travel landscape. Tourism and hospitality brands use technology to identify the geospatial context and improve customer engagement and help Tourist to plan Holiday trips.

- **Role of Technology for Formal Education in Bangladesh: Formal Education**

Education process with technology. We are using technology for e-learning platform, blended platform and formal education platform. Formal education is a structured and systematic form of learning. Formal education we can say face to face or on campus education. Formal education is classroom based, meaning everything a student learns comes books and other educational materials with the sole purpose of educating students. Internet give us option to meet around the world people to sit at home, for formal education technology is very importance. Internet distance education is a natural consequence of find siècle industrial transformations from a manufacturing economy, in which standard educational practices are based, to an information economy, in which greater autonomy, collaboration, flexibility and a project orientation to work are the norm. The Internet did not cause changes in education, but rather enabled educators to meet new demands for instructional practices and outcomes and adapt to a rapidly changing economic and social environment that was beginning to outpace the academy.

- **The Impact of Business Sophistication on Marketing Knowledge**

This study has analysed the impact of business sophistication on marketing knowledge. The research combines bibliometric literature review, Preferred Reporting Items for Systematic and Meta-Analyses (PRISMA) and empirical approach to collect extensive sample data GII (Global Innovation Index) of 50 countries' business sophistication technologic input-output framework. Furthermore, the research uses multiple linear regression analysis to tests the proposed hypotheses. Business sophistication impacts positively on marketing knowledge. However, each technological input pillar behaves differently. This study derives managerial strategies and policies from marketing knowledge.

- **The Relationship Between Organizational Innovation and Mobile Applications in Hotel Businesses: Organizational Innovation**

This study determines the effect of organizational innovation capabilities of hotel businesses on mobile applications. In line with this purpose, data were collected with a survey technique in March 2021 with 225 managers working in hotels with tourism operation licenses in the Cappadocia region. In the research, Pearson correlation analysis was used to determine the relationship between organizational innovation capabilities of hotel businesses and mobile applications use; Simple regression analysis was performed to determine the impact of organizational innovation on mobile applications. In this study conducted in the Cappadocia region, it was determined that the organizational innovation capabilities of hotel businesses affect the use of mobile applications. Therefore, these results show that the use of mobile applications by hotel businesses varies depending on their organizational innovation capabilities.

- **Employee Perception on the Effectiveness of Digitalized Performance Management System**

Performance management is a valuable tool for any organization to achieve its strategic objectives and align its resources. It is identified to lead a productive workforce and improves employee engagement. However, due to the disruption of technology in the various dimensions of the environment HRM systems have undergone many changes. Organizations have adapted to the technological outburst and synchronized their activity around it. Present times observe a heavy use of technology in the day-to-day HR functions. Performance Management has also been hugely impacted by the manifestation of technology, where many organizations have adopted the use of technology for the same. The stance of the management on the use of technology for Performance Management is often deliberated upon hence the outlook of employees on the use of technology for Performance management has been unclear. For this chapter, we consider the employees in the education sector and their perception of the effectiveness of the use of technology/software for Performance Management based on different parameters.

- **Digital Technologies and Intangible Cultural Heritage of the Rural Destination**

Rural tourism continues to evolve toward an experience economy. Along with rural tourism activities, travelers often enjoy intangible heritage as part of their cultural tourism experience. Digital technologies could aid in the development of online preservation, learning tool, and a set of guidelines based on intangible cultural heritage to assist small rural businesses in designing and promoting sustainable tourist products. The digital revolution has the potential to foster mutual learning among tour operators, tourists, and host communities, in addition to boosting access to cultural material and making it publicly available. However, there is a lack of digital technology in creating a favorable environment to promote the inheritance and enhancement of the value of intangible cultural heritage through rural tourism development. Moreover, the digital optimization of intangible cultural heritage and rural tourism development needs special attention. The chapter provides insights on digitalizing intangible cultural heritage and rural tourism for sustainable destination development.

- **Mobile Technology: Simplifying Tourism Business Operations and Facilitating Tourists**

Tourism industry is very dynamic and tourism businesses have witnessed drastic change in their operations since the inception and growth of technology. Mobile technology is one of the emerging segments which is facilitating tourism businesses on large scale. It saves time, effort, money and also provides ease, convenience & comfort. Mobile technology has enhanced tourism business operations and helps the tourism businesses in guided tours, navigation, reservation, payment, information search, content creation, product development, getting feedback, digital marketing etc. Mobile technology has also facilitated tourists for different purposes. It has made travelling convenient, easy and safe for tourists. Adoption of mobile technology is bound to grow in future for tourism businesses as well as for more tourists. The present study investigates the role of mobile technology for tourists and for various tourism related business organizations. With the help of review of literature, the study aims to highlight its importance.

- **Sustainability in the Gig Economy: An Indian Perspective**

A gig economy is a free market structure in which temporary positions are widespread and organizations employ independent workers for short-term commitments. The gig economy is fragmented and spans a wide diversity of workers like independent contributors, freelancers, self-employed, and part-time workers. The study highlights the major factors which influence the gig economy. The chapter discusses the same from every stakeholder's perspective e.g.: employers/organizations, gig workers, customers, and economy. The study explores the various common factors such as globalization, digitalization, and technological change, financial pressures, and emerging competition including different other factors about different stakeholders who are influencing the gig economy which is further propelling the entry of the next generation of workers in this system. The current scenario of coronavirus pandemic crisis has made survival even harder for gig workers. The chapter discusses the challenges from different aspects of all stakeholders with due consideration of industry 4.0 in detail.

The book aims to help students perusing Management courses in different service sector. For the faculties, it will act as a tool to guide the students and expose them to different Innovative and Technological practices. The book is also beneficial for service sector industries for improving their practices. For scholars the book opens new areas of research and further study

Pankaj Tyagi

Chapter 1
Impact of Mobile Technology to Enhance the Customer Service Experience in SME Hotels

Sajan Narayanan Chithradevi
University of Sunderland, London, UK

Vipin Nadda
https://orcid.org/0000-0002-2970-3709
University of Sunderland, London, UK

ABSTRACT

The aim of the chapter is to analyze the impact of mobile technology to enhance the customer service experience in the SME hotel sector. Most of the hotels use their mobile-enabled websites and third-party mobile platforms for supporting customer activities including booking and payment. They offer Wi-Fi services to their customers during their stay. Mobile technology-enabled applications have helped their customers to make online hotel bookings more easy and convenient as it helps customers to book hotel rooms from any geographical location with no hassle by eliminating tradition communication needs and reducing the time needed for booking and check in.

INTRODUCTION

According to Kotler and Keller (2012), In the highly customer driven global market,

DOI: 10.4018/978-1-7998-9194-9.ch001

customers are the major sources of organisational success as high level customer satisfaction leads to organisation success whereas poor level of customer satisfaction. For that reason, it is necessary for every organisation to achieve high level of customer satisfaction to be successful in competitive business environment. However, customer satisfaction is dependent in different issues (Fornell et al, 2010). Customer service experience is a significant determinant for customer satisfaction because if an organisation can provide better customer service experiences continuously to the customers, the organisation enjoys high level of customer satisfaction whereas if an organisation cannot provide better customer service experiences continuously to the customers, the organisation suffers from level of customer satisfaction (Tate and White, 2008). In modern business world, mobile technology is a significant strategic tool for organisations to enhance customer service experiences as it enables the organisations to design and deliver products, quality services and supports, reduce communication barriers between organisation and customers, and build better relationship with customers that increases better customer service experiences (Kursunluoglu, 2011).

Hudson and Hudson (2013) have said that hotel industry is one of the booming sectors in global economy. The industry has experienced significant growth with the fastest growing trend of tourism industry. The growth and success of hotel industry is also dependent on the level of customer satisfaction whereas customer satisfaction in hotel industry is significantly dependent on customer service experiences (Accenture, 2012). Positive customer service experiences of a hotel determine the success of it whereas poor customer service experience can lead poor performance of the hotel. In hotel industry, mobile technology is growingly used and some futurists have strongly urged that future success in hotel industry will be mainly dependent on mobile technology use (Brewer, 2008). It has been justified that better customer service experience in hotel industry is mainly dependent on the service quality and excellence, communication, enjoyable environment and better amenities whereas mobile technology can successfully deliver the better customer service experience and customer satisfaction by enabling hotels to design and deliver high quality and excellent customer services, attractive offerings and amenities, establish better communication and provide enjoyable environment (Avaya, 2011). The relation between the use of mobile technology use and customer service experience increase has been justified from the small and medium size hotels in UK hotel industry. The purpose of the research was to analysis the impact of mobile technology to increase customer service experience in small and medium sized Hotels in West London, UK. For the successful achievement of research purpose, organisational contexts of one small sized hotel Rising Sun Hotel in South Harrow and another medium sized hotel Novotel Hotels London Heathrow have been taken.

According to Warnock (2015), hotel industry is one of the significant parts of UK economy and growing rapidly. The industry is highly competitive and to sustain in the competition, hotels need to ensure high level of customer satisfaction, which is directly and indirectly influenced by customer service experiences. In UK hotel industry, most of the large hotels are using mobile technology (PWC, 2015). The reason behind it is that the rapidly growing mobile technology and its acceptance by the people and the use of mobile technology has significant impact to improve their customer service experience and satisfaction. Currently, different medium sized hotels as well as small sized using mobile technology to improve their customer service experiences. However, in which extent the use of mobile technology will be supportive for the small sized hotels compared to medium sized hotels in UK to increase their customer service experiences have not been assessed and justified yet (Hotel Industry Magazine, 2013), moreover, most of the small sized hotels in UK, owned by independent personals and in the case of medium sized hotels, it will be a part of a group, so researcher need to identify what extend these hotels can adopt mobile technology in customer service to enhance their customers' experience.

LITERATURE

The literature review has been prepared based on the funnel approach where it has been designed in a manner where discussions have been flown from broader perspective to precise.

Customers and Customer Satisfaction

According to Kotler and Keller (2012), in the customer driven global market, customers are the major stakeholder involved in business process. Customers are the recipient of goods or services or ideas, which are produced or collected from other parties, in exchange of money. In other way; all the parties purchase or consumes products or services and they have the ability to select between diversified products or suppliers. From the perspective of quality control, customers are the entity within a firm who establishes a process and accepts the output of that process from one or more internal and external suppliers. There are two types of customers including business customers and consumers. Business customers buy for further selling or use to produce products of services whereas the consumers buy for consumption or final use. Investors invest money to establish business firms for achieving profit (Kardes et al, 2015). However, for the successful achievement of business goal, they need to complete the business process. Customers are the significant part of the business process without them a business can never be successful or achieve desired profit or investment returned. Furthermore, customers are highly important for a business as they help repeat business whereas repeat business is the backbone of selling for its support for providing revenue and certainty for the business. Each and every organisation is highly dependent on customers as if organisations do not develop customer loyalty and satisfaction, they could lose their customers. Additionally, without customers, organisation would not exist as customers satisfies the fundamental need of business organisation (Mittal and Frennea, 2010).

Fornell et al, (2010) have said that customer satisfaction is the critical success factor for the business organisations as satisfied customers can bring desired growth and profitability whereas dissatisfied customers can make an organisation out of the market. Customer satisfaction is the state of mind of customers after having a product or service. When a customer purchases a product or service, the customer has some expectation about the value of the product or services. If the expectation of customers is met or exceeded after having a product or service, it will be considered as the customer satisfaction (Kotler and Keller 2012). For the successful business operation, an organisation needs to have more purchase and loyalty from customers whereas customer satisfaction works as the leading indicator of purchase repurchase intention and loyalty from customers. The organisation with high level of customer satisfaction enjoys differentiated views from customers. Customer satisfaction is an efficient tool for the organisation to reduce customer churn, which is harmful for business performance of the organisation. Customer lifetime value and word of mouth are two major factors strongly influence the success and growth of an organisation whereas high level of customer satisfaction enhances the customer lifetime value and increases positive word of mouth (Mittal and Frennea, 2010).

Customer Services

Kursunluoglu (2011) have explained that customer service is a significant concept in current business world as it is directly linked with the customer satisfaction, which is a critical success factor for an organisation in competitive market environment. Customer services are services delivered to customers for their satisfaction. More broadly, customers want services before, during and after purchase. For example, before purchasing product customers want different information and supports to make their purchase decisions whereas the organisations support the information to the customers as customer services to facilitate customers' purchase decision making. In the time of purchasing, customers' needs different supports, which are provided to the customers through customer services (Solis, 2011). After purchasing a product, customer may face troubles whereas customer services help customers to get the problems fixed after purchasing products. From this perspective, customer services are the services delivered to the customers before, during and after purchasing a product or services. High quality customer services are highly important for the successful operation of an organisation as continuous high quality customer service delivery keeps customers continuously satisfied, therefore, the continuous customer satisfaction makes customers loyal. Loyal customers make repurchase and make additional purchase by creating new customers. Consequently, the organisations can deliver high quality customer services can achieve desired growth and success. In contrast, if an organization fails to provide desired quality of customer services, the organization cannot achieve desired customer satisfaction and loyalty level. As a result, the organization lose its customers and get limited chance to have new customers, thus, the organization lose its market and desired success (Kotler and Keller 2012).

Fornell et al, (2010) have demonstrated that customer services are important for an organization as it increase customer loyalty and the amount of money each customer spend with business. High quality customer satisfaction helps an organization to increase customer repurchase frequency. It can help an organization to generate positive word of mouth and reduce negative word of mouth. Customer service can be successful link between customers and organizations and help to decrease the barriers to buy. For delivering better customer services, it is necessary for the organizations to treat their customers respectfully, following up on feedback, and handling complaints and returns gracefully. Organizations can be successful to deliver desired quality of customer services by understanding customers' needs and wants efficiently, exceeding customer expectations and going out of way organizations helps to their customers (Ryu et al, 2011).

Customer Service Experiences

As said in Jüttner et al, (2013), customer service experience is an important issue for the success and growth of organizations in the customer driven competitive global market. From the general point of view, customer service experiences is the percept that have customers have of their interaction with an organization or a set of interactions that consistently exceeds the needs and expectations of a customers. Customer service experience can be defined as the entirety of the interactions a customer has with a company and its products. Overall customer service experience is reflected how the customers feel about the company and its offerings (Tate and White, 2008). Customer service experience is the product of an interaction between an organization and a customer over the duration of their relationship whereas the interaction involves a customer's attraction, awareness, discovery, cultivation, advocacy and purchase and use of a service. Customer service experience is a highly important issue for an organization and it is measured by the individual's experiences during all points of contact against the individual's expectations (Nielsen, 2010).

Importance of Customer Service Experiences

Consistent with the study of Lemke (2009) customer service experience is crucial success factor as better customer service experience can generate unimaginable success for an organisation. In contrast poor customer service experience can lead miserable condition of an organisation. Better customer service experience makes customers satisfied. When an organisation can provide better customer service experience continuously, it increases customer loyalty and positive word of mouth (Khan et al, 2015). The loyal customers of the organisation make continuous purchase and additional purchase from the organisation. Additionally, positive word of mouth increases brand reputation and positive referrals. The positive brand reputation and positive referrals makes additional sales for organisation that enhances growth and success of the organisation. In contrast, when an organisation fails to deliver better customer service experience, the organisation cannot achieve desired level of customer satisfaction, suffers from poor customer loyalty and repeat purchase, negative customer referrals, increased customer churn and poor sales and relationship with customers (Tate and White, 2008).

From the study of Jüttner et al, (2013), improved customer service experience is highly important for an organisation as it improves customer satisfaction and foster repeat customers and customer loyalty. Not only can that but also positive customer service experience generates increased customer advocacy and customer loyalty, which contributes on gaining desired success of an organisation. Customer churn is highly harmful for an organisation whereas positive customer service experience can increase customer retention rate and reduces customer churn. Better customer service experience can create competitive advantage, which will generate better competitive positive for an organisation. Improved customer service experience can increase the revenues and sales of an organisation. Most importantly, when an organisation can be able offer better customer service experience to its customers, the organisation can enjoy strong customer relationships.

Factors Influencing Customer Service Experiences

Azila et al, (2014) have revealed that there are different factors that influences customer service experiences of an organisation. However, the major factors are the product, service, and environmental qualities and perceived value. An organisation can achieve desired level of positive customer service experiences from the customers by providing better product, quality services and enjoyable environmental to them. Perceived value is another major factor significantly influences the customer service experiences of the customers as if customer gets the desired values from the products or services, they get better experienced. In contrast, if an organisation fails to deliver better product, quality services, enjoyable environmental and perceived values to the customers, the organisation cannot provide desired level of positive customer service experiences (Tate and White, 2008). According to the customer experience framework, customer experience is dependent on some factors including level of customer need satisfaction, price reasonability, availability of products or services, level of convenience, necessary supports, quality products or services, environment, brand reputation and corporate social responsibility. If an organisation wants to increase customer experiences, the organisation should be successful to satisfy customer needs, high price reasonability, better availability of products or services, desired convenience, sufficient supports, quality products or services and environment, brand reputation and corporate social responsibility (Jüttner et al, 2013).

Ways to Improve Customer Service Experiences

In the light of Barrows (2015), there are different ways to improve customer service experience in an organization. The specific ways to improve customer service experiences are to strengthen customer skills; to support each and every customer n every touch points to interact with them; to enhance customer interactions; design and develop efficient customer service strategies; engage every skills and capacities of organisation to serve customers; and ensure swift customer feedbacks in an efficient way. For improving organisational customer service skills, it is necessary for the organisation to increase empathy, patience, consistency, adaptability and communication. In any stage of customer lifecycle, bad experience can be faced by customers (Tate and White, 2008). That's why it is necessary to improve customer service experiences at every touch points. For increasing positive customer service experiences, the first impression of customers must be positive and to make first impression of customers positive, organisations should consider some environmental aspects including accessibility, layout, cleanliness and personalized services. For achieving improved customer service experiences, customers should be provided product and services with exact needs of customers. To improve customer service experiences, an organization should increase the ability to meet the needs of customers and solve their problems efficiently. Organizations should ensure proper attention to complaints and dealing with them appropriately for increasing customer service experiences (Jüttner et al, 2013).

Customer Service in Hotel Industry

Gandolfo and Rosa (2010) have said that from the entering the room to check-out customer wants different customer services from every types of hotels along with small and medium sized hotels. Customers of hotels want warm greetings or welcome when they are searching for hotel information and checking-in whereas quality customer services of hotels will ensure proper greetings and desired information. It is necessary for hotels to offer enjoyable or memorable hotel experiences. However, hotels will offer desired level of enjoyable environment to the customers to satisfy them (Kotler, et al. 2010). Not only have customers of hotels want real-time feedback. For ensuring sufficient customer services delivery, hotels must provide desired level of customer services. Customers want personalized offerings and to ensure desired level of customer satisfaction, hotels will deliver personalized offerings and services when guests are staying in the hotels. Other customer services hotels should offer to its customers are providing desired information of the hotel facilities, desired amenities and enough entertainment opportunity and necessary information and support to travel within nearby destination that can enrich the satisfaction level of the customers (Vijayadurai, 2008).

Mobile Technology

In the light of Kumar and Zahn (2010), it has been revealed that the technology utilized for cellular communication is considered as mobile technology. Over the past years, mobile technology has become grown and widespread. From beginning of 21st century to now, a standard mobile device has gone from no more than a simple two way pager to being a mobile phone, GPS navigation device, an embedded web browser and instant messaging client and a hand held game console. It is believed that the future of computer technology rests in mobile computing with wireless networking and mobile computing by way of tablet computers are becoming more popular (Naismith, 2010). From another perspective, mobile technology normally defines the portable technology or mobile technology refers to any device that individuals can carry with them to perform a wide variety of task. The devices enables mobile technologies are cellular phone, PDA, vehicles, laptop etc. In last 10 years, mobile technology has improved a lot as the mobile gadgets have gotten smaller, more powerful, and very useful. In the lives of most everyone, they are everywhere and ply increasingly greater roles (Thakkar et al, 2010).

According to Jen-Her Wua and Shu-Ching Wanga (2009), Mobile technology is the technology which is portable and running an operating system optimized or designed for mobile computing. Whereas the mobile devices are the devices, which is small, hand-held computing device, typically having display screen with touch input or a miniature keyboard and less than two pound. Throughout the world the availability of mobile devices has been rapidly increased and spread. The improvement of mobile technology has changed different aspects of human lives. Mobile technology uses different media for activating it. For example, radio wave, microwave, infra-red, GPS and Bluetooth. These media allow for the transfer of data via voice, text, video, 2 dimensional barcodes and more (Haskin, 2007). The major devices help to activate the mobile technology are the laptop, tablets and netbook computers, smart phones, global positing system or GPS devices. These devices can be used based on wireless fidelity, which is a type of wireless local area network technology, Bluetooth, which connects mobile devices wirelessly, 3G, 4G, GSM and GPRS data services, which activate networking services for mobile phones, dial-up services, which enables data networking services using modems and telephone lines, and virtual private networks, which secure access to private networks. There are different mobile technologies are used by modern world. However, the most important mobile technologies are HTML, NFC, Platform independent application development tools, location and context devices, Bluetooth, 802.11ac, Machine to Machine (M2M), Smart products, Augmented Reality (AR), Multiple MDM, Long Term Evaluation (LTE) (Thakkar et al, 2010)

Characteristics of Mobile Technology

There are some specific characteristics of mobile technology and its devices including portability, social interactivity, context sensitivity, connectivity and individuality. The major characteristic of mobile technology is the portability and the devices of mobile technology are small in size and weight that means they can be taken to different sites or moved around within a site. Mobile technology is used for social interactivity and the devices of mobile technology enable social interactivity through data exchange and collaboration with other learners that can happen face to face (Warnock 2015). Mobile technology is context sensitive and the mobile devices can both gather and response to real or simulated data unique to the current location, environment and time. Connectivity is another major characteristic for mobile technology where a shared network can be created by connecting mobile devices to data collection devices, other devices or to a common network. Individuality is another important characteristic for mobile technology that scaffolding for tough actions can be customized for individual learners Hotel (Industry Magazine, 2013).

Basic Components of Mobile Technology

Mobile technology is enabled by different components. However, there are three major components that enable mobile technology. Hardwar device is the first component to enable mobile technology that include different low-end phones, which can only be used for phone calls and sending SMS and specialized devices such as point of sales terminal. Additional, hardware devices are smart phone, which can also be linked to add on devices such as bio-metric sensors, bar-code readers, and NFC and RFID3 chips (Naismith, 2010). Software is the second basic component of mobile technology. Different software is used for the successful enabling of mobile devices. Without proper software, it is impossible for getting a mobile technology successfully activated. Data transmission devices are other significant elements of mobile technology which enable the interconnectivity and communication with data transmission. The device can be set up in a centralized computer platform, mobile networks including SMS, voice and internet (Kumar and Zahn, 2010).

Importance of Mobile Technology in Business

Warnock (2015) explained that there are different reasons for which mobile technologies are being in the heart of the development and growth of business day by day. The technology will be a basic part of successful business operation. Now, the organizations in the globalized and technology based business environment can use the mobile technology efficient can achieve increased business success. There are some businesses which are fundamentally dependent on the mobile technology. The reasons which are making mobile technology as important part of current business organization are: in the modern business world, the organization with larger number of customer enjoys maximum business success whereas customers are people reside in society (Warnock, 2015). In case technological development, people are increasingly accessing internet through mobile devices that has made the technology significantly important for business organization. It is a growing trend that people are doing more e-commerce transaction through mobile devices that is making the technology a significant part of business operation and function (Wamba, 2008).

Kumar and Zahn (2010) said that business organizations must consider the efficient utilization of mobile technologies are mobile technology is changing the user's web surfing habits. Not only is that most the existing and potential customers now on the social media which is growingly used in mobile platforms. For that reason, for the increased attraction of customers and maintaining proper customer relationships, mobile technology is an important part for every business now. For business organizations, marketing is an important function as if organizations can market their products and services efficiently, the organization will enjoy higher success and growth. Mobile technology is an important and efficient marketing option for organizations as it allows location based, customized, and efficient marketing of an organization (Wamba, 2008). Now growingly, the use of mobile devices including smart phone and tablet are increasing that are removing barriers to mobile marketing. Mobile technology is replacing television and radio and organizations are being dependent on mobile technology for the basic promotional activities. The most valuable customer demographics are the young and educated customers who are liked with mobile technology. As a result, the technology has been more valuable for the business organizations. Furthermore, mobile marketing is becoming very cost effective and efficient to promote products and services. For that reason, mobile technologies are becoming more important for business organizations (Thakkar et al, 2010).

Small Sized Hotels and Medium Sized Hotels

In the study of Ahmad (2014), it has been revealed that modern hotels can be classified in different ways according to the size and shapes. However, without setting a standard for classification, it is very tough to classify hotels based on their differences. Normal standard for classify hotel is the size, where based on the size of hotels classifications are made. Based on the size, hotels can be classified counting the number of rooms. According to Ahmad (2014), there are four types of hotels including small, medium, large, and mega.

The small sized hotels will have 1 to 150 rooms whereas medium sized hotels will have 151 to 400 hotel rooms. From the study of Europa (2014), it has been clarified that based on the UK standard, small size hotels will have fewer than 25 rooms and mid-size hotel will have 25 to 99 rooms. The study has further revealed that from global standard, small size hotels will have rooms no more than 150 and medium size hotels will have 151 to 299 rooms.

The study reports by Pierret (2011) and RDCTO (2002) have revealed some features of small and medium sized hotels. The reports have explained that small size hotel will have reception desk open from 7:00 till 22:00 or on request, minimum size of single bed of 90 x190 cm, double bed of 140 x 190 cm, bed linen changed after gust's stay at hotel, at least one toilet for every ten rooms, and breakfast services. The medium size hotels have at least 40% of rooms with private bath, opened reception desk from 7:00 till 24:00 or on request, floor area of shower and toilet inside at least 3.3 M 2, separate public toilet for every 20 hotel rooms.

According to Travelodge, (2011), from the year of recession, the market for small and medium size hotels in UK has grown by 35% and the growth of market share has added 20000 rooms. From the other context, the market share for branded small and medium size hotels accelerated their accommodation with the growth from 12% to 16%. It is believed that the market share of hotel industry in UK will increase to 856750 rooms in which the 225000 will be small and medium size hotels. It is expected during the time, the small and medium size hotel market in UK will experience 26% of growth. Furthermore, the growth of small and medium size hotel market will be fuelled with new development, acquisition and conversion of independent small and medium size hotels in UK.

Mobile Technologies and Small & Medium Sized Hotels

Mobile technology is being developed rapidly; therefore, customers are doing more with their mobile devices. As a result, the customers want more from the companies they do business with. As like in most of the sectors of modern life mobile technologies are being domineering in customer operation, hotel industry also requires adopting sufficient mobile technology in their service delivery to support and satisfy the customers. In small and medium sized hotels sector, competition is growingly increasing where mobile technology use helps to attract more and more customers. Most of the hotels irrespective to size create and manage content; store and distribute the hotel digital marketing; and circulate special offers and packages, events and happenings through different mobile technology based channels including mobile website, tablet website, social media platform etc. (Strategicyearbook, 2015)

According to Appytech, 2016, most of the hoteliers all over the world are working to enhance their operational efficiency and for the successful increase of operational efficiency, they are increasingly using the mobile technologies. Like large hotels or hotel chains, small and medium hotels and hotel chains requires to have successful application of mobile technology as it reduces their failure to deliver maximum hotel service satisfaction to the customers. Worldwide small and medium size hotels and hoteliers are being conscious about the use of mobile apps and with the use of mobile technology they are getting multiple advantages. For example, most of the hotels have their own mobile apps and the mobile apps are permitting tourists and travellers to gather hotel information, direct Hotel Bookings, as travel guide, way to Hotel, information about local amenities, and the ability to check-in and receive the key for their rooms with very little hassle. Mobile apps helps hotels to serve the customers, who wants to avoid entire check-in process and head strait to their rooms and effective communication with room services and housekeeping during the stay in the Hotel and quick checkout facility and leave their valuable feedback, all these things can make possible just pressing their finger tip on the mobile devices. That leads high level of customer satisfaction (Ellis, 2015)

From a study by Google has revealed that irrespective to the size of hotels, the mobile technology use is highly important for its growth and profitability. The report has justified that the hotels only offered desktop based websites and ignore the use of mobile technology has lost their profit and the hotels used mobile technology along with desktop based technology have experienced significant increase in their profitability. The report has further demanded that the hotels will use updated mobile technologies over the next years; the hotels will experience high level of growth and success.

Small and medium size hotels like other types of hotels are using mobile technology in their different functions. For their booking management, they are using mobile technology friendly booking applications, which are enabled in different mobile devices. The use of mobile technology has simplified the booking engine with step by step processes, touch screen interfaces, easy dropdown menus, shorter product description and thumb-nail images. Mobile technology is becoming a fundamental part of hotel business as it has been found that during the year 2012, the number of customers used mobile devices to contact with hotels increased by 120% and the number of customers used tablet devices experienced 306% growth.

Like other categories of hotels, small and medium size hotels all over the world are facing high level of competitions. In this competitive environment, the hotels need to ensure real-time feed of specials, packages and promotions. Efficient uses of mobile technology can successful help the hotels to ensure real-time feed of specials, packages and promotions as mobile technology of hotels features these offers. Mobile technology can efficiently help small and medium size hotels to establish user friendly payment system by allowing for simplified reservation without the need to enter a credit card, and by entering and storing the credit card information in advance via the desktop website.

Some hotels are now using new Smartphone key technology where guests are enabled to bypass the front desk altogether. However, experts have claimed that it is not the beginning of the end for human interactions in the hotels. Another latest mobile technology are being used in hotel industry and it is the Express Check-In application where guests are allowed to check-in before arrival and simply picking up their keys when they arrive. The new checkout application adopted recently enables customers to make checkout with a push of button and receive bills through a mail.

Mobile Technologies in Customer Services in Hotels

According to Hudson and Hudson (2011), mobile technology is significantly changing the customer service delivery and experiences in hotel industry. It has been predicted that the use of mobile technology will bring revolutionary change in hotel services. From the initial contact to the check out, customers want different types of services from a hotel to get satisfied where mobile technology can enable the hotel to offer the services efficiently. Using mobile technology, hotels can offer efficient pre-purchase customer services to its guests. Potential guests for a hotel are using mobile technology increasingly to find out hotels, check on the availability of rooms and to read the reviews. When a hotel can successfully adopt mobile technology based pre-purchase services, the hotel can efficiently serve the customer to find out hotels, check on the availability of rooms and to read reviews through its mobile platform (Jin-zhao and Jing, 2009). When guests make check-in in a particular hotel, the guests expect different services. For example, once a guest checked-in, he/she wants to continue using his/her mobile devices, tablets, and laptops to do business, keep in contact with loved ones and be entertained. In this context, customers can be efficiently helped by the mobile technology based internet platform of the hotel. Not only that but also, mobile technology based application of a hotel can accelerate the experiences of guests highly by making their more available in the hotel. After check out of hotels, mobile technology can help customers to be connected with the hotels and increase the return propensity to the hotel again (Irvine and Anderson, 2008).

Koutroumanis (2011) have explained that the efficient use of mobile technology can enhance the customer service experience of hotel guest. A guest wants easy and standard payment system with desired level of security of his/her currency. With the mobile technology support, hotels can offer easiest option for customers to exchange currency and payment based on mobile wallet. Now hotels can provide excellent customer service to its customers in other different ways like replacement of hotel room keys and in-room phone with easiest method by using mobile technology and provision of internal and external guest facilities through mobile platform. With the use of locator in guest's phones, hotels can be enabled to offer services to its guests anywhere in the hotel property (Piccoli, 2008). If a hotel can efficiently use mobile technology, it can ensure non-printed and easy promotion of hotel services to their existing customers and enable guests to pick their best options of service to get maximum satisfaction. Mobile technology use can offer different entertaining offers to its customers that can satisfy those most (Oparanma et al., 2009).

According to Mittaland Frennea (2010) and Scottet al. (2009), customer service experience is highly important for every organisation in the highly competitive customer oriented global market as it is significantly linked with organisational success. There is a significant relationship between use of mobile technology and customer service experience as efficient use of mobile technology can enhance customer service experiences. In the recent years, the use of mobile technology is increasing to improve customer services. The use of mobile technology can significantly improve the customer service efficiency and customer service experiences. If an organisation can deliver services to its customers according to their needs, it will improve the customer services experiences and loyalty of customers (Jüttneret al.,2013). However, the use of mobile technology can successfully gather information regarding customers' service needs and help to design and desired customer services that improve customer service experiences and customer satisfaction (Hudsonand Hudson, 2011). The analysis can be presented as following.

Azilaet al. (2014) and Ford (2012) have said that efficient use of mobile technology can enhance customer service experiences as it enables organisations to personalise services for individual customers. The reason behind it is that the key to delivering the best customer service experiences through personalisation is to understand how customers behave, how they interact with a brand and how they use various channel as well (Jüttneret al.,2013). Use of mobile technology can easily deliver the information regarding individual customer to understand how customers behave, how they interact with a brand and how they use various channel. Based on the information, organisations can offer personalised services to its customers and enhance customer service excellence and customer service experiences (Kima et al.,2014). The analysis can be summarised as following.

Dennisand Dennis (2011) and Kotler et al. (2010) have explained that sometimes customers face troubles to achieve desired services from an organisation. However, these troubles can lead better customer service experiences and lead the customer dissatisfaction that can lead loss of sales and growth. Most of the customers in the modern time are using mobile platforms to express their feelings and feedback. Use of mobile technology, organisations will be able to collect feedbacks from customers and increase information collection about their service development and design. Based on the feedback and information, organisations will be able deliver improved customer service experience and customer satisfaction to the customers (Ahmad, 2014). There is a type of customers, who are task oriented, less likely to spend time browsing for services, and used to log on to the sites with a purpose to buy. To deliver great customer service experiences to those customers, mobile technology can help organizations efficiently as it can enable the organization to ensure easy, quick and consistent services (Karthikeyanand Balamurgan, 2012). The analysis can be expressed as following

Fornell et al., (2010) and Vijayadurai (2008) have found that before purchasing a product or service, customers need to access to the information about the product or services. Use of mobile technology can efficiently help organisations to be enabled to ensure easy customer access to their desired information regarding product and services. This easy access to the information before purchasing products or services can successfully enrich customer services satisfaction in pre purchase period (Jüttneret al.,2013). During the purchase of products or services, mobile technology can improve customer service experiences efficiently as mobile technology helps easy purchase process, enjoyable purchase environment, and first delivery of products or services. Not only that but also, use of mobile technology can ensure better customer service experiences after purchase of product or services as it makes after purchase services easy and fast, which is desired by customers (Caret al.2012). The analysis can be presented as following.

Gandolfo and Rosa (2010) have explained that from the perspective of hotel industry, mobile technology has increasingly important contribution to improve customer service experiences. In hotel industry, customers want easy and fast booking and payment process to develop better customer service experiences whereas mobile technology based booking and payment system can successfully ensure easy and fast booking and payment process by customers as well improve customer service experiences. Before check-in to the hotels, waiting time is a crucial factor for the organisations to increase customer service experiences (Hudsonand Hudson, 2011). Different studies have revealed that 5 minutes waiting time can develop better customer service experiences. However, use of mobile technology can successfully reduce the waiting time in the time of check-in period and increase better customer service experiences and customer satisfaction. It is believed that mobile technology has the ability to make customers' stays more enjoyable in a hotel by eliminating key cards and shorten waiting time during check-in (Koutroumanis, 2011).

Jin-zhaoand Jing (2009) have described that successful use of mobile technology in hotel operation can efficiently increase the customer service experiences as mobile technology based options for customers can ensure easy dealing with hotels that will reduce their hassel and waste of time. For example, with the help of in-app purchase, customers of a hotel can be able to buy a late check-out, order room services or call for housekeeping in a fastest and easiest manner (Koutroumanis, 2011). Complexity and time consumption in booking process can develop significantly negative service experiences among the customers. In contrast, customer service experiences among customers can be successfully increased by the use of mobile technology as the technology can efficiently simplified the booking engine with step by step processes, touch screen interface, easy dropdown menus, shorter product description, and thumb-nail images (Oparanmaet al., 2009).

In accordance with the study of Irvineand Anderson (2008), mobile technology can enhance the customer service experiences among the customers by offering real-time feedback for customers, delivering information of package and its selection and distribution of desired information to the potential and current customers. If hotels can use efficient mobile-friendly payment system, it improves customer service experience and satisfaction significantly as mobile friendly booking process allows simplified reservations without the need to enter a credit card (Piccoli, 2008).

CONCLUSION

The aim of the chapter was to is to analysis the impact of mobile technology to enhance the customer service experience in SME hotels in the UK.Most of the small and medium size hotels in UK are adopting mobile technology in their customer service like mobile enabled website, and third party mobile platforms for supporting customers' activities including booking and payment. They offer Wi-Fi services to the customers when they stay in the hotels.

The use of mobile enabled website has helped hotels to make online hotel bookings more easy and convenient as it helps customers to book hotel rooms from any geographical location with no hassle. The use of mobile apps has made Novotel Hotels' online booking more easy and convenient by eliminating tradition communication needs and reducing time needed for telephone booking. Additionally, the use of mobile technology has made the payment system more easy and convenient as customers can book rooms using mobile wallet.

The main aim for using mobile technology is to increase the hotel's customer service excellence and customer satisfaction. There is a significant relationship between the use of mobile technology and customer service experience. The use of mobile technology can enhance the customer service experience by increasing service design and delivery efficiency, operational efficiency, personalisation capacity, and service quality. Additionally, the use of mobile technology can improve customer service experiences by enhancing customers' convenience for booking and payment and reducing their waiting time. It can successfully gather information regarding customers' service needs by using mobile technology. The information about customer service needs can help the hotels to deliver high quality customer services to improve customer service experiences.

In terms of the recommendations, those hotels who don't have, need to develop own mobile apps to assure the privacy of customers information when they are involved in mobile technology based services of the hotel. The hotels need to work on mobile technology supported customer management system.

Further, the hotel should offer options to customers to request room service and housekeeping service through its mobile application as these options will reduce customers' waiting time for room service and housekeeping services. The hotel should reduce high dependence on third party mobile apps to have hotel reservation orders from customers. Also,to resolve the inefficiencies to use mobile technology in customer service, the hotels should provide sufficient bandwidth so as customers can get fast internet connection through the hotel's Wi-Fi.

REFERENCES

Accenture. (2012). *Getting Personal with Digital Mastering the digital revolution in the lodging industry*. Available at: https://www.cas-ag.eu/us-en/Documents/PDF/Accenture-Getting-Personal-Lodging-Master-Digital.pdf

Ahmad, S. Z. (2014). Entrepreneurship in the small and medium-sized hotel sector. *Current Issues in Tourism, 18*(4), 328–349. doi:10.1080/13683500.2014.934211

Avaya. (2011). *The Impact of Guest Experience on Hotel Revenues How the right technology can result in higher profitability*. Available at: https://www.avaya.com/usa/documents/impactguestexperienceshotelrevs.pdf

Azila, J. (2014). *Factors Affecting Customers' Experience in Local Fast Food Restaurant*. 2nd World Conference on Islamic Thought and Civilization, Perak, Malaysia.

Barrows, S. (2015). *Six Ways to Create a Memorable Customer Experience*. Available at: https://www.entrepreneur.com/article/206760

Brewer, P. (2008). *Current and Future Technology Use in the Hospitality Industry*. Available at: https://www.ahla.com/uploadedFiles/AHLA/Members_Only/Property_and_Corporate/Property_-_Publications/Current%20and%20Future%20Technology.pdf

Car, T. (2012). *Mobile marketing and advertising strategies in tourism and hospitality industry*. Faculty of Tourism and Hospitality Management Opatija, University of Rijeka.

Cohen, L. (2007). *Research methods in education* (6th ed.). Routledge. doi:10.4324/9780203029053

Collins, H. (2011). *Creative Research: The Theory and Practice of Research for the Creative Industries*. AVA Publications.

Cooper, D. R., & Schindler, P. S. (2006). *Business Research Method* (9th ed.). McGraw-Hill Irwin.

Creswell, J. W. (2009). *Research design: Qualitative, quantitative, and mixed methods approaches* (3rd ed.). Sage.

Creswell, J. W. (2012). *Qualitative inquiry and research design: Choosing among five traditions* (3rd ed.). Sage.

Creswell, J. W., & Clark, P. V. L. (2007). *Designing and conducting mixed methods research*. Sage.

Crowther, D., & Lancaster, G. (2008). *Research Methods: A Concise Introduction to Research in Management and Business Consultancy*. Butterworth-Heinemann.

Dominici, G., & Rosa, G., (2010). Customer Satisfaction in the Hotel Industry: A Case Study from Sicily. *International Journal of Marketing Studies, 10*(2).

Europa. (2014). *Classification Of Hotel Establishments Within The EU*. Available at: https://ec.europa.eu/consumers/ecc/docs/hotel_establishment_classification_EU_en.pdf

Ford, R. C. (2012). *Managing Quality Service in Hospitality: How Organizations Achieve Excellence in the Guest Experience*. Delmar, Cengage Learning.

Fornell, C., Rust, R. T., & Dekimpe, M. G. (2010). The Effect of Customer Satisfaction on Consumer Spending Growth. *JMR, Journal of Marketing Research*, *47*(1), 28–35. doi:10.1509/jmkr.47.1.28

Gandolfo, D., & Rosa, G., (2010). Customer Satisfaction in the Hotel Industry: A Case Study from Sicily. *International Journal of Marketing Studies, 2*(2).

Harmer, J. (2011). *Budget hotel market has grown by 35% during the recession.* Available at: https://www.thecaterer.com/articles/337431/budget-hotel-market-has-grown-by-35-during-the-recession

Hudson, S., & Hudson, L. (2011). *Customer Service for Hospitality and Tourism.* Goodfellow Publishers Limited.

Hudson, S., & Hudson, L. (2013). *Customer Service for Hospitality and Tourism.* Good Fellow Publishers Limited.

Huffcut, A. I. (2010). From science to practice: Seven principles for conducting employment interviews. *Applied H.R.M. Research*, *12*, 121–136.

Irvine, W., & Anderson, A. (2008). ICT (information communication technology), peripherality and smaller hospitality businesses in Scotland. *International Journal of Entrepreneurial Behaviour & Research*, *14*(4), 200–218. doi:10.1108/13552550810887381

Jen-Her Wua, B., & Shu-Ching Wanga, C. (2009). What drives mobile commerce?: An empirical evaluation of the revised technology acceptance model. *Information & Management*, *42*(5).

Jin-zhao, W., & Jing, W. (2009). Issues, Challenges, and Trends, that Facing Hospitality Industry. *Management Science and Engineering*, *3*(4), 53–58.

Jüttner, U., Schaffner, D., Windler, K., & Maklan, S. (2013). Customer service experiences: Developing and applying a sequential incident laddering technique. *European Journal of Marketing*, *47*(5/6), 738–769. doi:10.1108/03090561311306769

Kardes, & … . (2015). *Consumer Behavior* (2nd ed.). Cengage Learning.

Karthikeyan, N., & Balamurgan, T. (2012). Mobile Marketing: Examining the impact of Interest, Individual attention, Problem faced and consumer's attitude on intention to purchase. *Interdisciplinary Journal of Contemporary Research in Business*, *3*(6).

Khan, I., Garg, R. J., & Rahman, Z. (2015). Customer Service Experience in Hotel Operations: An Empirical Analysis. *Procedia: Social and Behavioral Sciences*, *189*, 266–274. doi:10.1016/j.sbspro.2015.03.222

Kima, S. (2014). Mobile Technology: An Exploratory Study of Hotel Managers. *International Journal of Hospitality & Tourism Administration, 15*(4), 417–446. doi:10.1080/15256480.2014.961795

Kotler, P. (2010). *Marketing for Hospitality and Tourism* (5th ed.). Pearson.

Kotler, P., & Keller, L. K. (2012). *Marketing Management (14th ed.).* Pearson Education Limited.

Koutroumanis, D.A. (2011). Technology's Effect on Hotels and Restaurants: Building a Strategic Competitive Advantage. *Journal of Applied Business and Economics, 12*(1).

Kumar, S., & Zahn, C. (2010). Mobile communications: Evolution and impact on business operations. *Technovation, 23*(6), 515–520. doi:10.1016/S0166-4972(02)00120-7

Kursunluoglu, D. E. (2011). Customer Service Effects on Customer Satisfaction and Customer Loyalty: A Field Research in Shopping Centers in Izmir City – Turkey. *International Journal of Business and Social Science*, 2(17).

Lemke, D.F. (2009). *What makes a great customer experience?* Available at: http://www.som.cranfield.ac.uk/som/dinamic-content/media/Yvonne/What%20makes%20a%20great%20customer%20experience%20with%20front%20.pdf

Liang, T.-P., Huang, C.-W., Yeh, Y.-H., & Lin, B. (2007). Adoption of mobile technology in business: A fit-viability model. *Industrial Management & Data Systems, 107*(8), 1154–1169. doi:10.1108/02635570710822796

McNiff, J., & Whitehead, J. (2002). *Action research: Principles and practice* (2nd ed.). Routledge Falmer. doi:10.4324/9780203199961

Merriam, S. B. (1998). *Qualitative research and case study applications in education.* Jossey-Bass Publishers.

Mittal, V., & Frennea, C. (2010). *Customer Satisfaction: A Strategic Review and Guidelines for Managers.* Marketing Science Institute: MSI Fast Forward (10-701).

Murname, R. J., & Willett, J. B. (2011). *Methods matter: Improving causal inference in educational and social science research.* Oxford University Press.

Naveed, M. (2012). Customer Relationship Management In Hospitality. *Journal of Good Governance And Sustainable Development, 1*(1), 40–47.

Nielsen, R. (2010). Customer satisfaction: The customer experience through the customer's eyes. *Total Quality Management & Business Excellence, 21*(11), 1229–1230. doi:10.1080/14783360903332361

O'Connor, P. (2004). A Review of Research on Information Technology in the Hospitality Industry. *International Journal of Hospitality Management, 23*(5).

Oparanma, O. (2009). Strategies for Managing Hospitality in a Turbulent Environment: Nigerian Experience. *International Journal of Management and Innovation, 1*(1), 24–37.

Patton, M. (2002). *Qualitative research and evaluation methods* (3rd ed.). Sage Publications.

Piccoli, G. (2008). Information technology in hotel management: A framework for evaluating the sustainability of IT-dependent competitive advantage. *Cornell Hospitality Quarterly, 49*(3), 282–296. doi:10.1177/1938965508320722

Pierret, F. (2011). *About hotel classification systems.* Available at: https://ec.europa.eu/consumers/ecc/docs/hotel_establishment_classification_EU_en.pdf

Ramphal, R. (2014). Service and quality and quality service: Satisfying customers in the hospitality industry. *African Journal of Hospitality, Tourism and Leisure, 3*(2).

Ryu, K. (2011). The influence of the quality of physical environment, food, and service on restaurant image, customer satisfaction, and behavioral intentions. *International Journal of Contemporary Hospitality Management, 24*(2), 200–223. doi:10.1108/09596111211206141

Saunders, M. (2007). *Research methods for business students* (4th ed.). London: Financial Times Prentice Hall.

Saunders. (2009). *Research Methods for Business Students.* Financial Times.

Scott, N., Laws, E., & Boksberger, P. (2009). The marketing of hospitality and leisure experiences. *Journal of Hospitality Marketing & Management, 18*(2-3), 99–110. doi:10.1080/19368620802590126

Sekaran, U., & Bougie, R. (2010). *Research Methods for Business: A Skill Building Approach* (5th ed.). John Wiley and Sons.

Solis, B. (2011). *Engage! The Complete Guide for Brands and Businesses to Build, Cultivate, and Measure Success in the New Web.* John Wiley & Sons.

Thakkar, M. (2010). *Mobile-based technology for monitoring & evaluation.* Available at: https://www.theclearinitiative.org/mobile-based-tech.pdf

Travelodge. (2011). *The UK budget hotel sector has grown by 35% during the recession*. Available at: http://www.melvingoldconsulting.com/2011%20Budget%20sector%20report%20press%20release.pdf

Vijayadurai, J. (2008). Service Quality, Customer Satisfaction and Behavioural Intention in Hotel Industry. *Journal of Marketing Communications*, *3*(3), 14–26.

Wamba, S. F. (2008). Exploring the impact of RFID technology and the EPC network on mobile B2B eCommerce: A case study in the retail industry. *International Journal of Production Economics*, *112*(2).

Warnock, C. (2015). *How mobile technology impacts both guest experience and hotel operations*. Available at: http://www.hotel-industry.co.uk/2015/04/how-mobile-technology-impacts-both-guest-experience-and-hotel-operations/

Zhou, K. Z., Yim, C. K. B., & Tse, D. K. (2005). The Effects of Strategic Orientations on Technology- and Market-Based Breakthrough Innovations. *Journal of Marketing*, *69*(2), 42–60. doi:10.1509/jmkg.69.2.42.60756

Chapter 2
Disruptive Innovations: A Mechanism for Achieving Business Distinction in the Hospitality Industry

Rajdeep Deb
Mizoram University, India

Pankaj Kumar
Mizoram University, India

ABSTRACT

The significant competitive environment around the hospitality industry triggers the exploration of novel ways and elements of coherent performance. Although disruptive innovations in the hospitality industry are complex, it provides compelling opportunities. Moreover, its emergence cannot be bestowed upon the current pandemic, since it is considered to be as old as business itself. The aim of the chapter is to capture the role of disruptive innovation in enabling the hospitality industry to engineer business excellence. Also, the chapter attempts to provide insights into the potential disruptions that will rule the hospitality industry in the future. The recent findings from this field show that the hospitality sector has already begun to adopt innovations gradually to respond to consumer behavior transition driven by on-demand services. Finally, the author concludes with the assertion that disruptive innovations are pivotal in the survival and sustenance of the hospitality businesses.

INTRODUCTION

The trademark of 21st century is the transformation of all kinds of organizational processes into a digital technology bed, as no disruption in business is workable

DOI: 10.4018/978-1-7998-9194-9.ch002

without imbibing a technological headway (Joshi, 2018). In colloquial language, the term 'disruption, is often identified with a sense of breakthrough that occurs in dynamic markets. However, the specificity of this understanding of disruption cannot be overemphasized, since it conveys different entities to different individuals. Despite this, the penetration of disrupting innovations has ushered in new era in service sector, and the resultant structural change is influencing market structure, the networks and the service that hospitality players are assumed to employ.

Over the past decade, the hospitality industry has witnessed rapid change, with novel technologies, virtual platforms and markets unfolding new capabilities of all kinds to the industry including mobile check-in and robots doing the job of housekeepers to self-ordering restaurant menus. These innovations are beginning to influence customer's experience in the service sector. In fact, disruptive innovations are introducing novel solutions and superior services to attract customers. Enterprising business models such as alternative accommodation (Airbnb, HouseTrip, etc.) and ride-sharing platforms (Uber) are leading from the front in influencing the individual's perceptions towards conventional hospitality businesses (refer to hospitalityinsights.ehl.edu).

The significant competitive environment around the hospitality industry triggers the exploration of novel ways and elements of coherent performance. One of the fundamental swings in this sphere is the development and application of a variety of innovations and new elements that can serve as a powerful stimulus for the growth of the hospitality industry. Innovations of all forms are pivotal for both the possibility and competitiveness of hotel enterprises. The methodical and pervasive usage of innovations to guarantee the growth of enterprise performance is now acknowledged by a diverse group of researchers and practicing managers (Dzhandzhugazova et al., 2015). Although disruptive innovations in the hospitality industry are complex, it provides compelling opportunities. Moreover, its emergence cannot be bestowed upon the current pandemic, since it is considered to be as old as business itself. It is generally looked at as a considerable change that tends to alter dramatically an industry. Also, it can take different forms, including product and service innovations, changes in operating processes and models. Ultimately, the intent is to continuously pay attention to novel and improved ways to cater to the needs of the customers and steer the market.

With this background, the current chapter endeavors to capture the role of disruptive innovation in enabling the hospitality industry to engineer business excellence. Also, the chapter has provided insights into the potential disruptions that will rule the hospitality industry in the future.

BACKGROUND

The Conceptualization of Disruptive Innovation

Society possesses liking as well as disliking for the phenomenon of disruptive innovation. The emergence of innovation as a widely researched topic is gaining momentum in diverse sectors such as manufacturing, finance, IT, and many more (Lu & Tseng, 2010; Biancolino et al., 2013). Several authors have defined innovation as the capacity to ground novel ideas, methods, products, or services, carrying the ability to alter and adjust (Meira et al., 2018). It is normally featured as everything that varies from normal activities or which depicts venturing out from earlier practices (Hjalager, 2010; Fraj et al., 2015; Divisekera & Nguyen, 2018). This delineation is in agreement with the Schumpeter's study (1985) that takes into account the economic significance and relevance of innovation. In the words Schumpeter, innovation refers to 'new products, new sources of supply, new methods of production, the exploitation of new markets and new ways to organize business (management)' (as cited in Dzhandzhugazova et al., 2016, p.10390). Even Zehrer et al. (2015) assert that innovation has economic competitive advantage, which firmly caters to the establishment of new products in the market or to the execution of new methods in the production cycle. Furthermore, the term innovation denotes the processes by which an organization transforms labor, capital, materials, and information into products and services of greater values (Christensen 1997). Alongside, the concept of 'disruption' is often broadly used by the media to specify a kind of reform that occurs in highly dynamic markets. It signifies different meanings to different people, along a continuum ranging from incremental change to radical transformation. There is no absolute definition for what traits define disruptive innovations. More often, they have been discussed as cheaper, simpler, smaller, and/or more convenient, but such statements are not accurate enough for measurement. Several studies anticipating or evaluating disruptiveness have tried to eliminate these ambiguities by finding whether a product aligns with the classic features of disruptive innovation. These studies have dependent on market research or industry experts (e.g., Keller & Hüsig, 2009). A significant development in the definition of 'disruptiveness' was regarding the term as relative, rather than absolute phenomenon i.e., a given innovation can mean a disruption to one particular firm and sustaining to another.

Christensen calls 'disruptive innovation' the change in technology and market structure (business models) that renders obsolete the management practices adopted by companies leading up to that moment. New technologies are broadly classified into 'sustaining technologies' and 'disruptive technologies'. The differentiation is based on the impact that technology bears on the personality of actors rather than on the 'pace of technological process.' The sustaining technologies are considered to be new technologies that stimulate growth in the efficacy of the product. On the other hand, the 'disruptive technologies' cause innovations that generally lead to a radical change in the rules of the competition between market players. In short, the disruptive technologies offer the market a distinct value proposition, which hardly existed before (Christensen 1997). The early version of the concept argued that in the initial phase an innovation fares worse than the core product or services in the market but with reduced prices, and only in the second phase, the quality of the innovation enhances and allures the hardcore consumers. However, in generalized form, a disruption appears just not from the 'low end', but also makes it appearance from 'high end' (Govindrajan & Kopalle, 2006), and from a new market (Christensen & Raynor, 2003). Besides, it might be proved that one of the fundamental features of disruptive innovations is their financial unattractiveness for the existing players (Christensen, 2006). Disruptive technologies—defined as potential technologies that result in a step change in the cost or access to products or services or that dramatically alter how information is gathered, products are manufactured, or are interacted—increasingly have been changing the development orbits of growing markets and of businesses that function in emerging markets. Examples of disruptive technologies include artificial intelligence (AI), block chain, robotics, 3D printing, genomics, and distributed power systems (World Bank).

Academic Debate on Disruptive Innovation

Despite the familiarity of the term disruptive innovation, its applications have taken on varying meanings. Clayton Christensen is an impact making author in the field, but his perspective has not been applied in a systematic and consistent manner (Kawamoto & Spers, 2019). The theory of disruptive innovations first appeared in management science (Bower & Christensen, 1995), and then later was accepted by researchers of other areas of social sciences (Trubnikov, 2017). Ever since the concept of disruptive innovation was introduced and then analyzed critically by Christensen (1997) in his seminal work, several academicians and practitioners have delineated the potential implications of the phenomenon within the scope of multiple management fields (Daneels, 2004). Adner (2002) argues that this concept:

Has had a profound effect on the way in which scholars and managers alike approach technology competition and has prompted a reassessment of the ways in which firms approach technological threats and opportunities. (p. 667)

However, one of the fundamental areas that call for further development of the Christensen's perspective is about the definition of disruptive innovation. In other words, the question of 'What can be regarded as disruptive innovation?' has been taken as partially answered by the work and the subsequent papers of Christensen. In fact, it has been exhibited that the concept of disruptive innovation encompasses varying meanings (Yu & Hang, 2011). For instance, Markides (2006) puts forward a finer categorization of disruptive innovation. He proposed three different disruptive innovation, anticipating that in each case it is plausible to detect different competitive effects, diverse responses from incumbents and diverse ways in which the disruptiveness of the innovation surfaces. Based on this, a triadic categorization is rolled out. He further highlights that along with the disruptive innovation mentioned by Christensen in his book and articles, two other disruptive innovations could be traced. In particular, in his work Markides illustrated 'disruptive business model innovation' and 'disruptive product innovation', and how they differ from 'disruptive technological innovation'.

In their study, Yu and Hang (2009) describe disruptive innovation as something that involves products, services or approaches that revolutionize the existing markets or create new ones by trading off raw performance to achieve simplicity, convenience, affordability and accessibility. They further argue that the main aim of disruptive innovation is not to encourage the best performance, product or service to surviving customers, but to bring below-par performance products or services to market by introducing other benefits. Therefore, it is quite evident that disruptive innovation theory relies on initial low-cost model but at the same time with lower performance features. Charitou & Markides (2003) stated that a response to disruptive innovation could differ from industry to industry or from market to market and determined five ways to respond. The first response suggests concentrating on the conventional business. The main idea behind this response is that a new method of doing business would not necessarily capture the entire market. Therefore, enhancing value proposition for the already targeted market could be the ultimate way to respond to disruptive innovation. The second way to respond is to overlook the disruptive innovation since it has a separate value proposition and targets different customer segments. This response represents an understanding that underestimates the threats that may be linked to this disruption. The third response proposes to exchange roles in order to disrupt the disruptor through playing an entirely different game. This response stresses upon still different product features than those of the disruptor. The fourth way of responding is to involve and scale up only the disruption at the cost of the old way of doing business. In this strategic choice the original disruptor is not disrupted by a new type of counter disruption but encounter a formidable challenge of intensified competition in its new market. The fifth response is to embrace the disruption while at the same time trying to keep the traditional business as is. This response necessitates holding two conflicting or seemingly conflicting positions, simultaneously. In this context, setting a separate organizational unit that is autonomous is a common approach (as cited in Gemici & Alpkan, 2015, p.800)

Nature of Innovation in the Hospitality Industry

The innovation studies in the service industries like hospitality sector are still at its nascent stage (Ottenbacher, 2007; Hjalager, 2010; Escobar & Parra, 2011; Tigu et al., 2013; Kessler et al., 2015; Zehrer et al., 2015; Divisekera & Nguyen, 2018). Hence, few of the conceptual and exploratory studies were evaluated with the intention of unearthing the varying aspects of the underlying theme. Some of the theoretical studies include: 1) Piccoli et al. (2004) establish a theoretical framework on the effect of innovation on customer relationship management; 2) Brunner-Sperdin and Peters (2004) put forward a theoretical construction regarding information in the economic environment.; 3) Sinclair and Sinclair (2009) explain 10 areas of project management; 4) Beesley and Davidson (2013) undertook a theoretical research about the part of academia, industry and government in the growth of innovative skills; 5) Kandampully et al. (2016) set forth a theoretical framework for exploiting creativity and innovation via human resource and technology. They regard employees, customers, and technology as the core constituents of out-of-the-box innovation and new leadership. To be precise, the hospitality sector can be regarded as a complex sector (Li & Hsu, 2016; Kallmuenzer, 2018; Kallmuenzer & Peters, 2018; Melhem et al., 2018). Zehrer et al. (2015) carried out a research to realize the extent to which internal and external factors influence innovativeness and focused the significance of fulfilling customer needs. Hence, in order to satisfy customers, and simultaneously to have the competitive edge globally and domestic market, the hospitality sector requires carrying out extended research with innovation as the core area (Lu & Tseng, 2010; Beesley & Davidson, 2013; Rio-Rama et al., 2017; Kallmuenzer, 2018). In 2015, Christensen incorporated "new market" disruptors in his theory, which refer to companies whose innovations support the creation of wholly new markets, rather than solely alluring the low end of a living market (Christensen et al., 2015). Disruption has triggered enormous innovation across every aspect of the hospitality industry from market offerings to marketing operations (Hotel Business, 2020).

Innovative pattern in the hospitality sector is generally expressed through the capability to create a wide range of innovations, which will make sure the successful development of a hotel (Zaitseva, 2013). In case, a hotel is reluctant to undertake any kind of innovative activities, the chances are very high that its performance and creditability will decline sooner or later and also its competitiveness will be hurt (Ilyenkova & Kuznetsov, 2009). No doubt, the role of innovation in hospitality industry is critical (Sipe, 2016), and it brings changes not only in various dimensions but also relationships among parties change with the change in their assigned roles (Vigila et al., 2016). This is evident from the instances such as hotels now make use of algorithms to devise revenue management action plans, track competition in real time (Vigila, et al., 2018) and also permit consumers to widely use mobile gadgets to avail of a whole array of services (Buhalis & Foerste, 2015). On the other hand, Christenensen et al. (2015) in their article claim that the disruption theory is likely to be engulfed by its own achieved success. Notwithstanding bigger scope, the theory's fundamental concepts have been vastly misunderstood and misinterpreted and its core aspects often misapplied. Furthermore, the use of disruptive innovation by many academicians, authors, and practitioners in describing any kind of situation in which an industry is awaken up and previously victorious occupants flounder is quite overwhelming. The revolution in technology and disruptive innovation has been acknowledged globally by separate manufacturing and service related industries (Adeyinka-Ojo & Abdullah, 2019). Table 1 depicts the particular ways of executing diverse types of innovations in the hospitality industry.

DISRUPTIVE INNOVATIONS IN PURSUIT OF BUSINESS EXCELLENCE IN THE HOSPITALITY INDUSTRY

Christensen (1997) analyzes the factors that led to the failure of companies that were popular cases of success. Companies occupying the number one spot in their respective industries often fail on account of radical changes in technology and market. Similarly, hospitality sector is also faced with considerable changes, but often in complex ways. Therefore, hoteliers must strategically concentrate on quickly adapting to new changes in the environment, so that they can be more effective in running business. The COVID-19 pandemic has punched a massive blow to the hospitality industry, propelling the industry into oblivion. However, the silver lining is that this disruption has triggered multifold innovation across each segment of the industry from market offerings to marketing strategies. As the hospitality industry is gearing up to revamp, hotel owners specially are resorting to disruptive innovations so that they can offer out of the box solutions and services to attract guests.

Few of the radical changes occurred in the hospitality industry that also determines the success level of the hospitality businesses are:

1) **Automation:** The complete check-in process can now be conveniently performed through a Smartphone, reducing significantly staff interactions and minimizing exposure to a crowded lobby. Guests can check-in with a single touch and make entry to their room within minutes and even without requiring a physical key card. Property automation system companies are catering specifically to the accommodations industry to make the integration of smart locks and devices easily accessible.

Table 1. Kinds of innovation in hospitality industry

No.	Innovation type	Description	Specific means to execute in hospitality industry
1	Physical and technical	Creation of new materials, products, services and technologies, novel ways to provide services, enhancing the old ones	Widening the range of specialized and contemporary accommodation provision types according to the tourists' needs
2	Economic	The growth of new markets resulting from the launch of new products or technologies, the generation of novel means to purchase and sell goods, and economic activities following the innovation process	Widening the hospitality industry organizations from the center to the fringe, eliminating "blank spots" in the geographical space of the hospitality industry
3	Organization and management	Fresh solutions and perspectives in managing or organizing the working procedures	Executable in the shape of enhancing the hospitality models employed by organizations in different continents such as European, Asian, American, Eastern European models
4	Legal	Introduction of new laws or regulations, as well as major alteration in the existing ones	Parallel execution of the global practices and national legislation in the area of hospitality, uniting the national legislation into the system of international law
5	Social	Novel ideas and solutions with the aim of redressing the social and cultural complexities which the society encounters	Executing current concepts based on the diverse types of tourism particularly business tourism, educational tourism, eco-tourism, pilgrimage, etc.
6	Marketing	New or highly refined marketing methods, involving the significant changes in the design and packaging of products, employing new sales techniques and product (services) presentations, exhibiting and promoting them on the markets, devising new pricing strategies	Executing the outcomes of market research, experience shared by experts, research by competitors, etc.

Source: Dzhandzhugazova et al. (2016, p.10390-91)

Few of the hotels are experimenting with robots for the purposes of cleaning and delivery. For example, a California-based hotel accommodates contactless deliveries through its robot ambassador,"Rosé," who can bring guests pillows, towels and groceries. So, for an industry that has long since dependent on its human staff to create and deliver customer services, are now relying on technology to create the same experience and enable generating a competitive advantage over other players of the industry. This has been regarded as a drastic innovation. So, an automated management system can enhance efficiency and overall guest experience.

2) **Marketing Promotions:** Employing branded apps, subscription services and in-room amenities as important part of the overall guest experience. In their efforts to bring massive innovations, hotels were starting to integrate branded apps as a marketing strategy to send push notifications. Now, these branded apps have emerged as a one-stop portal for everything from reservations to room service. Used properly, a branded app can enable streamline operations and develop a direct channel of communication between hotels and guests.

Furthermore, hotels are also becoming bolder in their decisions related to devising marketing strategies to allure new kinds of guests. For example, with the growth of the flexi work, several hotels in the United States have begun to be innovative in their offerings to attract guests. These innovations include including introducing subscription service models to give guests access to rooms, workspaces and facilities for a standard monthly fee. Some other hotels are attaching fitness equipment into each room instead of a gym, offering personalized breakfast deliveries as an alternative to the traditional continental breakfast and others are completely redesigning rooms to have kitchenettes.

3) **Smart Hotels:** Smart technology is a profitable investment for hotels since they help to minimize high touch points in rooms. Voice assistants have the capacity to control mostly everything in a room, such as temperature, lighting, alarm clocks, televisions and to order room service. It also generates an opportunity for hotels to gather knowledge about guest patterns and customize the experience even further.

In recent years, the hospitality sector has already begun to adopt innovations gradually to respond to consumer behavior transition driven by on-demand services. However, the onset of COVID-19 pandemic has accelerated the need to implement smart devices and automation on war-footing in the industry.

Potential Disruptions that will Rule the Hospitality Industry in the Future

The current chapter has also attempted to discuss the potential innovations that are most likely to redefine the hospitality industry. Since December 2019, the mankind has been passing through a difficult and new and unprecedented experience with the fast spreading of COVID-19 pandemic across the globe. There is hardly any doubt about the fact that the dreaded pandemic will have a long-term impact on accepted societal norms. This compels people to raise certain pertinent questions about the radical changes that will restructure and redeem the hospitality sector in a post-pandemic era. Now the questions are: Will the restructuring only be restricted to implementing basic health, hygiene and safety standards at hotels? Will social distancing norms be the new normal and change the very fundamental of hospitality operations? How will service delivery processes required to be adapted? Will mega transformations in guests' mindset and thinking push hotels towards a future controlled by process automation supported by tectonic technological advancements?

However, it is firmly believed that moving forward, fast innovations in technology and low-touch service delivery protocols will totally transform traditional hospitality operating approaches and models. In many ways, automation will also help hospitality businesses to fall back upon to their roots as a 'customer-first' industry. In place of a multitude of people doing rote behind-the-scenes tasks, well trained staff will perform as 'Care Ambassadors' optimizing customer experiences. So, the future of guest service delivery will transcend the traditional barriers and hospitality businesses will revolve around servicing the customer's core need for 'Health, Safety and Hygiene security'. Some of the disruptive innovations that may occur in the future are:

1) **Personalized delivery of low-touch services:** In the future, the guests in the hospitality sector will emphasize upon 'safe' delivery of all standard services within the business. The effective delivery of 'low-touch experiences' will emerge as a major driver of customer patronage. Similarly, hotels will have to redefine service delivery protocols for the complex yet significant task of providing service while maintaining safe distance and reducing physical touch points. Hotels will be required to increasingly invest in building and delivering on these new needs to cement patronage from the future traveler.
2) **Patronage of niche travel experiences:** Globally, there seems to be a significant shift towards exploring novel holiday ideas and the discovery of fresh destinations in niche markets, as travelers are expected to overlook holiday spots which are overcrowded. The hospitality business might have to re-think, re-invent and re-structure, on a continuous basis, to offer a distinctive but hugely delightful experience while following social distancing norms.
3) **Not only process but also people centric services:** Success of hotels will be very well decided by the situation where highly trained hotel staff can provide guests superior experiences such as provision of meals in unique, private setting within the hotel; permitting guests to have food in whichever location and at whatever moment they feel hungry etc.
4) **Digital Access Controls Systems (DACS) & Guest Room Automation** Becoming 'keyless' via digital access control systems will redefine Check-ins at hotels and restaurants. With the help of DACS guests will have the freedom to select the room or restaurant table of his/her choice depending on availability and move directly to the room/table upon reaching with limited or no

interactions with staff or physical surface contact at high density public areas. In-room Automation will be combined with voice technology to minimize the requirement for in-person interactions. Growing usage of DACS technology will enable hotels of the future to eliminate traditional lobbies with static reception desks and make staff available to involve in contact-less service delivery that will be absolutely need based.

5) **Artificial Intelligence, Neural Networks & Machine Learning**: The hospitality industry in a post COVID 19 pandemic era will witness a proliferation in the usage of Artificial Intelligence, Neural Networks and Machine Learning. The use of these disruptive technologies will bring about a complete transformation in the capacity of hotels in providing customized products and services.

Moreover, future service delivery will depend on targeted delivery programs, which will again be based on guest data using predictive analytics. For instance, in hotels, the usage of neural networks will help in identifying complex trends in consumer behaviour through statistical analysis. The role of Artificial Intelligence, Neural Networks and Machine Learning will involve the whole guest life cycle. Further, travel and hospitality management which is subject to constant changes in weather, epidemic outbreaks and geopolitical risks will be supported by growing use of artificial intelligence.

6) **Digital Display Systems:** In near future, the restaurant dining will be overwhelmed by growing usage of interactive smart tables that permits guests to custom select their food and wine preferences and also personalize their table-top food presentations, pay their bills and much more. Digital Display technology will play a pivotal role at Meeting and Conferences venues. Furthermore, RFID badges, registration through QR codes, augmented and virtual reality-based product displays, simultaneous multi-lingual virtual transmissions of events will prove to be the essential features at most MICE events.
7) **Robotics & Automated Processes:** Robotics will occupy a significant role in the hospitality industry, mainly on account of its ability to undertake traditional people-intensive functions at a faster pace, more consistently and without the requirement for in-person interactions. In hotels of the future, Robotics will automate standardized food production assembly lines and considerably reduce reliance on physical contact.

In more developments, Robotics will also be stationed at restaurants to efficiently and effectively administer the wine cellars and improve wine pairing functions. Large scale use of robotics and process automation will also considerably enhance store management and supply chain activities, thereby contribute massively to minimize costs, reduce human-made errors and offer superior efficiencies.

As hospitality related businesses continue to evolve and adapt to the changing environment, they need just as much focus on people as on systems and processes. While the adoption of low-touch service protocols and implementation of disruptive innovations will keep on growing, the very roots of hospitality are embedded in the idea of generating immediate and personal engagement that can improve guest experiences and drive loyalty and patronage. This is very unlikely to change. Personalized customer service delivery will always continue to rule the hospitality sector and guests will always derive solace and tranquility in the human greetings and soothing 'touch' of services (Hotelier India).

FUTURE DIRECTIONS FOR RESEARCH

This chapter portrays the role and the kinds of disruptive innovations that are determining the success of business firms operating in the hospitality sector. However, the chances of the disruptive innovations leading to pressing organizational issues were not considered in this chapter. The variation in the recommended strategies under such contexts therefore needs to be taken into consideration in future research.

Besides the issues concerned with the scope of the study, the qualitative approach employed in the study may not produce a broad scale generalization of the findings (Leung, 2015). Therefore, the possibility is that this may restrict the application of the outcome of this study. Having carried out a qualitative research, quantitative techniques are therefore required to be deployed in future research to assess the importance and significance of disruptive innovations in deciding the business excellence in the hospitality industry.

CONCLUSION

The current chapter elucidates on how disruptive innovations can lead to better performance of hospitality business. The chapter also enlightens on the potential innovations that will rule the hospitality industry in the future. Moreover, the ability to understand customers' needs and develop innovative services that offer social and environmental solutions can have an important implication on long-term economic success. Nowadays, a lot of existing dominant players and products eventually have to forfeit their position in the market due to excessive competition. Therefore, they have to continuously transform the products and services offered to the customers. The same is true for the hospitality industry as well.

The findings of the current study add substance to the role of disruptive innovations in the survival and sustenance of the hospitality businesses. Moreover the implications of the study find relevance to business stakeholders in hospitality business and strengthen the policy making. This could contribute towards social change via increasing the success rate of firms operating in the hospitality industry by enabling them to achieve a higher market share and to function relatively more profitably and sustainably. Additionally, it could also contribute towards creating more employment opportunities and improved livelihoods of the thousands of people that greatly rely on the business excellence of hospitality businesses to survive.

REFERENCES

Adeyinka-Ojo, S., & Abdullah, S. K. (2019). Disruptive Digital Innovation and Sharing Economy in Hospitality and Tourism Destination. *IOP Conference Series. Materials Science and Engineering*, *495*(012006), 1–7. doi:10.1088/1757-899X/495/1/012006

Adner, R. (2002). When are technologies disruptive? A demand-based view of the emergence of competition. *Strategic Management Journal*, *23*(8), 667–688. doi:10.1002mj.246

Beesley, L. G., & Davidson, M. (2013). A critical analysis of skilled labor supply and demand in the Australian hospitality industry. *Journal of Quality Assurance in Hospitality & Tourism*, *14*(3), 264–280. doi:10.1080/1528008X.2013.802552

Biancolino, C. A., Maccari, E. A., & Pereira, M. F. (2013). Innovation as a tool for generating value in the IT services sector. *Review of Business Management*, *15*(48), 410–426. doi:10.7819/rbgn.v15i48.1367

Bower, J. L., & Christensen, C. M. (1995). Disruptive technologies: Catching the wave. *Harvard Business Review*, *73*(1), 43–53.

Brunner-Sperdin, A., & Peters, M. (2004). Importance and measurement of entrepreneurial quality and processes in tourism. *Journal of Quality Assurance in Hospitality & Tourism*, *5*(1), 73–90. doi:10.1300/J162v05n01_06

Buhalis, D., & Foerste, M. (2015). SoCoMo marketing for travel and tourism: Empowering co-creation of value. *Journal of Destination Marketing & Management*, *4*(3), 151–161. doi:10.1016/j.jdmm.2015.04.001

Charitou, C., & Markides, C. (2003). Responses to Disruptive Strategic Innovation. *Sloan Management Review*, *44*(2), 55–63.

Christensen, C. M. (1997). *The innovator's dilemma: When new technologies cause great firms to fail*. Harvard Business School Press.

Christensen, C. M. (2006). The ongoing process of building a theory of disruption. *Journal of Product Innovation Management*, *23*(1), 39–55. doi:10.1111/j.1540-5885.2005.00180.x

Christensen, C. M., McDonald, R., Altman, E. J., & Palmer, J. E. (2018). Disruptive Innovation: An Intellectual History and Directions for Future Research. *Journal of Management Studies*, *55*(7), 1043–1078. doi:10.1111/joms.12349

Christensen, C. M., & Raynor, M. (2003). *The innovator's solution: creating and sustaining successful growth*. Harvard Business Review Press.

Christensen, C. M., Raynor, M., & McDonald, R. (2015). What is disruptive innovation? *Harvard Business Review*, *93*(12), 44–53. PMID:17183796

Danneels, E. (2004). Disruptive technology reconsidered: A critique and research agenda. *Journal of Product Innovation Management*, *21*(4), 246–258. doi:10.1111/j.0737-6782.2004.00076.x

Disruption Drives the Hospitality Industry to Innovation. (2020). Retrieved from https://www.hotelbusiness.com/disruption-drives-the-hospitality-industry-to-innovation

Divisekera, S., & Nguyen, V. K. (2018). Determinants of innovation in tourism evidence from Australia. *Tourism Management*, *67*, 157–167. Retrieved from https://www.researchgate.net/publication/323931154_Determinants_of_Innovation_in_tourism_Evidence_from_Australia

Dzhandzhugazova, E.A. (2015). Innovative marketing mix of hotels: Seven sensual notes of hospitality. *Russian Regions: Looking Into the Future*, *3*, 17–27.

Dzhandzhugazovaa, E. A., Ekaterina, A., Blinovaa, E. A., Orlovaa, L. N., & Romanovaa, M. M. (2016). Innovations in Hospitality Industry. *International Journal of Environmental and Science Education*, *11*(17), 10387–10400.

Escobar, A. E. S., & Parra, W. C. (2011). Matriz de Inteligência Hotelera - MIH: Una propuesta para el mejoramiento de la calidad em la prestación del servicio hotelero. *Pensamiento Y Gestión*, *31*, 211–246.

Fraj, E., Matute, J., & Melero, I. (2015). Environmental strategies and organizational competitiveness in the hotel industry: The role of learning and innovation as determinants of environmental success. *Tourism Management*, *46*(6), 30–42. doi:10.1016/j.tourman.2014.05.009

Gemini, E., & Alpkan, L. (2015). An Application of Disruptive Innovation Theory to Create a Competitive Strategy in Turkish Air Transportation Industry. *Procedia: Social and Behavioral Sciences*, *207*, 797–806. doi:10.1016/j.sbspro.2015.10.169

Govindarajan, V., & Kopalle, P. K. (2006). The usefulness of measuring disruptiveness of innovations ex post in making ex ante predictions. *Journal of Product Innovation Management*, *23*(1), 12–18. doi:10.1111/j.1540-5885.2005.00176.x

Hjalager, A. M. (2010). A review of innovation research in tourism. *Tourism Management, 31*(1), 1–12.

Hotelivate report: Disruptions that will redefine hospitality in a post-pandemic world. (n.d.). Retrieved from https://www.hotelierindia.com/business/10909-hotelivate-report-disruptions-that-will-redefine-hospitality-in-a-post-pandemic-world

Ilyenkova, S. D., & Kuznetsov, V. I. (2009). *Innovation Management*. Eurasian Open Institute.

Insights, E. H. L. Retrieved from https://hospitalityinsights.ehl.edu/leading-through-disruption-hospitality

International Finance Corporation. (n.d.). Retrieved from https://www.ifc.org/wps/wcm/connect/537b9b66-a35c-40cf-bed8-6f618c4f63d8/202009-COVID-19-Impact-Disruptive-Tech-EM.pdf

Joshi, B. P. (2018). Disruptive Innovation in Hospitality Human Resource. *Journal of Tourism and Hospitality Education*, *8*(48), 1–29. doi:10.3126/jthe.v8i0.20010

Kallmuenzer, A. (2018). Exploring drives of innovation in hospitality family firms. *International Journal of Contemporary Hospitality Management*, *30*(3), 1978–1995. doi:10.1108/IJCHM-04-2017-0242

Kallmuenzer, A., & Peters, M. (2018). Innovativeness and control mechanisms in tourism and hospitality family firms: A comparative study. *International Journal of Hospitality Management*, *70*, 66–74. doi:10.1016/j.ijhm.2017.10.022

Kandampully, J., Bilgihan, A., & Zhang, T. C. (2016). Developing a people-technology hybrids model to unleash innovation and creativity: The new hospitality frontier. *Journal of Hospitality and Tourism Management*, *29*, 154–164. doi:10.1016/j.jhtm.2016.07.003

Kawamoto, C. T., & Spers, R. G. (2019). A Systematic Review of the Debate and the Researchers of Disruptive Innovation. *Journal of Technology Management & Innovation*, *14*(1), 73–82. doi:10.4067/S0718-27242019000100073

Keller, A., & Hüsig, S. (2009). Ex ante identification of disruptive innovations in the software industry applied to web applications: The case of Microsoft's vs. Google's office applications. *Technological Forecasting and Social Change*, *76*(8), 1044–1054. doi:10.1016/j.techfore.2009.03.005

Kessler, A., Pachucki, C., Stummer, K., Mair, M., & Binder, P. (2015). Types of organizational innovativeness and success in Austrian hotels. *International Journal of Contemporary Hospitality Management*, *27*(7), 1707–1727. doi:10.1108/IJCHM-03-2014-0150

Leung, L. (2015). Validity, reliability, and generalizability in qualitative research. *Journal of Family Medicine and Primary Care*, *4*(3), 324. doi:10.4103/2249-4863.161306 PMID:26288766

Li, M., & Hsu, C. H. C. (2016). A review of employee innovative behavior in services. *International Journal of Contemporary Hospitality Management*, *28*(12), 2820–2841. doi:10.1108/IJCHM-04-2015-0214

Lu, I. Y., & Tseng, C. J. (2010). A study of service innovation activities of tourist hotels in Taiwan. *The International Journal of Organizational Innovation*, *3*(1), 156–172.

Markides, C. (2006). Disruptive innovation in need of better theory. *Journal of Product Innovation Management*, *23*(1), 19–25. doi:10.1111/j.1540-5885.2005.00177.x

Meira, J. V. S., Anjos, S. J. G. D., & Falaster, C. D. (2018). Innovation and performance in the hotel industry. *Journal of Quality Assurance in Hospitality & Tourism*, *20*(2), 185–205. doi:10.1080/1528008X.2018.1512936

Melhem, S. B., Zeffane, R., & Albaity, M. (2018). Determinants of employees' innovative behavior. *International Journal of Contemporary Hospitality Management*, *30*(3), 1601–1620. doi:10.1108/IJCHM-02-2017-0079

Ottenbacher, M. C. (2007). Innovation Management in the Hospitality Industry: Different Strategies for Achieving Success. *Journal of Hospitality & Tourism Research (Washington, D.C.)*, *31*(4), 431–454. doi:10.1177/1096348007302352

Piccoli, G., Anglada, L. D., & Watson, R. T. (2004). Using information technology to improve customer service: Evaluating the impact of strategic opportunities. *Journal of Quality Assurance in Hospitality & Tourism*, *5*(1), 3–26.

Río-Rama, M. C., Álvarez-García, J., & Coca-Pérez, J. L. (2017). Práticas de qualidade, responsabilidade social corporativa e o critério "resultados na sociedade" do modelo EFQM. *Revista Brasileira de Gestão de Negócios*, *19*(64), 307–328. doi:10.7819/rbgn.v0i0.3026

Schumpeter, J. (1985). *A teoria do desenvolvimento econômico*. Nova Cultural.

Sinclair, M., & Sinclair, C. (2009). Improving hotel efficiency through integration of service and project management cultures. *International Journal of Hospitality & Tourism Administration*, *10*(4), 344–360. doi:10.1080/15256480903337155

Sipe, L. J. (2016). How do senior managers influence experience innovation? Insights from a hospitality marketplace. *International Journal of Hospitality Management*, *54*(0), 75–83. doi:10.1016/j.ijhm.2016.01.009

Tigu, G., Iorgulescu, M.-C., & Ravar, A. S. (2013). The impact of creativity and innovation in the hospitality industry on customers. *Journal of Tourism Challenges and Trends*, *6*(1), 9–34.

Trubnikov, D. (2017). Analysing the Impact of Regulation on Disruptive Innovations: The Case of Wireless Technology. *Journal of Industry, Competition and Trade*, *17*(4), 399–420. doi:10.100710842-016-0243-y

Viglia, G., Pera, R., & Bigné, E. (2018). The determinants of stakeholder engagement in digital platforms. *Journal of Business Research*, *89*(C), 404–410. doi:10.1016/j.jbusres.2017.12.029

Viglia, G., Werthner, H., & Buhalis, D. (2016). Disruptive innovations. *Information Technology & Tourism*, *16*(4), 327–329. doi:10.100740558-016-0072-1

Yu, D., & Hang, C. C. (2009). A reflective review of disruptive innovation theory. *International Journal of Management Reviews*, *12*(4), 435–452. doi:10.1111/j.1468-2370.2009.00272.x

Yu, H., & Hang, C. C. (2011). Creating technology candidates for disruptive innovation: Generally applicable R&D strategies. *Technovation*, *31*(8), 401–410. doi:10.1016/j.technovation.2011.02.006

Zaitseva, N. A. (2013). *Management in service industry: tourism and hospitality*. Academia Publishing House.

Zehrer, A., Muskat, B., & Muskat, M. (2015). Enablers of corporate innovation in tourism. In H. Pechlaner & E. Innerhofer (Eds.), *Competence-based innovation in hospitality and tourism*. Gower Publishing.

KEY TERMS AND DEFINITIONS

Airbnb: An online marketplace that connects people who want to rent out their homes with people who are looking for accommodations in that locale.

Artificial Intelligence (AI): The ability of a computer or computer-controlled robot to perform tasks commonly associated with intelligent beings.

Competitive Advantage: A competitive advantage is the attribute that allows an organization to outperform its competitors.

HouseTrip: An online search portal for vacation rentals.

Value Proposition: A promise of value to be delivered, communicated, and acknowledged.

Chapter 3
Customer Perception and Brand Image Through Sensory Marketing

Pankaj Kumar Tyagi
https://orcid.org/0000-0001-9504-541X
Chandigarh University, India

Priyanka Tyagi
Chandigarh University, India

ABSTRACT

Firms can be seen as value facilitators, offering various types of services for consumer consumption, as well as value-generating methods, while following a service viewpoint. It has been proposed that a company's relationships with consumers are used to influence value generation processes. Different experiences influence the form and kinds of meaning that consumers interpret in terms of interactive, relativistic, preferential, or perception beliefs, as well as self- and other-oriented values, in these systems. The aim is to make the procedure easier by grouping alternative options into three main explanatory stages of means. Furthermore, the classification's aim was to include an exhaustive classification when none existed in the marketing literature. The three levels are paradoxically both connected to and independent of each other, according to a general observation made here. They can appear concurrently or independently of one another, but they can also be defined separately.

DOI: 10.4018/978-1-7998-9194-9.ch003

INTRODUCTION

Firms can be seen as value facilitators, offering various services for consumer consumption and value-generating methods while following a service viewpoint. It has been proposed that a company's relationships with consumers influence value generation processes (Gronroos, 2006). In terms of service logic, a company can assist consumers in their everyday operations and procedures by delivering products, facilities, secret services, facts, and so on, as long as this benefits the consumer (Gronroos, 2008). The importance of service as a brand name is believed to appear in this discussion when connections arise via the customer's sensory impressions in the value-generating processes. This picture depicts how consumers view and observe service and the procedure in the modern world. The customer's emotions and opinions regarding the service, which include both product and service materials and other aspects, all lead to a mental picture of the company (Gronroos, 2008). This aligns with Holbrook and Hirschmann (1982) and Schmitt (1999) 's concept of experiential marketing, which emphasises the importance of contexts, aesthetics, attitudes, and symbolic facets of consumer encounters.

This research aims to develop and investigate the multi-sensor brand-experience paradigm in generating consumer value, perceptions, and the image in connection to the human mind and senses - smell, sound, visuality, taste, and touch.

On the other hand, emotional branding seems to be more evident in the form of commodities or intangibles due to their intimate essence and the fact that the client is always more emotionally interested (Pullman and Gross, 2004).

A SM paradigm begins in the human mind and senses, with the resulting multi-sensory brand meetings of emotional flows, structures and psychological reactions. SM refers to a person who perceives and understands a multi-sensory brand encounter personally and emotionally.

The aim is to simplify the procedure by grouping alternative options into three main explanatory stages of means. Furthermore, the classification aimed to include an exhaustive classification when none existed in the marketing literature. They can appear concurrently or independently of one another, but they can also be defined separately.

1. CHOICE OF THEORY

The general marketing theory and sensory branding are discussed in this chapter. The analytical structure then starts by explaining the brand equity principle. In order to consider the effect of sensory branding on customers, brand equity is studied from customer perspectives. With an explanation of the science behind it, sensory branding

Figure 1. Disposition of theory

is added. In order to find out the flexibility of human senses and how effectively they can be used to mark, human senses are described in a marketing manner. For this study, the analysis process ends with the theory.

1.2 Brand Equity

As the emphasis is on customer experience, brand identity and, more specifically, customer equity, in this study, the effect of sensory branding on customers would be addressed to understand. The consumer-based market equity model explains how customer equity is evaluated and explains the various elements that build brand equity. 'To classify the products or services of one vendor or a community of sellers by differentiating such goods or services from the rivals' brands is a unique name and/or emblem (such as the slogan, trade name or packages designs). Branding improves the appeal of the commodity outside its practical purpose. It increases brand identity and differentiates brand characteristics through comparative advantages. Product characteristics are distinctive correlated with branding (Aaker 1991). If a commodity is in danger, a brand will protect consumers, reduce worry, and guarantee a certain quality standard (Kapferer 2004). Therefore, a company's credibility is of great significance because it will help the consumer decide through an acquisition. The buyer hopes to get the same advantages as prior orders and can spend more for this added value, making choosing between various brands simpler (Ind, 2003). Brand equality is a value additional provided to a commodity by a brand name and partnerships that do not have the same brand identification as a product (Elliot & Percy 2007; Keller, 2008). The difference between a product and a brand is the additional benefit. As a consequence of such additional qualities, labelled goods could be valued above the relevant unbranded products (de Chernatony & McDonald 1992).

Numerous markets, leading to a definition of the word, have identified and debated the idea of brand equity. Therefore, several brand equity facets occur today, which can be described in brief as "the marketing impact specific to the brand" concerning "the way buyers, clients and partners think about the brand" beyond its practical purpose (Knapp, 2000, p. 2) (Elliot & Percy, 2007).

'A good brand's true worth is its capacity to win customer loyalty and preference'. As the valuation of a brand is dependent, however, mostly on the feelings and opinions of consumers, which means that the actual value of a brand is challenging to measure rather than buyers that can determine the value of a brand (Ind, 2003). It is essential that a brand has visual features, such as the logo, and underlies its principles, concepts, and ideology with its goods. It must also be taken into account. According to Kapferer (2004), the connection between a company and its products is based on these principles, referred to as the 'brand faith.' Brand equity grouped in four groups by Aaker (1991), brand relationships and brand recognition, loyalty to the brands and product perceptions, arguing that maintaining each feature of the brand is crucial in order to attain high brand equity, as the combination of these variables leads to a higher overall added quality. The valuation of a brand is based on the brand's general image and the customer's appreciation (Knapp, 2000). Indeed, these aspects, which create brand equity, are closely related and can be seen as a reaction in the chain, from awareness to emotional associations, that lead to brand loyalty when the brand is positive.

These four definitions suggest that they evoke memories of a brand that thus relate powerful feelings to a brand that creates brand equality (Elliot & Percy, 2007). A brand equity indicator (McQueen, 1991) is the added benefit that can be assessed financially or as a client's brand experience (Elliot & Percy, 2007). Kapferer (2004) says that all financial and customer dimensions of brand equity measurement can merge. The research, however, is only based on investors' point of view, as a result of market perceptions of additional benefit, is financial performance. Indeed, the brand would create demand towards buyers who perceive positive brand loyalty, and if brands can attract loyal customers through powerful brand equity, the brand would probably command higher rates and retain a larger market share which then turns into economic growth.

1.2.1 Customer-Based Brand Equity

'The buyer needs to understand brand equity, as this would directly influence brand performance. (Elliot & Percy, 2007, p. 82). The way customers settle about a brand's choice depends on their understanding of the added benefit that gives them a sense of the brand. Brand value is based on customers as the buyer is comfortable with the brand and retains some favourable, powerful and special brand organisations.

Two aspects are possible in measuring customer-based brand stock; they can be integrated indirectly, directly and eventually. The indirect method is to identify the fundamental causes for changes in customer-based brand stock through assessing brand awareness, while the direct approach attempts to clarify the consequences of the transformation. Keller (1993) notes that customer brand equity means that campaign measures are consistent with brand awareness, not that the customer brand equities are analysed numerically. There is no consumer quality equity if a customer does not have a brand consciousness and thus may not remember and appreciate the company. This would be the commodity recognised without connection with a brand (Heding, Knudtzen & Bjerre, 2009).

1.2.1.1 Brand knowledge

Brand recognition and brand picture can be separated (Keller, 1993). It applies to the relations which have been taken into account concerning the commodity group concerned. Brand awareness is crucial because it is the foundation for brand equity, particularly consumer reactions to marketing efforts. In reality, Brand Awareness consumers would likely respond favourably to a brand's marketing efforts, while brand and unbranded commodity consumers are likely to get considerably less influenced by the same marketing efforts. Moreover, the chance to choose a brand is higher with high brand awareness, remaining faithful and resisting the temptation of rival products.

1.2.1.2 Brand awareness

Brand recognition is around the memory of a brand in the customers' minds and is referred to as the "likelihood and convenience" of a brand name (Keller, 1993). Brand identification is the belief of a consumer's prior reference to a brand and the possibility to correctly identify a brand by connection to a brand knowledge through the previous exposition of facts such as product group. These considerations are the basics of brand recognition (Keller, 1993). Moreover, Keller (1993) suggests that the degree of recall, coupled with identification to achieve the maximum interest, relies, in particular, on the company and the items involved, on how consumers are confronted with brand exposure choices. The market recognition of brands has an impact on customer decision making, according to Keller (1993), "by shaping brand creation and strength in the brand picture." Brand recognition developments include intentional and latent encouragement of customer relationships (Zaltman, Braun, Puccinelli & Mast, 2001). Observations can calculate implicit awareness; a company may see if their marks have favourable or negative connections by observing implicit consumers' interactions with a certain logo compared to other marks (Fioroni &

Titterton, 2009). The observation was carried out by experimenting in this study to test brand awareness.

1.2.1.3 Brand image

The brand image is described by Keller (1993) as "the impression of brands that the connections hold in the mind of consumers" The brand logo implies a broader sense of the brand in the minds of customers as regards various connections (Keller, 1993). Each individual has several connections that together form a brand from his or her point of view. These organisations, of course, differ personally, but the organisations' qualities, advantages and attitudes are grouped into three main categories (Keller, 1993). Either they are specifically linked to product features such as practical aspects or not connected to products such as prices, packages or images, the consumer's characteristics correspond to what the brand thinks about (Keller, 1993). The user's imagination is an image of someone else using this product, whereas images of use are comparisons of the use of this product (Keller, 1993). These relationships are highly individual and based on a personal comparison framework, which allows a brand name to differ depending on past product assessment experiences. Imagery helps to create a brand personality, and these partnerships are not just about the qualities of the brand but rather about the sensations of the brand (Keller, 1993). The benefits, though, are what the company will provide for the customer and, therefore, the personal qualities associated with the label (Keller, 1993). In conclusion, a brand stance must be viewed as a general impression of a brand that is the basis of how consumers conduct themselves, for example, in the decision-making phase in the case of several products (Keller, 1993).

1.2.1.4 Brand perception

Perception is described as 'the act of only using one's senses to acquire knowledge of the world, to communicate and to experience it' (Boothe 2002, p.2). Perception is of the utmost significance in terms of branding. Brand awareness of customer quality and values, for example, can influence a brand's long-term performance (de Chernatony & McDonald 1992). The quality perceived as the perception of supremacy in quality of a commodity concerning competitors of a brand is described by Aaker (1991). Perceptions do not constantly change yet constantly (Buchholz & Wördemann, 2000). It is important to consider that interpretation is individual and varies between receivers based on their personal preferences. The way an item is perceived is, in effect, highly dependent on the meaning and relevance of the item addressed (Lindström, 2005). However, the view of customers that a brand "may be revised or overwritten to connect a brand to a persuasive purchasing motive" is changing over time (Buchholz & Wördemann, 2000). In other terms, the view of a customer may be influenced by marketing campaigns to enhance the appearance and role of a company in accordance with its identity towards a particular goal. In order to estimate their answers to various types of stimuli, understanding brand perceptions is critical (Fioroni & Titterton 2009). It may be challenging to identify underlying perceived influences, including patterns, rituals and behaviours. In certain ways, however, human experience may be influenced. Thus, these considerations can be established after consumers.

1.2.1.5 Brand loyalty

Brand loyalty is a "measure of a customer's commitment to a brand" (Aaker, 1991 p.39), thereby showing how often a buyer is possible, especially in light of improvements in the brand (Aaker, 1991). It was described as what happens when "favourable beliefs and attitudes are expressed by repeated purchasing behaviour" (Keller, 1993, p.8). Strong brand loyalty implies that consumers immediately choose a commodity without considering the buying decisions on their part (Kapferer, 2008) so that if some of the product features shift, there is no chance of 'losing' a consumer to a rival. Customer commitment to a brand shows how keen the customer is to sustain a connection to the brand, and it is crucial that the business respects and gives due consideration to the brand's original characteristics, which first and foremost attract customers (Kapferer, 2008). The main reason for strong brand loyalty is that it is time-intensive and generally more expensive to acquire new clients than to satisfy them (Aaker 1991). Furthermore, a strong level of consumer satisfaction influences profits in the long run (Robinette & Brand, 2001). Consumer loyalty is reached when product perceptions meet customers' needs (Kotler et al., 2008). Consumer happiness should not ensure brand loyalty; even consumers are ready to turn to a different brand if obstacles to transition are low enough, thus repeat sales (Elliot & Percy 2007).

Therefore, creating obstacles to change will help enterprises maintain their brand loyalty level as it complicates the change for the customer and makes it more connected to the company (Elliot & Percy, 2007). Brand equity consists of the brand name in the memory of the buyer and the feeling in the core of the brand (Czerniawski & Maloney, 1999), which can also be regarded as a function of an intangible connection between the brand and its consumers. Consistency of brand name and brand image must be achieved to create a solid brand, which entails high brand loyalty, how the brand wants to be viewed, and how customers currently view it. This continuity is vital to ensure that consumers are confident because loyalty is based upon confidence. Moreover, it does not ignore the emotional component of brand loyalty, as emotions greatly impact the view of a brand by customers (Robinette & Brand, 2001). Indeed, personal relationships with a company are also part of loyalty, and these 'feelings' should not always be closely related to the real product characteristics (Haig, 2005).

1.3 Sensory Branding

The key to sensory branding is the emotionally interactive relation of a customer and a brand between five human senses; vision, hearing, taste, scent, and touch (Lindström, 2005). Today, it is a "hot subject" in the marketing world, and the numbers of businesses who use it rise rapidly (A. Pasila, personal communication, 2009). He argued that customers appear to take practical qualities such as price and cost for granted in individualistic, contemporaneous cultures. Hultén, Broweus & Dijk (2008). With the overload of knowledge that users are confronted everyday with thousands of texts, the interest of consumers is more difficult to obtain (Lindström 2005).

Moreover, technical advances, such as the Internet, have allowed consumers to buy goods or services and bring them to their homes without leaving the building. Therefore, businesses must deliver more than just the main commodity to allow the commission to make the purchasing reality (Rieunier, 2009). In Schmitt and Simonson (1997), positive intangible qualities such as interactions are dominant decision drivers in the eyes of the consumers, whether traditional attributes of a service or product are insufficient to distinguish the brand. Hultén et al. (2008) conclude that a buying experience may be gained from the subjective connection through human sentiments to a brand. It is essential to recognise the feelings to elicit when identifying the targets for the sensory branding approach and what message should be conveyed by the brand. The aim should be to carefully analyse the impacts of the activities and create a fundamental message to perfectly describe the aims of the sensory brand (Lindström 2005). An analogy with a buddy may be created to clarify the significance of involving the senses. According to Rieunier (2009), a sense of marketing will improve the environment through the shops, in which a 'soul' of the location should be created, and good connections can be brought about for the shoppers. S

1.3.1 The marketing perspective

The value of human senses is presented in a marketing framework in Figure 2 below. Vision and scent, voice, taste and contact are of most significance in the senses (Lindström, 2005).

Figure 2. Sensory Importance
(Lindström, 2005, p. 69)

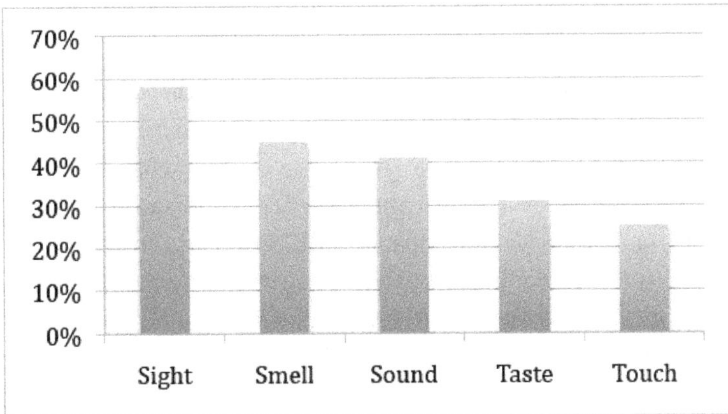

1.3.1.1 Smell

"The eyes may be closed, the ears covered, the contact rejected, and the taste rejected, however the scent remains part of the air we respire." (Switzerland, 2005, p.25) Laird already noticed a favourable correlation in 1932 between consistency and the use of fragrance (Bone & Jantrania, 1992). The close correlation between scent and memory allows it a competitive weapon for connecting consumers to a brand. Furthermore, the argument is that scent can be used as a strategic branding tactic to reassure implicit thought and manipulate it to influence consumers' behaviour and mood (Lorig & Schwartz, 1988). Smelling associations are highly individual, meaning that anything good may be harmful for one person. This is therefore critical to be seen as a strategic instrument when using smell since the expected reaction could differ between people and cultures (Lindström, 2005). The scent is strongly associated to society and history, according to Fox (2006), which contributes to the ethnic variations in the perceived smell. Sweeter scents like cocoa and cinnamon are favoured in the USA, for example, while the most favourite in Scandinavia is the normal scents such as chocolate, woodland and freshly cured grass. This illustrates the need to tailor the fragrance to various audiences and find a concomitant aroma that evokes dented reactions and associations.

Ambient scents may be used to draw buyers in a shop by affecting their attitude and association (Shifferstein & Blok 2002). For shoppers to be attracted and various divisions to be highlighted in the shop, different ambience fragrances may be diffused to differentiate the departments. For instance, imagine the washing powder section smelling of lemon throughout the summer. The washing powder section smells of wood and forest, while the garden equipment section smells of peach. Similarly, a sports store will have the football shoes or golf clubs felt with the distinctive scent of a new lawn. A beauty store can use the smell of the cocoon to draw attention to the tanning lotion. Spangenberg et al. (1996) surveyed a ready to carry store to study the impact of environmental fragrances.

A smell that was perceived to be feminine, vanilla in this case and another scent that was perceived to be male, 'Moroccan Rose,' were distributed across the shop, showing that consumers preferred to pay more money when the smell matched their gender. In the case of a congruent fragrance, shoppers purchased goods for an average of roughly 55 USD compared with 23 USD, in which the aroma was inconsistent. To make an odour effective as a marketing weapon, the sense in which it has diffused must be consistent (Rieunier, 2001). In order to obtain the desired effects by adding an ambience smell, the coherence of stimulation and targets are important. It is also important that the target consumers are considered and that their tastes and responses to various fragments are carefully analysed. The mixture of calming smells and soft music improves purchasing momentum and consumer loyalty, according to Rieunier (2001), whilst no incongruous modification of music and scent in customer behaviour has been observed. A soft drink analysis found that when the appearance of a drink matched the flavours, the taste was easier to recognise when the colour, the true flavour, was not apparent (Lindström, 2005).

1.3.1.2 Taste

Great taste is the most particular feature of all of the five human senses because what they consume is strongly connected with our life. Smell and taste are strongly related and called chemical sensations (Korsmeyer, 2002). Indeed "different preferences are marked by different variations and a more elaborate scent sense". An individual can be attracted to ascent without a taste, but anything can hardly be tasted without tasting them (Lindström, 2005), as you can feel as you enjoy a tasty meal with a flue. In this respect, consumers either prefer to enjoy the scent and the taste or despise the smell and the taste, and seldom like one, and they dislike another.

Gobé (2001) believes that food and drink are closely connected to happy and optimistic experiences, one explanation for not neglecting the taste factor of marketing. Adding brand flavour enhances customer satisfaction, and the presumed advantage of a symbolic act like giving a cup of coffee to the shop can make a positive difference to shoppers' minds (Gobé, 2001). The taste factor can also provide things to eat or drink when purchased or in including cafés and restaurants in a shop, which build an enjoyable environment around the brand, making the customer feel more comfortable (Gobé, 2001). Even though a commodity is not specifically related to oral usage. Skin is the human being's biggest organ. It is both our alarm mechanism and a strong medium for non-verbally conveying our ideas and emotions. Contact is the most important means of identifying and manipulating artefacts while view and hearing are removed (Wolfe, 2006).

However, this sense has been regarded in comparatively few ads, but it requires more intervention than any other sense. According to Gobé (2001), the lower their name awareness, the more brands consumers choose to look for by touching on. Touching a commodity is, in effect, a way to ensure the consistency of a product and is even more relevant in the face of unknown brands. In the sensory phase, weight and material are essential considerations. The perceptions are influenced by the texture of a substance (Schmitt & Simonson, 1997). You will in fact find yourself more addicted and more ready to purchase a commodity if you contact it. The brand feeling is strongly related to the sense of product consistency, claims Lindström (2005).

A product's weight will represent a certain quality level; hi-tech firms are making their goods harder for high-end consumers (Lindström, 2005). There may be a more significant feeling for the device, like the weight of a mobile phone, than look in the purchase decision. The usage of touch screens in the buying phase is one way to include touch to a company. This is growing and can be seen in many shopping points today, such as McDonald's' having customers place orders through touchscreens. The personal bond with the company increases the participation of the consumer in the buying phase by contact. Gobé (2001) reports that even the contact component of businesses is most likely to achieve outstanding loyalty with customers.

1.3.1.4 Sight

Vision is the strongest of the senses when brains and eyes cooperate more than any computer that has ever been created (Winter & Winter, 2003). The sight often overrides those in the most seductive sense; it was, therefore, historically the most used visual stimulus in ads (Lindström, 2005). Vision has an important function in the experience of a brand, and tests have shown that an individual attracted to a product preferred it over the like, even though the consumer may not recall seeing the product (Bornstein, 1987). E.g., logo, style, usage of colours and lighting influence the brand by perception. Vision is mostly about illumination, and colours are just distributions that are analysed by our sensory system of the various wavelengths (Wolfe et al., 2006). Importantly, visuals are more difficult to modify since they are stable if attempts are not taken for their modification, with the exception of film. This is to be compared to other sensations such as music, which evolves continuously and means greater variety at a lower rate (Schmitt & Simonson, 1997).

Colours are central to a brand's perception and may emphasise a commodity's main characteristics and associations. It is used for "setting the brand's tone by means of logos and packings" (Gobé, 2001 p. 79). These characteristics are also one of the main focus areas that implies the thorough selection of colours. In order to enhance and express the ideal brand logo, colours that are selected appropriately (Gobé, 2001). Besides colours, the brand name and ideals of the brand can be reflected by the lighting in the shop. At a point of buying, the use of lights can turn a climate that can be quickly adjusted according to the season.

1.3.1.5 Sound

Sound tends to create atmosphere by the creation of emotions. It "has the immediate impact on memories and feelings" (Gobé, 2001, p.71) and can be used as a catalyst for the creation of the response needed when an emotional connection to a brand is created. Sound is used in brand building as a traditional feature (Lindström, 2005). The mixture is known as audio-visual branding and for several businesses today it is the basis of marketing activities. Due to the potential to influence the mood and brand value by feelings, a sound at the buying stage has become a necessity in recent years (Rieunier, 2009).

Music is an effective instrument to evoke emotions and actually produces feelings of joy by listening to music through endorphins. Due to these good emotions from endorphins utilising sound as an atmospheric stimulant, consumers may be an emotionally strong way to connect to a brand (Schmitt & Simonson, 1997). As sound triggers the emotional portion of the brain more than logical, it may effectively communicate the customers' latent impulses (Gobé, 2001). A wine shop survey found that 77% of clients preferred French wine while French music was playing. The rest of customers ordered German wine when German music was played. In addition, ambient music may be used to manipulate consumers' shopping speeds (Gobé, 2001).

The aims of utilising ambient sounds can, according to Rieunier (2009), be divided into emotional, cognitive and comfortably. She believes that affective goals involve engaging the emotional user to create feelings like joy and gladness while the cognitive goal is to show the goal and the place by producing a matching mood and utilising music to attract attention to a commodity or situation. The behavioural aims, finally, at improving customer behaviour, where time spent in a shop can depend optimally on the music performed. Relaxing music can make you hang in a store longer, whereas faster music can speed up shopping. Indeed, the understanding of the customer of the time spent in the shop may be changed (Rieunier, 2009). According to Lindström (2005), the value of branding sound cannot be overlooked and can even be decisive for consumers' preference. It's relatively simple and inexpensive to add a dimension of tone, making it a versatile option to strengthen a brand image (Schmitt & Simonson, 1997). In addition to using ambient sound at purchase points, the distinctive tone of a company is an essential factor to remember as making brand unique product features increases competition distinction (Lindström, 2005).

1.4.1 Gestalt Psychology

The Gestalt Movement responded to scientists and experimental psychological ideas in the early 1900s (Koffka, 1999). Gestalt psychology thinks that is greater than the number of the components of the whole, or Gestalt. The whole of Gestalt matters. However, minor differences in fundamental aspects or their relationships will result in huge changes in Gestalt (Schmitt & Simonson, 1997). Gestalt's hypothesis may be applied more specifically to sensory branding and holistic views where a minor shift of sensory stimuli can lead to a major change in brand experience. In other words, using both senses in a branding phase will lead to a better result relative to just one sensation. This is called 5-d branding since it covers all the senses of human beings and has a five-dimensional brand. For sensory marketing, the ultimate objective is to build a complete brand.

1.4.2 Bonding with consumers

Lindström (2005) argues that the aim of sensory brands is to stimulate the relationship between customers and the brands and 'optimise impulse buying behaviour'. He says it will contribute to an optimised correspondence between understanding and the facts by establishing an intimate relationship between customers and a company for potential product extensions. The end aim of sensory branding is that the senses build synergies, leading to a chain reaction where the participation of one sense stimulates the usage of another, called a synthesis. In fact, the use of senses reminds the recipient that marketing activities will help to build the desired brand picture. 'Emotional drives contribute to actions that bridge the distance between the implicit desires of customers and their behaviour' (Brand & Lenz, 2000, p.33). Robinette et al. (2000) argue that corporations may bring long-term strategic benefits by the addition of emotional meaning. The greatest improvement is achieved if the action is intuitive and sensorial branding will provide the best possible connection between a customer and a brand if properly handled.

This is achieved when sensory stimulation is new and constant, such that users can familiarise it and perceive it as a regular preference. The customer's loyalty will continue, and the company will be perceived as being a differentiation from rival if the brand excels in a relaxing sense in an inimitable way (Lindström, 2005). If customer loyalty to the company grows, the connection with the brand becomes better and the consumer is moving upwards in the pyramid. The consumer's link to the brand is increasing. The 'market breakthrough' often increases as brands pass the

Figure 3. Sensory Brand Pyramid
(Lindström, 2005)

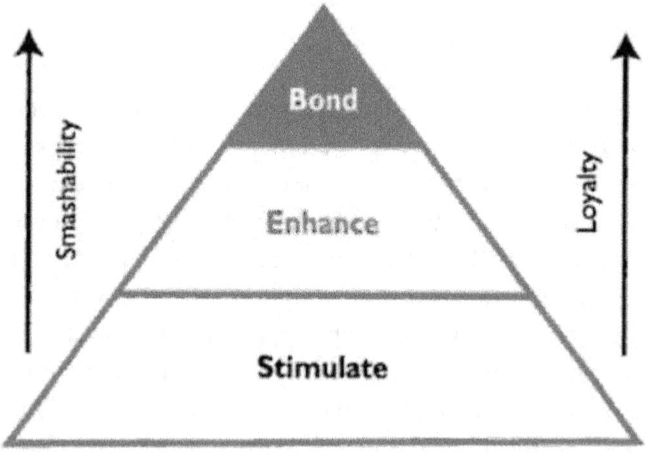

sensory pyramid because the more 'brand breakthrough' the greater the connection between consumers and the brand. The more the brand is breaking down.

1.4.3 Consistency Between Sensory Elements

Each sensory component should be marketed in order to enhance the sensory platform in the brand to render it exclusive to the brand. Each feature should embody its core values and communication to create clear connections between sensory contact points. They can, though, always be uniquely identifiable. Consistency need not be monitored and coherence persuades customers to have faith in the brand and can contribute to loyalty. If a sensory branding campaign is involved, it is only feasible to attain the maximum potential as synergies exist around the sensory contact points.

In reality, Lindström (2005) believes that the impact of the brand contact can be doubled with the inclusion of sensory synergies. The use of five senses to form a clear connection between the brand and customers would require multi-dimensional access to a brand The Flow of Linds (2005). It is also crucial that the five senses are consistently integrated in communication, goods and services since it helps to enrich the product and deepen the relationship between customers and the company. This bond's strongness depends on how much the senses synergise (Lindström, 2005). As discussed previously, bundling consumers with the brand induces emotional loyalty above and beyond critical thought by affecting customers on a multi-dimensional level (Lindström 2005).

Using the senses in every part of the company aims to split the brand down into many sensory contact points, supporting the brand's core values. Subsequently, these contact points can be merged to build a convergence that needs to be extended and shared around the brand. "Emotions are dependent on knowledge obtained from our senses", Lindström (2005) says, which is how sensual arousal reinforces the customer's connection with the company. Many clients may not know the sensory sensations; however, they must have complete knowledge of the stimuli results by the sender, i.e., the brand (Gobé, 2001). Therefore, it is critical that the sensory points of contact (Lindström 2005) should be encouraged to hold the brand special in the customers' minds for this will attract consumers' attention in the brand and affect their reasoned purchasing behavior through an emotional attachment to the brand.

2. BRANDING AND EXPERIENCES

The definition of brand identity is described in branding literature as a specific series of brand connections created or maintained by a company. It may provide an idea of meaning with functional, emotional or self-expressive advantages. It does not matter if the relations are concrete or emotional/symbolic, or both (Anselm and Kostelijk, 2008). In creating strong brands, the emotional connection between the brand and the customer is suggested as critical. Data has also indicated that users are seeking and buying emotional impressions about purchases and not buying goods and services alone (Brembeck and Ekströ̈m, 2004; Ratneshwar and Mick, 2005). There appears to be a desire to concentrate more on tangible products (product brands) than intangible in scholarly discussions on emotional brandings (services brands). Emotional branding seems evident in the service or intangible sense of their intimate essence and when the client is also more individually concerned (Pullman and Gross, 2004).

In addition, in building interpersonal bonds, the atmosphere in which service meetings take place is essential. This covers the features of the physical and related environment in which the service is consumed and the components with which the user interact (Gupta and Vajic, 1999). The sights, the noises, the textures and the smells of the world tend to produce stimulus in the physique sense, and in the connection context, the people and their actions emanate from stimuli.

In the marketing literature, the focus is constantly being paid to user engagement and customer experience ideas. Pine and Gilmore (1999) emphasise the customer's importance of knowing what an encounter is. There is an insight as a company designs one to involve its clients purposefully. Klaus and Maklan (2007) argue that the company has no option as to whether it is linked to its customers. Both coordination, use and consumer interactions eventually lead to a customer's experience.

In the last place, consumer satisfaction is found not in the purchased commodity but in the consumer experience(s) from the purchased product, not in the selected name, not in the item possessed. Essentially, the logic in this sense is that both products provide resources to generate needs or want-satisfactory interactions. All marketing in this context is "marketing facilities." This positions the importance of knowledge at the heart of customer value creation. In particular, feelings and contextual, symbolic and non-utilitarian consumption elements are underlined in experiential consumption research (Arnould and Thompson 2006).

In this analysis, a sensory experiment is described as a picture that challenges the mind and sense of man perceiving products or services or other elements within a service phase. Brakus et al. (2009) draw the conclusion that all such interactions affect customers actively or indirectly and are distinguished between products and buying, service experiences and consumption experiences. Schmitt (1999) proposes consumer interactions in acting, knowing, relating, sensing and thought.

The multiple sense brand experience relates to the five human senses, which are too often ignored in marketing literature, considering their role in producing consumer value, sensory perceptions and the brand as a picture. Scholars also shown that diverse sensory impressions influence customer behaviour and products and services perceptions. For instance, Orth and Malkewitz (2008) and Smith and Burns have addressed empirical studies concerning visual perceptions (1996). The sense of vision is the strongest way to discover environmental shifts and variations and the most basic sense of the perception of products or services. A multi-sensory brand awareness occurs as more than one of the five senses relates to the meaning processing (Hulte'n et al., 2009).

The concept of multi-sense brand experience is as follows: Amulti-sensory brand experience encourages individual value formation and indicates how people respond to their company interactions by including 5 human senses in creating customer value, perceptions and branding as an icon to promote their purchasing and consuming process. Another research has shown that different methodologies define multi-sensory convergence areas in the human brain and that "links with other senses may influence one sense" (Driver and Noesselt, 2008). The human brain's visual, emotional and cognitive functions are often linked to neuromarketing, a new scientific field that explains and enhances our perception of customer behaviour.

3. CONSUMER'S PERCEPTION AND RELATION WITH FIVE SENSES

The five human senses are very important to the various buying and consuming processes of a person. By means of the senses people become aware of companies, goods and labels and experience them. The senses experience all sorts of sensory sensations while the awareness takes place. The styles, quantities and the way these sensations influence the individual's vision mechanism. In actual fact, the senses are the starting point for interpretation, and marketers realise the significance of the shopping experience to use these sensations to influence consumer perception. The key results, such as sound, scents, the environment, touch and taste, have been studied in past studies. In an environmental psychology analysis, Mehrabian and Russell (1974) demonstrated that the environmental factors contribute to emotional reactions, resulting in a customer response. This is really the reaction model for the stimuli – organism. The model proposes that customers have three emotional reactions according to these environmental stimuli; enjoyment, excitement and superiority (Mehrabian and Russell, 1974). Incidentally, certain cognitive reactions lead to two distinct approaches and avoidance behaviours. Most research has been carried out using the model Mehrabian and Russell on the effect of environmental factors, such as extra time spent in a shop, buying decisions, the quest for variety and real expenses.

These experiments have shown that smell can affect purchases, production time and range, and time spent in a shop. Colour also influences so-called shopping, shopping prices, time spent in-store, nice feelings and excitement. (Hite and Bellizzi, 1992) As a previous study has shown, the senses' sensations impact the consumer's reaction. This chapter will examine how these stimuli influence consumers' experiences and, therefore, their buying choice.

CONCLUSION

Perception is the method of attempting by five senses to perceive the environment. Sense organs can be characterised as instruments for gathering information from our environment. Indeed, customers like, before finally buying a product they want to see, touch, hear, smell or taste a commodity, in other words to experience it. The root cause of this mechanism is the need to mitigate market perception of risks and to strive to find the optimal way to meet needs. (Christian Democrats, 2012) Due to this feeling an individual begins to perceive in tandem with perceptions, memories of the past and motivations. The stimulants are pictures, noises, tastes, smells, and contact through five senses as well as human stimulants such as perceptions, motivations and memories in the past.

As stimulants are called products, labels, containers, advertising, designs for a shop. Consumers are subjected to these stimulants while in close interaction with them. Sense organs are the main forces mediating a mechanism through which sensory organs can be subjected to stimuli from the environment and feeling.

Consequently, the user pays attention to and then interprets the stimulants generated by the environment, depending on the factors and function of the stimulants. Finally, sensory factors play a key role in the vision phase.

The emotional effects that 80% of the surrounding knowledge get are colours, illumination, patterns, products, shop designs, and arrangements, which affect moods and consumer buying behaviour. Researchers claim that four roles perform the visual architecture of a shop. The first feature is 'watchfulness.' In other words, a shop with its graphic style draws interest. "Drawing and impression" is the second feature. An excellent graphic interface, for example, attracts shoppers into the shop and impresses clients. If "being well" implies that a customer quickly searches for a product and facts. The last feature is "visual equilibrium between supply and expectations of customers." The most powerful methods to describe and classify colours and statistics.

As competition in globalising markets grows, on the one hand, due to increased product and service diversity and on the other due to fast-moving technology, it becomes more difficult for businesses to influence and attract more information for consumers. Traditional marketing methods are proving insufficient to influence buying decisions. On the other hand, the findings show that it is possible to influence customer choices by changing customer perception. Consumer perceptions start with extrinsic physical stimulation, expectations, experiences and motivation. The sensory marketing theory begins with customer feelings forced to purchase behaviour by bodily stimulation by marketing practitioners. Personal stimulants are really objecting marketing specialists can organise that, but physics stimulants of our environment. In fact, consumers may sense physical stimulants via senses, and consumer decision-making may be influenced by perception if the senses are aroused.

More empirical study is required in more diverse circumstances to expand information regarding the effect of sensory stimulation on purchase behaviours. Future research must use higher age and occupation samples and analyse the moderating effects of switching costs on important structures for the reanalysis of the brand-experience-brand intention link. A model may acquire added value if other sectors like tourism or the travelling industry are to use the model for their understanding, since there are necessary distinctions between goods and services, of how the singularity of services may impact buying habits. For example, it might be helpful to understand how less sensory goods like air-travel goods vary more from sensory services related to tourist activities. Given the importance of creating emotional brand experiences, the greater study is essential to understand how companies interact with consumers and how they vary in pre-or post-purchase phases. While sensory marketing is crucial to generating distinctive brand experiences, it can be added to understanding how marketing support influences the link between brand experience and repetitive purchasing behaviour and between brand equity and repetitive purchasing behaviour. Finally, qualitative data that may better understand the effects of sensory cues on procurement behaviours might be part of future studies.

As customers now cannot spend time on TV publications and other conventional advertising tactics, marketers should use part of their marketing budget to reach people's minds and hearts by giving a pleasant shopping experience and a transcendental sensation. Despite significant research, marketers have discovered that human senses have a key function for purchasing and that customer purchasing behaviour is changed in such an inventive manner by intentional stimulation. Sensory marketing places the human brain at the heart of its five senses and shows corporations and merchants that they can positively influence five consumers using diverse senses like colour, smell, music, taste, and texture.

REFERENCES

Ackerman, D. (1990). *A natural history of the senses*. Random House.

Adolphs, R., Damasio, H., Tranel, D., Cooper, G., & Damasio, A. R. (2000). A role for somatosensory cortices in the visual recognition of emotion as revealed by three-dimensional lesion mapping. *The Journal of Neuroscience: The Official Journal of the Society for Neuroscience*, *20*(7), 2683–2690. doi:10.1523/JNEUROSCI.20-07-02683.2000 PMID:10729349

Areni, C. S., Duhan, D. F., & Kiecker, P. (1999). Point-of-purchase displays, product organisation, and brand purchase likelihood. *Journal of the Academy of Marketing Science*, *27*(4), 428–441. doi:10.1177/0092070399274003

Areni, C. S., & Kim, D. (1993). The influence of background music on shopping behavior: Classical versus top-forty music in a wine store. Academic Press.

Aydinoğlu, N., & Krishna, A. (2011). Guiltless gluttony: The asymmetric effect of size labels on size perceptions and consumption. *The Journal of Consumer Research*, *37*(6), 1095–1112. doi:10.1086/657557

Baker, J., Levy, M., & Grewal, D. (1992). An experimental approach to making retail store environmental decisions. *Journal of Retailing*, *68*(4), 445–460.

Bell, S. (2007). Future Sense: Defining Brands Through Scent. *Market Leader*, 60-62.

Biedekarken, O., & Henneberg, S. (2006). Influence of brands on taste acceptance: ice cream brand versus discount brand; brand recognition influences sensory acceptance positively or negatively, an effect that can sometimes be quite dramatic. Food Engineering and Ingredients, 9(1).

Bosmans, A. (2006). Scents and sensibility: When do (in) congruent ambient scents influence product evaluations? *Journal of Marketing*, *70*(3), 32–43. doi:10.1509/jmkg.70.3.032

Brown, B. L., Strong, W. J., & Rencher, A. C. (1973). Perceptions of personality from speech: Effects of manipulations of acoustical parameters. *The Journal of the Acoustical Society of America*, *54*(1), 29–35. doi:10.1121/1.1913571 PMID:4731646

Bublitz, M. G., Peracchio, L. A., & Block, L. G. (2010). Why did I eat that? Perspectives on food decision making and dietary restraint. *Journal of Consumer Psychology*, *20*(3), 239–258. doi:10.1016/j.jcps.2010.06.008

Cahill, L., Babinsky, R., Markowitsch, H. J., & McGaugh, J. L. (1995). The amygdala and emotional memory. *Nature*, *377*(6547), 295–296. doi:10.1038/377295a0 PMID:7566084

Chandon, P. (2010). Estimating Food Quantity: Biases and Remedies. In A. Krishna (Ed.), *Sensory marketing: Research on the sensuality of products*. Routledge.

Chandon, P., & Ordabayeva, N. (2009). Downsize in 3D, supersize in 1D: Effects of dimensionality of package and portion size changes on size estimations, consumption, and quantity discount expectations. *JMR, Journal of Marketing Research*, *46*(6), 725–738.

Christopher, M., Payne, A., & Ballantyne, D. (1991). *Relationship Marketing*. Butterworth Heinemann.

de Chernatony, L., Cottoma, S., & Segal-Horn, S. (2006). Communication service brands' values internally and externally. *Service Industries Journal*, *25*(8), 819–836. doi:10.1080/02642060601011616

Driver, J., & Noesselt, T. (2008). Multi-sensory interplay reveals cross modal influences on 'sensory specific' brain regions, neural responses, and judgments. *Neuron*, *57*(1), 11–23. doi:10.1016/j.neuron.2007.12.013 PMID:18184561

Eichenbaum, H. (1996). Olfactory perception and memory. In R. R. Llinas & R. Smith Churchland (Eds.), *The mind-brain continuum* (pp. 173–202). MIT Press.

Elder, R., & Krishna, A. (2010). The effect of advertising copy on sensory thoughts and perceived taste. *The Journal of Consumer Research*, *36*(5), 748–756. doi:10.1086/605327

Elder, R., & Krishna, A. (2012). The "Visual Depiction Effect" in advertising: Facilitating embodied mental simulation through product orientation. *The Journal of Consumer Research*, *38*(6), 988–1003. doi:10.1086/661531

Engen, T., Kuisma, J. E., & Eimas, P. D. (1973). Short-term memory of odors. *Journal of Experimental Psychology, 99*(2), 222–225. doi:10.1037/h0034645 PMID:4715315

Engen, T., & Ross, B. M. (1973). Long-term memory of odors with and without verbal descriptions. *Journal of Experimental Psychology, 100*(2), 221–227. doi:10.1037/h0035492 PMID:4745452

Epstein, L. H., Temple, J. L., Roemmich, J. N., & Bouton, M. E. (2009). Habituation as a determinant of human food intake. *Psychological Review, 116*(2), 384–407. doi:10.1037/a0015074 PMID:19348547

Fisher, J. D., Rytting, M., & Heslin, R. (1976). Hands touching hands: Affective and evaluative effects of interpersonal touch. *Sociometry, 39*(4), 416–421. doi:10.2307/3033506 PMID:1006362

Galak, J., Redden, J. P., & Kruger, J. (2009). Variety amnesia: Recalling past variety can accelerate recovery from satiation. *The Journal of Consumer Research, 36*(4), 575–584. doi:10.1086/600066

Gardner, M. P. (1985). Mood states and consumer behavior: A critical review. *The Journal of Consumer Research, 12*(3), 281–300. doi:10.1086/208516

Gilbert, D. T., & Gill, L. J. (2000). The momentary realist. *Psychological Science, 11*(5), 394–398. doi:10.1111/1467-9280.00276 PMID:11228910

Goldkuhl, L., & Styfve'n, M. (2007). Scenting the scent of service success. *European Journal of Marketing, 41*(11/12), 1297–1305. doi:10.1108/03090560710821189

González, J., Barros-Loscertales, A., Pulvermüller, F., Meseguer, V., Sanjuán, A., Belloch, V., & Ávila, C. (2006). Reading cinnamon activates olfactory brain regions. *NeuroImage, 32*(2), 906–912. doi:10.1016/j.neuroimage.2006.03.037 PMID:16651007

Gro¨nroos, C. (1982). An applied service marketing theory. *European Journal of Marketing, 16*(7), 30–41. doi:10.1108/EUM0000000004859

Gro¨nroos, C. (2000). *Service Management and Marketing: A Customer Relationship Management Approach*. Wiley.

Gro¨nroos, C. (2006). Adopting a service logic for marketing. *Marketing Theory, 6*(3), 317–333. doi:10.1177/1470593106066794

Gro¨nroos, C. (2008). Service logic revisited: Who creates value? And who co-creates? *European Business Review, 20*(4), 298–314. doi:10.1108/09555340810886585

Gro¨nroos, C. (2009). *Service logic: Value creation and co-creation and marketing implications*. Paper presented at the 14th Biennial World Marketing Congress, Academy of Marketing Science, Oslo, Norway.

Gro¨nroos, C., & Ravald, A. (2009). *Marketing and the logic of service: value facilitation, value creation, and their marketing implications*. Working Papers Series No. 542/2009, Hanken School of Economics, Helsinki.

Hagtvedt, H., & Patrick, V. M. (2008). Art infusion: The influence of visual art on the perception and evaluation of consumer products. *JMR, Journal of Marketing Research*, *45*(3), 379–389. doi:10.1509/jmkr.45.3.379

Harlow, H. F. (1958). The nature of love. *The American Psychologist*, *13*(12), 673–685. doi:10.1037/h0047884 PMID:4984312

Havas, D. A., Glenberg, A. M., Gutowski, K. A., Lucarelli, M. J., & Davidson, R. J. (2010). Cosmetic use of Botulinum Toxin-A affects processing of emotional language. *Psychological Science*, *21*(7), 895–900. doi:10.1177/0956797610374742 PMID:20548056

Herz, R. (2007). *The scent of desire: Discovering our enigmatic sense of smell*. William Morrow.

Herz, R. S. (1997). The effects of cue distinctiveness on odor-based context dependent memory. Memory & Cognition, 25(3), 375–380.

Herz, R. S. (2004). A naturalistic analysis of autobiographical memories triggered by olfactory visual and auditory stimuli. *Chemical Senses*, *29*(3), 217–224. doi:10.1093/chemse/bjh025 PMID:15047596

Herz, R. S., & Engen, T. (1996). Odor memory: Review and analysis. *Psychonomic Bulletin & Review*, *3*(3), 300–313. doi:10.3758/BF03210754 PMID:24213931

Hoch, S. J., & Ha, Y. (1986). Consumer learning: Advertising and the ambiguity of product experience. *The Journal of Consumer Research*, *13*(2), 221–233. doi:10.1086/209062

Hoegg, J., & Alba, J. W. (2007). Taste perception: More than meets the tongue. *The Journal of Consumer Research*, *33*(4), 490–498. doi:10.1086/510222

Holmberg, L. (1975). The influence of elongation on the perception of volume of geometrically simple objects. *Psychological Research Bulletin*, *15*, 1–18.

Homburg, C., Koschate, N., & Hoyer, W. D. (2005). The interplay of cognition and affect in the formation of customer satisfaction: a dynamic perspective. *American Marketing Association Conference Proceedings*, 16.

Hulte'n, B., Broweus, N., & van Dijk, M. (2009). *Sensory Marketing*. Palgrave Macmillan. doi:10.1057/9780230237049

Hung, I. W., & Labroo, A. A. (2011). From firm muscles to firm willpower: Understanding the role of embodied cognition in self-regulation. *The Journal of Consumer Research*, *37*(6), 1046–1064. doi:10.1086/657240

Kahn, B. E., & Isen, A. M. (1993). The influence of positive affect on variety seeking among safe, enjoyable products. *The Journal of Consumer Research*, *20*(2), 257–270. doi:10.1086/209347

Kellaris, J. J., & Kent, R. J. (1992). The influence of music on consumers' temporal perceptions: Does time fly when you're having fun? *Journal of Consumer Psychology*, *1*(4), 365–376. doi:10.1016/S1057-7408(08)80060-5

Kellaris, J. J., & Kent, R. J. (1993). An exploratory investigation of responses elicited by music varying in tempo, tonality, and texture. *Journal of Consumer Psychology*, *2*(4), 381–401. doi:10.1016/S1057-7408(08)80068-X

Keller, K. L., & Lehmann, D. R. (2006). Brands and branding: Research findings and future priorities. *Marketing Science*, *25*(6), 740–759. doi:10.1287/mksc.1050.0153

Kinney, J. A. S., & Luria, S. M. (1970). Conflicting visual and tactual–kinaesthetic stimulation. *Attention, Perception & Psychophysics*, *8*(3), 189–192. doi:10.3758/BF03210203

Klink, R. R. (2000). Creating brand names with meaning: The use of sound symbolism. *Marketing Letters*, *11*(1), 5–20. doi:10.1023/A:1008184423824

Krishna, A. (2006). Interaction of senses: The effect of vision versus touch on the elongation bias. *The Journal of Consumer Research*, *32*(4), 557–566. doi:10.1086/500486

Krishna, A. (2010). *Sensory marketing: Research on the sensuality of products*. Routledge.

Krishna, A., Elder, R. S., & Caldara, C. (2010). Feminine to smell but masculine to touch?: Multi-sensory congruence and its effect on the aesthetic experience. *Journal of Consumer Psychology*, *20*(4), 410–418. doi:10.1016/j.jcps.2010.06.010

Krishna, A., Lwin, M. O., & Morrin, M. (2010). Product scent and memory.\. *The Journal of Consumer Research*, *37*(1), 57–67. doi:10.1086/649909

Krishna, A., & Morrin, M. (2008). Does touch affect taste? The perceptual transfer of product container haptic cues. *The Journal of Consumer Research*, *34*(6), 807–818. doi:10.1086/523286

Labroo, A. A., & Nielsen, J. (2010). Half the thrill is in the chase: Twisted inferences from embodied cognitions. *The Journal of Consumer Research*, *37*(1), 143–158. doi:10.1086/649908

Laird, D. A. (1932). How the consumer estimates quality by subconscious sensory impressions: With special reference to the role of smell. *The Journal of Applied Psychology*, *16*(3), 241–246. doi:10.1037/h0074816

Landau, M. J., Meier, B. P., & Keefer, L. A. (2010). A metaphor-enriched social cognition. *Psychological Bulletin*, *136*(6), 1045–1067. doi:10.1037/a0020970 PMID:20822208

Lawless, H., & Cain, W. (1975). Recognition memory for odors. *Chemical Senses*, *1*(3), 331–337. doi:10.1093/chemse/1.3.331

Lawless, H., & Engen, T. (1977). Associations to odors: Interference, mnemonics, and verbal labeling. *Journal of Experimental Psychology. Human Learning and Memory*, *3*(1), 52–59. doi:10.1037/0278-7393.3.1.52 PMID:845551

Leclerc, F., Schmitt, B. H., & Dubé, L. (1994). Foreign branding and its effects on product perceptions and attitudes. *JMR, Journal of Marketing Research*, *31*(2), 263–270. doi:10.1177/002224379403100209

Lee, L., Frederick, S., & Ariely, D. (2006). Try it, you'll like it: The influence of expectation, consumption, and revelation on preferences for beer. *Psychological Science*, *17*(12), 1054–1058. doi:10.1111/j.1467-9280.2006.01829.x PMID:17201787

Mattila, A. S., & Wirtz, J. (2001). Congruency of scent and music as a driver of in-store evaluations and behavior. *Journal of Retailing*, *77*(2), 273–289. doi:10.1016/S0022-4359(01)00042-2

Mehrabian, A., & Russell, J. A. (1974). *An Approach to Environmental Psychology*. Massachusetts Institute of Technology.

Milliman, R. E. (1982). Using background music to affect the behavior of supermarket shoppers. *Journal of Marketing*, *46*(2), 86–91. doi:10.1177/002224298204600313

Milliman, R. E. (1986). The Influence of Background Music on the Behavior of Restaurant Patrons. *The Journal of Consumer Research, 13*(September), 286–289. doi:10.1086/209068

Morewedge, C. K., Huh, Y. E., & Vosgerau, J. (2010). Thought for food: Imagined consumption reduces actual consumption. *Science, 330*(6010), 1530–1533. doi:10.1126cience.1195701 PMID:21148388

Morrin, M., & Ratneshwar, S. (2003). Does it make sense to use scents to enhance brand memory? *JMR, Journal of Marketing Research, 40*(1), 10–25. doi:10.1509/jmkr.40.1.10.19128

Morrison, S., & Crane, F. G. (2007). Building the service brand by creating and managing an emotional brand experience. *Journal of Brand Management, 14*(5), 410–421. doi:10.1057/palgrave.bm.2550080

Paivio, A. (1969). Mental imagery in associative learning and memory. *Psychological Review, 76*(3), 241–263. doi:10.1037/h0027272

Peck, J., & Childers, T. L. (2008). If it tastes, smells, sounds, and feels like a duck, then it must be a....: Effects of sensory factors on consumer behaviors. In C. P. Haugtvedt, P. M. Herr, & F. R. Kardes (Eds.), *Handbook of consumer psychology* (pp. 193–219). Psychology Press.

Peck, J., & Shu, S. B. (2009). The effect of mere touch on perceived ownership. *The Journal of Consumer Research, 36*(3), 434–447. doi:10.1086/598614

Peck, J., & Wiggins, J. (2006). It just feels good: Customers' affective response to touch and its influence on persuasion. *Journal of Marketing, 70*(4), 56–69.

Peck, J., & Wiggins, J. (2006). It just feels good: Customers' affective response to touch and its influence on persuasion. *Journal of Marketing, 70*, 56–69.

Raghubir, P., & Krishna, A. (1999). Vital dimensions in volume perception: Can the eye fool the stomach? *JMR, Journal of Marketing Research, 36*(3), 313–326. doi:10.1177/002224379903600302

Raghunathan, R., Naylor, R. W., & Hoyer, W. D. (2006). The unhealthy=tasty intuition and its effects on taste inferences, enjoyment, and choice of food products. *Journal of Marketing, 70*(4), 170–184. doi:10.1509/jmkg.70.4.170

Rauscher, F. H., Krauss, R. M., & Chen, Y. (1996). Gesture, speech, and lexical access: The role of lexical movements in speech production. *Psychological Science, 7*(4), 226–231. doi:10.1111/j.1467-9280.1996.tb00364.x

Rolls, E. T. (2005). Taste, olfactory, and food texture processing in the brain and the control of food intake. *Physiology & Behavior*, *85*(May), 45–56. doi:10.1016/j.physbeh.2005.04.012 PMID:15924905

Rozin, P., & Fallon, A. E. (1987). A perspective on disgust. *Psychological Review*, *94*(1), 23–41. doi:10.1037/0033-295X.94.1.23 PMID:3823304

Schab, F. R., & Crowder, R. G. (1995). Implicit measures of odor memory. In F. R. Schab & R. G. Crowder (Eds.), *Memory for odors* (pp. 72–91). Pyschology Press.

Scott, M. L., Nowlis, S. M., Mandel, N., & Morales, A. C. (2008). The effects of reduced food size and package size on the consumption behavior of restrained and unrestrained eaters. *The Journal of Consumer Research*, *35*(3), 391–405. doi:10.1086/591103

Shepard, R. N. (1967). Recognition memory for words, sentences and pictures. *Journal of Verbal Learning and Verbal Behavior*, *6*(1), 156–163. doi:10.1016/S0022-5371(67)80067-7

Shiv, B., & Nowlis, S. M. (2004). The effect of distractions while tasting a food sample: The interplay of informational and affective components in subsequent choice. *The Journal of Consumer Research*, *31*(3), 599–608. doi:10.1086/425095

Simmons, W. K., Martin, A., & Barsalou, L. W. (2005, October 1). Pictures of appetising foods activate gustatory cortices for taste and reward. *Cerebral Cortex (New York, N.Y.)*, *15*(10), 1602–1608. doi:10.1093/cercor/bhi038 PMID:15703257

Spangenberg, E. R., Crowley, A. E., & Henderson, P. W. (1996). Improving the store environment: Do olfactory cues affect evaluations and behaviors? *Journal of Marketing*, *60*(2), 67–80. doi:10.1177/002224299606000205

Spangenberg, E. R., Grohmann, B., & Sprott, D. E. (2005). It's beginning to smell (and sound) a lot like Christmas: The interactive effects of ambient scent and music in a retail setting. *Journal of Business Research*, *58*(11), 1583–1589. doi:10.1016/j.jbusres.2004.09.005

Stout, P., & Leckenby, J. D. (1988). Let the music play: Music as a nonverbal element in television commercials. In S. Hecker & D. W. Stewart (Eds.), *Nonverbal communication in advertising* (pp. 207–233). Lexington Books.

Sweeney, C.J., & Wyber, F. (2002). The role of cognitions and emotions in the music approach-avoidance behaviour relationship. Journal of Services Marketing, 16(1), 51–70. doi:10.1108/08876040210419415

Thesen, T., Vibell, J., & Calvert, G., & Osterbauer, A. (2004). Neuroimaging of multi-sensory processing in vision, audition, touch and olfaction. *Cognitive Processing, 5*(2), 84–93. doi:10.100710339-004-0012-4

Wells, G., & Petty, R. (1980). The effects of overhead movements on persuasion: Compatibility and incompatibility of responses. *Basic and Applied Social Psychology, 1*(3), 219–230. doi:10.120715324834basp0103_2

Willander, J., & Larsson, M. (2006). Smell your way back to childhood: Autobiographical odor memory. *Psychonomic Bulletin & Review, 13*(2), 240–244. doi:10.3758/BF03193837 PMID:16892988

Williams, L. E., & Bargh, J. A. (2008). Experiencing physical warmth promotes interpersonal warmth. *Science, 322*(5901), 606–607. doi:10.1126cience.1162548 PMID:18948544

Wolfe, J. M., Kluender, K. R., Levi, D. M., Bartoshuk, L. M., Herz, R. S., Klatzky, R. L., & .... (2006). *Sensation & perception*. Sinauer Associates.

Woodruff, R. B., & Gardial, S. (1996). *Know Your Customers – New Approaches to Understanding Customer Value and Satisfaction*. Blackwell.

Wyer, R. S. Jr, Hung, I. W., & Jiang, Y. (2008). Visual and verbal processing strategies in comprehension and judgment. *Journal of Consumer Psychology, 18*(4), 244–257. doi:10.1016/j.jcps.2008.09.002

Yalch, R. F., & Spangenberg, E. R. (2000). The effects of music in a retail setting on real and perceived shopping times. *Journal of Business Research, 49*(2), 139–147. doi:10.1016/S0148-2963(99)00003-X

Yorkston, E. (2010). Auxiliary auditory ambitions: Assessing ancillary and ambient sounds. In A. Krishna (Ed.), *Sensory marketing: Research on the sensuality of products* (pp. 157–167). Routledge.

Zajonc, R. B., & Markus, H. (1982). Affective and cognitive factors in preferences. *The Journal of Consumer Research, 9*(2), 123–131. doi:10.1086/208905

Zampini, M., & Spence, C. (2005). Modifying the multi-sensory perception of a carbonated beverage using auditory cues. *Food Quality and Preference, 16*(7), 632–641. doi:10.1016/j.foodqual.2004.11.004

Zatorre, R. J., & Halpern, A. R. (2005). Mental concerts: Musical imagery and auditory cortex. *Neuron, 47*(1), 9–12. doi:10.1016/j.neuron.2005.06.013 PMID:15996544

Zhang, S., & Schmitt, B. H. (2004). Activating sound and meaning: The role of language proficiency in bilingual consumer environments. *The Journal of Consumer Research*, *31*(1), 220–228. doi:10.1086/383437

Zhu, R., & Meyers-Levy, J. (2005). Distinguishing between the meanings of music: When background music affects product perceptions. *JMR, Journal of Marketing Research*, *42*(3), 333–345. doi:10.1509/jmkr.2005.42.3.333

Zucco, G. M. (2003). Anomalies in cognition: Olfactory memory. *European Psychologist*, *8*(2), 77–86. doi:10.1027//1016-9040.8.2.77

Chapter 4
Evaluation of E-Service Satisfaction Among Online Travel Agency (OTA) Users

Sunil Kumar
Chandigarh University, India

Shiv Kumar Gupta
HNB Garhwal Central University, India

Abhishek K. Vaishnav
HNB Garhwal Central University, India

Pankaj Kumar
Mizoram Central University, India

ABSTRACT

Online travel agencies (OTAs) are online travel platforms like Expedia.Com, Make My Trip, Booking.com, and Travelzoo, etc., which sell travel-related products and services such as hotels, flights, travel packages, rentals, amenities, and activities to customers. OTAs work as an intermediary between suppliers and customers and help both in selling and buying the products and services. Over the period, due to technological advancement, OTAs have captured an average of 40% to 50% of the total global travel market. Users of online travel agencies are also increasing significantly as they are getting numerous benefits like saving of time and money, cheapest fares, best travel options and deals, customize packages, and superior value propositions. The present study is empirical in nature and has measured the perception and satisfaction level of uses towards various products and services of online travel agencies (OTAs).

DOI: 10.4018/978-1-7998-9194-9.ch004

INTRODUCTION

Information and communication technology has transformed the ease of business and opened the opportunities for business enterprises to facilitate consumers at large. Online travel agency business is growing fast. It has been observed that internet enabled ICT has accelerated the volume of business transactions of travel and tourism enterprises and to the diverse range of potential and existing visitors in last few years. ICT has transformed tourism information and products to all stakeholders of the industry through its application by distribution channels and travel and tourism intermediaries' viz online travel agencies/tour operators. The technological innovation of the internet as a medium has an intense impact on tourism business enterprises from producer to distributor. It has enabled purposeful information about the products and services to countless users. The internet has accelerated the search pattern and easily update a tourist about travel information or purchase of travel products. The digitalization in India has equipped tourist to travel anywhere with required belongings and have eliminated traditional travel practices. Due to ease of online travel and tourism business large number of OTAs are opening every year and at the same time many of them are dying as well. There might be several reasons behind that. These OTAs are offering e-services in terms of selling individual services viz. air ticket, accommodation, etc. or varieties of predesigned tour packages and customized tour packages. In order to sustain in the increasingly competitive environment the company needs to satisfy the users. A satisfied customer spends more money thus the chance of profits is always on the higher side. Customer satisfaction has a direct impact on, as well as purposeful post-purchase indicator for, future profitability. In modern competitive market, customer satisfaction is a key factor for being profitable irrespective of size or volume of business organization. In this study a strong relationship between customer care, customer satisfaction, and profitability is found as customer satisfaction has significant influences on the growth of an organization and its financial outcomes.

REVIEW OF LITERATURE

Tourism and information communication technology (ICT) have emerged as strong drivers of the global economy since tourism products and services are leading commodities on the online platforms (Connolly, Olsen, & Moore, 1998; Kozak, & Rimmington, 2000). Therefore, it becomes important to understand the factors affecting the customer satisfaction and their experiences online (Fiore, & Jeoung, 2007; Sparks, & Browning, 2010; Sharma, & Baoku, 2013; Confente, 2015; Möhlmann, 2015). Consumer satisfaction deeply influences the growth of any business. As tourism business is dynamic in nature, it is essential for tourism businesses to continuously monitor the performance in terms of the delivery of products and services (Bowen, & Clarke, 2002; Prebensen, 2004). Oliver, (1980) stated that 'satisfaction is an emotional state arising from the non-confirmation of positive or negative expectations for the experience of consumption. A number of researchers have defined e-satisfaction differently. Anand, (2007) conceptualized e-satisfaction in terms of relationship marketing through media technology" whereas Anderson, and Srinivasan (2003) considered pre-purchasing experiences on travel websites as a basis of e-satisfaction.

There is a dearth of literature specific to the e-service satisfaction in general and in context of online travel agencies/portals in particular as much of the research work is confined to general sales and marketing management (Szymanski, & Hise, 2000; Burke, 2002; Gómez, McLaughlin, & Wittink, 2004; Evanschitzky, Iyer, Hesse, & Ahlert, 2004; Law, Leung, & Buhalis, 2009; Wang, Zhang, Gu, & Zhen, 2009; Flint, Blocker, & Boutin, 2011). There have been plenty of studies related to tourists' satisfaction in the traditional (offline) model of tourism including those conducted by Haber and Lerner, (1998), Law, and Leung, (2000), Akama and Kieti, (2003), Mills, and Morrison, (2004); Kim, and Lee, (2005), Matzler, Waiguny, Toschkov, and Mooradian, (2006), Guan, et.al, (2007); Wang, Zhang, Gu, and Zhen, (2009), Alegre, and Garau, (2010), Dutta, Chauhan, and Chauhan, (2017). In order to understand the determinants of e-service satisfaction, a number of constructs and measures have been proposed by different authors (Zeithaml *et al.,* 2002; Masoomeh, Tahayori, & Sadeghian, 2013; Anderson, & Srinivasan, 2003) and moreover, there is no unanimity about the parameters of e-service quality and e-satisfaction (Masoomeh, *et al.* 2013). Cho, and Agrusa, (2006) suggested that information related factors, technology, and usability related factors, price-related factors, convenience related factor, and brand name factors are the major factors affecting the e-satisfaction towards the online travel portal or website. Mohammed, et, al. (2016), in her study, discussed three models for measuring e-satisfaction including Weber et al.'s Model proposed by Weber, Murphy, Schegg, and Murphy, (2005); Kim et al.'s scale, developed by Kim, Ma, & Kim, (2006), and E-Satisfaction Model of Masoomeh, (2013). Measuring E-Tourism Service Quality is crucial for understanding the underlying factors of e-satisfaction and researchers like Zeithaml, Parasuraman, and Malhorta, (2002); Parasuraman, Zeithaml, and Malhotra, (2005); Swaid, and Wigand (2007); Ho, and Lee (2007); Hongxiu *et al.* (2009); and Iliachenko (2006 b) have developed models for evaluating e-tourism service quality. Further, attributes related to e-service evaluation were studied by scholars like Finn, (2011) and Parasuraman *et al.,* (2005). They proposed four categories of e-service attributes perceived by online buyers, namely- product perceptions/expectations, shopping experience, customer services, and consumer risks. As researchers have not found enough literature regarding the e-service satisfaction of tourists purchasing tour packages from Online Travel Agencies in India, this study is significant.

OBJECTIVE AND HYPOTHESIS OF THE STUDY

On the basis of review of literature and research gap, following research objective and hypothesis have been formulated.

1. To measure the satisfaction level of online travel service users towards various services offered by online travel agencies (OTAs).
    - **H1** There is a high satisfaction among online travel service users towards various services offered by online travel agencies (OTAs).

RESEARCH DESIGN AND METHODOLOGY

This research is based on an empirical study, by analysing and critically examining the relevant information and statistics, collected from primary as well as secondary sources. Primary data were collected by using a structured questionnaire in the form of 'Google Form' which was circulated to the OTA users of Delhi, capital city of India. The email ids were chosen from a pool of e-mail Ids collected through convenient sampling method. The email Ids were identified with the help of tourism professionals and online travel agencies in the study area. The response rate of the questionnaire (Google forms e-mailed to identified users) was quite discouraging as after sending e-mails followed by reminders to 2400 respondents only 554 responses were received from the respondents. After scrutiny of the responses, only 500 responses were coded for the final analysis. The opinion of respondents was recorded on a five point Likert scale. The descriptive analysis and expectation-experience gap analysis was used for evaluation of tourist satisfaction towards online travel agencies. Further, the association of overall satisfaction level with demographic variables including age and occupation level was performed by cross tabulating these variables and the results were confirmed using chi-square statistics. The satisfaction of the respondents was analysed by performing Mean Gap Analysis between the expectations and perceptions of the respondents about the product and services attributes. The data analysis was performed by using SPSS 20.

DATA ANALYSIS AND INTERPRETATION

The mean scores for the expectations and perceptions of the respondents for the 21 identified product or service attributes were compared using paired sample t-test and the results are displayed in the following Table- 1 A close look on the t-statistics shown in the table reveals that out of a total 21 pairs of attributes 16 pairs of attributes are significantly different from each other at $P< 0.05$. The highest gap (.982) is recorded for the attribute 'user control of transactions 'while the smallest gap (.050) is recorded for the attribute 'FAQs'. The negative values for the gap (mean difference) suggest that respondents were having higher expectations in comparison to their perception resulting in dissatisfaction whereas positive values denote that the respondents' perception exceeded their expectation hence resulted in

Table 1. Paired-sample t-tests for User Satisfaction

Item	Perception Mean	Satisfaction Mean	Mean Difference	t-ratio	P-value
Product diversity	3.536	3.550	0.014	-0.18	0.855
Clear specification of Products with Images	3.340	3.942	0.602	-8.96	0.000
Comparison of Products/Services	3.098	3.622	0.524	-7.86	0.000
Virtual Tours of destination and amenities, facilities	3.126	3.598	0.472	-6.79	0.000
Search Speed	3.364	3.450	0.086	-1.23	0.218
Navigation Quality	3.670	3.228	0.442	6.51	0.000
Interactive design	2.990	3.276	0.286	-3.75	0.000
Ease of Use	3.120	3.442	0.322	-4.48	0.000
Authentic Reviews	3.118	3.620	0.502	-7.32	0.000
Refinement/exquisite page design	3.596	3.260	0.336	-4.77	0.000
User Control of Transactions	2.776	3.758	0.982	13.45	0.000
Lower prices of product and service	3.514	3.548	0.034	-0.44	0.654
Secure payment gateways	3.388	3.560	.0172	-2.67	0.008
User Information Security	2.868	3.576	0.708	-8.89	0.000
Clear Terms and Conditions	3.356	3.686	0.330	-5.30	0.000
Wish list/cart option	3.242	3.612	0.370	-5.74	0.000
FAQs	3.266	3.216	0.050	0.63	0.529
Efficient 24*7 Customer Support	3.300	3.712	0.412	-6.37	0.000
Compensation policy	2.958	3.812	0.854	11.74	0.000
Target User Service	3.364	3.452	0.088	-1.18	0.237
Website Linking	3.338	3.490	0.152	-2.28	0.023

Source: Primary Data.

satisfaction. Significant p values for the attributes including 'diversity of products and services', 'search speed', 'lower prices of products and services', 'FAQs' and 'target user service' indicate that there is no significant difference between the mean values for perceptions and expectations and any visible difference if occurred that was just by chance.

The data from above Table-1 suggests that the perception level of the respondents exceeded their expectations in case of the attributes including 'virtual tours of destination, amenities, facilities'; 'navigation quality'; 'user control of transactions'; and 'FAQs' with positive mean gap values resulting in high satisfaction. However, their perception could not meet their expectations in the case of remaining attributes. Hence, OTAs need to improve upon these attributes for fostering higher satisfaction among the users.

Figure 1. User Perception and Satisfaction Means differences

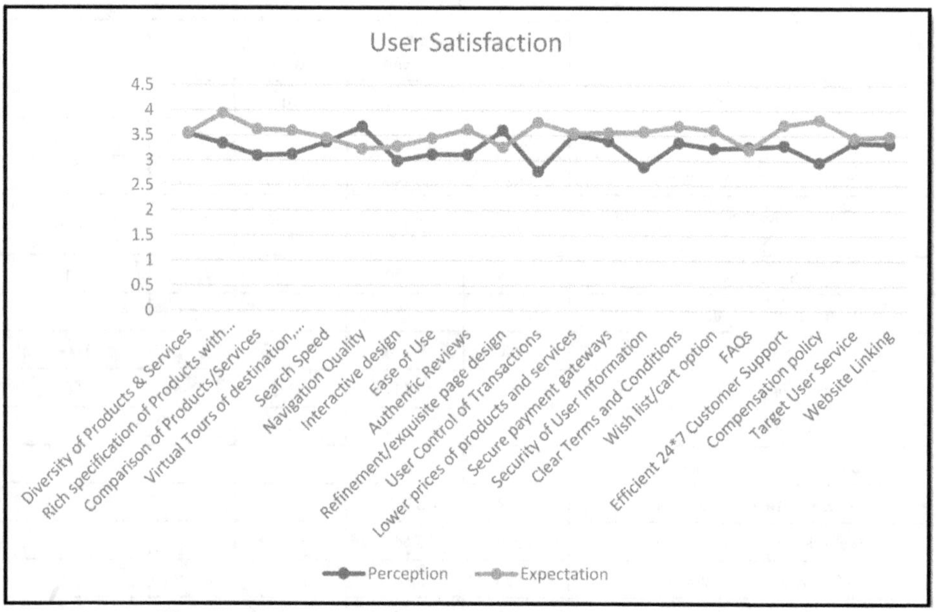

The respondents were asked to record their overall satisfaction with OTAs. The distribution of responses about overall satisfaction is provided in the following Table 2. The data from the table presents that 49.8% of the total 500 respondents were 'satisfied' with the overall attribute of the OTAs while 7.6%, 9.2%, 20.2% and 13.2% of the respondents were 'fully dissatisfied', 'dissatisfied', 'neither satisfied nor dissatisfied' and 'fully satisfied' respectively.

Table 2. User Overall Satisfaction about OTAs

Satisfaction	Frequency	Percentage
Fully dissatisfied	38	7.6
Dissatisfied	46	9.2
Neither satisfied nor dissatisfied	101	20.2
Satisfied	249	49.8
Fully satisfied	66	13.2
Total	**500**	**100.0**
Mean = 3.51		**S.D. = 1.075**

Source: Primary Data.

In order to understand the association between demographic variables of respondents and their overall satisfaction with OTAs, a cross-tabulation between the variables was performed and the results were interpreted with the help of the chi-square test. The following Table-3 displays the cross-tabulation between the

Table 3. User Age wise distribution pertaining to the overall Satisfaction about OTAs

Age	Satisfaction					Total
	Fully Dissatisfied	Dissatisfied	Neither	Satisfied	Fully Satisfied	
18-25 Years	0	7	4	3	2	16
	(0.0)	(43.8)	(25.0)	(18.8)	(12.5)	(100.0)
26-33 Years	13	8	41	50	33	145
	(9.0)	(5.5)	(28.3)	(34.5)	(22.8)	(100.0)
34-41 Years	13	23	36	142	19	233
	(5.6)	(9.9)	(15.5)	(60.9)	(8.2)	(100.0)
42-49 Years	10	6	3	32	7	58
	(17.2)	(10.3)	(5.2)	(55.2)	(12.1)	(100.0)
50-57 Years	2	2	15	18	3	40
	(5.0)	(5.0)	(37.5)	(45.0)	(7.5)	(100.0)
66 + Years	0	0	2	4	2	8
	(0.0)	(0.0)	(25.0)	(50.0)	(25.0)	(100.0)
Total	38	46	101	249	66	500
	(7.6)	(9.2)	(20.2)	(49.8)	(13.2)	(100.0)
χ = 88.12, df=20, Sig.= .000						

Source: Primary Data. The figures in brackets are the percentages of row total.

age groups of the respondents and overall satisfaction with OTAs. The data reveal that a single largest group of respondents (43.8%) belonging to the age group of '18-25 Years' was dissatisfied with OTAs while a majority of the respondents (34.5%) belonging to the age group '26-33 Years' were satisfied. Further, in the case of the age group of falling between '34-41 Years, 60.9% of respondents were satisfied whereas, 55.2% of respondents from the age group of '42-49 Years' were also satisfied with OTAs. Half of the respondents belonging to the age group of 'above 66 years' were satisfied with OTAs.

The significant value of chi-squire (χ = 88.12) with degrees of freedom 20 suggests that there is a significant relationship between the age of the respondents with the level of their overall satisfaction with OTAs.

The following Table-4, represents the occupation wise distribution of overall satisfaction reported by respondents about OTAs.

Table 4. User Occupation Wise Distribution of Overall Satisfaction Level About OTAs

Occupation	Fully Dissatisfied	Dissatisfied	Neither	Satisfied	Fully Satisfied	Total
Student	4	1	8	12	10	35
	(11.4)	(2.9)	(22.9)	(34.3)	(28.6)	(100.0)
Government Service	4	4	22	69	9	108
	(3.7)	(3.7)	(20.4)	(63.9)	(8.3)	(100.0)
Private Service	17	22	38	58	27	162
	(10.5)	(13.6)	(23.5)	(35.8)	(16.7)	(100.0)
Business	9	19	33	110	20	191
	(4.7)	(9.9)	(17.3)	(57.6)	(10.5)	(100.0)
Agriculture	4	0	0	0	0	4
	(100.0)	(0.0)	(0.0)	(0.0)	(0.0)	(100.0)
Total	38	46	101	249	66	500
	(7.6)	(9.2)	(20.2)	(49.8)	(13.2)	(100.0)
χ = 91.15, df=16, Sig.= .000						

Source: Primary Data. The figures in brackets are the percentages of row total.

In-depth examination of the data obtained from the table reveals that a single largest group of students (34.3%), Government servants (63.9%), private servants (35.8%) and businessmen (57.6%) were satisfied while all of the agriculturists were fully dissatisfied with OTAs. Again, the significant value of chi-square (χ = 91.15) with degrees of freedom 16 suggests that there is a significant relationship between the occupation of the respondents with their overall satisfaction with OTAs.

CONCLUSION

The result of the study reveals that the expectations of the respondents were high for almost all the attributes and even after having satisfactory performance their perceptions could not match their expectations in the case of most of the attributes. In view of this, it is suggested that the service providers must try hard to keep the satisfaction level high among the OTA users. The study analysed the overall satisfaction of users towards OTAs and the results suggest that a single largest group of respondents with half of the users was found satisfied towards the overall features of OTAs. The results also suggest that the overall satisfaction is significantly dependent on the age groups and occupation of the users. However, the users are having higher expectations from online travel products and services and need to improve the perception of users towards the online travel products and services offered by OTAs.

REFERENCES

Akama, J. S., & Kieti, D. M. (2003). Measuring tourist satisfaction with Kenya's wildlife safaari: A case study of Tsavo West National Park. *Tourism Management, 24*(1), 73–81. doi:10.1016/S0261-5177(02)00044-4

Alegre, J., & Garau, J. (2010). Tourist satisfaction and dissatisfaction. *Annals of Tourism Research, 37*(1), 52–73. doi:10.1016/j.annals.2009.07.001

Anand, A. (2007). E-*Satisfaction: A Comprehensive Framework*. International Marketing Conference on Marketing and SocietyIMK.

Anderson, R. E., & Srinivasan, S. S. (2003). E-satisfaction and e-loyalty: A contingency framework. *Psychology and Marketing, 20*(2), 123–138. doi:10.1002/mar.10063

Bowen, D., & Clark, J. (2002). Reflections on tourist satisfaction research: Past, present and future. *Journal of Vacation Marketing, 8*(4), 297–308. doi:10.1177/135676670200800401

Burke, R. R. (2002). Technology and the customer interface: What consumers want in the physical and virtual store. *Journal of the Academy of Marketing Science, 30*(4), 411–432. doi:10.1177/009207002236914

Cho, Y., & Agrusa, J. (2006). Assessing use acceptance & satisfaction toward online travel agencies. *Journal of Information Technology and Tourism, 8*(3/4), 179–195. doi:10.3727/109830506778690795

Confente, I. (2015). Twenty-five years of word-of-mouth studies: A critical review of tourism research. *International Journal of Tourism Research, 17*(6), 613–624. doi:10.1002/jtr.2029

Connolly, D. J., Olsen, M. D., & Moore, R. G. (1998). The Internet as a distribution channel. *The Cornell Hotel and Restaurant Administration Quarterly, 39*(4), 42–54. doi:10.1177/001088049803900408

Dutta, S., Kumar Chauhan, R., & Chauhan, K. (2017). Factors affecting customer satisfaction of online travel agencies in India. *Tourism and Hospitality Management, 23*(2), 267–277. doi:10.20867/thm.23.2.3

Evanschitzky, H., Iyer, G. R., Hesse, J., & Ahlert, D. (2004). E-satisfaction: A re-examination. *Journal of Retailing, 80*(3), 239–247. doi:10.1016/j.jretai.2004.08.002

Flint, D. J., Blocker, C. P., & Boutin, P. J. Jr. (2011). Customer value anticipation, customer satisfaction and loyalty: An empirical examination. *Industrial Marketing Management, 40*(2), 219–230. doi:10.1016/j.indmarman.2010.06.034

Gomez, M. I., McLaughlin, E. W., & Wittink, D. R. (2004). Customer satisfaction and retail sales performance: An empirical investigation. *Journal of Retailing, 80*(4), 265–278. doi:10.1016/j.jretai.2004.10.003

Guan, H., & Yin, M. (2007). Empirical study of user satisfaction of travel website information resources-take C-trip as an example. *Journal of Beijing International Studies University, 151*(11), 64-68.

Haber, S., & Lerner, M. (1998). Correlates of Tourist Satisfaction. *Annals of Tourism Research, 25*(4), 197–201.

Ho, C., & Lee, Y. (2007). The development of an E-Travel Service Quality Scale. *Tourism Management, 28*(6), 434–1449. doi:10.1016/j.tourman.2006.12.002

Hongxiu, L., Yong, L., & Reima, S. (2009). *Measurement of e-service quality: an empirical study on online travel service.* 17th European Conference on Information Systems (ECIS, 2009), Verona.

Iliachenko, E. Y. (2006 b). *Customer needs with Tourism websites: Tourism Consumer requirements for Electronic Service Quality (E-SQ) Characteristics of Tourism websites, Department of Business Administration and social Science.* Lulea University.

Kim, W. G., & Lee, H. Y. (2005). Comparison of web service quality between online travel agencies and online travel suppliers. *Journal of Travel & Tourism Marketing, 17*(2-3), 105–116. doi:10.1300/J073v17n02_09

Kim, W. G., Ma, X., & Kim, D. J. (2006). Determinants of Chinese hotel customers' e-satisfaction and purchase intentions. *Tourism Management, 27*(5), 890–900. doi:10.1016/j.tourman.2005.05.010 PMID:32287716

Kozak, M., & Rimmington, M. (2000). Tourist satisfaction with Mallorca, Spain, as an off-season holiday destination. *Journal of Travel Research, 38*(3), 260–269. doi:10.1177/004728750003800308

Law, R., & Leung, R. (2000). A study of airline's online reservation service on the Internet. *Journal of Travel Research, 39*(2), 202–211. doi:10.1177/004728750003900210

Law, R., Leung, R., & Buhalis, D. (2009). Information technology application in hospitality and tourism: A review of publication from 2005-2007. *Journal of Travel & Tourism Marketing, 26*(5-6), 599–623. doi:10.1080/10548400903163160

Möhlmann, M. (2015). Collaborative consumption: Determinants of satisfaction and the likelihood of using a sharing economy option again. *Journal of Consumer Behaviour, 14*(3), 193–207. doi:10.1002/cb.1512

Masoomeh, M., Tahayori, H., & Sadeghian, A. (2013). Drivers of customer satisfaction in online tourism-the case of uropean countries. *Middle East Journal of Scientific Research, 13*(9), 1172–1179.

Matzler, K., Waiguny, M., Toschkov, A., & Mooradian, T. A. (2006). Usability, emotions, and customer satisfaction in online travel booking. In Information and Communication Technologies in Tourism (pp. 135-146). Springer-Wien. doi:10.1007/3-211-32710-X_21

Mills, J. E., & Morrison, A. M. (2004). Measuring customer satisfaction with online travel. In *Information and Communication Technologies in Tourism* (pp. 11–28). Springer-Wien.

Mohammed, E. M., Wafik, G. M., Abdel Jalil, S. G., & El Hasan, Y. A. (2016). The Effects of E-Service Quality Dimensions on Tourist's Satisfaction. *International Journal of Hospitality and Tourism Systems*, (9), 1221.

Oh, H., Fiore, A. M., & Jeoung, M. (2007). Measuring experience economy concepts: Tourism applications. *Journal of Travel Research, 46*(2), 119–132. doi:10.1177/0047287507304039

Oliver, R. L. (1980). A cognitive model of the antecedents and consequences of satisfaction decisions. *JMR, Journal of Marketing Research, 17*(4), 460–469. doi:10.1177/002224378001700405

Parasuraman, A., Zeithaml, V. A., & Malhotra, A. (2005). ES-QUAL: A multiple-item scale for assessing electronic service quality. *Journal of Service Research*, *7*(3), 213–233. doi:10.1177/1094670504271156

Prebensen, N. K. (2004). *Tourist Satisfaction with a Destination: Antecedents and Consequences. Finmark College*. Department of Hospitality and Tourism.

Sharma, G., & Baoku, L. (2013). Customer satisfaction in web 2.0 and information technology development. *Information Technology & People*, *26*(4), 347–367. doi:10.1108/ITP-12-2012-0157

Sparks, B. A., & Browning, V. (2010). Complaining in cyberspace: The motives and forms of hotel guests' complaints online. *Journal of Hospitality Marketing & Management*, *19*(7), 797–818. doi:10.1080/19368623.2010.508010

Swaid, S. I., & Wigand, R. T. (2009). Measuring the quality of e-service: Scale development and initial validation. *Journal of Electronic Commerce Research*, *10*(1), 13–28.

Szymanski, D. M., & Hise, R. T. (2000). E- satisfaction: An initial examination. *Journal of Retailing*, *76*(3), 309–322. doi:10.1016/S0022-4359(00)00035-X

Wang, X., Zhang, J., Gu, C., & Zhen, F. (2009). Examining antecedents and consequences of tourist satisfaction: A structural modeling approach. *Tsinghua Science and Technology*, *14*(3), 397–406. doi:10.1016/S1007-0214(09)70057-4

Weber, N., Murphy, H., Schegg, R., & Murphy, J. (2005). An Investigation of Satisfaction and Loyalty in the Virtual Hospitality Environment. In A. Frew (Ed.), *Information and Communication Technologies in Tourism* (pp. 452–461). Springer Verlag.

Zeithaml, V. A., Parasuraman, A., & Malhotra, A. (2002). Service quality delivery through web sites: A critical review of extent knowledge. *Journal of the Academy of Marketing Science*, *30*(4), 362–375. doi:10.1177/009207002236911

Chapter 5
Geospatial Application in Tourism Study on Geoportals as an Expedient Tool for Holiday Trip Planning

Malini Singh
Amity University, Noida, India

Sudipta Mukherjee
Jamia Millia Islamia, India

Madhumita Mukherjee
Indian Institute for Human Settlements, India

ABSTRACT

Geospatial technology refers to data and information that identifies the location of specific features on the Earth's surface. The term refers to collective data in which the technologies involved have geographic or locational dimensions. Geospatial information is attached to any information related to space (i.e., locational component [latitude and longitude]). When location information is added to any dataset, it is transformed into geospatial data. For example, if the population of a region's various districts is stored in a spreadsheet, it is not spatial. If a population map is created for this region, it becomes geospatial data. Geospatial technology is widely used in tourism and has changed the travel landscape. Tourism and hospitality brands use technology to identify the geospatial context and improve customer engagement and help Tourists to plan holiday trips.

DOI: 10.4018/978-1-7998-9194-9.ch005

INTRODUCTION

Technological advancement has always been helpful in the planning process. Planning in different stages in tourism was carried out with the technology. Geospatial technology in tourism is not a very old practice, but this modern technology has widely experimented in the tourism industry for planning, maintenance, conservation, monitoring and supporting tourism-related business and their stakeholders. Geospatial Technology refers to data and information that identifies the location of specific features on the earth's surface (Dibiase & Kidwai, 2010). The term refers to collective data in which the technologies involved have geographic dimensions. Geospatial information is attached to any information related to space, i.e., locational component (latitude and longitude) (Roche, 2016). When location information is added to any dataset, it is transformed into geospatial data. For example, if the population of a region's various districts is stored in a spreadsheet, it is not spatial. If we create a population map for this region, it becomes geospatial data.

Geospatial technology is widely used in tourism and has changed the travel landscape. Tourism and hospitality brands use technology to identify the geospatial context and improve customer engagement creatively through co-creation. The term 'Geospatial' is used interchangeably by scientists, engineers, planners, and laypeople. It was first used in literature in the late 1980s and quickly became popular (Haklay et al., 2010)

Geographic Information System (GIS) is the engine that power processes and use geospatial data (Haslett, 1990). They collect, store, manipulate, analyse, and visualise geospatial data, converting it into information. It is a framework for storing information and geographic location in a database for management and analysis processes (Peuquet & Duan, 1995). GIS incorporates a wide range of datasets (Arvanitis et al., 2000). They use maps to analyse spatial locational data and organise multiple layers of information into two and three-dimensional visualizations (Kwan, 2000; Wang, 2014). The combination of spatial and attribute data enables GIS to initiate processes and become a practical geospatial problem-solving tool through spatial analysis. GIS layers can represent various environmental attributes such as soil layer, geology layer, land cover layer, river layer, road layer, and so on (Mahiny, 2012). Geographers can use spatial analysis (overlay analysis) to find a suitable location with a particular rock type, soil, and land cover, such as a river with road access (Mussa & Suryabhagavan, 2019). Both geospatial and GIS work together to indicate location and support decision making related to particular contexts. GIS supports the use of various geographical data layers to carry out spatial analysis and derivative maps for depicting information. Geospatial refer to all kinds of data, technologies and applications related to spatial/locational/geographic data. For example, Google Earth describes the features/land covers of the earth surface and can tag any related information.

Tourism is primarily a location-based industry (Talpur & Zhang, 2018). Geospatial data and GIS processes have significant implication for the operations of the industry (Sigala & Marinidis, 2012). For example, geospatial data may indicate the location of a moving train or an aircraft. That information is then used by GIS to create a range of processes, including to predict Estimated Time of Arrival (ETA) and to indicate requirements at each particular location (Jeong et al., 2006)

Various helpful mapping applications are being created using geospatial data and technology. This includes urban mapping, disaster mapping, surveying, wetland mapping, geological mapping, agricultural applications, land cover change detection, natural resource management, land information systems, asset management, coal fire mapping and monitoring, ocean-related applications, climate change, defense-related mapping and applications, and tourism information systems (Phiri et al., 2020 ; Pradhan et al., 2009; Kar & Singh, 1997; Gupta & Dogra, 2017). Municipal governments may use the GIS system and parcel mapping to create useful applications such as a digital tax collecting system. Satellite or aerial imaging is advantageous during natural catastrophes (Drummond & French, 2008; Ganapati, 2011). During a storm, for example, organizations can identify flooded regions, estimate the depth of the water, and take appropriate action. Some governmental authorities, such as NASA's forest fire site and the United States' Drought Management System, have employed web-based GIS to develop information systems based on geospatial technology (Wang & Yuan, 2010) ; (Emrich et al., 2011).

Geospatial technology provides several opportunities for developing new tourist applications based on digital maps. These applications integrate geospatial data retrieval with map-based information processing. It is a useful instrument that adds to both visitor safety and policy development. Spatial Decision Support System (SDSS) allows travellers to organize their journey more effectively and enjoy their time at the destination (Coutinho et al., 2011).

Geoportal is one of the most significant GIS – guided application which can bring remarkable change in visitor's perception in trip planning (Singh, 2015). Government attempts to promote the industry and keep it a key source of income for development in the country has been underway through tourist institutions. The tourism potential of the nation has not been adequately explored and commercialized (Prebensen, 2007).

The following approach must be used during the construction of the spatial database; purchase of graphic maps covering the region' digitalisation of paper maps and creation of topology to link the characteristics of the map. To construct tourism maps, textual information and pictures should be incorporated, including vector graphic forms. The subject-specific layer is to be assigned to every item.

The relevant items such as roads, construction, or watercourses are combined in every stratum. For the integration of tourist data, the typical model layer should be extended with other tourism areas, such as hotels, restaurants, sights, and further infrastructure layers with layers such as roads, builders, greenery, stretches, and so on.

The chapter has begun with the concept of geospatial technology and its application, especially geoportal. The second phase described the importance, process, and implementation of geoportal in the tourism industry and the conceptual framework of a geoportal. The chapter also depicted the structure of geoportal by using ArcGIS software. A practically-oriented case study of Sikkim is projected at the end of the chapter for demonstration purposes.

The digital revolution has greatly influenced the tourism sector. Therefore, web-based technology, such as the geoportal approach, should be incorporated in the context of Indian tourism.Technology is essential for businesses in the tourism and hospitality sectors and their clients. Today, hundreds of technological aids have changed the average person's traditional travel and lodging experiences by moving the power of choice from the hands of service providers to the customer (Kasriel, 2016).The incorporation of ICTs has aided chiefly in the facilitation of experiences. With the development of new technology, new forms of tourist activities were developing that can change traditional experiences and lead to the emergence of new types of tourism experience (Neuhofer et al., 2014). Legitimate scientific tourism management and planning may be accomplished with the aid of cutting-edge technology (Moyo, 2000), yielding a productive outcome in resolving the above mentioned tourism-related issues.

Concept of Geo-Portal

A geo-portal is an online portal used to locate and access geographical information and related geographic resources (display, editing, research, and so on) (Singh et al., 2021). As a crucial feature, geo portals are essential for the efficient use of Geographic Information Systems (GIS) and Spatial Data Infrastructure (SDI) (Goodchild, 2007). A geo-portal gives a single point of entry to search and download information from a variety of sources. The geo-portal must be distinguished from other techniques for processing geographic data on the Internet. Geographic information, for example, is a critical enabler for web-based mapping programs such as Google Maps and Yahoo Maps. Specialized mapping does not rely on the incorporation of official geodata, such as land use categories, temperature, rainfall, slope, elevation, landslide, population density zones. This lacks access to geographic data using standard software interfaces such as Web Map Services (WMS) or the Web. On the other hand, Geoportal provides geographic information for further study of the data presented.

Geo-portal combines Web GIS capability with internet accessibility (Nowak, 2006). Decision making is a crucial component for the Tourism Sector, investors, and tourists in the current situation (Timothy & Tosun, 2003). By combining diverse types of datasets on a single platform, geoportal improves decision-making capability (Giuffrida et al., 2019). Another distinguishing feature of Geoportal is its ability to communicate quickly over the web. It can help enhance the distribution of tourism resources, which leads to scientific planning. It may assist visitors with open communications, allowing them to acquire an accurate image of the location or state they want to visit in the near future. Tourism components are a combination of man-made and natural objects (Jovanovic, 2016). The geo-portal allows for the control of both resources at the same time. Another feature of Geoportal is its graphical map representation, which will enable travellers to see a clear image of a tourist attraction even it is created with complex layer data.A few developed and developing countries have adopted the practice of implementing geoportal in the tourism industry. The Maldives is one of them which has converted their tourism portal into a geoportal (Chaudhuri, 2016). The Isfahan Council of Tourism in Iran studied GIS application in Tourism Research in storing, manipulating, and evaluating large amounts of tourism data and survey results (Omid et al., 2019). The ICT in IRAN conducted Network Analysis, Network Allocation, Network Routing, and Network Tracing for this research (Tourism and GIS: Mapping and Promoting Places, 2019). Another example is cited by Ghana Tourism Authority. They developed the tourism portal with help of ESRI ARC GIS software. With the help of web-based tourism geoportal, the tourists were able to solve the challenge of identifying all historic monuments along the major road.'The Tourism Information and Promotion System (TIPS) were created in Turkey based on a tourism-related GIS application(https://www.ukessays.com, 2015).In this system, a 'Digital Tourist Information Bank' and a detailed map of all primary, secondary, and other roads providing access to significant historical and natural sites, political boundaries, all cities, essential towns, historical and archaeological places, Wilderness Areas, spa services, tourism centres, ports of entry, and physical limitations are established. The ArcGIS Network analyzer queries and displays the shortest distance and travel time between the provided origin and destination places since all road segments are given lengths in miles and kilometres and road quality and level of service. "SIGTUR " for tourism planning through GIS was established in 1997 for looking for the boundaries and qualifications of possible tourism locations and converting them into digital map (www.proceedings.esri.com, 2021).Many other countries have also developed tourism geoportal in recent day.

Background of the Research

To improve India's tourist operations, tourism agencies must decide on the creation of a web-based geo-portal. The primary goal is to build a geoportal that will provide travellers with aggregate information through a single portal that will explain the aspects of the locations and their services, such as hotels, restaurants, and so on. Furthermore, it saves both money and time by accelerating the decision-making process compared to other existing solutions. The concept of geoportal is used for extensive promotion, management, control and monitoring of tourism related services because it has the capacity of design, management and analysis tourism database for solving all related problems. The recent advancement of geoportal provides the various potential for making trip preparation least difficult and time-consuming, more effective, interactive, cooperative, and pleasant for tourists. Web-based tourism geoportal and the provision of online map services have also become commonplace for many tourist websites and e-tourism apps. Tourists may obtain all trip information faster, accurately, and correctly by using web map services to organize their trips.

Geoportal provides a centralized location for browsing and downloading Web GIS data from disparate sources. These quick, low-cost, interactive, and multi-layer online mapping services give visitors new geospatial tools and information for route planning. Geoportal generally gathers data from multiple sources and show it as a map. The map may be either static or dynamic. In the case of tourism, maps are typically employed in the selection of tourist sites and the planning of travel arrangements. Maps are used by potential visitors to navigate on or before their travels and plan their vacations. Geoportal' interactive web maps take advantage of the two-dimensional capabilities of human vision to portray information in a practical, accurate, and easily readable way.

Web-based geoportal can also enhance the quality of visitor's experience. The main principle of any destination is to showcase its product in a presentable manner. It is only possible when all the tourism-related information are presented on the website, and visitors can collect it as per their desire. For example, a tourist wishes to know about the scenic spots of a city and the location of nearby five star hotels and multi-cuisine restaurants or may want to visit a wildlife sanctuary with a stay at jungle huts to collect all information in a single digital map. Publishing this information on a single layer map is possible with the help of geoportal.

Quick retrieval of information is another characteristic of geoportal. For example, a tourist who would like to know the most shortcut way of visiting a tourist spot along with an Indian restaurant on his way should be available with a digital map.

The geoportal is also capable of retrieving multiple information in a single web platform. For example, a tourist needs to know about the most promising tourist spots of a city, best quality hotels, super-specialty dining arrangements, travel time between all the places of interest, entertainment facilities at the destination, climatic condition, nearest airport, railway station, bus stand, authorized tour operators and government tourist information centres can be retrieved and presented in a single digital map.

Security is one of the prime factors of travel. If the visitors do not feel that the place is safe and secured, they become hesitant to plan their trip. Confidence building of the potential visitors is another principle aspect of tourism. Geoportal can enhance the process of confidence-building by offering the actual situation of the destination. For example, the study area of this research, Sikkim, is vulnerable. The occurrence of frequent landslides is widespread in the state. However, a geoportal can provide information with a hundred per cent accuracy that there are many places where no landslide took place since few years. It is also evident that Sikkim is located in an earthquake zone and had a history of earthquakes in many areas. If tourists wish to know about significant earthquake locations of the state against famous tourist places can be retrieved by a geoportal. Once the sites are visible, they can avoid tourist spots located in disaster-prone zones and choose alternative options. Tourism geoportal can be a catalyst for building the tourist's confidence and enhancing the opportunity for the destinations and tourism stakeholders.

Many people love to visit places with low temperatures and enjoy snowfall. All the tourist places can be plotted on the temperature zone of the state, can a digital map be presented to the potential tourists. This way, geoportal can help in location suitability for the visitors.

Geo portal can also help tourists fixing their trip duration by providing accurate information. For example, a couple wishes to visit a state and is confused about finalizing their trip duration; geoportal can allow them to fix the final itinerary most suitably by providing distances between different cities, the time required to cover the major sports, and indicating spots which are isolated from the primary circuit and need extra days to protect them. This way, geoportal becomes an interactive portal and capable of answering all the quarries of the tourists.

In a general tourism website, circuit development and circuit creation usually are not possible. It is observed that tourism authorities display few pre-selected circuits on their website, creating discomfort for tourists. A geoportal has the capacity of creating a new tourist circuit or tailor-made vacation of their choice. Tourists can retrieve information about relevant information of a state and can identify the places of their likings and finally can prepare a new tourism circuit as per their choice. The portal offers the facility of displaying, storing and printing options for the same. For example, tourists can decide on an eco-tourism trip or adventure tourism trip or a Buddhist circuit.

Tourism is also related to cross-selling auxiliary products such as handicrafts, ethnic products, and organic products. It helps and supports the locale and enhances their income. For example, a group of tourists wish to buy organic products while visiting Sikkim as the state is crowned as the first organic state of India. With the help of an interactive geoportal, tourists can select a route approaching their sightseeing spots through an organic firm and experience those products.

Siliguri and Gangtok's highway links are affected by the landslide problem, especially in monsoon months and summer. Few kilometres in the Kalijhora area is very vulnerable. Geoportal can provide real-time information to the tourists about any incident, maybe through a web-based application, to avoid the problem. Geoportal can also help provide updated disaster-related information to the tourists and save their time and offer them security during or before the trip. Besides, tourists can find out emergency evacuation routes during sudden disasters during their sightseeing trip or transportation between two cities.

Geoportal can offer better visitor database management for both planners and tourists. By clicking on the portal, visitors can visualize the number of tourists who visited the place during a particular year, month or day. There could be a provision of updating tourists' footfall on a specific tourist place, which would be plotted against the spot. The popularity of the tourist spot can be enhanced in this way.

Foreign tourists face major problems while entering Sikkim as there are limited entry permit centres, and a heavy rush is experienced by the tourists, which creates a negative impression on them. The registration facility can be done online through the proposed geoportal, where tourists can complete their registration during their travel to Sikkim from the mainland and save time. Geoportal can also help keep visitors records on a day-to-day basis and display them to the authorities or the tourists.

The majority of the tourist places have some special restrictions imposed either by a state government or by the local authority. A general website can display all rules and restrictions on a single web page, but geoportal has a unique capacity of displaying the information against the specific location. For example, a special permit is required to obtain by the tourists when they plan a trip to Tsomgo Lake. Sikkim tourism website displays the information on a specific page. As geoportal is an interactive portal, the same information can be shown as a "pop –up" when tourists click on the Tsomgo Lake and can also get the location from where they can obtain the necessary permit. They can also get accurate information of distance between their present location, i.e. hotel and the office of permit-issuing authority, along with driving direction and distance, and travel time – all in a single digitized map.

Marketing and promotion of tourism products is another critical aspect of the tourism business. All the fairs, festivals, special events with their photographs and descriptions can also be displayed against the tourist spots through the web-based geoportal. For example, Losar, the Tibetan New Year, celebrated in February at Rumtek Monastery, Gangtok can be plotted on the digital map, and tourists can easily access relevant information as per their choice.

Moreover, the entire world is suffering from a deadly pandemic, COVID-19, and there are several related guidelines and restrictions in India and Sikkim that can be displayed through this portal. The travel style of the people has been changed due to the effect of the pandemic, and they generally avoid overcrowded cities, instead prefer to visit less populated destinations. With the help of geospatial technology, tourist destinations can be plotted over the population density map so that more minor populated tourist spots can be easily identified. COVID related infrastructures like COVID hospitals, quarantine zones, and other medical facility centres can be plotted against the tourist spots and hotels for avoiding if necessary.

As the geoportal has a digital base, all information can be updated, compared, monitored and retrieve regularly. A transparency on the present situation can be maintained through the portal. Besides, it would help to maintain a real time data for future analysis. The portal can be accessed from anywhere by tourists, planners tourism professionals and stakeholders with an internet connectivity.

Need of Geo-Portal for Sikkim

Sikkim is a mountainous state with a low population density. Significant parts of the state are not accessible and unexplored due to improper infrastructure and poor flow of information. Tourists only receive information on Sikkim's tourism destinations through Govt. of the Sikkim website and few other websites created by tour operators and travel agents. It is evident that "all information in a single platform" is not available for tourists. For example, a tourist who wants to plan his trip for about a week in Sikkim needs to browse few websites to obtain information. HE may learn about few tourist spots through govt. Website, accommodation can be searched through booking.com or similar hotel booking sites, for transport, need to seek information from various travel agent's portals.

Sikkim is a disaster-prone state, as mentioned earlier. Disaster-related information can be obtained from the Sikkim Government web portal, and information on the climatic condition can be received from Indian Meteorological Department's website or maybe from www.weather.com. Moreover, all this information are not visible at a time on a single website. Some information might be accurate and authentic, but a significant number of information might not be authentic, and nodal agencies do not validate them. So a question of gentility also arises.

On the other hand, all information received through geoportal is absolutely accurate as they are incorporated scientifically and has a spatial base (already validated through coordinates). The chance of error is negligible and has the capacity of producing real-time information to solve specific problems. So Sikkim has a necessity of constructing a web-based geoportal for better tourism management of the state. The conceptual architecture of a geoportal of Sikkim is discussed in the next section.

METHODOLOGY

According to Singla (Sigala, 2009) the repercussions of Web-GIS 2.0 on geoportal usher in a new era known as neogeography, and many latest papers (De Longueville, 2010; Goodchild, 2007; Sigala, 2010) examine multiple research papers demonstrating how the two features of Web-GIS 2.0. These are basically collective intelligence and social networking, and they have revolutionalised the creation and diffusion of information. Tait (Tait, 2005) highlighted four critical functions of tourism-related geoportal in 2005. He proposed broadening the essential elements to incorporate Web 2.0's social and collaborative capabilities in hospitality and tourism management. These four geoportal capabilities, namely Search, Mapping, Publishing, and Administrative Capabilities, have significant consequences for trip planning and decision making. They serve as a virtual tour guide and planning tool for potential travellers.

The research was carried out in two phases in this study. In the first phase, all tourism and GIS related data were collected. Tourism related data are mentioned in a table (Table 7.1):

The second phase was the design phase. Sikkim, especially East Sikkim District was taken as the study area which is located within the coordinates of 27°04' to 28°07' North and 88°00' to 88°55' East. After deciding on the most appealing tourist destination during the design phase, data processing and physical design were carried out using ArcGIS 10.2. Backend was filled up by spatial RDBMS.

In this example, boundary maps, actual maps, images, roads, and their names are incorporated as graphical components of GIS Design and Application for Tourism. Centre lines of highways with vector and graphical properties for network analysis, historical and tourism sites, and all geographical objects deemed necessary for tourism was built as point layers. Only the building layer was created as a polygon layer. Disaster-related datasets were also taken into account. Different levels of analysis were employed. It also includes basic information about the country's entrance criteria, the climate, road laws, and COVID-related information.ArcGIS network analyzer is used to find the shortest path between two points and produce directions. This was done to assist travellers in determining the best place for them. Distance between points of interest and hotels, the distance between two cities, and many other components were also included. A conceptual design is shown in Fig 7.1.

Table 1. Major Tourism Parameters for Geoportal

Types of user	Functionality	Concerned Dept.	Issues Related to travel	Parameter / Datasets
		State transport Authority/ State Tourism Board	Information on transport operators	Detail of certified transport operators and their location coordinates and descriptions.
		State/ Central Tourism dept./ Hotel Association	Different types of accommodation	Hotels and their location coordinates, photograph and descriptions
		Central Govt. census Department	Destination wise population density	District wise population density datasets.
		Municipality or local authorities	Detail of local amenities like restaurants, shopping malls etc.	Zone division for Corona free area where restaurants and shopping malls are located
		State / central Tourism Dept.	Information on visiting places of interest	Location of places of interest with their latitude and longitude
		Health Department	Lack of information about COVID and non COVID Hospitals &testing centers	Detail of medical facilities for COVID treatment
		Health Department	Risk and rumors	Detail of contentment Zones, hotspots with their latitude and longitude
		Department of Culture and Heritage	Information related fairs and festivals, events etc	Detail of concerned places with their coordinates, photographs and descriptions.
Administrator	Controller of the geo- portal, & has got all control over the publisher 's data. Can review and approve posted resources	Tourism Department, India Government.	All related issues	All datasets
Anonymous user	End user, who has the public functions of the geo- portal, including : search, view results,	Tourists / Visitors	All travel related issues	Receives all sorts of information in a single display (map & graphical presentation)

Figure 1. Conceptual Architecture of Geoportal

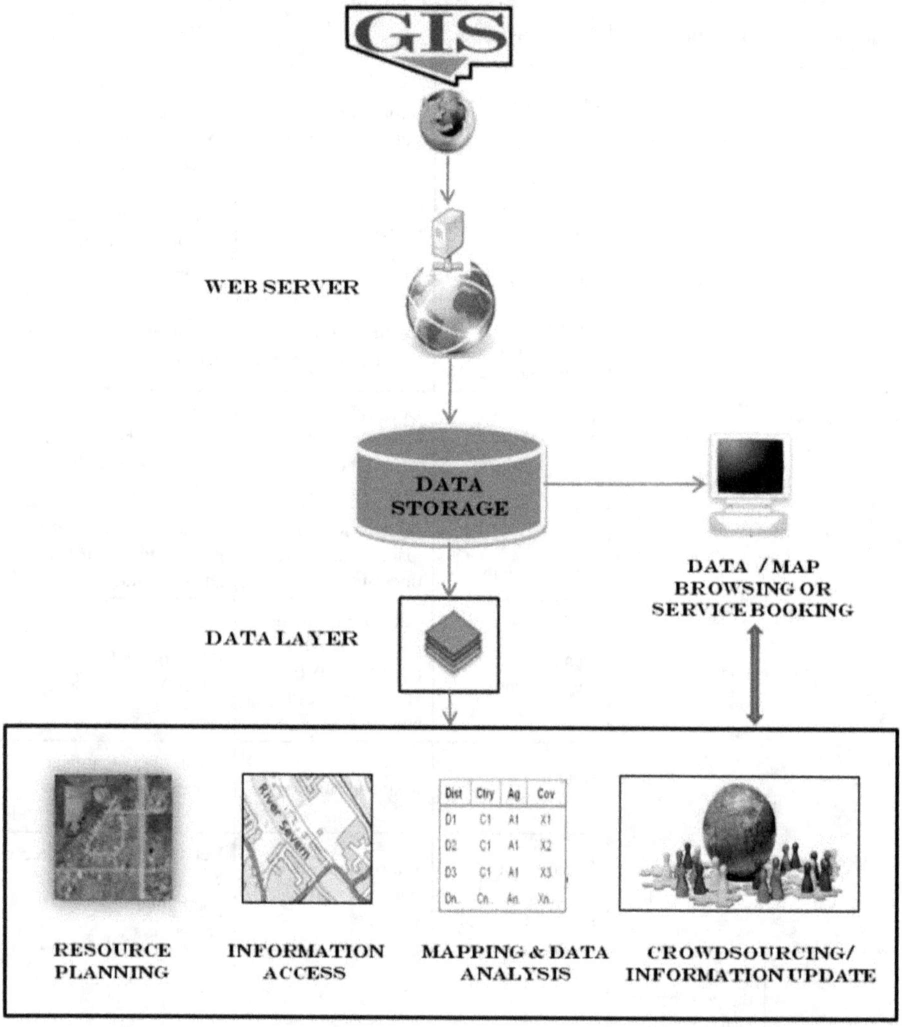

RESULTS AND DISCUSSION

In this section, the researcher has narrated different digitalized information in respect of geoportal. Different famous tourist destinations (Fig 2) are visible and respective road networks are also plotted against the them. It will help tourist to find out their approachable road to the tourist place.

Tourist spots were plotted against the accommodation and road; so that they can find out require information on the location of the spots, their connectivity, and

Figure 2. Major Cities and Road Network

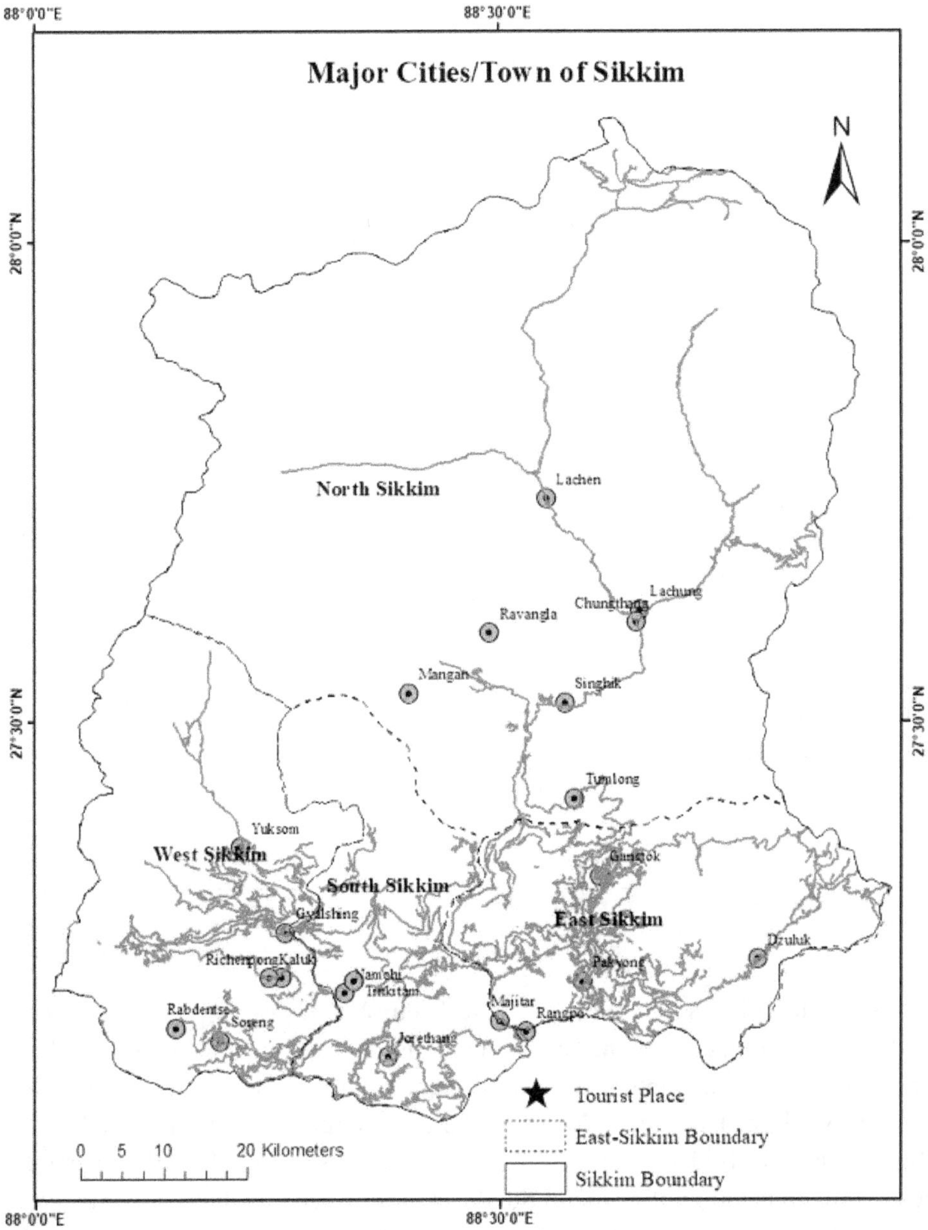

nearest accommodation facility at a glance (Fig 3). Any description and photograph can be inserted against each object for better understanding.

Figure 3. View of Some Tourist Places, Hotels and road Network of Sikkim

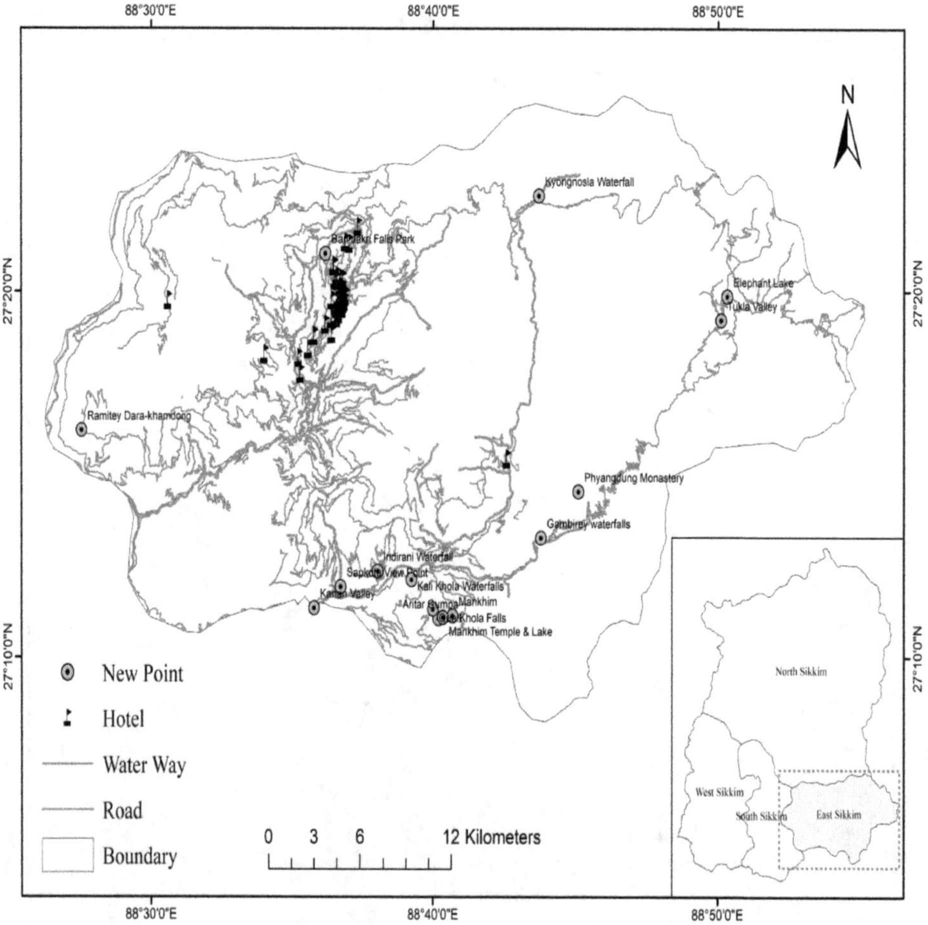

Some classified hotels (Fig 1.4) have been plotted in this phase for a better understanding of the research. The photographs, description of the individual hotel can be retrieved in this interactive portal according to the need of the tourists.

Tourist places have been plotted on the temperature map of Sikkim (Fig 1.5). Tourists can quickly identify their summer and winter destinations from this interactive map. The temperature of East and South Sikkim is moderate throughout the year. So people can visit these destinations even in summer. It helps visitors planning their trip in a better way.

Display of festivals, special events with their photograph (Fig 6) can be available in the portal, and tourists can retrieve detail information at the time of their trip planning.

Figure 4. Hotel Detail of Sikkim in Geoportal

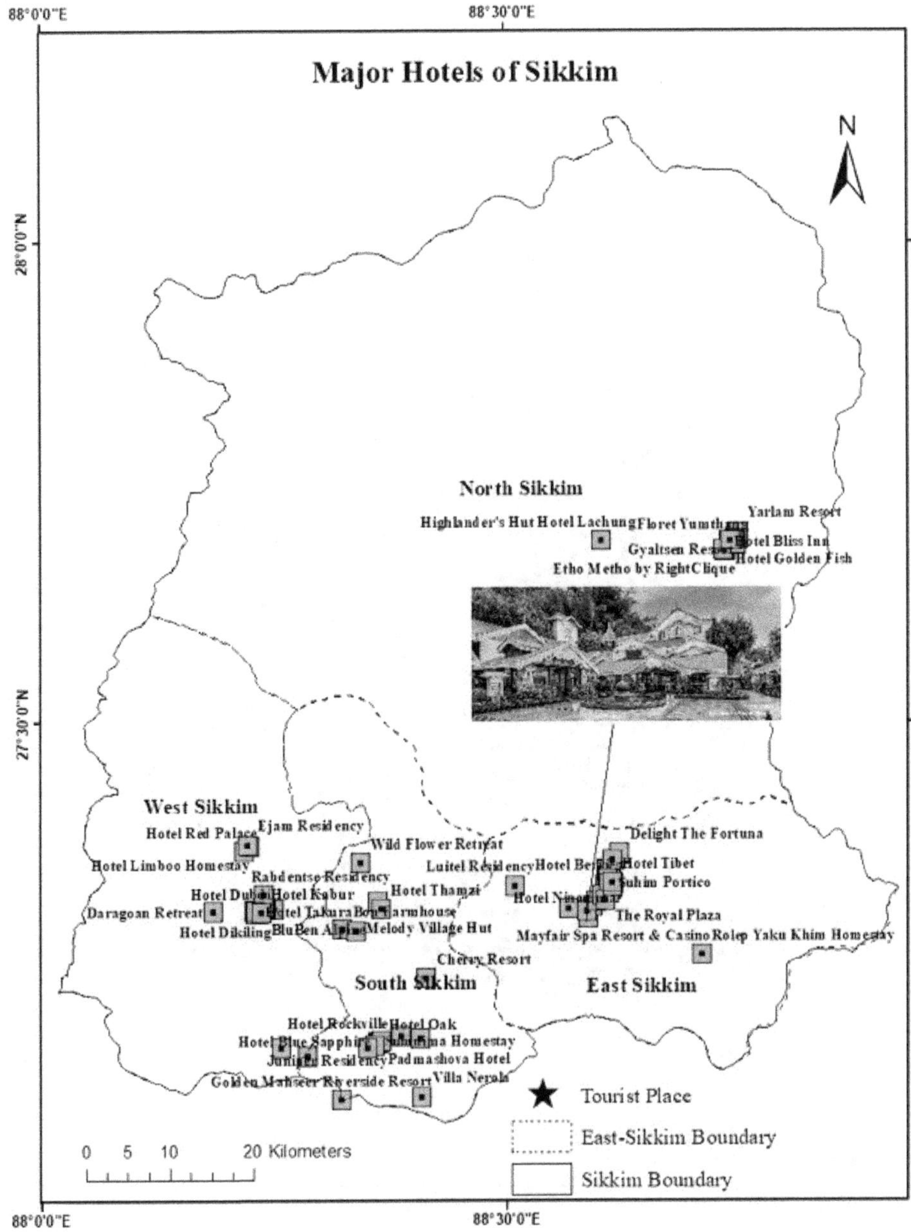

This map (Fig 7) shows the concentration of tourism places in a specific place. Visitors have a liberty of choosing places as per their interest.

Figure 5. Tourist Maps are plotted on the Temperature Zone of Sikkim

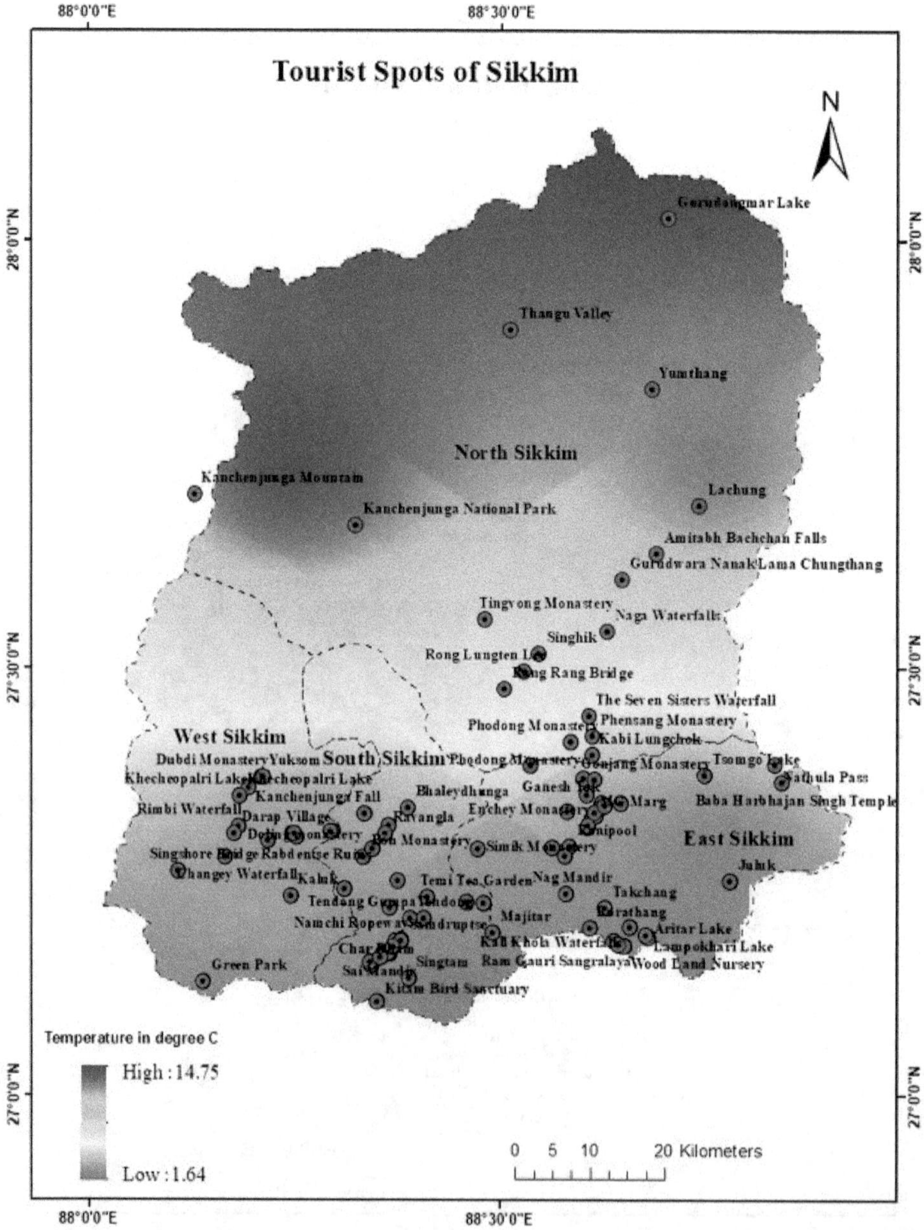

Tourist can also find out new location by browsing the portal and can develop their own circuit (Fig 8). This digital map would be available for printing and storing in the form of a soft copy

Figure 6. Display of Festival Related Information on the Geoportal

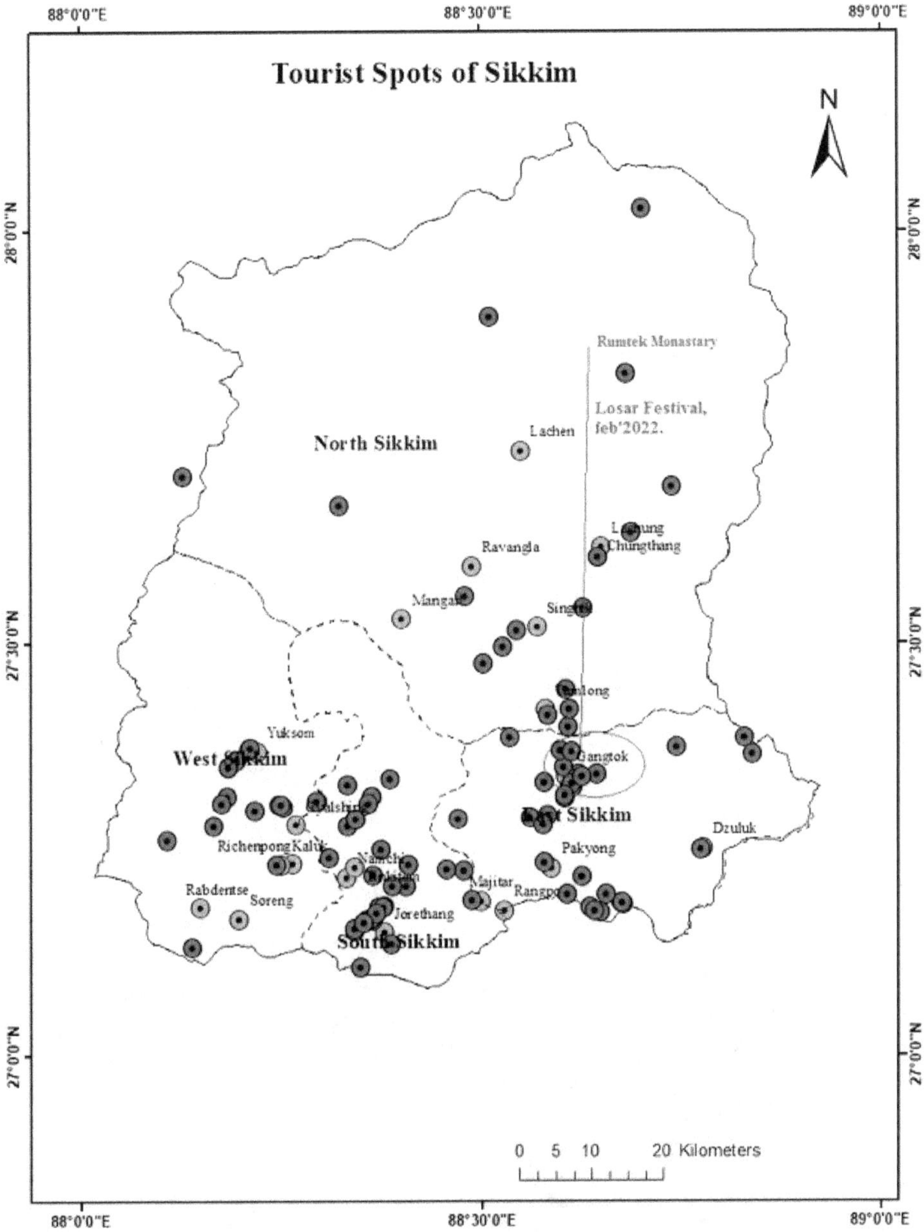

The Indian tourism sector is highly affected due to the pandemic situation. Visitors are planning their trips to less populated destinations. Geoportal can offer an authentic picture of the population in a particular city or the state as an entire state (Fig 9). This will help visitors to avoid crowded places and can do effective trip planning in the post-pandemic phase.

Figure 7. Interactive Tourist Map of Sikkim

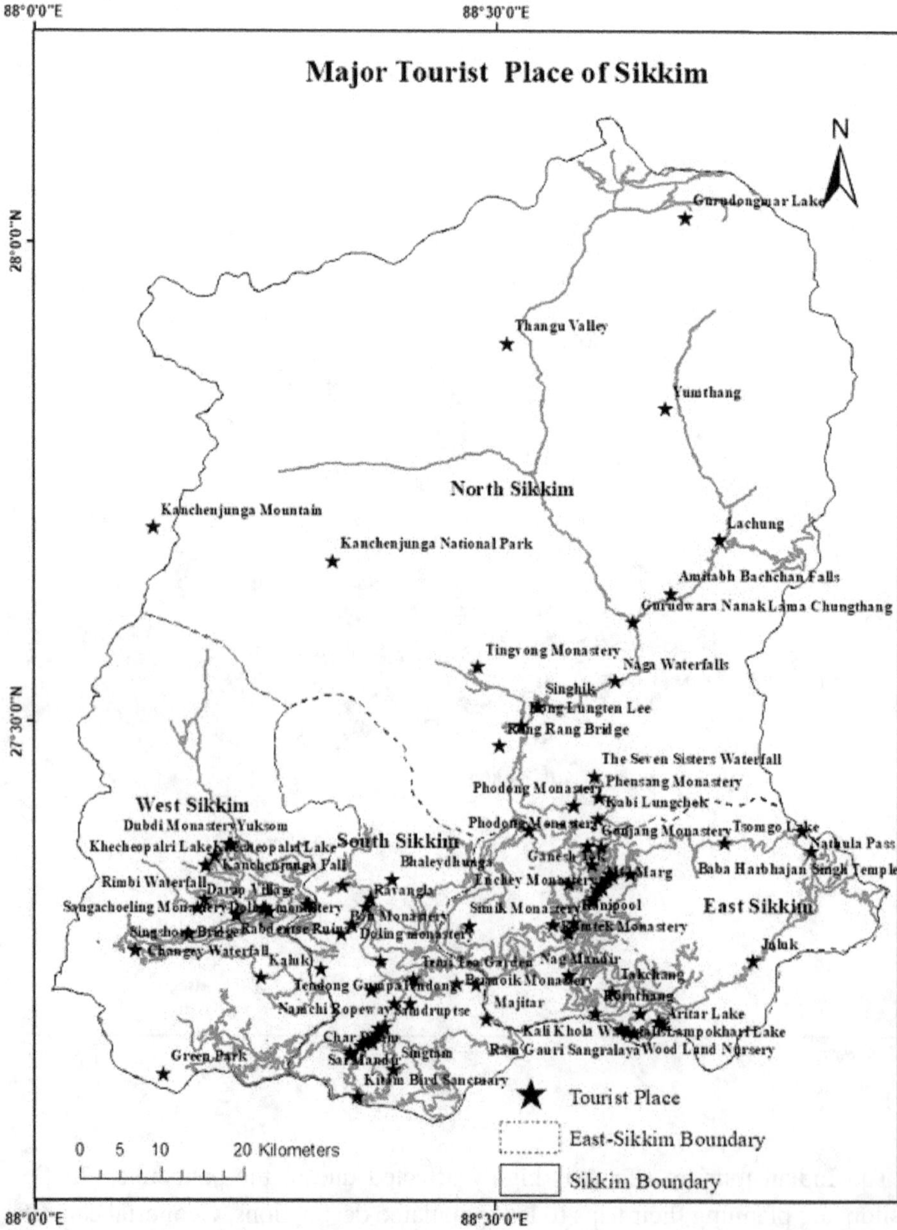

Figure 8. Tourism Circuit Development through Geoportal

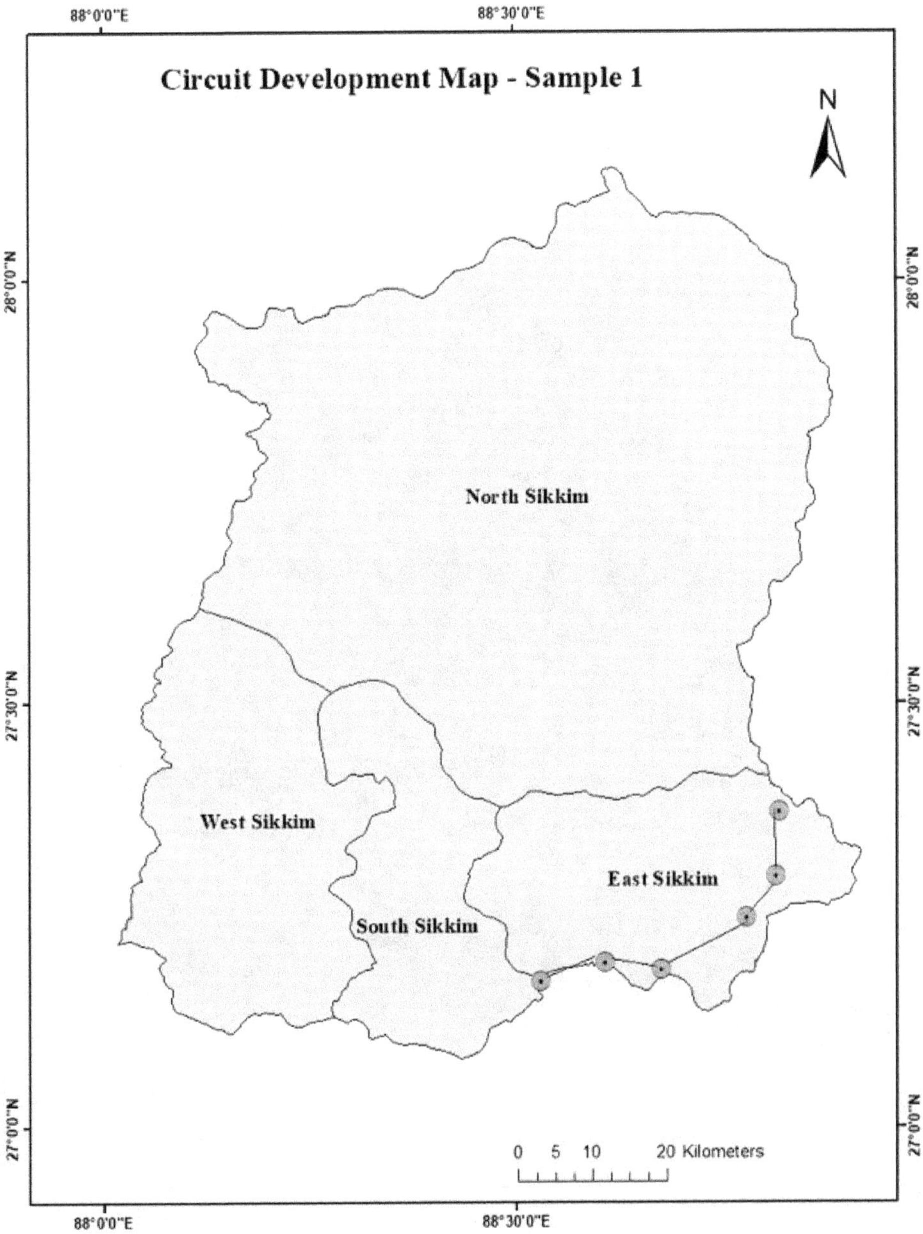

The state is disaster prone. Landslide issue is quite common in the tourist destination. But tourists can avoid landslide zones (Fig 10) and plan a safe trip in near future.

Figure 9. Tourist Spots of Sikkim are projected on the Population Map

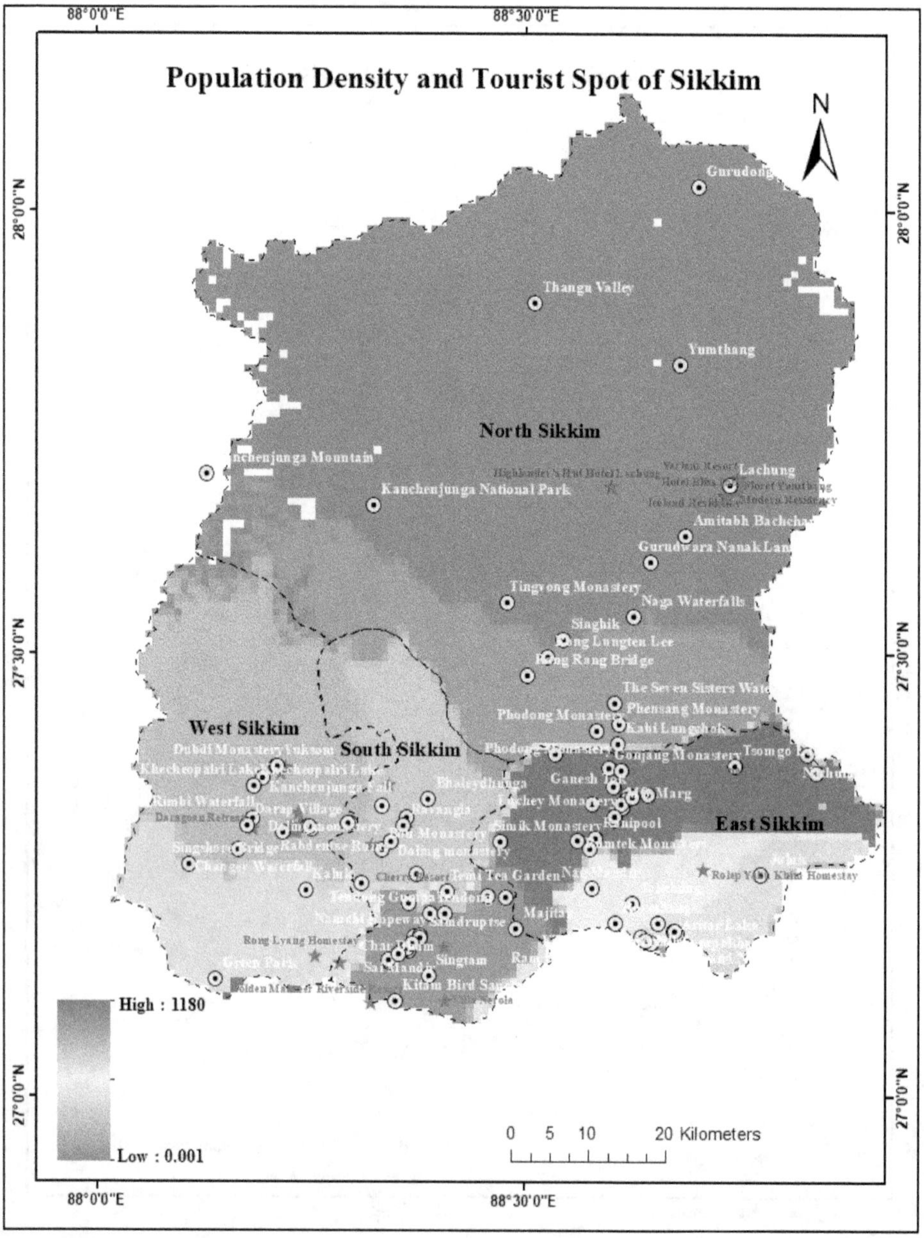

Transportation is another important aspect of trip planning which influence tourists in their decision making process. Visitors can retrieve authentic transport operators, their locations, and other necessary detail from the interactive geoportal (Fig 11).

Figure 10. Landslide Risk Zone Map of Sikkim

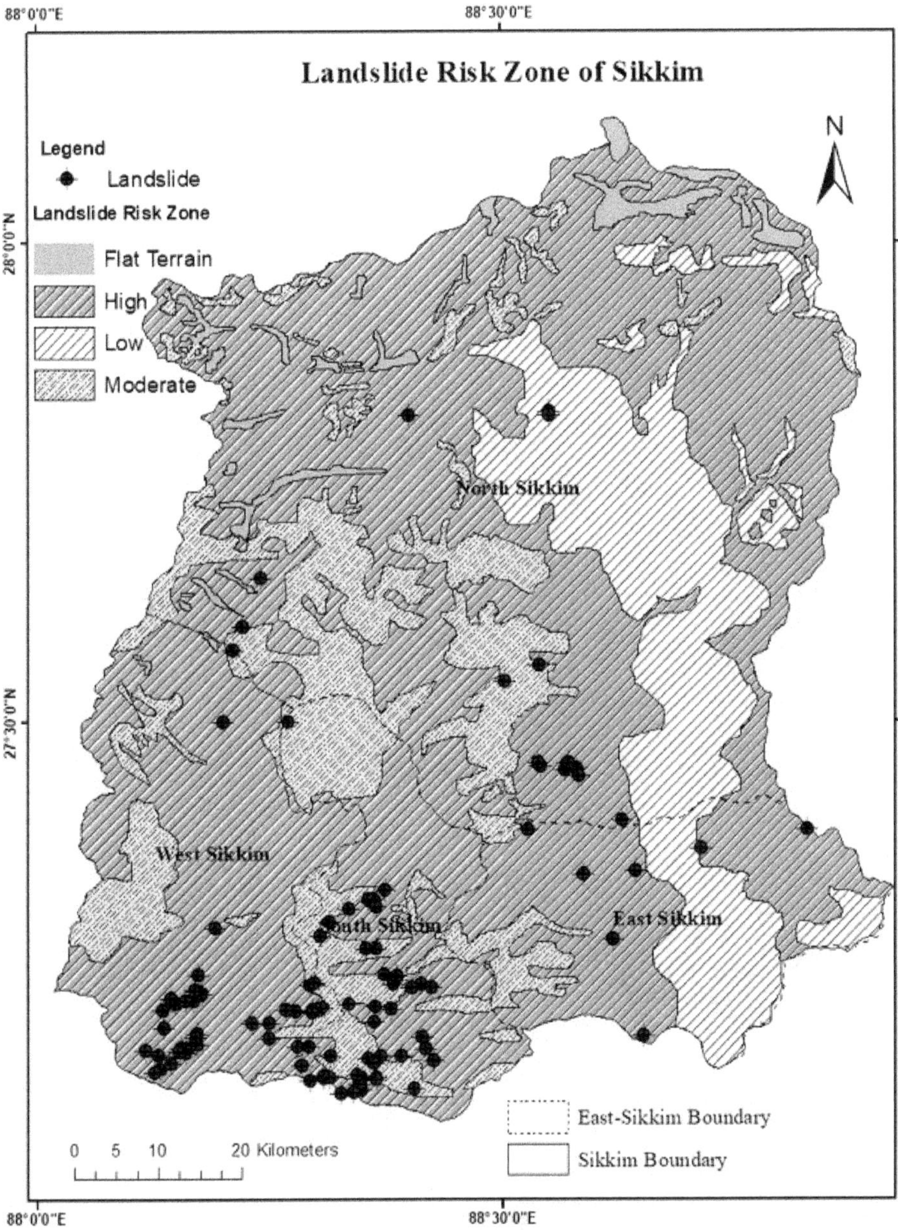

Tourists enjoy shopping and other entertainment facilities during their trip to a destination. Detail of shopping centers, restaurants and other facilities (Fig 12) can be incorporated in the portal. Tourists can retrieve information as per their requirement.

Figure 11. List of Transport Operator of Sikkim

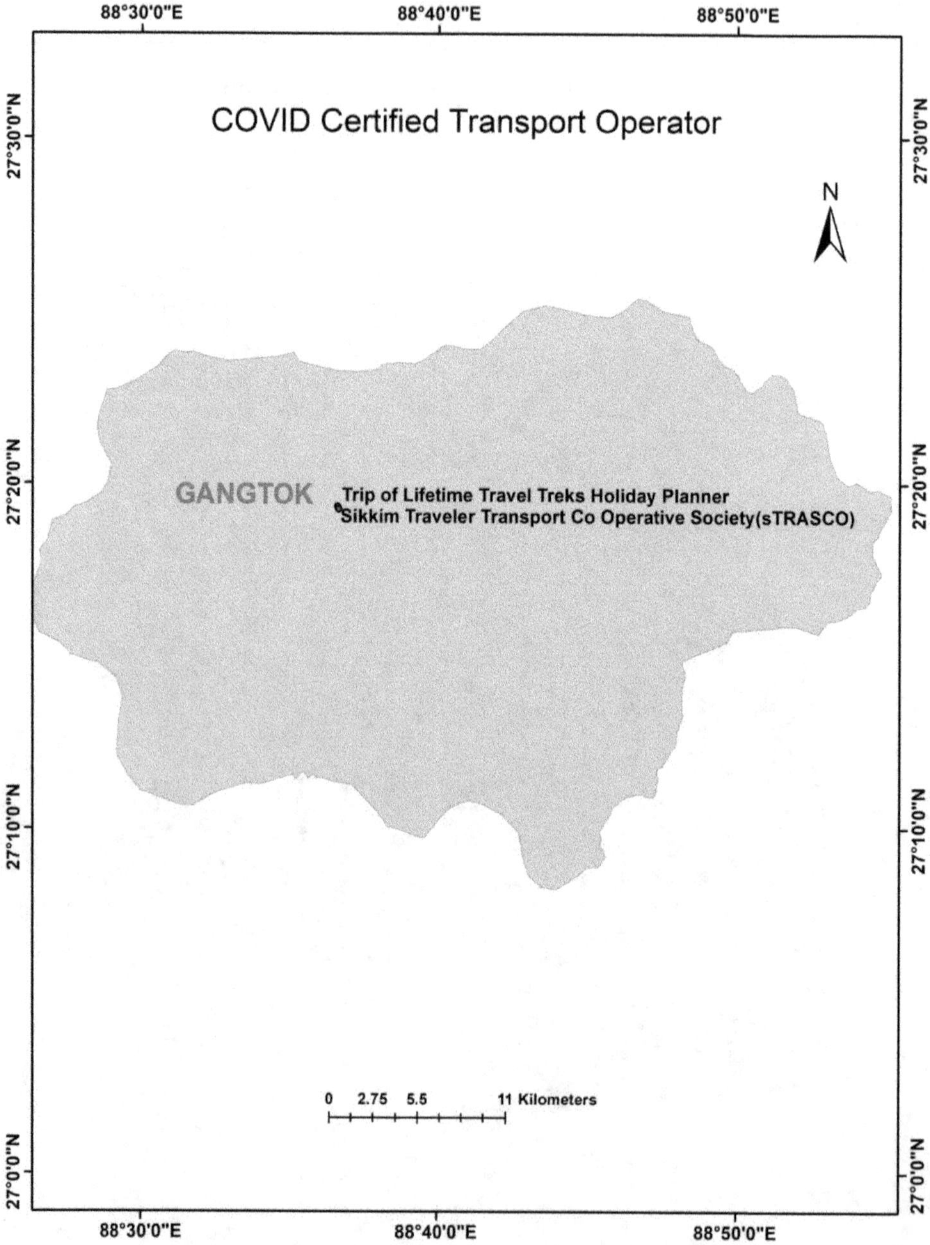

Tourists can also receive other necessary information and location of those facilities such as COVID hospitals etc. through the geoportal (Fig 13).

Figure 12. Display of Shopping Centers of Sikkim

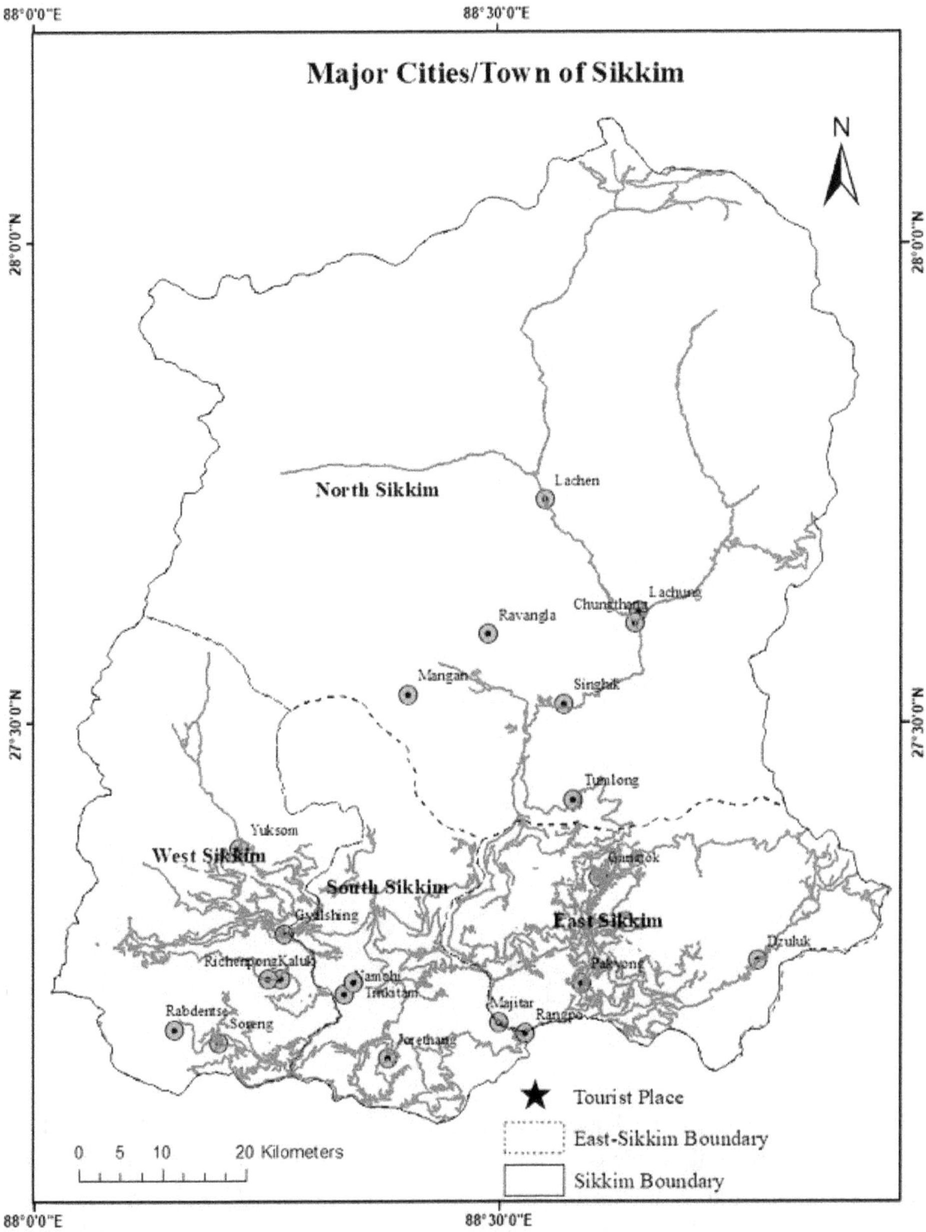

CONCLUSION

The applicability of geoportal in tourism can be fully understood based on the

Figure 13. List of COVID Hospitals in Sikkim

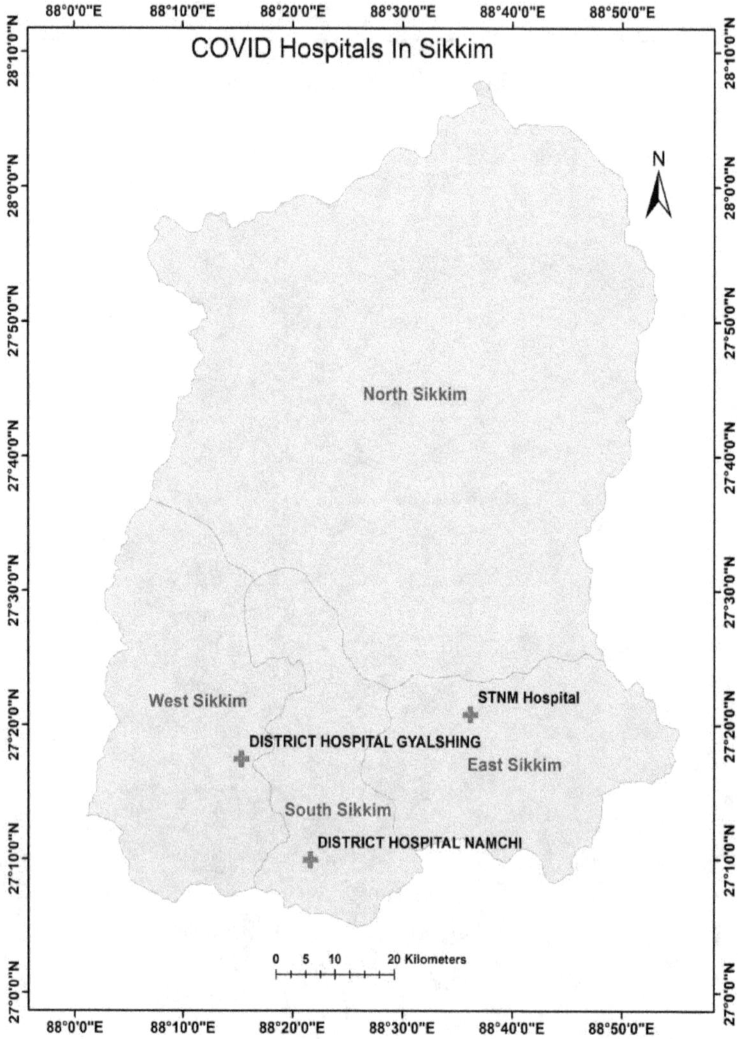

examples provided above. There are numerous other uses of GIS geoportal in the tourism and hospitality sector. Entering, storing, and manipulating digital map creation, database administration, Data queries and requests, Decision assistance, spatial analysis, spatial modelling, Location, structure, and routing are all critical considerations. When it comes to the use of geoportal in tourism, exciting patterns come to mind. It helps identify the ideal tourist spots for development, measuring the impact of tourism in various sections, visitor management and flow, analyzing linkages, and evaluating possible implications of tourist growth. The tourism potential of Sikkim is not yet appropriately explored. The tiny state has many more to offer to visitors, but the information about those places is not mentioned on the present website of the Sikkim Tourism Department. People encounter a massive problem which they would like to retrieve information on the state. It is also observed that disaster-related real-time information does not reach the visitors, and they get stuck in the nearby location where the disaster occurred. They lose their day due to lack of information, and visitors' experience is also spoilt.

Moreover, the number of tourist information centres is also not adequate in the state. As a result, tourists cannot seek relevant information during their visit. A web-based geoportal can solve the problem instantly. Tourists can browse the portal or an application downloaded on their smartphone and easily search for desired information. Budget allocation for tourism is not also sufficient for the state. So, it becomes difficult for the state government to spend huge money on developing manual assistance systems for the tourists at various places, but they can afford to build a web-based geoportal which can be an alternative solution for this problem. Promotion is another part that the state is lacking. Sikkim tourism products have not been adequately highlighted at the national and international levels. Especially, international visitors suffer from the clarity of information before their trip planning. A geoportal can be the appropriate solution for this issue as it can show all required information against each other on a digital platform.

Moreover, it helps to build an image for the destination. If visitors experience that the destination is well-equipped with modern technology, they feel comfortable taking interest and initiative in visiting the destination. This way, geoportal can hold building "brand image" for Sikkim. The state has a positive approach towards tourism development, and the state tourism authorities are willing to project Sikkim as an "all season's destination" in the near future. Their motive is to showcase the state's tourism potentials at the domestic and international level and project the state as a year-round destination. Geoportal can eventually help the authorities to be successful with its unique features. Sikkim with high tourism potential can be highly benefitted with the proposed geoportal.

REFERENCES

Arvanitis, L. G., Ramachandran, B., Brackett, D. P., Abd, R. E., Hesham, A., & Du, X. (2000). Multiresource inventories incorporating GIS, GPS and database management systems: A conceptual model. *Computers and Electronics in Agriculture*, *28*(2), 89–100. doi:10.1016/S0168-1699(00)00124-1

Chaudhuri, S. (2016). Geographic Information Portals: Maldives Tourism Perspective. *6th Int'l Conference on Advances in Engineering Sciences and Applied Mathematics*.

Coutinho, R., Joao, L., Simao, A., & Antunes, C. H. (2011). GIS-based multicriteria spatial decision support system for planning urban infrastructures. *Decision Support Systems*, *51*(3), 720–726. doi:10.1016/j.dss.2011.02.010

De Longueville, B. (2010). Community-based geoportals: The next generation? Concepts and methods for the geospatial Web 2.0. *Computers, Environment and Urban Systems*, *34*(4), 299–308. doi:10.1016/j.compenvurbsys.2010.04.004

Dibiase, D., & Kidwai, K. (2010). Wasted on the young? comparing the performance and attitudes of younger and older US adults in an online class on geographic information: JGHE annual lecture. *Journal of Geography in Higher Education*, *34*(3), 299–326. doi:10.1080/03098265.2010.490906

Drummond, W. J., & French, S. P. (2008). The future of GIS in planning: Converging technologies and diverging interests. *Journal of the American Planning Association*, *74*(2), 161–174. doi:10.1080/01944360801982146

Emrich, C. T., Cutter, S. L., & Weschler, P. J. (2011). GIS and emergency management. The SAGE handbook of GIS and society, 321-343. doi:10.4135/9781446201046.n17

Ganapati, S. (2011). Uses of public participation geographic information systems applications in e-government. *Public Administration Review*, *71*(3), 425–434. doi:10.1111/j.1540-6210.2011.02226.x

Giuffrida, N., Le, P., Inturri, G., & Ignaccolo, M. (2019). Mapping with stakeholders: An overview of public participatory GIS and VGI in transport decision-making. *ISPRS International Journal of Geo-Information*, *8*(4), 198. doi:10.3390/ijgi8040198

Goodchild, M. F. (2007). Citizens as voluntary sensors: Spatial data infrastructure in the world of Web 2.0. *International Journal of Spatial Data Infrastructures Research*, *2*(2), 24–32.

Goodchild, M. F. (2007). Citizens as voluntary sensors: Spatial data infrastructure in the world of Web 2.0. *International Journal of Spatial Data Infrastructures Research*, *2*(2), 24–32.

Gupta, A., & Dogra, N. (2017). Tourist adoption of mapping apps: A UTAUT2 perspective of smart travellers. *Tourism and Hospitality Management*, *23*(2), 145–161. doi:10.20867/thm.23.2.6

Haklay, M., Basiouka, S., Antoniou, V., & Ather, A. (2010). How many volunteers does it take to map an area well? The validity of Linus' law to volunteered geographic information. *The Cartographic Journal, 47*(4), 315-322.

Haslett, J. R. (1990). Geographic information systems. A new approach to habitat definition and the study of distributions. *Trends in Ecology & Evolution*, *5*(7), 214–218. doi:10.1016/0169-5347(90)90134-Y PMID:21232358

Jeong, C. W., Chung, J. Y., Joo, C. S., & Lee, J. (2006). Tourism guided information system for location-based services. *Asia-Pacific Web Conference*, 749-755. 10.1007/11610496_101

Jovanovic, V. (2016). The application of GIS and its components in tourism. *Yugoslav Journal of Operations Research*, (18), 2016.

Kar, A., & Singh, S. (1997). Remote sensing data products and visual interpretation tools for land resources and grazing land studies. *Silvipastoral Systems in Arid and Semi-Arid Ecosystems, 87.*

Kasriel, A. D. (2016). *Top 10 global consumer trends for 2015*. Euromonitor International.

Kwan, M. P. (2000). Interactive geovisualization of activity-travel patterns using three-dimensional geographical information systems: a methodological exploration with a large data set. *Transportation Research Part C: Emerging Technologies, 8*(1 - 6), 185-203.

Mahiny, S. A., & Clarke, K. C. (2012). Guiding SLEUTH land-use/land-cover change modeling using multicriteria evaluation: Towards dynamic sustainable land-use planning. *Environment and Planning. B, Planning & Design*, *39*(5), 925–944. doi:10.1068/b37092

Moyo, S. (2000). *Land reform under structural adjustment in Zimbabwe: land use change in the Mashonaland provinces*. Nordic Africa Institute.

Mussa, A., & Suryabhagavan, K. (2019). *Solid waste dumping site selection using GIS-based multi-criteria spatial modeling: a case study in Logia town, Afar region.* Geology, Ecology, and Landscapes.

Neuhofer, B., Buhalis, D., & Ladkin, A. (2014). A typology of technology-enhanced tourism experiences. *International Journal of Tourism Research*, *16*(4), 340–350. doi:10.1002/jtr.1958

Nowak, J. (2006). *Public Access to Remotely Accessible Spatial Information. Geographic Information Systems Conference and Exhibition*. GIS Odyssey.

Omid, G., Samereh, P., Thomas, B., & Bakhtiar, F. (2019). Mapping potential nature-based tourism areas by applying GIS-decision making systems in East Azerbaijan Province, Iran. *Journal of Ecotourism*, *18*(3), 1–23.

Peuquet, D. J., & Duan, N. (1995). An event-based spatiotemporal data model (ESTDM) for temporal analysis of geographical data. *International Journal of Geographical Information Systems*, *9*(1), 7–24. doi:10.1080/02693799508902022

Phiri, D., Simwanda, M., Salekin, S., Nyirenda, V. R., Murayama, Y., & Ranagalage, M. (2020). Sentinel-2 data for land cover/use mapping: A review. *Remote Sensing*, *12*(14), 2291. doi:10.3390/rs12142291

Pradhan, B., Lee, S., & Buchroithner, M. F. (2009). Use of geospatial data and fuzzy algebraic operators to landslide-hazard mapping. *Applied Geomatics*, *1*(1), 3–15. doi:10.100712518-009-0001-5

Prebensen, N. K. (2007). Exploring tourists' images of a distant destination. *Tourism Management*, *28*(3), 747–756. doi:10.1016/j.tourman.2006.05.005

Roche, S. (2016). Geographic information science II: Less space, more places in smart cities. *Progress in Human Geography*, *40*(4), 565–573. doi:10.1177/0309132515586296

Sigala, M. (2009). Geoportals and Geocollaborative Portals: Functionality and Impacts on Travellers' Trip Panning and Decision Making Processes. *International CHRIE Conference-Refereed Track, 28.*

Sigala, M. (2009). Geoportals and Geocollaborative Portals: Functionality and Impacts on Travellers' Trip Panning and Decision Making Processes. *International CHRIE Conference-Refereed Track, 28.*

Sigala, M. (2010). *The Role of Customers in Sustainable Supply Chain Management in Tourism*. Academic Press.

Sigala, M., & Marinidis, D. (2012). Web map services in tourism: A framework exploring the organisational transformations and implications on business operations and models. *International Journal of Business Information Systems*, *9*(4), 415–434. doi:10.1504/IJBIS.2012.046293

Singh, M., Mukherjee, S., & Mukherjee, M. (2021). Recent Development in Geospatial Platform and its significance in Tourism Planning. *ICIEM*, 40-45.

Singh, P. (2015). *Role of geographical information systems in tourism decision making process: a review.* Academic Press.

Tait, M. G. (2005). *Implementing geoportals: Applications of distributed GIS.* Academic Press.

Talpur, A., & Zhang, Y. (2018). A Study of Tourist Sequential Activity Pattern through Location Based Social Network (LBSN). *2018 International Conference on Orange Technologies (ICOT)*, 1-8. 10.1109/ICOT.2018.8705895

Timothy, D. J., & Tosun, C. (2003). Arguments for community participation in the tourism development process. *Journal of Tourism Studies*, *14*(2), 2–15.

Tourism and GIS: Mapping and Promoting Places. (2019, October). Retrieved June 14, 2021, from https://www.vmap.rocks/blog-detail/tourism-and-gis-mapping-and-promoting-places

Wang, F., & Yuan, H. (2010). Challenges of the sensor web for disaster management. *International Journal of Digital Earth*, *3*(3), 260–279. doi:10.1080/17538947.2010.484510

Wang, Y. Q. (2014). MeteoInfo: GIS software for meteorological data visualization and analysis. *Meteorological Applications*, *21*(2), 360–368. doi:10.1002/met.1345

Chapter 6
Role of Technology for Formal Education in Bangladesh

Md Hussin Alam
https://orcid.org/0000-0002-0652-3334
University of Wroclaw, Poland

ABSTRACT

We are using technology for e-learning platforms, blended platforms, and formal education platforms. Formal education is a structured and systematic form of learning. For formal education, we can say face-to-face or on-campus education. Formal education is classroom based, meaning everything a student learns comes from books and other educational materials with the sole purpose of educating students. Internet gives us the option to meet around the world. Internet distance education is a natural consequence of industrial transformations from a manufacturing economy, in which standard educational practices are based, to an information economy, in which greater autonomy, collaboration, flexibility, and a project orientation to work are the norm. The internet did not cause changes in education, but rather enabled educators to meet new demands for instructional practices and outcomes and adapt to a rapidly changing economic and social environment that was beginning to outpace the academy.

INTRODUCTION

Bangladesh formal education system is divided pre-primary or early education, primary (grades I-V), secondary (grades VI-XII, of which the first three grades are considered junior or lower secondary, grade IX-X as secondary, and grade XI-XII as higher secondary), and tertiary education (grades VI-XII, of which the first

DOI: 10.4018/978-1-7998-9194-9.ch006

three grades are considered junior or lower secondary, grade IX-X as secondary, and grade XI-XII as higher secondary), and four-year bachelor's degree courses, and one-year master's degree courses. The basic structure of these educational systems is depicted in the figures and tables below. For Muslim students, madrasah education is a separate system of official religious education. Dakhil, Alim, Fazil, and Kamil correlate to primary, secondary, higher secondary, bachelor's, and master's degrees, respectively, in Madrasah education. Madrasah education has undergone various changes in recent years to put it more in line with Bangladeshi general education system. Madrasah education currently enrolls nearly 3 million students. Bangladesh's government made primary education compulsory for all children aged six to 10 years old after implementing education for all (EFA). This had a considerable impact on the system, with the gross enrolment rate increasing from 75% to 95% by 1996. Bangladesh has 18 million children enrolled in 62,000 primary schools, making it one of the largest primary school systems in the world. a lot more than 65 percent of primary schools are government schools, with the remaining portion being registered non-government schools that are facilitated by the government. The government of Bangladesh provides free books and education equipment to all primary school students. There are also some private schools that fulfil to the social elite, though they are much fewer in number. Many secondary schools have primary school sections as well (Sarkar,2013)

The Department of Primary Education (DPE) is in charge of implementing and managing the education system. At the end of the fifth year, there is no national examination. On the other hand, government education boards hold a scholarship examination at the end of year 5. Secondary education in Bangladesh is divided into three categories: general, technical, and Madrasah education. Following the end of the primary cycle, general education begins in grade VI and continues through grade XII. This seven-year cycle is divided into three stages: secondary school grades VI-VIII; secondary school grades IX-X; and a national public examination, the Secondary School Certificate Examination (SSC), held at the end of grade X. In the case of upper secondary grades XI-XII (known as HSC), a second national public test, the higher secondary certificate examination, is administered at the end of grade XII. Madrasah education includes programmers that operate alongside regular schooling. As a result, Madrasah Dakhil education corresponds to the educational system's grades VI-X. E-learning system in Bangladesh is very poor. Student list and other information still not on the online database. For any kind of information students need to move one office to another office. The main goal of this research is to investigate how technology to help for formal education might help Bangladesh's rural population transform in terms of significant socioeconomic indices. The higher education is closely connected with technology every where in the world, but in Bangladesh higher education is connected with print textbook

(Saarbrücken,2018). Technology base higher educational opportunities will open new facilities door for formal education sector.

BACKGROUND OF RESEARCH

Every year around 1.8 million people are entering to existing workforce in Bangladesh. Youth labour force will be nearly reach 30 million by 2015. As the forces of globalization become stronger, the need for formal education and human capital investment (Haider,2015). If Bangladesh want to get ahead in this modest world, Bangladesh has to develop linkage formal education with technology, this linkage will demand our formal education and economy. We have to improve our formal education technology based from every level of education. Formal education is a major driving force of development in any modern society (Haider,2015). Technology base education paly vital role to unemployment reduction. A positive link between formal education and technology will provide smooth education sector that will process educational growth for every level of study.

Bangladesh is moving towards technology vile educationalization (Motiur, 2019). Bangladesh has one of the largest primary education systems in the world, according to the Directorate of Primary Education (DPE). There are a total of 37,672 government primary schools in the country with an estimated 10.7 million primary school aged children (6 to10 years). Nearly 6,300 primary schools around the country do not have a headmaster and over 35000 primary school no not teach technology base education. On the other hand, international standard teacher/ student ratio is 30:1 (Haider, 2015). If I look through deeply in Bangladesh there is one teacher for every 53 students so questions come up mind by the limitation of teachers to teach huge number of students, how education system can be international standard.

Bangladesh is attempting to educate and skill its inhabitants in order to engage in the global world as a least developed country. Both the public and private sectors are collaborating to give the greatest possible higher education. Bangladesh open University is the country's only public distance education institution (BOU). The traditional system, which includes brick-and-mortar campuses, is used by the all-public universities in the Bangladesh. Only a few of the private institutions provide online learning in addition to regular classroom instruction. Bangladesh Open University use technology, such as electronic gadgets, to reach individuals all over the country, rather than employing campus-based instruction. This technique allows students to learn regardless of time, location, or age. The university's main purpose is to use a range of approaches, including digital technology, to extend all levels of education in science, agriculture, humanities, and social science, as well as all other disciplines that lie under the umbrella of human knowledge and understanding. Its goal is to raise educational standards. so that people from all socioeconomic backgrounds can benefit from it. to develop efficient and well-trained workers from diverse origins The Bangladesh Open University provides two types of courses. Seven distinct schools provide formal and non-formal education. There are presently 21 formal and 19 non-formal programmes available at Bangladesh Open University (BOU). Certificate, diploma, degree, and master's degree are the four levels of formal education. specifically for students participating in formal programmes (TC) can be obtained via Regional Resource Centers (RRC), Co-ordinating Offices (CO), and Tutorial Centers. There are also audio cassettes available. Open university has been able to plan daily radio broadcasts of 25 minutes and television broadcasts of 20-25 minutes five days a week since BOU began creating audio-visual content. Every year, BOU gives two examinations for each formal programmed, one for each semester. Most of the universitas do not use technology for formal education. Primary education and high-school and college level education technology use very few.

Bangladesh government's continued commitment to employing in education, various challenges prevent it from being adopted in schools. Teachers encounter a number of difficulties, one of which is a lack of understanding of ICT technologies. CLT always favours technology-based self-directed learning. Integrating 10 in language instruction refers to the use of ICT technology such as a computer, whiteboard, audio devices, internet, television, and other devices to make an any classes a success. Bangladesh is trying to establish a Digital Bangladesh. M. Khan, M. Hasan, M. Clement, as a result, the ICT division drafted the National ICT Policy 2009 which was incorporated into the National Education Policy in 2010. It emphasises the use of information and communication technology (ICT) to improve educational quality. As a result, UNESCO has been assisting Bangladesh's government in the use of information and communication technology (ICT) in education. Following the realization of ICT's educational potential, a number of private and non-governmental organisations are attempting to include technology as an innovative approach to teaching. Through efforts such as the In-Service Secondary School, BRAC (Bangladesh Rural Advancement Committee) and Grameen Bank, in particular, have taken steps to integrate ICT into education. Computer-Aided Learning, Gonokendros (Union Library), and Teachers' ICT Training Program Furthermore, the National Education Policy (NEP) 2010 placed a strong emphasis on promoting ICT-enabled teaching and learning, as well as teacher professional development.

Information and communication technology (ICT) literacy for students, ICT-enabled education-related services, and ICT use in school administration are all things that ICT can help with. ICTs can be used to process data, build knowledge bases, and make them accessible wherever and whenever needed. Despite the condition of the economy, Information and Communication Technologies (ICTs) have been quite successful in delivering low-cost services to people's homes. ICTs play a similar role in lowering the cost of higher education across the country for people from all walks of life. On the one hand, people will have access to higher education, as well as vital information, skills, and experience. on the other, allowing them to serve the nation and develop as a result. In the twenty-first century, it is rare to find a country where distance education is not available. It's something that's been done for a long time. As a result of improvements in ICTs, higher education via distance mode has become more feasible and widely accepted by people all over the world. It is now referred to as "virtual learning." People in industrialized countries are becoming more interested in learning online rather than on campus. A virtual campus is an ICT-enabled campus where students can attend classes remotely, communicate with teachers, access learning resources, take tests, join forums/clubs, submit assignments. Most essentially how we can practice technology for formal education. Still Bangladesh education flow formal education system. If Bangladesh education ministry use technology for formal education it could be benefited all students and teachers.

Bangladesh first education commission was established 1972 by the Kudrat-i-Khuda.This education commission was highest significance education policy in Bangladesh. This commission main focus was "To develop and nurture the child's moral, mental and social personality; to bring up the child as a patriotic, responsible, inquiring and law-abiding citizen, and develop in him/her love for justice, dignity, labour, proper conduct and uprightness; to learn to read and write in the mother tongue and to be able to count and calculate; to be able to acquire the fundamental knowledge and skills needed for a future citizen; to prepare for the next stage of higher education"(Prodhan, 2016). If I look through deeply this commission didn't add technology for formal or non-formal education. Technology base education was missing from 1971 to till 2010 in Bangladesh. However, 2010, Bangladesh government were changed first education commission and formed a new education commission by Dr. Kabir Choudhury (Prodhan, 2016). This education commission goals were below list

- to develop a curricula and textbooks imbued with the national spirit with a view to cultivate the humanistic values. A congenial and joyful environment need to be created in the schools to promote healthy physical and mental development of the children:
- to initiate a uniform and mandatory syllabus for some basic subjects to be taught in diverse types of schools delivering primary education:
- to help the students inculcate moral and spiritual values like idea of justice, sense of duty, discipline and etiquettes, non-communalism, human rights, accommodative attitudes toward corporate living, curiosity, friendliness and

perseverance, and to encourage them to acquire scientific, cultural and human values and to shun superstitions;

- to ignite in them the spirit of our national liberation movement and encourage them with patriotism to dedicate themselves to nation-building;
- to make them motivated and capable of pursuing higher education through ensuring the qualitatively adequate marginal skills at respective levels of studies; To achieve this, adequate number of quality teachers will be appointed. Besides, the development of physical infrastructure, favorable social ambience, competent pedagogy, warm teachers students relationship and the respectable status of women have to be ensured.
- to take effective steps to ensure the acquisition of essential knowledge, subject-based knowledge, life skills, attitudes, values and the sense of social awareness to meet their basic learning needs that will enable them to move ahead to the next level of education;
- Pre-vocational education will be in place from Classes VI to VIII to develop respect for manual labour and to give them some idea of vocational education.
- to facilitate learning in the mother languages of the indigenous peoples and small ethnic groups at the primary level of education (Sarkar, 2013)

After carefully read all points, I found out still on this commission not add technology for formal education in Bangladesh education system. That's why teachers and students have lack of knowledge about technology. Still, most of the students and teachers have very poor knowledge to use technology for formal education. Only 2% school and college use technology for projector, even they do not use email, online library. My focus for formal education technology base like email communication, online meeting, online library, online syllabus, online marks, online class timetable, online result and online school/ university activities. All mentioned pointes will reduce cost and time. There is a long run relationship between economic growth and higher education (Sarkar, 2013). In Bangladesh, there are few education commissions have theoretically emphasized on unlocking potential at all levels of the society and creating a pool of highly trained individuals, who could contribute to the nation building (Shakhawat Hossain Sarkar, 2013). But in practice the academic technology standard of Bangladeshi universities are very weak and as such they have measurably failed to bring positive forma education change (Mobasser and Muhammed, 2010). Better technology practice among teachers can improve the quality technology base formal education in Bangladesh (Mobasser and Muhammed, 2010).

Education Process with Technology

Technology is a tool that has always been used in the formal educational. 2020/2021 all business, education and communication put in to fully online because of covid-19. Covid-19 give us lesson how we can continuation our formal education or non-formal education and business through online. Technology was only way to keep stable education during covid-19. Bangladesh education was affected lot more than 20 months school and university was closed and online practice was very limited. On the other hand, "the World Bank estimated the levels of learning poverty across the globe by measuring the number of 10-year-old children who cannot read and understand a simple story by the end of primary school. In low- and middle-income countries learning poverty stands at 53%, while for the poorest countries, this is 80% on average. With the spread of the Coronavirus disease (COVID-19), 180+ countries mandated temporary school closures, leaving 1.6 billion children and youth out of school at its height and affecting approximately 85% of children world-wide. While most countries are working towards re-opening schools, there are still intermittent closures and use of hybrid learning" (world bank Sep 24, 2021).

According to Devon C. Duhaney "technologies are increasingly being adapted and integrated into the educational process. The use of technology for formal education has greatly increased the quality of education. Through the technology many important tasks can be done easily. The growing use of technologies in formal education has given significant interpersonal relations among teachers and students. Technologies are changing the old traditional teaching approach to formal education. On the other hand, technology is changing traditional educational strategies techniques and integration education process. Interactive technology activities are making potential value for formal education. Appropriate technology teaching tools give our formal education huge change. Benefits to practice technology for education learning and teaching we can achieve communication tools, cooperation and collaborative (Salmon, 2000). To use technology as a communication tool for formal education learning to improving relationships between the tutor and student and between student parents and teachers. Student will benefit of using learning technologies such as the ability to learn at their own pace, to learn independently. Technology is especially useful for formal education, any universities can access technology for traditional education. Non-traditional students are often more easily addressed through the flexibility of online learning, as it releases time for other responsibilities related to work and family (Hill & Rivera, 2001). 2021 education will be not completed with out technology. Education process with technology.

Education Platform

On the grap I draw up three type of education platform, On-campus, E-Learning and Blended teaching. We are learning every day different way. Institutionally we are learning with fix syllabus by teachers. On the other hand, we are learning also by TV, Radio and social media. We also learning by environment, over all education is lifetime process that will never end. Question is which way learning process or practice is best. Formal learning, non-formal learning or technology base learning. However, formal education is currently facing the challenge to provide lesson traditional way and more challenges for formal education of adapting to new technology. There are so many debates about formal, non-formal education and online education. I will not focus others; my main focus is formal education with technology.

E- Learning Platform

1994, the Open University of Catalonia has been geared to the offer of non-presence-based education. Education process through an internet-based methodology that provides students the resources and tools necessary for them to be able to learn, without requiring them to be physically present in a classroom or to coincide, in terms of time, with others involved in the educational process. This is achieved with the intensive use of ICTs, leading to a virtual learning process through the exchange of information in common virtual spaces. Consequently, academic objectives are accomplished in a flexible, continuous manner, which does not depend on coinciding in time or space (E.Rimbau 2020) E-learning education is operating microelectronic technologies to approach education course external of a conventional classroom. Covid-19 issue all education system become an e-learning. We can also find almost any book, article, movie, or song, and all our educational instrument through online. "One of the easiest ways to gain information is through the media. In one UK study, 79% of all adults interviewed reported that they used some kind of media for learning on average, spent about eight and a half hours a week engaged in such learning (Hague and Logan 2009). Since that time, there has been an enormous rise in the use of the Internet, computers and social media, enabling even more informal learning through technology" (Mobassern and Muhammed, 2010)

Blended Platform

Blended teaching is an instructional approach that uses digital strategies in tandem with best practice in the classroom. In some blended classrooms, digital and face-to-face teaching may alternate according to a fixed schedule. For example, students might take one class on campus and another one entirely online. For example, Vanderbilt

Table 1.

	Public	Privet	Teachers	Students
Primary school	65620	63638	721801	20122337
High-school)	675	19985	246845	10349323
College	651	3900	127767	4385210
Madrasah education	3	9275	113577	2491268
Professional education	121	350	14545	143553
Public teacher education	84	132	3060	35039
Technical vocational institution	894	6154	53684	1100177
University	45	103	30730	1179796

Source: Bangladesh bureau of educational information and statistics BANBEIS) Bangladesh education statistics book 2020

University, The University of Rhode Island use blended platform. More recent example around the world all medical university and formal university conducted classes blended platform because of Covid-19. My university we provided classes 50% online and 50% stationary.

Formal Education in Bangladesh

"Formal education is a structured and systematic form of learning. This is the education of a certain standard delivered to students by trained teachers. To make sure formal learning is standardized and all learning institutions (e.g. schools, colleges, universities, etc.) comply with these standards, formal education in a country is governed by organizations" (Through education, 15 dec 2019. Formal education is institutional and classroom base education that a student learns from textbook by the teachers with rules and time. Formal education all teachers are appointed by government those teachers are well trained and qualified for teach. Formal education is popular education. I give the table below for formal education in Bangladesh total amount of school, college and universities and total amount of teachers and students.

Based on the table 171530 school, college and university provide formal education among 21696603 students. All institution included primary and high-school, college, madrasa and university conduct formal education. Formal education

Table 2.

	Formal Education	Non-formal Education
Organization	Government	NGO and 3rd sector
Found	Government	NGO and 3rd sector or by self
Structure/ learning channel	Institutional full time	Part-time
Syllabus/ curriculum	Institutional base	Specific labor market base
Study duration	Fix time	Life time study
Aim	To achieve certificate	To achieve experience

Table created by author

a place where learning is more formal and better regulated (Zervas, 2017). Human are learning from born to end. We are learning everyday different way by books, internet, environment, society, culture and nature. Over the centuries, information and knowledge were adapted so that we could adjust to the constant changes occurring in our world. The arrival of the modern age brought about new inventions, ideas, and ways of living and learning, all of which were created by humankind and built over the centuries from a passing on of information from one generation to the next (Zervas, 2017).We can communicate with teachers, classmates, colleagues, friends, and family members through a formal education.Through formal education students not only read and write books they also learn behavior, culture, communication skill, leadership and cooperative and collaborative work. For the modern world we are learning via internet and books. Learning has truly become boundless, and its possibilities are endless. If we are looking long time benefit for education sector, we should handover technology for formal education.

Below the table I am showing differences between formal and non-formal education

Base on the table formal education organize by government and nonformal education lead by non-government organization (NGO), international development agencies, for-profit providers, employer and employee groups give disadvantaged children access to basic education, and prepare them to enter or re-enter formal education (Saarbrücken,2018). Formal education funded by the government and non-formal education funded by NGO. Formal education is time base and systematic base study. Students learns by the system during the fix time, on the other hand non-formal education parttime or unsystematic learning process that anyone can learn any age or anywhere. Formal education has institutional base syllabus or curriculum that teacher make the syllabus base on the student's level and subject but non-formal education doesn't have any syllabus or curriculum for teach. Formal education has fix time duration that student needs to finish study level during time, for example, bachelor study, 3/4 years and master 1/2 years but non-formal education is life time education there no fix time. Formal education aims to achieve to get academic certificate to get job. On the other have non-formal education aims to get experience.

Technology for Formal Education

We use technology every day. Technology makes our life very first and easy. We can use graph mentioned technology for formal education. Valcon and librus technology that use in Poland for primary education. With access both side students can see their exams marks, educational activities, daily present result and teachers' comments. On the other hand, parents directly communication with school authority and each teacher. Panopto and Kerboodle use in UK primary education for same prepose. I am not going to talk all tools that I mentioned on the above. I want to focuses about university study-oriented system (USOS)

RECOMMENDATIONS

University Study-Oriented System (USOS) For Formal Education in Bangladesh

Technology doesn't use for formal education in Bangladesh. Primary school, high school and college students still don't have email excess to technology. Some of university student use email for different purpose, example University of Dhaka and other few universities use their own website but not full of the information. On the other hand, primary school and high school and college still do not practice technology. If Bangladesh educational board use USOS for educational purpose there will be huge impact for formal education. The incorporation of ICT in education has led in substantial changes, as Dash and Kuddus (2020), and Kuddus (2013) note out, particularly in English Language Teaching (ELT). The Bangladesh government has taken a number of initiatives to integrate ICT into classroom learning in order to support these developments. Rather than focusing exclusively on linguistic literacy, the government has already made ICT-based ELT a priority in education. The National Education Policy (NEP) of 2010 supports the use of information and communication technology to improve educational quality (ICT). Similarly, NEP 2010 identifies a variety of ICT-related strategies for all stages of education: elementary, secondary, and post-secondary. Bangladesh government trying to develop technology for education sector but still not enough to reach all education sector.

From the above discussion it is clear that limited technology and insufficient facilities are the major challenges for formal education in Bangladesh. Here are key elements (USOS) which will be influence technology base formal education in Bangladesh. This element is modern teaching technology tools that will help for registration/admission facilities, time table facilities, exam facilities, course facilities, final grades facilities, information facilities, promotion facilities, scholarship decision facilities, course exchange facilities, student mobility facilities, dormitory facilities and exam result and certificate facilities etc. I would like to mention here practice level of USOS in Poland is 99% base on the University of Wroclaw survey 2020. On the other hand, use of technology for formal education in Bangladesh is 2% that why most of the students miss the information and co-communication with teachers and friends. As a result, four years bachelor study compilated with in 6/7 years and 2 years master study finish with in 3/4 years and for an admission form or letter student need to come from hundred and hundred mile far way. In order to increase the formal education facilities of the above and below mentioned key points the government should take necessary step to implement this tool for formal education in Bangladesh and respective universities, colleges and schools' authority should ensure proper utilization of this USOS.

University Study-Oriented System (USOS)

University Study-Oriented System (USOS) is a student management information system used in 70 Polish universities like technical universities, higher vocational institutions, university schools of physical education and other types of high education institutions. USOS is based on an approach that implement formal education. According to university of Wroclaw usos website "The USOSweb system is one of many web-based applications in usos referred to as virtual office to which students, PhD students and teaching staff have access. For students and PhD students the login is their index number while for the employees usually their first and last names act as their login".To learn the understandings about Usos students reached formal way to distinguish all educational information. Usos tools accordingly acknowledge the fact that learning takes place through different kinds of experience, example registrations, results, tests, promotions, final grades, decision, scholarship and diploma. Usos focus on after login news, director, my usosweb, students' section, staff section and common section. Through the news part student and staff will able to know all update information.

USOS Director

Directory sector logger will discover all students list with full name and email, on the other hand also will find all academic staff full name with email and photo. Students and teachers will identify approaching each courses access to directory. Faculties is one of the key important for students and teachers for this section students will comprehend individually faculty dean and professor be able to catch every faculty student. Polish every university has dormitories, all students will stepped dormitory registration link, payment link, dormitory name with room number and date of chick in and check out all information across directory and any kind of help issue students and teachers be able to get help by directory. **USOS, Student's Section**

Student able to know registration subject and faculty, this section student also identifies about tests date with time, student can pay tuition fee from this section will able to know dew payment amount, Polish all universities and high school give best student rector scholarship base on achievement, after apply for scholarship student able to see decision about scholarship. Students will know final grads through this section. Finally, from this section student able to download each semester marksheet and diploma certificate. Use the technology make students life move comfortable even student can see all inform after 20 or 30 years later also. On the other hand, staff section, all teachers able to publish test date with group name and time, after tests teacher put grades an usos. If any teacher want to change any course teacher edit in the usos. Teacher also able to know how many students register for exam if any student comes from others universities for short period teacher can identify them.

Usos, Staff Section

The basic goals by use of university study-oriented system (USOS) for formal education in Bangladesh below

1. Student will know all academic information through USOS account
2. Administration committee and teachers can provide syllabus and class time table by USOS
3. Student will able to know admission conformation by USOS
4. Administration committee or teacher will able to put exam date and time through USOS
5. Students will know exam date and result through USOS
6. Student will able to do exam registration through USOS
7. Students will able to pay tuition fee through USOS
8. Students will able to apply for scholarship through USOS
9. Students will able to apply for exchange course through USOS
10. Student will know final result and will get certificate through USOS
11. Teacher's will know all internal information through USOS
12. Students will able to exchange study one county to other countries

Over all by use of USOS our formal education will be standardization and modernization. Students and teachers will have smooth communication that will have positive effect for our formal education. On the other hand, by practice of USOS students, teachers and university staff will able to reduce time and cost.

USOS essential to developing the knowledge and skills for formal education. I found seven achieve by USOS for formal education. Seven achieve are blew

Achieved

1. To exterminate communication gap
2. To achieve world stander quality formal education
3. To encourage technology base formal education
4. To decrease time and travel cost
5. To combat against of lack of knowledge about educational technology
6. To ensure technology base formal education stability
7. To ensure develop a global partnership for development formal education through technology

Education Issue in Bangladesh

Technology for formal education is a much-debated issue in Bangladesh nowadays. It is observed that insufficient budgetary provision and lace of the quality information for the key elements has been affecting the technology base formal education in Bangladesh. Bangladesh as a developing country needs to develop and ensure minimum facilities for technology base formal education in every sector education. Abu Afeaful Haider, mentioned four education issues in Bangladesh on the daily star newspaper,2014. His four issue is below

1. Lack of qualified teachers
2. poor school facilities in terms of the number of schools classrooms
3. libraries and playgrounds are responsible for poor quality education at primary schools.
4. A recent DPE internal report shows that around 70 percent of children are unable to read or write properly, or perform basic mathematical calculations even after five years at primary school. Based on his issue I like to add few issues here for formal education in Bangladesh. All those issues are affected our formal education
5. Poor educational policy
6. Short tram and undeveloped educational curriculum
7. Lack of knowledge about educational technology
8. Poverty
9. Unqualified educational policy maker

10. Insufficient budget for education
11. Corruption
12. Political and business base education issue

Grameen Phone Connect with Formal Education and Rural Business

The Village Phones are self-contained pay phones with complete connectivity and the ability to make and receive phone call. The significance of the Grameen Bank's Supervisor a micro-credit product in politically and economically benefiting rural women is examined in this research. Through the supply of a very little amount of microcredit, the study adds to a better understanding of how a technical and financial collaboration led to village women's economic and social participation and improved social status and increased role in decision-making). It also shows how an association arrangement within the Grameen group of organisations such as house old solution and mutual support for the common business model helped village phone succeed in the prepayment market while keeping telecom service inexpensive to poor rural clients. The village phone (VP) model could serve as a model for ICT practitioners who are pro-poor.

Grameen phone meaning is village phone. Village Phone is a new concept, it is an extension of Grameen Bank's 23-year-old microcredit programmer. Between 1976 and 1996, the Grameen Bank loaned $2 billion. These loans were primarily used for village economic activities such as rice threshing, goat raising, vegetable cultivation, and irrigation, all of which were safe, familiar, and low-risk and, in most cases, low-value added and had no effect on stimulating other business activities or the growth of non-traditional small and medium businesses. Grameen Bank, on the other hand, has expressed an interest in continuing to invest in high-risk businesses by 1996. Grameen wanted to leverage its future loans to promote a wider range of high-value firms, including information technology and the Internet. Employees at Grameen recognised that there were several options. Massive investments in technology and communications technology research and development had been made by wealthy developed-world companies.

Only Grameen Bank members roughly 95% of whom are women are now eligible for a GT village phone and they must meet certain requirements, including a minimum of two years as a Grameen Bank employee, a track record of on-time payments, English digit knowledge, a centrally located house or place of business, one or two other sources of income, and access to electricity (to charge the phone). If she meets the criteria, she is given a $220 loan with a 22% interest rate to purchase a Grameen phone (the phone and accessories cost around $420). she will pay back the money in three years Grameen Telecom, which operates out of adjacent Grameen Bank branches, primarily provides village phone in rural areas. There are approximately 1000 phones now in operation, with approximately 60,000 users. Grameen Grameen Telecom plans to have placed 40,000 village phones. Villagers who run such phone businesses are said to earn an average of more than $700 per year.

Beginning in the year 2003, Grameen Shikkha has created a scholarship management scheme to help disadvantaged rural boys and girls continue their education and improve their IT abilities. It pinpoints how and where this demographic change might take place. Published and unpublished records, research material, reports, and professional papers given at seminars were used as secondary data sources in this study. Thanks to the help of 180 individuals and institutions, Grameen Shikkha was able to provide financial assistance to approximately 5,300 impoverished students in Bangladesh as of 2018. Thousands are currently pursuing degrees in medicine, engineering, and textile technology. To mention a few, there are business administration, law, economics, and the arts. Bangladesh is a Southeast Asian country with a population of over a hundred million people. Sixty percent of them are female. Among the contributors and sponsors of the Grameen Shikkha Scholarship Management Program are the Hunter Foundation, H&M, Citi Foundation, and Mr. Vidar Jorgensen of the United States. The Green Children Corporation of the United States, Grameen Foundation of the United States, Grameen Phone Limited is a company based in Bangladesh. Monica Yunus, GSRD Foundation of the Netherlands, Small Planet Fund of the United States, NOKIA, Rotary International District 2670 Japan, Hessnatur Germany, Holcim Bangladesh Ltd., SOLAS Italy, Her Majesty Queen Sofia of Spain, Rotary International District 2670 Japan, Rotary International District 2670 and Saudi Arabia's Muhammed Abdul Latif Jameel. With the help of these sponsors, In Bangladesh, GS is able to grant scholarships to the children of GB borrowers. Thanks to the generosity of numerous sponsors, GB is able to grant Tk scholarships to ten students. Fifty students in Bangladesh receive monthly Tk. 500 and monthly Tk. 2,5000 scholarships. GS provides student scholarships in accordance with the agreement with GB. Individual donors contribute to the GB educational system. education scholarship programme, which is deposited under the GB monthly profit system. Many people do not want to earn interest on their money, but GB does so in order to support Bangladesh's poor children. People (both domestic and international) are being urged to invest in this scheme by the United Kingdom. GS is funded by philanthropists to provide scholarships to the children of GB debtors. Grameen Shikkha is currently operational.

Since 2008, Grameen Shikkha has worked with C&A International to provide vocational training in Bangladesh. The overall goal of this training programme is to improve Bangladesh's human resources in order to accelerate the country's economic development.The main goal of this vocational training programme is to offer low-cost professional skills to disadvantaged young men and women from rural areas and urban slums so that they can find meaningful work, either as self-employed individuals or as wage workers, and therefore succeed in life. One of the world's leading sourcing firms, Thomas Edward Stockwell Company (TESCO) International Sourcing Ltd. The programme benefits the children of Tesco garment manufacturing workers in Bangladesh. Scholars are undergraduate students enrolled in public universities or colleges, as well as those in higher secondary schools who are preparing for higher education. Each of the TESCO scholars receives a BDT 3000.00 monthly stipend. The program's implementing partner is Grameen Shikkha. Grameen Shikka gives TESCO scholarships to a hundred students each year whose parents are GB borrowers. In April 2008, Grameen Shikkha built a full-fledged career training centre in Talbag, Savar, near Dhaka City. GS has its own vocational training site in Asolia Savar, which it owns and operates.The GS vocational centre educates poor Bangladeshi youth how to repair cell phones, radios, televisions, refrigerators, fans, ovens, computers, and automobiles, among other trade skills. It also provides training in areas such as food preparation, garment tailoring, and electrical device assembly. Since 2008, more than 8,500 young men and women have been trained at this vocational training institution (Grameen Shikka, 2019). Grameen Shikka provides scholarships to several vocational trainees at the GS vocational centre to aid them with their expenses. There are costs associated with occupational training as well as living expenses. Grameen Shikka selects students for sponsorship of vocational training expenses (or scholarships) depending on sponsor criteria. Scholarship money is awarded to students on a regular basis by GS, but only after a comprehensive review of their academic achievements. A new student receives a scholarship or bursary when an existing scholar completes his or her studies. Once a year, Grameen Shikka informs sponsors of academic achievement.In its publications and on its website, it provides information on GS's different programmes and services. Grameen Bank and Grameen Shikka support the development of schools, pre-schools, and day-care centres for their borrowers and beneficiaries. Grameen Shikka sets up a school system for Grameen Bank borrowers, offering a complete basic education curriculum for village children. Women have long played a significant part in the economic life of their communities. They demonstrated their entrepreneurial and business skills by using and repaying their vocational training loans. Women, especially poor mothers, must divide their time between productive job and family reproductive roles. Their donations were considered as additional cash for family survival or as a chance to improve their living conditions in Bangladesh's dominating male society. In the meantime, their unintentional participation in microfinance efforts has enhanced their business potential. The field officer's accountability and honesty, as well as that of the borrowers, is one of the reasons for success.

For example, Taskia Parveen is a secondary school student in Magura, Bangladesh. Taskia Parven received a government scholarship in the talent pool category after being selected the best student in Class eight. Taskia school have over 1000 students but her school doesn't have any computer lab or technology base study and 1000 students doesn't know what is email and her school doesn't have website with school information. This school move on with formal education. Any students need help from school or need to collect information or certificate students need to be school physically. As a result, student expend all day for an information its make constable, time affection, herdable and not profitable. If school practice Librus and Vulcan tools student able to catch all information from home with in finger click. Above I just give one example all university and college still do not practice technology. Bangladesh education ministry can take step to use USOS for formal education.

CONCLUSION

The research has successfully identified the main challenges and key elements of technology for formal education in Bangladesh. "Technology base formal education should not be written paper only. It should be the commitment and willingness of the government and all concerned. If Bangladesh could successfully address the existing challenges of technology base education and ensure essential facilities for the same through budgetary provision, it could provide world class higher education at moderate cost and it could be an example to the whole world" (Saarbrücken, 2016). Technology's benefit for formal education that used over the world. For formal education in Bangladesh USOS can be an incredible asset. Usos one of the tool for formal education, by using Usos will increase quality education. By using "Usos" teachers and students will be able to complete many difficult tasks very easily. Through the Usos employees and students will be able to know all information about university any part of the world with an a very short time. Bangladesh formal education will be change to use technology.

REFERENCES

Rimbau-Gilabert. (2014). Article. *E-learning in Economics and Business*, *11*(2).

Bangladesh Bureau of Educational Information and Statistics (BANBEIS). (2020). *Bangladesh education statistics book*. Author.

Dash, A., & Kuddus, K. (2020) Leveraging the benefits of ICT usage in teaching of English language and literature. In Smart intelligent computing and applications, vol 160. Smart innovation, systems and technologies. Springer.

Duhaney. (2005). Technology and Higher Education: Challenges in the Halls of Academe. Academic Press.

Grameen Bank. (2004). *Opening Speech by Muhammed Yunus, 30th Zonal Manager Conference*. Dhaka: Grameen Bank.

Grameen Bank. (2005). Opening Speech by Muhammed Yunus, *30th Zonal Manager Conference*. Dhaka: Grameen Bank

Grameen Bank Shikka Barta. (2009). *Five highest scholars' faces from the children of GB members in 2009*. Grameen Bank.

Grameen Shakka Bartta. (2014). *Talented children stories*. Grameen Bank.

Grameen Shikka, . (2006). *Grammen Shikka Activities*. Grameen Shikka.

Grameen Shikka, . (2019). *Arsenic mitigation program in Bangladesh*. Grameen Shikka.

Grameen Shikka Bartta. (2008). *Proud mothers from the borrowers of GB*. Department Administration, Grameen Bank.

Grameen Shikka Bartta. (2009). *Proud mothers from the borrowers of GB*. Department Administration, Grameen Bank.

Grameen Shikka Bartta. (2014). *Grameen Bank talented Scholars*. Department Administration, Grameen Bank.

Hague & Logan. (2009). *Informal Learning and Non-Formal Education for Development*. Academic Press.

Hill & Rivera. (2001). How Is the Liver Primed or Sensitized for Alcoholic Liver Disease? Academic Press.

Khan, M., Hasan, M., & Clement, C. K. (2012). Barriers to the introduction of ICT into education in developing countries: The example of Bangladesh. *Online Submission*, *5*(2), 61–80.

Kuddus, K. (2013). Role of mass media and technology in fostering English language acquisition. *Proceedings of the UGC national seminar on English language acquisition development and environment*, 107-116.

Mobasser & Muhammed. (2010). Higher Education in Bangladesh: Status, Issues and Prospects. Academic Press.

Motiur. (2019). *Pulsed flow-through cultivation of Margaritifera: Effects of water source and food quantity on the survival and growth*. Academic Press.

Report, G. A. (2005). *Grameen Bank scholarship program*. Grameen Bank.

Rimbau-Gilabert, E., & Ficapal-Cusı, P. (2008). The power of technology for learning. Academic Press.

Saarbrücken. (2016). *Transition from Nonformal to Formal Education in Bangladesh: An Exploration of the Challenges Student Face*. LAMBERT Academic Publishing.

Wahid, A. N. M. (1999). The Grameen Bank and women in Bangladesh. *Challenge*, *42*(5).

Zervas. (2017). Formal and informal education during the rise of Greek nationalism. Academic Press.

Chapter 7
The Impact of Business Sophistication on Marketing Knowledge

Francisco Xavier Pedro
https://orcid.org/0000-0001-8947-8980
Universidade do Minho, Portugal

Ricardo Gouveia Rodrigues
Universidade da Beira Interior, Portugal

ABSTRACT

This study aims to analyze the impact of business sophistication on marketing knowledge. The research combines bibliometric literature review, preferred reporting items for systematic and meta-analyses (PRISMA), and empirical approach to collect extensive sample data GII (Global Innovation Index) of 50 countries' business sophistication technologic input-output framework. Furthermore, the research uses multiple linear regression analysis to test the proposed hypotheses. Business sophistication impacts positively on marketing knowledge. However, each technological input pillar behaves differently. This study derives managerial strategies and policies from marketing knowledge.

INTRODUCTION

This research aims to analyze and describe *the impact of business sophistication on marketing knowledge.* Several revolutions have happened in the past. As a result, the Information Technology (IT) Industry is multiplying and transforming

DOI: 10.4018/978-1-7998-9194-9.ch007

the business standards of tomorrow. First industrial revolution (1.0, 1700) drove steam engines' discovery to optimize the industry's production process. The second industrial revolution (2.0, 1800) was the precursor of electricity for mass production. Third industrial revolution (3.0, 1900) was the hallmark of the use of Information and Communication Technology (ICT), the internet, and electronic elements that automated production processes; Fourth industrial revolution - better known as 4.0 (intelligence – digital transformation) - is the junction of technologies, speed and intelligence.

IT industry has already gained much traction at the global level shifting towards the fourth industrial revolution (4.0) by adhering to cutting-edge technologies through digital enterprise transformation. The fourth industrial revolution (4.0) on digitizing all its processes allows the interaction between physical and digital systems, thereby achieving real-time information for making timely decisions (Riola, J.M. et al. 2020). The Fourth industrial revolution involves several changes in the workforce's key features. The fourth revolution catalyzes welfare, socio-economic changes, cross-sector boundaries (e.g., water service, health, business), and new business models that will influence job marketing knowledge. With the fourth industrial revolution, the marketing strategies of companies are disruptive when the world manages the pandemic crisis of COVID-19. Digital technologies have dramatically changed the business sophistication and, as a consequence, there is an urgent need to redefine the impact of business sophistication on marketing knowledge for *Disruptive Innovation and Emerging Technologies for Business Excellence in the Service Sector.* In addition, companies experience significant managerial transformations. The digital enterprise transformation needs to plan and produce disruptive innovations for traditional business management tools and challenge integrating the marketing knowledge of companies' management processes and strategies.

Kirikkaleli and Ozun (2019) explore the linkages between business sophistication and macroeconomic stability within OECD countries. If policymakers intend to accelerate business sophistication, then their attention should be directed towards maximizing the economic indicators in the long run. Zhou and Li (2012) examine how the existing knowledge base interacts with external and internal market knowledge to affect radical innovation. Business sophistication and knowledge marketing are a matter of concern for business excellence in the service sector because business sophistication support competitiveness in order for it to reach the advanced level requirements needed for global competitiveness. Business sophistication and innovation have bilateral impacts as they are seen as central pillars of competitiveness, especially if an economy is innovation-driven (Kirikkaleli & Ozuna, 2019, p. 352). However, there is no relationship between business sophistication and marketing knowledge in the service sector in these studies. Therefore, what is *the impact of business sophistication on marketing knowledge* in the service sector? According to Global Innovation Index (GII) framework, we assume that the proxy for business sophistication is knowledge, innovation linkages and knowledge absorption, and these variables in a broad pillar that we designate as input - Digital Enterprise Transformation - in the institutional environment, human resources and research, infrastructures to support the business environment. Business sophistication refers to the market through access to credit, investment, competition and market scale. Furthermore, we assume as a proxy for knowledge marketing the outputs of the GII framework, namely welfare - measured by the number of goods and services produced. Thus, when referring to marketing knowledge, within the framework of the GII, we assume as a proxy knowledge and technology outputs - therefore knowledge creation, knowledge impact and knowledge diffusion; when referring to the dimension of creative outputs, that is, goods and services such as in health, we assume intangible assets, creative goods and services and online creativity (see figure 12; table 7 and 8).

Based on theory, multiple regression techniques, the study develops panel data, grouped on the Global Innovation Index (GII) encompassing 50 countries during 2019. The model assumes the independent variables, the *institutions, human capital, research, infrastructure, market sophistication* and *business sophistication*. Furthermore, it assumes *marketing knowledge* as the output. Through data analysis, multiple linear regressions and empirical analysis, this study has two objectives: (1) Analyze the impact of business sophistication on marketing knowledge. (2) Investigate the impact of each technological input on marketing knowledge. These instruments provide policymakers with a panoply of relevant information on managerial strategies and practices that need to be adapted to meet the *marketing knowledge* challenges in service sector. The management and strategies for the digital transformation framework rely on the distinction between *technological inputs and outputs* to measure the absorption of technological intensity and deriving policies from marketing knowledge in service sector. Thus, *"inputs"* are the national economy elements that allow innovatively business activities and *"outputs"* the results of innovative activities in the economy, which results in marketing knowledge. The GII framework aggregates the indicators into *21 sub-pillars and seven pillars, respectively. Five* of *them are input pillars*, consisting of *Institutions, Human Capital and Research, Infrastructure, Marketing Sophistication and Business Sophistication.* Simultaneously, *two are outputs pillars, referring to knowledge and technology outputs and creative outputs*. Finally, the *inputs* and *outputs* pillars aggregated to form *the input* and *output sub-indices* (Figure 12).

In the disruptive era, - *innovation and emerging technologies for business excellence in the service sector* - business sophistication significantly influence marketing knowledge. Developing marketing knowledge help companies to have a well-defined path and benefit from business sophistication for sector service. A positive impact of business sophistication on marketing knowledge is not a self-standing process. This process is dependent on the technological intensity and innovation that a given country can absorb and managerial strategies for companies. The results showed that not all pillars – inputs - had the same impact; many had adverse effects and insignificant contributions in the service sector.

The research covers the *introduction, methodology, solutions and recommendations (results and discussions), future research directions, conclusions and references*.

LITERATURE REVIEW

In this section, we review previous studies of *global innovation index, disruptive and emerging technologies in service sector, business sophistication in service sector,and marketing sophistication in service sector.*

Global Innovation Index

The *Global Innovation Index* (GII) is a set of innovation determinants *(inputs)* and *outputs,* collects annual datasets and proposes a global ranking for countries based on their capacity to innovate (Hamidi, S, & Berrado, A., 2018). *Connell University, INSEAD* and the *World Intellectual Property Organization* (WIPO, a specialized agency of the United Nations) co-publish the GII (Dutta & Lanvin 2013; Sohn, SY et al., 2016). In the GII, there are *five pillars under the input sub-index: institutions, human capital and research, infrastructure, market sophistication, and business sophistication*. The *innovation output sub-index* is divided into two pillars: *knowledge and technology output and creative output.* Innovation essential role in economic growth and success in the global economy, in which knowledge and intangibles are increasingly essential and encourage investment in research and development. Thus, these previous studies consider various aspects of innovation measurement, and an innovation index can be used to represent the performance of the technological advances and innovation capacities of different countries. Furthermore, the GII index is calculated by taking the simple average of the innovation input and output sub-indices. Furthermore, this may seem to be a straightforward approach. It requires no transition from macroeconomics to microeconomics levels to explore the potential of the GII with a focus on marketing and considering the relationships among the components of complicated national innovation systems. Therefore, in this study, we propose and test hypotheses based on the *impact of business sophistication on marketing knowledge.*

Disruptive and Emerging Technologies in Service Sector

As Schmidthuber, Maresch and Ginner (2020) stated, mobile payment is an example of a situation in which the potential of new disruptive technology is not tapped by the masses even though it offers substantial benefits. Schmidthuber, Maresch and Ginner's study investigates the factors influencing using disruptive technology. As results indicate that the intention to use mobile payment services is positively affected by perceived usefulness, perceived compatibility, perceived personal innovativeness, and perceived social influence, but is negatively affected by perceived risk. Both perceived costs and risk mitigate the positive impact of several other characteristics. Their findings provide leverage points to better tap the potential of mobile payment in contexts such as Europe (Schmidthuber, Maresch, & Ginner, 2020 p. 1).

Disruptive and emerging technologies differ from incumbent technologies by introducing a new performance dimension for products altering the basis of competition; the emerging technology replaces the incumbent technology from the mainstream market despite the new technology often performing worse in one or two of the performance dimensions that are particularly important to mainstream customers. Research has explored why individuals choose to adopt disruptive and emerging technologies. According to Schmidthuber et al. (2020), among the most popular models analyzing individual adoption decisions are the technology acceptance model explores the factors that affect individuals' intention to adopt new technologies by extending the theory of reasoned action (Schmidthuber, Maresch, & Ginner, 2020 p. 2).

Different indicators influence business performance in disruptive and emerging technology and competitive business environment. Gaile-sarkane and Andersone (2011) analyze one of the most critical company stakeholders – their customers. The research evaluates and analyzes existing consumer behaviour models. The authors have developed a mathematical model for modelling consumer behaviour and investments in communication with customers based on this research. The model assumption stated the existence of two groups – people and goods. A series of parameters characterize each group. The Gaile-sarkane and Anderson model contains only three variable parameters (a consumer and a product). It is also necessary to determine each parameter's coefficients of mutual impact, which experts should indicate to perform an accurate calculation. The Gaile-sarkane and Andersone model would be suitable for practical application within the business to analyze the return of the company investments and identify perspective and less prospective areas of investment towards *business sophistication* (Gaile-sarkane and Andersone, 2011 p. 1).

Business Sophistication in Service Sector

Business sophistication analyses how competent companies develop and apply new technologies in their practices, products, and services. It also reflected the general quality of manufacturing and domestic services and how companies are receptive to the market (Amon-Há, R. et al., 2019). According to Sohn, SY et al. (2016), *business sophistication* indices measure *knowledge workers, innovation linkages and knowledge absorption.* Salas-Velasco (2018) empirical analysis of macroeconomic performance stated that OECD countries with a higher capacity for innovation and greater sophistication production processes tend to be less inefficient. Furthermore, non-parametric methods for evaluating the impact of process and contextual variables on efficiency also confirmed that business sophistication and innovation contribute to efficiency improvements across OECD countries (Salas-Velasco, 2018, p.60). Sohn, Kim and Jeon, (2016), using a structural equation model (SEM), hypothesizing national innovation structure among seven inputs (institution, human capital and research, infrastructure, market sophistication, and business sophistication) and outputs (knowledge and technology outputs, and creative outputs). Using GII data from 2013, they discovered that business sophistication and infrastructure have the most substantial direct and indirect effects on creative output, respectively (Sohn, Kim & Jeon, 2016, p. 2). These results provided a Research and & Development (R&D) infrastructure for innovation and marketing knowledge transfers. Innovation has an essential role in the economic growth and success of a global economy in which marketing knowledge and intangibles are increasingly crucial in the world. Therefore, it is necessary to enhance the levels of marketing knowledge workers, innovation linkages such as joint ventures, strategic alliance and knowledge absorption (e.g. high-tech imports) to improve innovation performance (Sohn, Kim & Jeon, 2016, p. 12). Hathaivaseawong, Mohamad and Ramayah (2004) focus of their study is the transfer of marketing knowledge within joint venture firms. The transfer incidence is the highest for activities in strategic marketing management, followed by price management (Hathaivaseawong, Mohamad and Ramayah, 2004, p. 1), and therefore, *Marketing Sophistication in Service Sector.*

Marketing Sophistication in Service Sector

According to Peòalba-Aguirrezabalaga et al. (2021), the importance of marketing knowledge management is integrating internal and external knowledge into the product/service innovation process. Therefore, they analyze *marketing departments' role in accessing internal and external knowledge resources (i.e., marketing-specific relational capital [RC]) to reach improved product and service* innovation performance. Their study makes a *valuable contribution to marketing and management literature by revealing the types of social interactions in the marketing function that enable access to knowledge sources that promote successful product/service innovation* (Peòalba-Aguirrezabalaga et al., 2021, p.1).

In the *'outputs'* context, the *knowledge creation* pillar reflected the degree to which a country can develop and apply knowledge to increase the components of added value in products and services and, in general, to an economy driven by innovation (Amon-Há, R. et al., 2019). According to Eisend, M (2015), *marketing knowledge* follows a discontinuous model of progress: knowledge has increased over time, but at a decreasing rate. *Marketing knowledge* has triplex dimensions: *knowledge creation, knowledge impact and knowledge diffusion* (Duarte, M.P., & Carvalho, F.M.P.O., 2020).

In the subsequent section, we present the research methodology.

RESEARCH METHODOLOGY

This research follows a (1) *systematic, a (2) bibliometric literature review and (3) empirical application method* to identify, evaluate and synthesize all relevant studies following a PRISMA statement *(Preferred Reporting Items for a Systematic Review and Meta-analysis)* (Moher et al., 2009). According to Grant, M. J., & Booth, A. (2009), a systematic review seeks to systematically search for, appraise, and systematically synthesise research evidence. It also aims for exhaustive, comprehensive searching, the quality assessment that may determine inclusion/exclusion, typically narrative with tabular accompaniment, known and unknown knowledge, uncertainty around findings and recommendations for practice for future research. The literature review process involves time and lacks completeness and involuntary omissions (Nazarko, L., 2019). We adopted three approaches to reduce the potential (bias): (a) *a qualitative approach based on bibliometric analysis;* (b) *a quantitative approach focused on analysing the content present in the literature and* (c) *practical application from GII (global innovation index) framework and linear regression to analyze the impact of business sophistication on marketing knowledge.* The three approaches are complementary and have advantages and disadvantages. Generally, using more than two databases is necessary to achieve an in-depth systematic review of the literature. Meanwhile, this research chose only two databases - *Web of Science Core Collection* (one of the most extensive abstracts and citation databases of peer-reviewed literature - multidisciplinary, comprehensive) and *Scopus (2017-2021).* First of all, the search equation "*business sophistication*", "*global innovation index*", and "*knowledge marketing*" was established in the WOS and Scopus databases.

Sample. The sample is 186 final articles from WOS and Scopus. First, the study sample was established by the application of the limitation criteria: year (2017-2021), *articles, the final stage, subject area, exact words and publisher hybrid gold access, ("business sophistication", "global innovation index", "knowledge marketing").* By applying the search equation in the two databases, a final study sample with the application of the inclusion criteria is shown in figure 1. The analysis was based on journal articles indexed in WOS and Scopus (n = 186). First, the study sample was established by the application

Search strategy. This search strategy was tailored to 2 databases: Scopus and Web of Science, and the search terms used were the following: *"business sophistication"* and "*global innovation index*" or "*knowledge marketing*." All searches spanned from database inception until 2021 and included journal articles published in english only.

Selection criteria. PRISMA *(Preferred Reporting Items for Systematic Reviews and Meta-Analyses)* statement (Moher et al., 2009) was the selection criteria. The search mainly focused on mapping existing literature on *"business sophistication"* and" *global innovation index"* or *"knowledge"* in the field of social sciences, *business and economics.* The search then narrowed to the subject areas business and economics fields. The span was from the year 2017- 2021.

Furthermore, we exclude from the search ll articles before 2017. We get a total of 186 (Wos=68, Scopus=118) research articles. There were 125 (Wos=15, Scopus=110) records extracted at this stage. At the final stage were 106 (Wos=10, Scopus=96) records extracted.

Quality assessment. The study is based only on original research articles. For maintaining the quality of the research, all duplications we checked out thoroughly. Abstracts of the articles were checked deeply for the articles' analysis and purification to ensure the quality and relevance of academic literature included in the review process. Furthermore, we carried out a careful evaluation of each research paper. The following exclusion criterion was to limit the papers published in the English language only.

Data extraction. In the data extraction phase, we selected 16 articles and the characteristics extracted were: (a) Article Must be an original paper. Published reports, case studies were included. (b) The article must be in English language and from the field of business and economics. (c) We extracted articles published between 2017 to 2021

Figure 1. Scientific yearly production in Scopus
Source: author

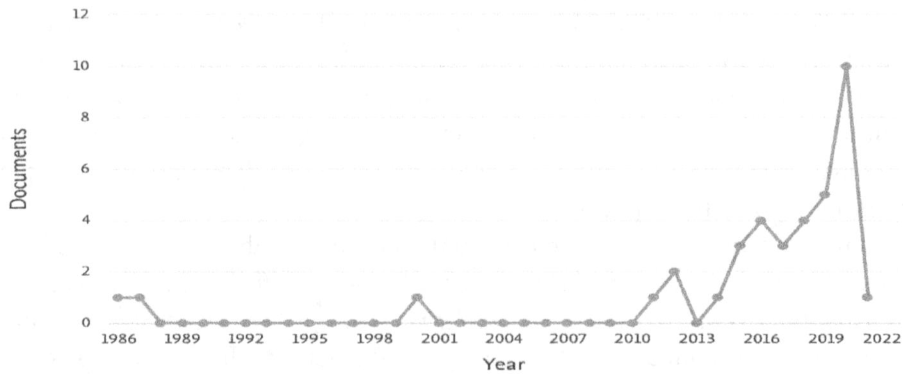

FINDINGS

Quantitative Results and Analysis (Scopus)

Although the number of papers on *business sophistication* and *marketing knowledge* evolved, it was only after 2019 that their numbers increased significantly (Figure 2). The scientific publications grew and reached a peak in the year 2020. Since 2020 *business sophistication* and *marketing knowledge* is connected in the literature; this trend appears to increase until 2020. In 2020 there was a peak of publication in the topic: new ways of *marketing knowledge* (education, conditioning, institutions, performance) resulting from the accelerated digital transformation in the pandemic phase of covid-19. The impact of *business sophistication* on *marketing knowledge* was identified in the recent literature as a vehicle for better understanding education, institutions, infrastructure and performance. A better understanding of *business sophistication* results in an ever more outstanding customer commitment through the *knowledge of its macroeconomic indicators.*

Riga Technical University is the institution that more contributed to *business sophistication and marketing knowledge literature.*

The countries that most contributed to these publications are *Iran* and *the United Kingdom,* each innovation leader (Figure 4). The reason behind these numbers, in those countries, reinforces the importance given to *business sophistication* and *marketing knowledge* in particular contributed with the institutional framework that justifies networking in the innovation processes moreover these Academia's are traditionally open and prove to develop new knowledge at a fast pace. Therefore,

Figure 2. The PRISMA Statement
Source: author

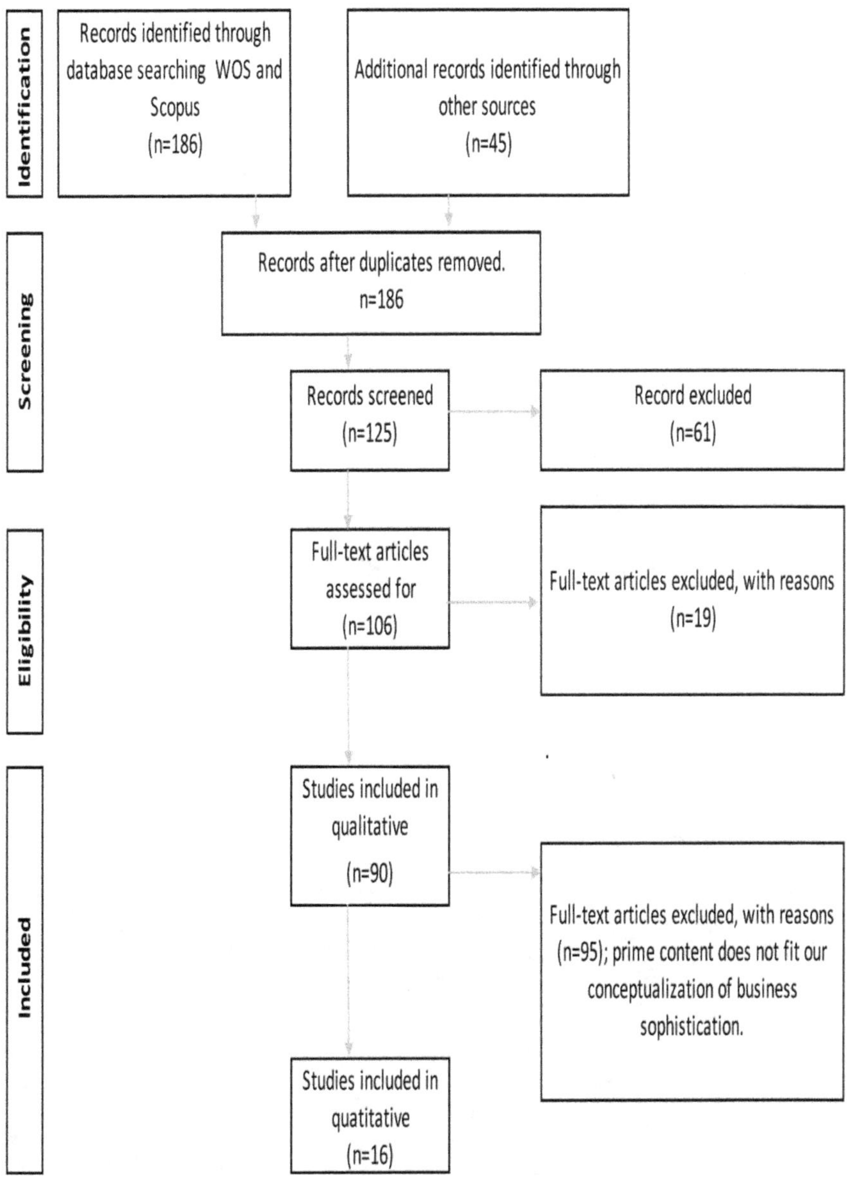

countries in which Academia has a dynamic role capture the publishers and authors' interest in those topics.

Figure 3. Scientific affiliation production in Scopus
Source: author

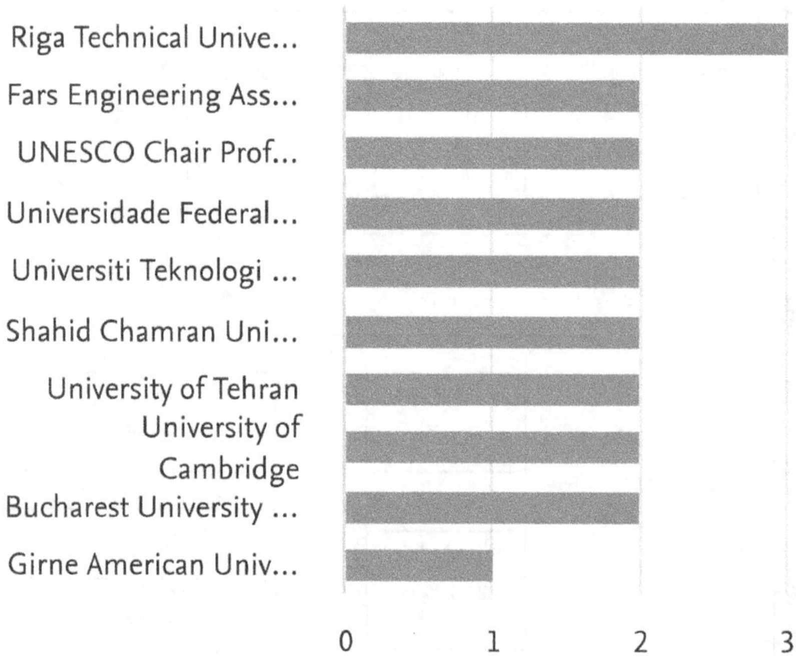

Figure 4. Scientific production by country in Scopus
Source: author

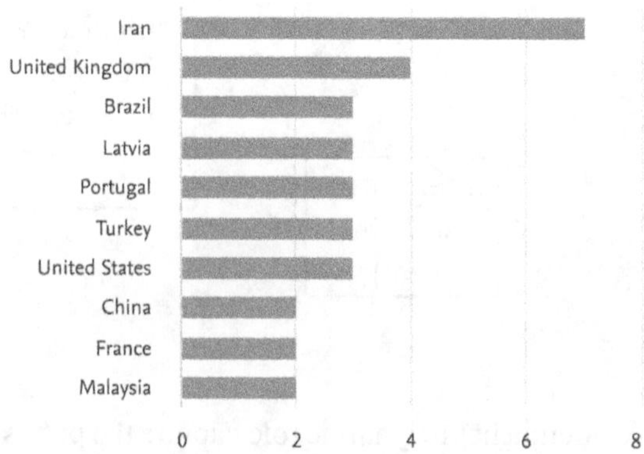

Figure 5. Scientific production by subject area
Source: author

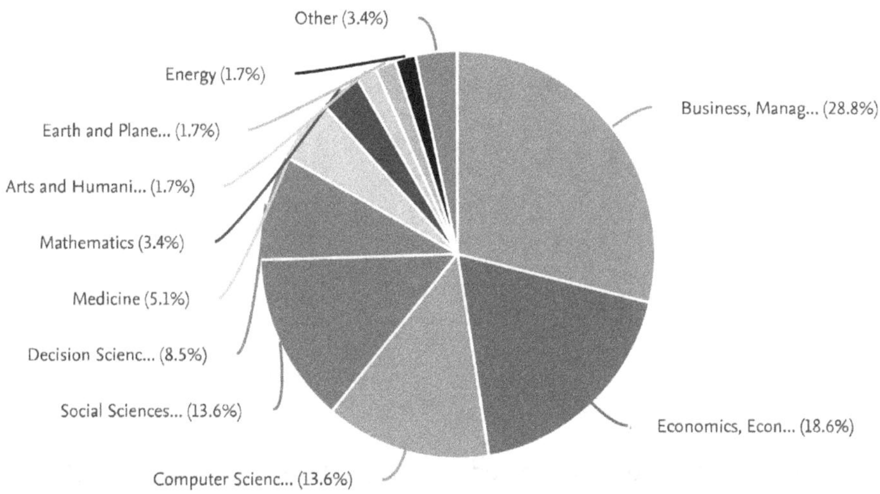

At current days, business sophistication and marketing are advancing new theories under the subject areas of "*Business, Management and Accounting*", "*Economics*", "*computer science" and "social science"*. Moreover, Scopus automatically provided the results according to minor subject areas, as shown in Figure 5. Not surprisingly, 28,0% of the articles published in titles that classified under the "*Business, Management and Accounting*" – which is still the predominant subject area; 18,6,4% to Economics; and 13,6% to "*computer science*" and "*social science",* respectively. This result goes a long cloth the previous generations of business sophistication models and frameworks justified by connecting to marketing knowledge and customer commitment.

Web of Science

In the *web of science*, scientific production on *business sophistication* and *knowledge* followed a process opposite to *Scopus* and with a decreasing trend. The reasons are that the GII indicators are static and refer to the past. The accelerated *digital transformation* catalyzed by covid-19, may be the explanation for this sharp decrease from 2019.

The natural institutions to collaborate for *business sophistication* and *marketing knowledge* is *Stare University of Florida* (9%), *Swansea University* (9%) and *University of Pennsylvania* (6%).

Figure 6. Scientific yearly production in WOS
Source: author

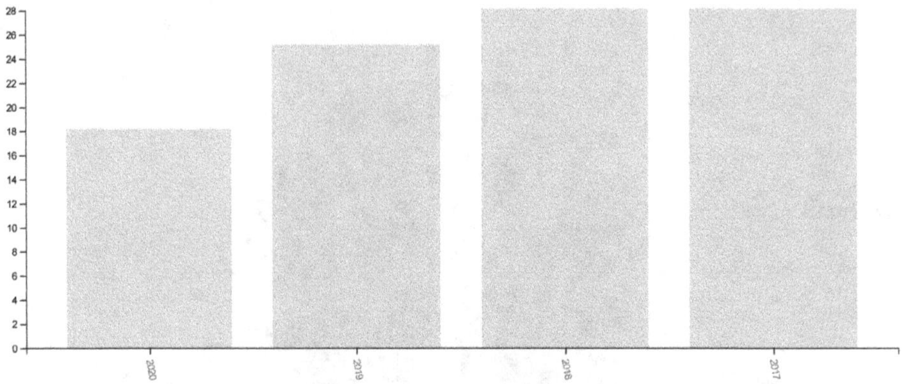

The countries that most contributed to these publications are *USA, England and China (Figure 9).*

At current days, *business sophistication* and *marketing* are advancing new theories under the subject areas of "*Business*", "*Management*", "*Hospitality Leisure*". Not surprisingly, 49,5% of the articles published in titles classified under the "*Business*" – which is still the predominant subject area and 16% to *Management*. This result goes a

Figure 7. Scientific affiliation production in WOS
Source: author

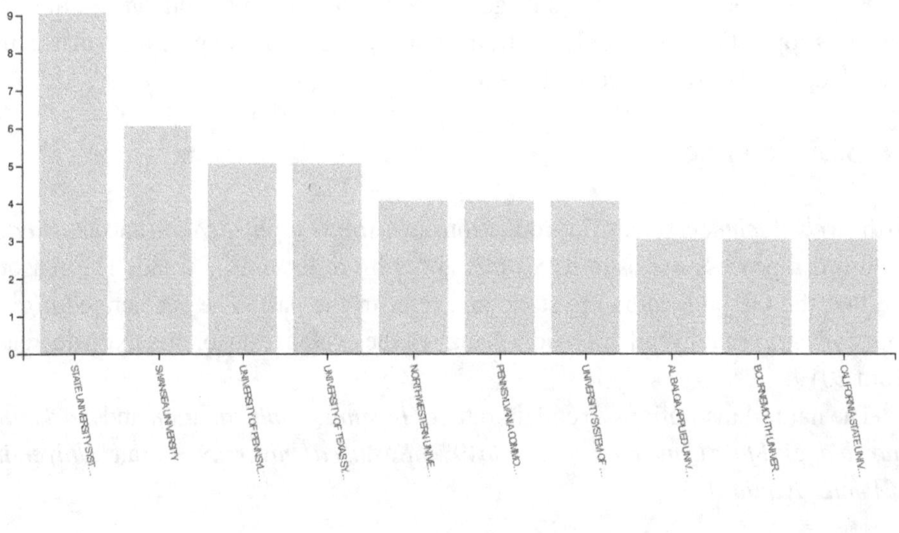

Figure 8. Scientific production by country in WOS
Source: author

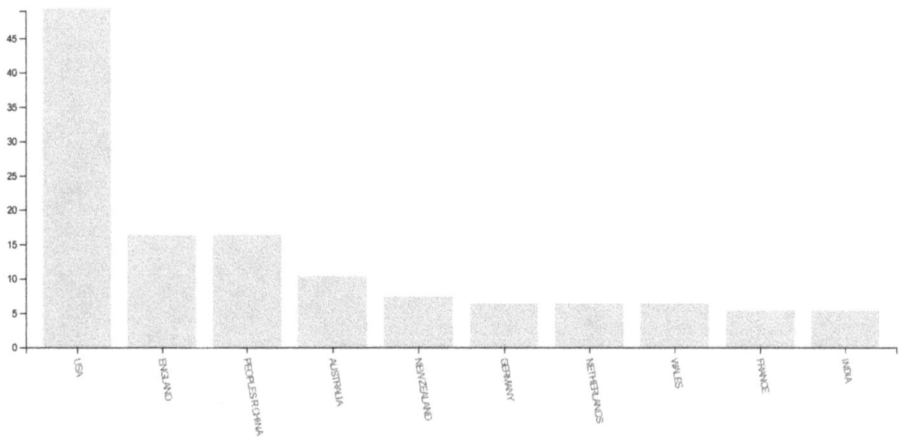

long cloth the previous generations of business sophistication models and frameworks justified by connecting to marketing knowledge and customer commitment.

Figure 9. Scientific production by subject area
Source: author

The source titles presented strongly emphasize original empirical work and theoretical articles exploring how business sophistication impacts marketing knowledge practice. The Tourism *management published* 16%; *Journal of Retailing and Consumer Services*, and *Journal of the Academy of Marketing Science 10%* respectively. These articles are very recent, meaning these journals are relevant to the topic's research under study (Figure 10).

Figure 10. Scientific production by journal
Source: author

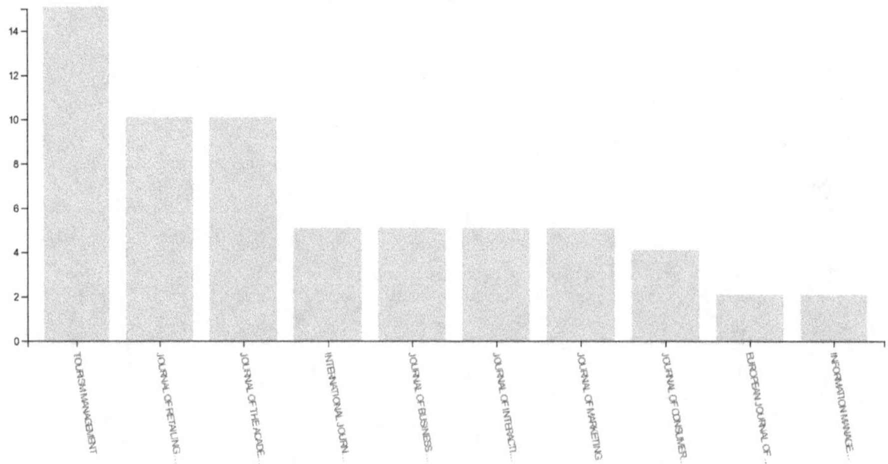

Qualitative Results and Analysis

To improve our argument, we present five tables that summarize the *theoretical trend - business sophistication, education, condition infrastructure, institution and performance. Thus, exploring the five trends and how business sophistication impacts marketing knowledge*. This categorization allows us to observe the most valuable points of view (Table 1-5).

According to Vlasova, V. et al., (2017), Russia demonstrates positive dynamics in aggregate rankings. However, these relatively high positions are provided by the resource-related to education, e.g., various forms of R&D and innovation expenditure, the share of university graduates in the total population (Table 1).

Jankowska, B. et al. (2017), the inconclusive condition theory explains how national innovation systems may transform innovation input into innovation output in different marketing knowledge (Table 2). Institutions have a significant and positive effect on innovation output (Table 3). These findings are useful for national innovation policies since they emphasize the need to promote better innovation incentives to promote customer commitment (Reis, D.A.,2018).

Using GII data from 2013, the studies discovered that business sophistication and infrastructure have the most substantial direct and indirect effects on creative output, respectively. (Sohn, S.Y., 2016). According to Pence, I. et al. (2019), the infrastructure can help the countries achieve long-term output growth and improve

Figure 11. Theoretical trend - business sophistication
Source: author

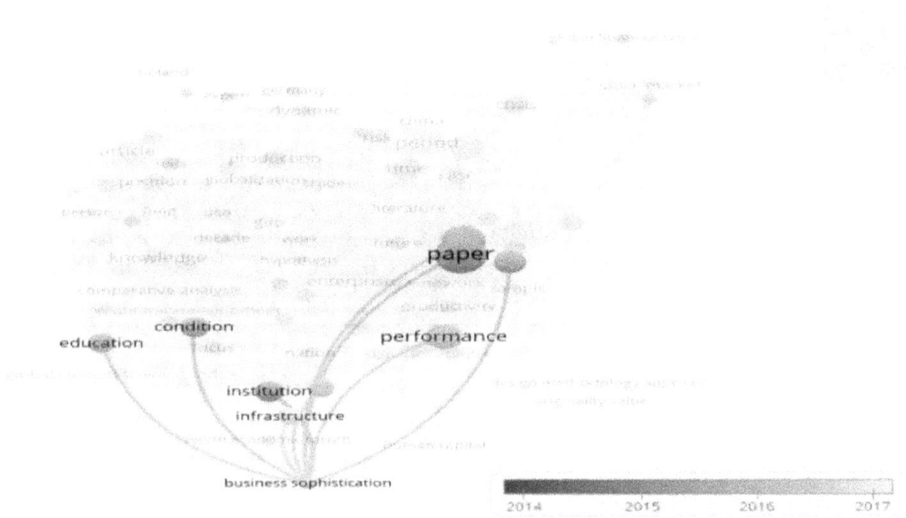

Table 1. Education

Authors	Title	Focus	Objective
Vlasova, V., et al. (2017)	*Drivers and limitations of Russia's development based on the evidence provided by the Global Innovation Index*	The emphasis on the resource elements reflects the instability of competitive advantages and the prevailing development model.	Russia demonstrates positive dynamics in terms of the aggregate rankings. However, these relatively high positions are provided by the resource-related dimensions, e.g. various forms of R&D and innovation expenditure, the share of university graduates in the total population.

Source: author

Table 2. Condition

Authors	Title	Focus	Objective
Jankowska, B., et al. (2017)	*Efficiency of National Innovation Systems - Poland and Bulgaria in The Context of the Global Innovation Index*	Explains how national innovation systems may transform innovation input into innovation output in different countries.	The inconclusive theory

Source: author

their innovation capabilities, business sophistication, and marketing knowledge (Table 4).

Table 3. Institution

Authors	Title	Focus	Objective
Reis, D. A., et al. (2018)	*The Linkage between Input and Output in the Global Innovation Index*	Using annual country data, this study estimated a quantile regression model to identify the (hypothesised) structural relationship between innovation input and output. The model includes control variables such as GDP (PPP) per capita.	Shows that innovation input has a significant and positive effect on innovation output. These findings are useful for national innovation policies, since they emphasise the need to promote better innovation incentives.

Source: author

Table 4. Infrastructure

Authors	Title	Focus	Objective
Sohn, S. Y., et al., (2016)	*Re-evaluation of global innovation index based on a structural equation model*	Proposes a structural equation model (SEM) based on seven factors representing inputs (institution, human capital and research, infrastructure, market sophistication, and business sophistication) and outputs (knowledge and technology outputs, and creative outputs).	Using GII data from 2013, the studies discovered that business sophistication and infrastructure have the most substantial direct and indirect effects on creative output, respectively.
Pence, I., et al. (2019)	*Estimation of the Country Ranking Scores on the Global Innovation Index 2016 Using the*	The significance of this paper is that; it is the first curve fitting and estimation of the score processes on GII 2016 dataset.	The final results can assist the countries in achieving long-term output growth and improving their innovation capabilities.

Source: author

Crespo, N.F., & Crespo, C.F. (2016) finds that several causal combinations of conditions lead to high innovation performance in the context of marketing knowledge. In order to obtain better innovation performance, low-income countries show more multifaceted solutions. The innovational process should involve market knowledge for all members, including considerable business sophistication (Oveshnikova, L. et al. 2017) (Table 5).

Table 5. Performance

Authors	Title	Focus	Objective
Oveshnikova, L., et al. (2017).	*Studying the Sector of the Russian High-Tech Innovations on the Basis of the Global Innovation Index INSEAD*	The authors analyze dynamics and perspectives of development of the high-tech innovations market.	The innovational process should involve all market members, including large business.
Hamidi, S., et al., (2017)	*Segmentation of Innovation determinants: Case of the Global Innovation Index*	The purpose of this paper is to study and verify the relevance of the determinants proposed by the GII in order to develop the best possible model to predict and explain national innovation outputs.	A new reduced determinant set is defined allowing a better specification of factors and/or policies to explain the variation of the innovation intensity between countries.
Crespo, N. F., et al., (2017)	*Global innovation index: Moving beyond the absolute value of ranking with a fuzzy-set analysis*	This study applies a fuzzy-set qualitative comparative analysis to data from the Global Innovation Index (GII).	By defining two subsamples of countries (high-income and low-income), this study finds that several causal combinations of conditions lead to high innovation performance in both groups. In order to obtain better innovation performance, the low-income countries show more multifaceted solutions.

Source: author

THE IMPACT OF BUSINESS SOPHISTICATION ON KNOWLEDGE MARKETING-EMPIRICAL APPROACH

Theory, Data and Methods Issues, Controversies, Problems

We define *business sophistication* according to GII framework. *Business sophistication* is indices that measure knowledge workers, innovation linkages and knowledge absorption. Furthermore, according to Eisend, M (2015), *marketing knowledge* is defined by triplex dimensions: *knowledge creation, knowledge impact and knowledge diffusion* (Duarte, M.P., and Carvalho, F.M.P.O., 2020). Evaluating the impact of *business sophistication* on marketing knowledge, allows a greater commitment from customers in the context of marketing.The models built in this empirical approach of *business sophistication* on marketing knowledge were based on theories, literature review, and tested from the GII database. These models - tested on the GII data (released by INSEAD - European Institute of Business Administration)- served to build the research design. The INSEAD - launched the GII in 2007 to improve measurement of innovation readiness as a component of strategies better understand the business sophistication and its impact on marketing knowledge. Its framework distinguishes inputs and outputs. Inputs are elements of the national economy that enable business sophistication activities, namely, *knowledge, innovation linkages and knowledge absorption.* Outputs results of innovative economic activities on marketing knowledge, namely, *knowledge creation, knowledge impact and knowledge diffusion.*

Indicators aggregated in 21 sub-pillars, in turn, are aggregated under seven pillars.

Five of those are input pillars, consisting in institutions, human capital and research, infrastructure, market sophistication, and business sophistication, while two are output pillar, namely knowledge and technology outputs, and creative outputs. Both input and output pillars then aggregated to form the input and the output sub-indices (Table 14). Theory, previous literature, and empirical studies show, in most cases, the existence of a positive correlation between, business sophistication and marketing knowledge. However, this empirical approach aims to understand how and which business sophistication variables impact marketing knowledge. Knowing these variables enable customer commitment. Figure 12 shows the proposed conceptual model, in which arrows represent the hypothesis developed below.Duarte M.P. et al. (2007) argues that there is a positive impact of innovation inputs on creative outputs in every income group. However, the impact of business sophistication on marketing knowledge is unclear. We define *business innovation inputs* as the element of the national economy that enable innovative activities, such as *institutions, human capital and research, market sophistication, business sophistication*. Furthermore, *business innovation outputs* as results of innovative activities within the economy, such as *knowledge, technology and creative outputs* (Duarte, MP, & Carvalho, F.M.P.O., 2020). Hence the question is: What is the impact of *business sophistication on marketing knowledge?*

Therefore, we propose the following hypothesis:

H1: *Business innovation input* has a positive impact on *business innovation output;*
H2: *Business sophistication* has a positive impact on *marketing knowledge*;
H3: *Business innovation input* has a positive impact on *business innovation creative output;*

Based on the longitudinal GII. framework, we have developed a pooled O.L.S. regression models to test the proposed hypothesis. We then applied the models to a sub-sample composed exclusively by top 50 ranking countries to analyze the impact of business sophistication on marketing knowledge.

Data and sample. As mentioned above, we have developed a panel dataset composed of 50 countries (Table 14) during 2019. The study uses G.I.I. data exclusively.

We chose the 50 countries because they are the ones best positioned in the G.I.I. index. So, we avoid an analysis in very asymmetric countries. The models assume no heterogeneity because our goal is not to explore differences between countries

Figure 12. Conceptual model
Source: author

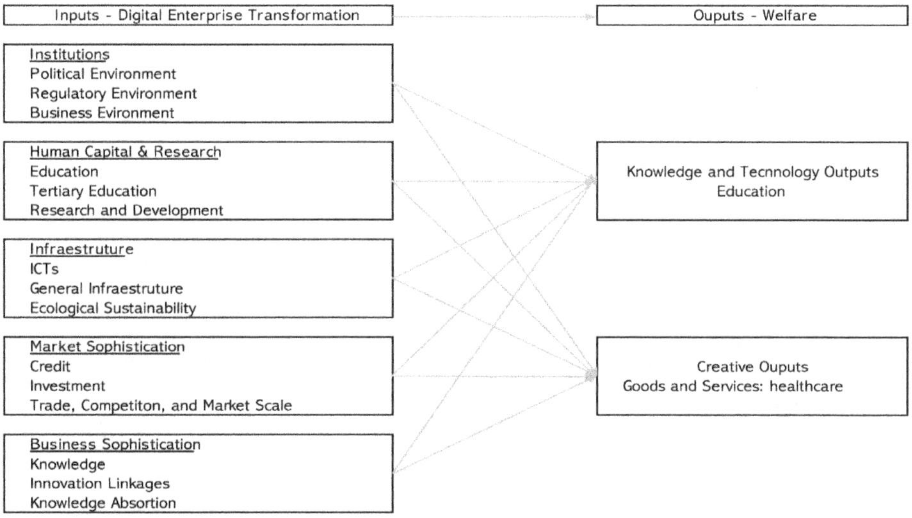

or possible fixed or variable effects, but from the database analyzing the impact of business sophistication on marketing knowledge.

Variables and codebook. Tables 5 and 6 show the variables and codebook.

We reconstructed the database from each country's reports, generated by the G.I.I. in 2019, taking into account the score in a ranking of 1-100 points. Then we developed a codebook to clarify the relationship between the variables, based on the reports and database of the G.I.I. for the year 2019.

Table 6. Sample

1°	Switzerland	11°	Republic of Korea	21°	Austria	31°	Slovenia	41°	Greece
2°	Sweden	12°	Ireland	22°	Australia	32°	Portugal	42°	VietNam
3°	United States of America	13°	Hong Kong, China	23°	Belgium	33°	Hungary	43°	Thailand
4°	Netherlands	14°	China	24°	Estonia	34°	Latvia	44°	Croatia
5°	United Kingdom	15°	Japan	25°	New Zealand	35°	Malaysia	45°	Montenegro
6°	Finland	16°	France	26°	Czech Republic	36°	United Arab Emirates	46°	Russian Federation
7°	Denmark	17°	Canada	27°	Malta	37°	Slovakia	47°	Ukraine
8°	Singapore	18°	Luxembourg	28°	Cyprus	38°	Lithuania	48°	Georgia
9°	Germany	19°	Norway	29°	Spain	39°	Poland	49°	Turkey
10°	Israel	20°	Iceland	30°	Italy	40°	Bulgaria	50°	Romania

Source: author

Table 7. Codebook - independent variables

Indepentent Variables: Technological Inputs	Code	Description / Proxy
Institutions	InX1	Discrete variable form 1-100
Political Environment	InX1,1	Measurement Political Environment score
Regulatory Environment	InX1.2	Measurement Regulatory Environment score
Business Evironment	InX1.3	Business Evironment
Human Capital & Research	InX2	Discrete variable form 1-100
Education	InX2.1	Measurement Education score
Tertiary Education	InX2.2	MeasurementTertiary Education score
Tertiary Education	InX2.3	MeasurementTertiary Education score
Infraestruture	InX3	Discrete variable form 1-100
ICT's	InX3.1	Measurement ICT's score
General Infraestruture	InX3.2	Measurement General Infraestruture score
Ecological Sustainability	InX3.3	Measurement Ecological Sustainability score
Market Sophistication	InX4	Discrete variable form 1-100
Credit	InX4.1	Measurement Ecological Sustainability score
Investment	InX4.2	Measurement Investment score
Trade, Competiton, and Market Scale	InX4.3	Measurement Trade, Competiton, and Market Scale score
Business Sophistication	InX5	Discrete variable form 1-100
Knowledge	InX5.1	Measurement Knowledge score
Innovation Linkages	InX5.2	Measurement Innovation Linkages score
Knowledge Absortion	InX5.3	Measurement score Knowledge Absortion score

Source: author

Codebook and dependent variables. To analyze the relationship between innovation inputs and outputs, we used two dependents' variables in the model (Knowledge and Technology Outputs (OX6)) and Technological Innovation Outputs (OX8).

Codebook and independent variables. The explanatory variables used are the scores of the innovation input sub-index (In) and the five innovation input pillars, Institutions (InX1), Human Capital and Research (InX2), Infrastructure (InX3), Market Sophistication (InX4), Business Sophistication (InX5), and three sub-input pillars within Market Sophistication (InX4), namely Credit (InX4.1), Investment (InX4.2), Trade, Competition, and Market Scale (InX4.3).

Model specification. Considering the available data and the conceptual model presented - the linear regressions - using several estimators, the most common the pooled ordinary least squares, best fit (Baltagi, 2015; Wooldridge, 2016). Furthermore, we developed three models in the pooled OLS.To build the models, we used the method based on theoretical reasons. Answering the initial research question, we formulated three hypotheses. The study developed three models corresponding to each hypothesis. Each model was built hierarchically using the software. The models were assembled by gradually inserting an explanatory variable.

Model 1

First, we performed a linear regression of *business innovation input* (innovation input pillars), namely, *Institutions (InX1), Human Capital and Research (InX2), Infrastructure (InX3), Market Sophistication (InX4), and Business Sophistication*

Table 8. Codebook - dependent variables

Dependents Variables : Ouputs	Code	Description / Proxy
Knowledge and Tecnnology Outputs	OX6	Discrete variable form 1-100
Knowledge creation	OX6.1	Measurement Knowledge creation score
Knowledge impact	OX6.2	Measurement Knowledge impact score
Knowledge diffusion	OX6.3	Measurement Knowledge diffusion score
Creative Ouputs	OX7	Discrete variable form 1-100
Intagible assessts	OX7.1	Intagible assessts score
Creative goods & services	OX7.2	Creative goods & services score
Online creativity	OX7.3	Online creativity score
(OX6+OX7)/2	OX8	Technologial Innovation Output score
(InX1+InX2+InX3+InX4+InX5)/2	InXO	Techonogical Innovation Input score

Source: author

(InX5) against *business innovation output* (InX8) to assess *business innovation input* impact on *business innovation output (OX8).*

Therefore, to test hypothesis H1, we developed the following models:

$$OX8_{it} = \beta_0 + \beta_1 InX_{1it} + \beta_2 InX_{2it} + \beta_3 InX_{3it} + \beta_4 InX_{4it} + \beta_5 InX_{5it} + \mu_{it};$$
i=1,2,...50; t=2019 (1)

Where, Ox8it is the dependent variable business innovation output, measured by *Business Innovation Output* (OX8) for each country (i=1,2....50) in the year 2019, β0 is the intercept, β1, β2, β3, β4, β5 are the slope of the variable of interest and the coefficients of InX1, InX2, InX3, InX4, and InX5, which stand for *Inputs of Institutions, Human Capital and Research, Infrastructure, Marketing Sophistication, Business Sophistication,* respectively, and μit as a stochastic error.

Model 2

Secondly, we perform a linear regression between *business innovation input,* measured by all input pillars, *Institutions (InX1), Human Capital and Research (InX2), Infrastructure (InX3), Market Sophistication (InX4), and Business Sophistication (InX5)* against *knowledge marketing*, measured by the output sub-index *Knowledge and Technology Outputs (InX6)* to assess *business sophistication impact on marketing knowledge; (OX6).*

Therefore, to test hypothesis H2, we developed the following models:

$$OX6_{it} = \beta_0 + \beta_1 InX_{1it} + \beta_2 InX_{2it} + \beta_3 InX_{3it} + \beta_4 InX_{4it} + \beta_5 InX_{5it} + \mu_{it};$$
i=1,2,...50; t=2019 (2)

Table 9. Descriptive statistics and correlation matrix

Variables	Cod	Mean	S.D	N	OX8	InX1	InX2	InX3	InX4	InX5
Tecnological Innovation Ouputs	OX8	4.3	9.319	50						
Institutions	InX1	79.1	10.533	50	.611					
Human Capital & Research	InX2	47.1	10.503	50	.632	.700				
Infraestruture	InX3	57.4	7.242	50	.677	.824	.700			
Market Sophistication	InX4	57.2	10.215	50	.498	.632	.581	.498		
Business Sophistication	InX5	47.1	11.339	50	.900	.705	.761	.739	.510	

Source: author

Where, Ox6it is the dependent variable knowledge marketing (OX6) for each country (i=1,2.....50) in the year 2019, β0 is the intercept, β1, β2, β3, β4, β5 are the slope of the variable of interest and the coefficients of InX1, InX2, InX3, InX4, and InX5, which stand for Inputs of Institutions, Human Capital and Research, Infrastructure, Marketing Sophistication, Business Sophistication, respectively, and μit as a stochastic error.

Model 3

Third, we perform a linear regression between business innovation input, measured by all input pillars, Institutions (InX1), Human Capital and Research (InX2), Infrastructure (InX3), Market Sophistication (InX4), and Business Sophistication (InX5) against Creative Outputs (OX7).

Therefore, to test hypothesis H3, we developed the following models:

$$OX7_{it} = \beta_0 + \beta_1 InX_{1it} + \beta_2 InX_{2it} + \beta_3 InX_{3it} + \beta_4 InX_{4it} + \beta_5 InX_{5it} + \mu_{it};$$
$$i=1,2,...50;\ t=2019 \qquad (3)$$

Table 10. Coefficients and variance inflation factors (VIF)

Model 1 (a)	Unst. Coefficients B	Std. Error	St. Coefficients Beta	t	Sig	Collinearity Statistics Tolerance	VIF
Constant	3,249	5,218			0,623	0,537	
inX1-Institutions	-0,132	0,111	-0,149	-1,183	0,2243	0,246	4,066
inX2-Human Capital & Research	-0,155	0,095	-0,174	-1,633	0,109	0,341	2,932
inX3-Infraestruture	0,186	0,157	0,145	1,88	0,241	0,262	3,817
inX4-Market Sophistication	0,118	0,077	0,13	1,545	0,129	0,552	1,812
inX5-Business Sophistication	0,793	0,089	0,964	8,92	0,000	0,332	3,009
(a) dependent variable - Technological Outputs							

Source: author

Table 11. Descriptive statistics and correlation matrix

Variables	Cod	Mean	S.D	N	OX8	InX1	InX2	InX3	InX4	InX5
Knowledge & Technology Outputs	OX6	39.33	12.458	50						
Institutions	InX1	79.088	10.533	50	.501					
Human Capital & Research	InX2	47.056	10.503	50	.634	.700				
Infraestruture	InX3	57.394	7.242	50	.568	.824	.700			
Market Sophistication	InX4	57.190	10.215	50	.498	.632	.581	.498		
Business Sophistication	InX5	47.071	11.339	50	.858	.705	.761	.739	.510	

Source: author

Where Ox7it is the dependent variable *Creative Outputs* – Goods and Services (OX7)) for each country (i=1,2….50) in the year 2019, β0 is the intercept, β1, β2, β3, are the slope of the variable of interest and the coefficients of InX1, InX2, InX3, InX4, and InX5, which stand for *Inputs of Institutions, Human Capital and Research, Infrastructure, Marketing Sophistication, Business Sophistication,* respectively, and μit as a stochastic error.

SOLUTIONS AND RECOMMENDATIONS

Results and Discussion

Tables 9 - 14 show the main descriptive statistics, the correlation matrix, and variance inflation factors (VIF). An analysis of the correlation matrix reveals the existence of significant correlations between the variables. The existing correlations between the variables could result in multicollinearity. However, the highest VIF value (4.066

Table 12. Coefficients and variance inflation factors (VIF)

Model 2 (b)	Unst. Coefficients B	Std. Error	St. Coefficients Beta	t	Sig	Collinearity Statistics Tolerance	VIF
Constant	3,545	7,884	-0,325	0,450	0,655		
inX1-Institutions	-0,385	0,168	-0,325	-2,292	0,027	0,246	4,066
inX2-Human Capital & Research	-0,024	0,143	-0,02	-0,167	0,868	0,341	2,932
inX3-Infraestruture	0,042	0,237	0,025	0,179	0,859	0,262	3,817
inX4-Market Sophistication	0,248	0,116	0,203	2,143	0,038	0,552	1,812
inX5-Business Sophistication	1,078	0,134	0,981	8,032	0,000	0,332	3,009
(b) dependent variable - Knowledge and Technology Outputs							

Source: author

Table 13. Descriptive statistics and correlation matrix

Variables	Cod	Mean	S.D	N	OX7	InX1	InX2	InX3	InX4	InX5
Creative Outuputs	OX7	41.302	8.269	50						
Institutions	InX1	79.088	10.533	50	.621					
Human Capital and Research	InX2	47.056	10.503	50	.469	.700				
Infraestruture	InX3	57.394	7.241	50	.670	.824	.700			
Market Sophistication	InX4	57.190	10.214	50	.371	.632	.581	.498		
Business Sophistication	InX5	47.0714	11.338	50	.735	.705	.761	.739	.510	

Source: author

for variable InX1) is below the standard rule of thumb of 10 (Wooldridge, 2016), which indicates that multicollinearity should not be a problem.

Model 1

Descriptive statistics, correlation matrix, and variance inflation factors (VIF): Tables 18 and 19 show the main descriptive statistics, the correlation matrix, and variance inflation factors (VIF). An analysis of the correlation matrix reveals the existence of significant correlations between the variables. The existing correlations between the five input pillars could not result in multicollinearity issues when regressed together. However, the highest VIF value (4.066 for variable InX1 - Institutions) is below the typical rule of thumb of 10 (Wooldridge, 2016), which indicates that multicollinearity should not be a problem.

We found that business innovation input can predict knowledge marketing. The analysis resulted in a statistically significant model. Following that business sophistication is described as follows: I F (5, 44) = 42,689; p< 0,001; = 0,911) I. The model shows that Business Sophistication (β=0,964; t=8,920; p<.001) are

Table 14. Coefficients and variance inflation factors (VIF)

Model 3 (b)	Unst. Coefficients B	Std. Error	St. Coefficients Beta	t	Sig	Collinearity Statistics Tolerance	VIF
(Constant)	2,953	6,856		0,431	0,669		
inX1 - Institutions	0,122	0,146	0,155	0,835	0,408	0,246	4,066
inX2 - Human Capital and Research	-0,286	0,124	-0,363	-2,297	0,026	0,341	2,932
inX3 - Infraestruture	0,33	0,206	0,289	1,602	0,116	0,262	3,817
inX4 - Marketing Sophistication	-0,011	0,101	-0,014	-0,112	0,911	0,552	1,812
inX5 - Business Sophistication	0,507	0,117	0,695	4,342	0,00	0,332	3,009

(b) dependent variable - Creative Outputs

Source: author

able (firmly) to knowledge (Knowledge & Technology and Creative Outputs). The exegesis of the results of this first model points to the confirmation of our initial hypothesis. This excessive weight may be an open path for policymakers to focus on marketing knowledge, enabling customer commitment by promoting knowledge workers, innovation linkages, knowledge absorption. In this model, we expected Institutions and Human Capital and Research to have a positive impact. This result does not happen since these variables' impact is negative (Institutions, β = -.149; Human Capital and Research β = -.179); however, it is statistically insignificant with p> .05.

Then, from Model 1, the equation (1) becomes

$$OX8_{it} = \beta_0 + \beta_1 InX_{1it} + \beta_2 InX_{2it} + \beta_3 InX_{3it} + \beta_4 InX_{4it} + \beta_5 InX_{5it} + \mu_{it};$$
i=1,2,...50; t=2019 (1)

Knowledge marketing = 3,249 - 0,132 *(Institutions) - 0,155(Human Capital & Research,) + 0,186 (Infrastructure)+0,118(Marketing Sophistication) +0,793 (Business Sophistication) + μit*

Model 2

Carried out multiple regression to verify whether the impact of *business sophistication has a positive impact on marketing knowledge*; Again, we confirm Hypothesis 2.

Then, from Model 2, the equation (2) becomes:

$$OX6_{it} = \beta_0 + \beta_1 InX_{1it} + \beta_2 InX_{2it} + \beta_3 InX_{3it} + \beta_4 InX_{4it} + \beta_5 InX_{5it} + \mu_{it};$$
i=1,2,...50; t=2019 (2)

Business sophistication (Knowledge & Technology) = 3,545 - 0,385 (Institutions) - 0,024(Human Capital & Research,) + 0,042 (Infrastructure)+0,248(Marketing Sophistication) +(1) (Business Sophistication) + μit.

Model 3

We have carried out multiple linear regression to verify whether business innovation input positively impacts business innovation creative output.The analysis resulted in a statistically significant model, (F (5, 44) = 14.683; p <0.001; = 0.625)).The model shows that business innovation input, - *Institutions (β = 0.155; t = 0.835; p> 0.001), Human Capital and Research (β = -0, 363; t = -0.297; p> 0.001), Infrastructure (β = 0.289; t = 1.602; p> 0.001), Marketing Sophistication (β =*

-014; t = -0.112; p> 0.001), and Business Sophistication (β = 0.695; t = 4.342; p <0.001), - has a positive impact on Creative Output, i.e., intangible assets, creative goods and services, and online creativity.

Taking into account the available data and statistics, we emphasize that *business sophistication* (β = 0.695; t = 4.342; p <0.001), has the most powerful and most significant impact on marketing knowledge. Then, from Model 3, the equation (3) becomes:

$$OX7_{it} = \beta_0 + \beta_1 InX_{1it} + \beta_2 InX_{2it} + \beta_3 InX_{3it} + \beta_4 InX_{4it} + \beta_5 InX_{5it} + \mu_{it};$$
$$i=1,2,\ldots 50;\ t=2019 \qquad (3)$$

Then, from Model 3, the equation (3) becomes: Creative Outputs = 2,953 + 0,122 (Institutions) - 0,286 (Human Capital & Research,) + 0,33(Infrastructure) – 0,011(Marketing Sophistication) + 0,507 (Business Sophistication) + μit. Again, we confirm Hypothesis 3, according to which there is a positive impact of business innovation input on creative output; If we analyze Table 23, of the coefficients and the Variance Inflator Factors (VIF), we will notice that although the impact is positive, each factor or variable's contribution levels differ. Thus, business sophistication that significantly explains the marketing knowledge (creative outputs). Furthermore the management variable or for policymakers, it will be *business sophistication*, which corresponds to knowledge, innovation linkages, and knowledge absorption in our codebook.

Theoretical Implications

Knowledge marketing in the context of business sophistication is crucial. Several technological input factors impacts on knowledge marketing. Establishing relations and integrating stakeholders' knowledge is crucial for limited knowledge resources. Furthermore, knowing which technological input factor of business sophistication is crucial for marketing activity.

Practical Implications

At the time of business sophistication, digital and holistic marketing, knowledge is an essential determinant of consumer purchasing decisions. Within the digital forms of sales support tools used, knowledge is crucial for maintaining a portfolio of customers.

FUTURE RESEARCH DIRECTIONS

Limitations and Future Directions of Research

Despite the importance of this research, our results have some limitations. First, the studies choice the top 50 countries of GII. A random selection of countries, regardless of their digital involvement, would likely lead to a different conclusion. The data was limited to the year 2019, and the study needed to cover a time horizon of 10 years to compare the results taking into account the fixed and variable effects over time. Future studies should better explore the differences in the framework input-output technological intensity of countries and their ability to absorb knowledge regardless of their ranking and region.

CONCLUSION

In the era of accelerated digital enterprise transformation economy, business sophistication, significantly influence marketing knowledge. Developing marketing knowledge help companies to have a well-defined path and benefit from business sophistication. A positive impact of business sophistication on marketing knowledge is not a self-standing process. This process is dependent on the technological intensity and innovation that a given country can absorb and managerial strategies for companies. The results showed that not all pillars – inputs - had the same impact; many of them had adverse effects and insignificant contributions. Nevertheless, in aggregate, the study confirms that business sophistication predicts marketing knowledge. Therefore, the study confirms the hypotheses stated: the impact of business sophistication on knowledge marketing.

REFERENCES

Alkhaleefah, A. (2018). What to do to improve the international saudi innovation Rank/Score. *International Journal of Mechanical Engineering and Technology*, *9*(3), 435–442.

Aydin, E., Polat, A., & Ergene, L. T. (2016, November). Vector control of DFIG in wind power applications. In *2016 IEEE International Conference on Renewable Energy Research and Applications (ICRERA)* (pp. 478-483). IEEE. 10.1109/ICRERA.2016.7884383

Baltagi, B. H., Egger, P. H., & Kesina, M. (2016). Bayesian Spatial Bivariate Panel Probit Estimation', Spatial Econometrics: Qualitative and Limited Dependent Variables (Advances in Econometrics, Volume 37). Emerald Group Publishing Limited.

Bloomberg, J. (2018). Digitization, digitalization, and digital transformation: confuse them at your peril. *Forbes*.

Bousquet, J., Bedbrook, A., Czarlewski, W., Onorato, G. L., Arnavielhe, S., Laune, D., ... Morais-Almeida, M. (2019). Guidance to 2018 good practice: ARIA digitally-enabled, integrated, person-centred care for rhinitis and asthma. *Clinical and Translational Allergy*, *9*(1), 1–19.

Canonica, G. W., Antó i Boqué, J. M., Mullol i Miret, J., & Valero Santiago, A.MASK study group. (2019). Guidance to 2018 good practice: ARIA digitally enabled, integrated, person-centred care for rhinitis and asthma. *Clinical and Translational Allergy*, *9*, •••.

Cantú-Ortiz, F. J., Sánchez, N. G., Garrido, L., Terashima-Marin, H., & Brena, R. F. (2020). An artificial intelligence educational strategy for the digital transformation. *International Journal on Interactive Design and Manufacturing*, 1-15.

Castagna, F., Centobelli, P., Cerchione, R., Esposito, E., Oropallo, E., & Passaro, R. (2020). Customer Knowledge Management in SMEs Facing Digital Transformation. *Sustainability*, *12*(9), 3899. doi:10.3390u12093899

Chandler, A. D. (1990). *Strategy and structure: Chapters in the history of the industrial enterprise* (Vol. 120). MIT Press.

Correani, A., De Massis, A., Frattini, F., Petruzzelli, A. M., & Natalicchio, A. (2020). Implementing a digital strategy: Learning from the experience of three digital transformation projects. *California Management Review*, *62*(4), 37–56. doi:10.1177/0008125620934864

Crespo, N. F., & Crespo, C. F. (2016). Global innovation index: Moving beyond the absolute value of ranking with a fuzzy-set analysis. *Journal of Business Research*, *69*(11), 5265–5271. doi:10.1016/j.jbusres.2016.04.123

Duarte, M. P., & Carvalho, F. M. (2020). *Portugal in the Global Innovation Index: A panel data analysis* (No. 0144). Gabinete de Estratégia e Estudos, Ministério da Economia.

Faghih, N., & Sazegar, M. (2019). A Taxonomy of Country Performance Based on GDP and Innovation Indicators for the Group of Twenty (G20). In *Globalization and Development* (pp. 163–200). Springer. doi:10.1007/978-3-030-14370-1_7

Fischer, M., Imgrund, F., Janiesch, C., & Winkelmann, A. (2020). Strategy archetypes for digital transformation: Defining meta objectives using business process management. *Information & Management*, *57*(5), 103262. doi:10.1016/j.im.2019.103262

Frennert, S. (2018). Lost in digitalization? Municipality employment of welfare technologies. *Disability and Rehabilitation. Assistive Technology*. PMID:30264649

Gaile-sarkane, E., & Andersone, I. (2011). Modeling of Consumer Behavior for Business Sophistication. *The 15th World Multi-Conference on*. https://www.iiis.org/CDs2011/CD2011SCI/SCI_2011/PapersPdf/SA275VH.pdf

Garrido-Baserba, M., Corominas, L., Cortés, U., Rosso, D., & Poch, M. (2020). The fourth-revolution in the water sector encounters the digital revolution. *Environmental Science & Technology*, *54*(8), 4698–4705. doi:10.1021/acs.est.9b04251 PMID:32154710

Ghobakhloo, M. (2020). Determinants of information and digital technology implementation for smart manufacturing. *International Journal of Production Research*, *58*(8), 2384–2405. doi:10.1080/00207543.2019.1630775

Hanelt, A., Bohnsack, R., Marz, D., & Antunes, C. (2020). A systematic review of the literature on digital transformation: Insights and implications for strategy and organizational change. *Journal of Management Studies*.

Hasibović, A. Ć., & Tanović, A. (2019, May). PRINCE2 vs Scrum in digital business transformation. In *2019 42nd International Convention on Information and Communication Technology, Electronics and Microelectronics (MIPRO)* (pp. 1514-1518). IEEE. 10.23919/MIPRO.2019.8756716

Hathaivaseawong, N., Mohamad, O., & Ramayah, T. (2004). *Acquisition of Marketing Knowledge in Thai International Joint Venture Firms*. Preliminary research. https://ramayah.com/journalarticlespdf/acquisitionofmarketing.pdf

Khan, S. (2016). *Leadership in the digital age: A study on the effects of digitalisation on top management leadership*. Academic Press.

Kirikkaleli, D., & Ozun, A. (2019, February). Innovation capacity, business sophistication and macroeconomic stability: Empirical evidence from OECD countries. *Journal of Business Economics and and Management, 252*(2), 351–367. doi:10.3846/jbem.2019.9602

Korachi, Z., & Bounabat, B. (2020). *Towards a Frame of Reference for Smart City Strategy Development and Governance*. Academic Press.

Lankshear, C., & Knobel, M. (Eds.). (2008). *Digital literacies: Concepts, policies and practices* (Vol. 30). Peter Lang.

Larsson, Z. Y., Di Gangi, P. M., & Teigland, R. (2019). Sharing my way to success: A case study on developing entrepreneurial ventures using social capital in an OSS community. *Information and Organization, 29*(1), 23–40. doi:10.1016/j.infoandorg.2018.12.001

Limani, Y., Hajrizi, E., Stapleton, L., & Retkoceri, M. (2019). Digital Transformation Readiness in Higher Education Institutions (HEI): The Case of Kosovo. *IFAC-PapersOnLine, 52*(25), 52–57. doi:10.1016/j.ifacol.2019.12.445

Matt, C., Hess, T., & Benlian, A. (2015). Digital transformation strategies. *Business & Information Systems Engineering, 57*(5), 339–343. doi:10.100712599-015-0401-5

Mesas-Carrascosa, F. J., de Castro, A. I., Torres-Sánchez, J., Triviño-Tarradas, P., Jiménez-Brenes, F. M., García-Ferrer, A., & López-Granados, F. (2020). Classification of 3D point clouds using color vegetation indices for precision viticulture and digitizing applications. *Remote Sensing, 12*(2), 317. doi:10.3390/rs12020317

Mintzberg, H. (1979). Patterns in strategy formation. *International Studies of Management & Organization, 9*(3), 67–86. doi:10.1080/00208825.1979.11656272

Mutanov, G., Mamykova, Z., Kopnova, O., & Bolatkhan, M. (2020). Applied research of data management in the education system for decision-making on the example of Al-Farabi Kazakh National University. In *E3S Web of Conferences* (Vol. 159, p. 09003). EDP Sciences. doi:10.1051/e3sconf/202015909003

Nair, H., Staat, H. J., Tran, T., van Houselt, A., Prosperetti, A., Lohse, D., & Sun, C. (2014). The Leidenfrost temperature increase for impacting droplets on carbon-nanofiber surfaces. *Soft Matter, 10*(13), 2102–2109. doi:10.1039/C3SM52326H PMID:24651906

OECD. (2016). *Energy and Air Pollution: World Energy Outlook Special Report 2016*. OECD.

Peòalba-Aguirrezabalaga, C., & Ritala, P. (2021). Putting marketing knowledge to use: Marketing-specific relational capital and product/service innovation performance. *Journal of Business*. https://www.emerald.com/insight/content/doi/10.1108/JBIM-07-2020-0369/full/html

Reis, D. A., de Moura, F. R., & de Aragao Gomes, I. M. (2019, May). The Linkage between Intellectual Property and Innovation in the Global Innovation Ecosystem. In *European Conference on Intangibles and Intellectual Capital* (pp. 218-XIII). Academic Conferences International Limited.

Salas-Velasco, M. (2018). Production efficiency measurement and its determinants across OECD countries: The role of business sophistication and innovation. *Economic Analysis and Policy*. https://www.sciencedirect.com/science/article/pii/S0313592616302417

Schmidthuber, L., Maresch, D., & Ginner, M. (2020). Disruptive technologies and abundance in the service sector-toward a refined technology acceptance model. *Technological Forecasting and*. https://www.sciencedirect.com/science/article/pii/S0040162517308430

Sohn, S. Y., Kim, D. H., & Jeon, S. Y. (2016). Re-evaluation of global innovation index based on a structural equation model. *Technology Analysis & Strategic*. https://www.tandfonline.com/doi/abs/10.1080/09537325.2015.1104412

Sohn, S. Y., Kim, D. H., & Yoon, J. H. (2016). Technology credit scoring model with fuzzy logistic regression. *Applied Soft Computing*, *43*, 150–158. doi:10.1016/j.asoc.2016.02.025

Tekic, Z., & Koroteev, D. (2019). From disruptively digital to proudly analog: A holistic typology of digital transformation strategies. *Business Horizons*, *62*(6), 683–693. doi:10.1016/j.bushor.2019.07.002

Vrooman, J. C. (2009). *Rules of relief: Institutions of social security, and their impact*. Academic Press.

Wang, H., Feng, J., Zhang, H., & Li, X. (2020). The effect of digital transformation strategy on performance. *International Journal of Conflict Management*, *31*(3), 441–462. doi:10.1108/IJCMA-09-2019-0166

Wang, H., Feng, J., Zhang, H., & Li, X. (2020). The effect of digital transformation strategy on performance. *International Journal of Conflict Management*, *31*(3), 441–462. doi:10.1108/IJCMA-09-2019-0166

Williams, W., & Elmore, R. F. (Eds.). (2014). *Social Program Implementation: Quantitative Studies in Social Relations*. Academic Press.

Wooldridge, J. M. (2016). *Introductory econometrics: A modern approach*. Nelson Education.

Zhou, K. Z., & Li, C. B. (2012). How knowledge affects radical innovation: Knowledge base, market knowledge acquisition, and internal knowledge sharing. *Strategic Management Journal*. Retrieved from https://onlinelibrary.wiley.com/doi/abs/10.1002/smj.1959

KEY TERMS AND DEFINITIONS

Business Sophistication: Is an innovation and greater sophistication production processes. Empirical analysis of macroeconomic performance stated that OECD countries with a higher capacity for innovation and greater sophistication production processes tend to be less inefficient. Furthermore, non-parametric methods for evaluating the impact of process and contextual variables on efficiency also confirmed that business sophistication and innovation contribute to efficiency improvements across OECD countries (Salas-Velasco, 2018, p.60).

Digital Transformation: Is the adoption of new digital technologies to capture change in the performance of an organization with a focus on disruptive technologies.

Digitalization: Derives from the Latin word *digitus*, which means categorized, integer, countable and discrete in value and time.

Digitization: Is transforming analog data into digital data. For example, taxpayers can enter their data online and from anywhere, and after the input confirmation, the online form automatically forwarded to the responsible tax office.

Educational Institution: Is where school ages attend education, providing a wide variety of teaching and learning process.

Fourth Industrial Revolution (4.0): Digitizing all enterprise processes allows interaction between physical and digital systems, thereby achieving real-time information for making timely decisions.

Global Innovation Index: The Global Innovation Index (GII) is a set of innovation determinants *(inputs)* and *outputs*, collects annual datasets and proposes a global ranking for countries based on their capacity to innovate (Hamidi, S, & Berrado, A., 2018). Connell University, INSEAD and the World Intellectual Property Organization (WIPO, a specialized agency of the United Nations) co-publish the GII (Dutta and Lanvin 2013; Sohn, SY et al., 2016).

Knowledge Creation: Is the pillar that reflects the degree to which a country can develop and apply knowledge to increase the components of added value in products and services and, in general, to an economy driven by innovation.

Marketing Knowledge: The importance of marketing knowledge management is integrating internal and external knowledge into the product/service innovation process. Therefore, they analyze marketing departments' role in accessing internal and external knowledge resources (i.e., marketing-specific relational capital [RC]) to reach improved product and service innovation performance. Their study makes a valuable contribution to marketing and management literature by revealing the types of social interactions in the marketing function that enable access to knowledge sources that promote successful product/service innovation (Peòalba-Aguirrezabalaga et al., 2021, p.1).

World Intellectual Property Organization: WIPO is a specialized agency of the United Nations that co-publish the GII.

Chapter 8
The Relationship Between Organizational Innovation and Mobile Applications in Hotel Businesses

Ebru Kemer
Nigde Omer Halis University, Turkey

ABSTRACT

The purpose of this study is to determine the effect of organizational innovation capabilities of hotel businesses on mobile applications. In line with this purpose, data were collected with a survey technique in March 2021 with 225 managers working in hotels with tourism operation licenses in the Cappadocia region. In the research, Pearson correlation analysis was used to determine the relationship between organizational innovation capabilities of hotel businesses and mobile applications use. Simple regression analysis was performed to determine the impact of organizational innovation on mobile applications. In this study conducted in the Cappadocia region, it was determined that the organizational innovation capabilities of hotel businesses affect the use of mobile applications. Therefore, these results show that the use of mobile applications by hotel businesses varies depending on their organizational innovation capabilities.

INTRODUCTION

Many changes in the field of technology started the “mobile age” era (UNESCO, 2014) and affected many sectors. The human-oriented tourism sector also follows

DOI: 10.4018/978-1-7998-9194-9.ch008

the developments and applications in information technologies (Atay, et al., 2018). In this age, hotel businesses aim to provide better service to their guests and gain a competitive advantage by using new technologies (Şanlıöz et al., 2013). Therefore, innovation is important for organizations to remain competitive and successful (Smith & Tushman, 2005). The use of new technologies in the provision of services in the service sector constitutes service innovation (Elçi, 2007: 7). The increase in internet use, the development of social media platforms and social networks, and the widespread use of smartphones have brought new social networks (Colombo et al., 2012). With the development of technology, hotel businesses have both created the opportunity to offer different services to consumers by using social networks and have the opportunity to express themselves and offer different opportunities by using the media (İşlek, 2012).

It is stated that the tourism sector is among the areas where mobile applications are most common (Brown & Chalmers 2003). It has been determined that hotel businesses prefer mobile applications more because of the time-saving benefit of travelers (Carlsson et al. 2005). For example, 83.61% mobile, 15.34% desktop, and 1.05% tablet are preferred for the distribution of bookings made in hotel businesses by the device; 69.16 percent mobile, 29.95 percent desktop, and 0.89 percent tablets are preferred for reservation. As for the operating system, Android 50.49 percent, iOS 34.11 percent, and others 15.40 percent; It is seen that Android is preferred by 35.18 percent, iOS 34.23 percent, and others by 30.59 percent (Online Hotel Reservation Platform, 2020).

Due to the portability and easy accessibility of the mobile internet, tourists can use these applications whenever they want and wherever they want. In this way, users can easily make transactions such as hotel and airline reservations, tour organizations, or car rentals (Ercan & Önal 2007; Wang & Wang 2010). Hotel businesses enrich mobile applications by making their websites compatible with mobile devices with mobile applications (Can et al., 2017). This research is important both in terms of determining the point of view of hotel business managers on organizational innovation, and for hotel, businesses to carry out basic promotion and marketing activities and gain sustainable competitive advantage. Therefore, the fact that organizational innovation and the use of mobile applications are applied to hotel managers and the limited number of studies on the relationship between these variables reveal the importance of the study. Also, the analysis made on the relationships between the relevant variables in the research is a methodological contribution. The study aims to determine the effect of organizational innovation capabilities of hotel businesses serving in the Cappadocia region on the use of mobile applications. For this purpose, firstly, the relevant literature review of the variables was made and the theoretical background between the variables was revealed. Then, necessary analyzes were made to test the hypotheses established within the research and the results were interpreted in detail.

BACKGROUND

Organizational Innovation

In this study, Schumpeter's approach (creative destruction) Schumpeter (1934) was used to explain the concept of organizational innovation. According to this approach, innovation plays an important role in businesses with a dynamic structure where there are intense entries and exits in the market, in parallel with the developments in markets where innovation is frequent and where technological development is rapid. It is claimed that enterprises that enter the market by making radical innovations can ensure continuity in the market and will stay fresh in the developments made for the market (Schumpeter, 1934). Innovation, which is a function of entrepreneurship, is to generate welfare by creating new resources or to provide prosperity by increasing the use potential of existing resources (Drucker, 1998). Schmookler (1966) stated that innovation is innovation, an action that a business takes by developing a new product or service for itself, using a new method or input for itself. According to a different definition, it is defined as "the first presentation or use of an idea, tool, system, policy, program, product, service or process by the enterprise" (Öğüt et al., 2007). Innovation requires some features such as "having an innovative perspective, entrepreneurial thinking, dynamic planning, breaking the rules, being ambitious and choosing the right leader". Therefore, innovation is relative, the innovation to be made suitable for the business, it can be tried, and the innovation is observable are among the innovation characteristics (Akgöz, 2014: 3).

Innovation is basically divided into four types: product, process, marketing, and organizational innovation. Product innovation includes product innovation, rebuilt or improved product that meets the demands and needs of consumers. Product innovation is considered as the replacement or improvement of a new or existing product. Making and applying significant changes in the components, materials, performances, promotion, and marketing of all products and services owned explains product innovation (Akgöz, 2014). Innovation is not just a simple renewal, it is also considered as a process that includes the innovation product starting from the theoretical stage of renewal and accepts its marketable quality (Horuz, 2012). Process innovation arises from the need for a certain time, method, and planning for a product or service to emerge. Changes made in the production and delivery method of a new product or service are defined as process innovation (Sabuncu, 2014). Marketing innovation is the process of making serious changes in product design, product placement, promotion, and pricing developing and improving new marketing methods, or applying a different marketing method (Zerenler et al., 2007). Organizational innovation is a type of innovation that management is closely related to. General strategies of businesses are closely related to technological innovations and research and development strategies. Organizational innovation is the strategies implemented by the organization to see the dangers of developing technologies or new products and to evaluate the lives of newly developed products in the market (Sabuncu, 2014: 108). Businesses make innovations to survive and maintain their competitiveness. Making innovations; ensures minimizing costs, developing new products and services, diversifying, and increasing product and service quality. Therefore, innovation is the key to economic growth, employment, and welfare increase (Elçi, 2007). The most important reason why innovation is gaining importance in businesses day by day is customer requests and needs. Meeting the changing demands and needs of customers and creating elements that will create demand by offering different alternatives to the customers become important in the innovation competition race. Research and development and technology lie on the basis of this (Üstel & Kabatepe, 2006).

Using Mobile Applications

To explain the concept of using mobile applications in the research, Venkatesh et al. (2003), Technology Acceptance and Use Unified Model was used. The combined technology acceptance and use model is about the research on the effects of performance expectation from the technology used, effort expectation, social use intention effects, facilitating conditions, and usage intention. Advances in communication technologies "started with wireless telegraphy in the 1890s, entered the era of the mobile revolution with fixed telephone systems in the 1910-1980s, analog mobile systems in the 1980s, digital mobile systems after the 1990s and multimedia systems in the 2000s" . and continued to improve (Steinbock, 2005: 2). With the rapid development of technology, the use of smartphones has increased and has enabled the use of new applications in many different sectors. The five-fold increase in the number of mobile devices and reaching five billion users increased the number of internet users from 400 million to two billion (Verma & Bashir, 2015). Therefore, the increase in the number of mobile devices has increased the use of mobile applications. Mobile applications consist of a set of software and programs that run on mobile devices and perform specific tasks for the user. Mobile applications are the field in which the developing global information and communication technologies are new and rapidly developing. (Charland, 2011). Mobile application is defined as "end-user software application programs designed for operating systems of mobile devices that increase the capacity of the phone by enabling the user to perform certain tasks" (Kim et al., 2013, p. 53). Various applications in smartphones; Its use in many areas from commercial transactions to communication, from entertainment to shopping provides ease of access to both customers and businesses (Verma & Bashir, 2015). In addition, mobile applications enable businesses to establish behavioral and positional relationships with consumers and provide them with enjoyable experiences (Lamberton & Stephen, 2016).

Consumers' rate of digital media usage has increased significantly and mobile devices are among the most preferred in this increase. Mobile devices are among the sine qua non of today with both the entertainment elements they contain and the applications they provide. According to a study conducted in 2019, the number of people using mobile devices worldwide reached 4 billion, and 48% of their internet usage was made on mobile devices (Clement, 2019). Mobile phone users spend most of their hours on mobile applications. Mobile applications quickly meet user needs by providing ease of access (Gezici, Tarhan & Chouseninoğlou, 2018) increases the importance of mobile applications for businesses. The use of mobile technologies in all areas of life creates significant changes, and after the digital revolution, human life is greatly changed. Therefore, fast, easy, and low-cost communication not only creates advantages for individuals but also significantly affects the way they do business, their efficiency, and profitability (Kırova, 2015). The increase in the rate of mobile application users every year contributes to the fulfillment of the requests and needs of the users by using conscious resources (Wijesekera et al., 2018). Easy access to information has led to the emergence of many different needs in individuals. The fact that mobile phones are always with us and they can communicate with audio and video has facilitated direct access to the user. As in all sectors, the use of mobile applications to reach a strong market in the market has provided important developments in the tourism sector (Şanlıöz, Dilek & Koçak, 2015). With these important developments, businesses started to look for new channels to increase their profitability and strengthen the consumer experience, and one of these channels emerged as mobile applications (Wang et al., 2016).

MAIN FOCUS OF THE CHAPTER

The Relationship between Organizational Innovation and Mobile Applications in Hotel Businesses

The relationship between organizational innovation and mobile applications use in the research Schumpeter Approach Schumpeter (1934) and Venkatesh et al. (2003) based on the Technology Acceptance and Use Unified Model. The basic rule for innovation is that businesses continuously improve their products and services and make innovations in line with the trends of the day. Organizations that are open to changes and researches develop faster than other organizational structures (Henard & Dacin, 2010). Innovation in the service sector is different from the manufacturing sector. While enterprises in the manufacturing sector prefer product and process innovation, organizational innovation gains importance in the service sector (Tether, 2005: 159). Because organizational innovation creates innovation and difference in the delivery or distribution of the service by offering a new or significantly changed service. The use of new technologies by businesses increases their technological and organizational capabilities (Simonceska, 2012).

New services, new products, supporting new ideas with technological processes contribute to the increase of the innovation approach. To ensure the realization of innovative applications, an innovative approach and appropriate structure should be established in organizations. (Lumpkin & Dess, 1996). Establishing the appropriate structure, working in harmony with the employees of the organization can be achieved by developing new products and processes and increasing the competitive advantage of the enterprise by gaining customer loyalty (Serçeoğlu, 2014). Therefore, managers in the tourism sector, where competition is important, should encourage their employees towards innovation (Çoşkun et al., 2013). Differentiation and new ideas are accepted as important strategies in the sector due to the intense competition of the tourism sector and the constant threat of new competitors (Tajeddini & Trueman, 2008).

In the service sector, enterprises carry out innovation in order to provide customer satisfaction and attract customers' attention (Çeliktaş, 2008). On the other hand, innovations are carried out in hotel businesses, which are a part of the service sector, to get rid of the uniform service delivery, to differentiate and to gain competitive advantage (Can, 2009). Innovations in the service sector cover many areas and product and process innovation cannot be considered separately in the service sector (Carvalho & Costa, 2011). For example, Point Hotel in Istanbul, which determines its target audience as businessmen, has brought a special understanding for business meetings by using "home comfort and office technology" together. He differentiated himself in other hotel businesses by using the information infrastructure and technologies that support this understanding (Demirkaya & Zengin, 2014). On the other hand, Peninsula Beverly Hills makes its guests feel special by adopting an excellent service concept during the check-in process. The hotel offers a manager service with all accommodation information about the guest who knows the name of the guest. In this way, guests bypass the procedures performed at the reception (Turizmde Bu Sabah, 2021). Many hotel businesses around the world have started to take advantage of this technology and increasingly use mobile devices to communicate with their guests (Kwon et al. 2013). Based on these propositions, the hypothesis developed within the scope of the research is intended to test the impact of the organizational innovation capabilities of hotel businesses on the use of mobile applications. While

Figure 1. Research model

developing the hypothesis, the theories on which the variables are based and the studies in the literature were taken as a basis.

H1: Organizational innovation capabilities of hotel businesses positively and significantly affect the use of mobile applications.

Hotel businesses aim to provide better service to their guests by following technological innovations, creating differences in their products and services. Also; It aims to retain its customers and gain potential customers by using information technologies to exist in the sector, to gain competitive advantage and to increase its profitability, and to ensure its continuity in the current market (Şanlıöz et al. 2013). Therefore, hotel businesses use mobile applications to carry out promotional and marketing activities and achieve a sustainable competitive advantage, and enrich their applications on their websites by making them compatible with mobile devices (Can, Yesilyurt & Sancaktar, 2017). The tourism sector is among the areas where mobile applications are used the most (Brown & Chalmers 2003). For example, transactions such as hotel airline reservations, tour organizations, or car rental are carried out by users with mobile devices (Wang & Wang 2010).

The most commonly used features in related mobile applications used by hotel businesses are reservation, hotel information and hotel search, location, and interactive maps. It has been observed that customers use campaigns and notifications for guest relations, and users who prefer hotels' own applications use these applications for reservation and loyalty programs (Wang et al., 2016). In this context, travel apps are ranked 7th among the most downloaded apps (Mickaiel, 2011). Also, QR code applications are used by hotels; In areas such as room cards, elevator announcements, welcome desks, and message boards in the lobby, it offers guests suggestions such as what to do or where to eat during their stay. Users can access different services such as events and recommendations by scanning the QR code or by being directed to the hotel website (Landman, 2013).

METHODOLOGY

In the research, the relational scanning model, one of the quantitative research methods, was used. The research aims to determine the effect of organizational innovation capabilities of hotel businesses on mobile applications. The main problem of the research is "What is the impact of organizational innovation on mobile applications in hotel businesses?" The universe of the research consists of managers working in 4 and 5-star hotels operating in the Cappadocia region. The research data were obtained in March 2021 from hotel businesses that were selected by the convenience sampling method and allowed the application. The Cappadocia Region is a world-renowned tourism center, which is on the UNESCO world heritage list in the internationally recognized National Park Status (UNESCO, 2019). Cappadocia region; It consists of Nevşehir, Aksaray, Niğde, Kırşehir and Kayseri provinces. Also Cappadocia region of Turkey after 2019. According to the Minister of Culture and Tourism Ministry data on visitor statistics, Istanbul and Antalya province are in third place (Ministry of Culture and Tourism Ministry, 2019). For this reason, the universe of the research consists of 4 and 5-star hotel managers in the Cappadocia region. 16 (4-star) in Nevşehir, 6 (5-star), 3 (4-star) in Aksaray, 1 (5-star), 2 (4-star) in Kayseri, 2 (5-star), 3 (4-star) in Niğde. star hotel business. Data were collected through face-to-face interviews with 225 senior and lower-level managers who agreed to participate in the study.

The questionnaire form used in the study consists of three parts. The first part includes questions to determine the demographic characteristics of the managers participating in the research, and the second part includes questions to measure the organizational innovation capabilities of hotel businesses. In the third part, there are questions about the use of mobile applications by hotel businesses.

In the research, the "Business Innovation Scale" created by Calantone, Cavusgil, and Zhaob, (2002) was used to measure organizational innovation. The scale consists of 4 items and one dimension. Scale items were subjected to a 5-point Likert scale (1 = strongly disagree…., 5 = strongly agree). The reliability of the scale was calculated as $\alpha = .925$.

To measure the use of mobile applications by hotel businesses, Adukaite et al., Which consists of 13 basic categories and 8 sub-categories. (2014) and Baloğlu and Pekcan (2006) used the scale of mobile applications used in their studies. The reliability of the scale was calculated as $\alpha = .825$.

SOLUTIONS AND RECOMMENDATIONS

22.2% of the research participants are women, 77.8% are men; 45.3% of them are married and 54.7% are single. 35.8% of the participants stated that they have a monthly income between 5000-6000 TL, 22.5% between 6001-7000 TL, and 41.7% of them have a monthly income of 7001 TL and above. 31.8% of the participants are high school graduates, 15.7% are associate degree graduates, and 52.5% are

Table 1. Descriptive Statistics Regarding the Data Regarding the Organizational Innovation Ability of Hotel Business Managers

	Ort. *	*Standart Sapma*
A new idea is often tried out in our hotel.	3.39	1.16
Our hotel is creative in its working methods.	3.46	.916
Our hotel is often the first to market new products and services.	3.62	.739
The introduction of new products of our hotel has increased in recent years.	3.51	.856

undergraduate. When the participants are evaluated in terms of their age, 14.8% are between the ages of 31-40, 21.7% are between the ages of 41-50 and 63.5% are between the ages of 51 and over. Also, 36.7% of the participants work in the tourism sector for 6-15 years, and 63.3% who work in the tourism sector for 16 years or more.

When the findings are examined, hotel business managers stated that the organizational innovation skills of the hotel businesses they work with are above the average. Your most positive opinions; "Our hotel is generally the first company to market new products and services", "Our hotel has increased the introduction of new products in recent years" can be evaluated as hotel businesses attach importance to innovation practices especially in recent years.

When the findings are examined, it is determined that the most mobile applications use by hotel businesses are "Mobile reservation". Later, it was determined that mobile applications were used on the subjects of "Hotel Information (Hotel introduction, room information, activities, eating and drinking, meeting rooms, beauty, and spa, pools, hotel services)". Therefore, these data show that mobile applications are widely used in hotel businesses in the Cappadocia region.

Explanatory Factor Analyzes Regarding the Scales Used in the Study

Before determining the construct validity of the scale used in the research, whether there are missing values in the data set and its extreme values were examined and it was determined that the data set was suitable for analysis. To decide whether the data are suitable for factor analysis or not, the skewness and kurtosis coefficients were examined to test whether they met the normality assumption and to test the sample size fit. Coefficients and results are given in the table below.

If the coefficient of skewness and kurtosis of the data is divided by the standard error of skewness and kurtosis, respectively, if the values are between -1.5 and +1.5, the distribution is accepted as normal. Organizational innovation scale skewness

Table 2. Descriptive Statistics Regarding Data Regarding The Use of Mobile Applications by Hotel Enterprises

	Ave *	St. Dev.
Mobile booking	4.76	1.33
Hotel Information (Hotel introduction, room information, activities, eating and drinking, meeting rooms, beauty, and spa, pools, hotel services)	3.89	1.16
Campaigns and offers	3.66	.916
Guest relationships.	3.92	.939
How to reach the hotel	3.51	.856
Social media	3.96	1.05
Photo gallery	4.30	1.27
Contact	3.60	.821
Language option	3.65	.880
Information about the destination	3.70	.870
Other information and services	3.68	.868
In-hotel use	3.52	.855

value -0.73 and kurtosis value 0.68; On the mobile applications usage scale, we can state that the data with the skewness value of 0.58 and the kurtosis value of 0.99 show a normal distribution (Tabachnick & Fidell, 2007).

As a result of the explanatory factor analysis of the organizational innovation scale used within the scope of the research. The resulting dimensions and reliability (Cronbach alpha) values are listed below. In this study, while explanatory factor analysis was performed, the Principal Components method was used as the estimation method and the Varimax method was used as factor rotation method. Also, Kaiser-Meyer-Olkin sample size and Bartlett sphericity test results were checked for the suitability of the data to factor analysis. In determining the appropriate number of factors, factors with an eigenvalue greater than 1 and a variance explanation rate

Table 3. Skewness and kurtosis values

Organizational Innovation	Statistics	Standard Error
Kurtosis	.009	.132
Skewness	-.23	.314
Mobile Applications Usage		
Kurtosis	0.21	.212
Skewness	0.13	.222

Table 4. Explanatory Factor Analysis

Scale / Items	Factor Loadings	Total Variance
	F1	
A new idea is often tried out in our hotel.	0.945	88.690
Our hotel is creative in its working methods.	0.967	
Our hotel is often the first to market new products and services.	0.918	
Our hotel's new product introduction has increased in recent years.	0.937	
Eigenvalues	3.548	
Variance Description Ratios (%)	82.177	
KMO = 0.823; Bartlett Test of Sphericity = 1113.544, p <0.001		

above 5% were taken into account. However, while determining the total number of factors, the factors were chosen so that the total variance explanation rate would be more than 50%. In determining the factors, attention has been paid to adherence to the literature. In the distribution of the items to the factors, attention has been paid to have the factor load higher than 0.50.

When the assumptions were examined to make an explanatory factor analysis regarding the organizational innovation scale, the Kaiser-Meyer-Olkin scale, which represents the adequacy of the sample size, was found to be 0.823, and it was determined that the sample size was sufficient. Also, according to Bartlett's sphericity test result, which is used to determine whether the correlation matrix for the variables is a unit matrix, it has been observed that the correlation matrix for the variables is not a unit matrix ($\chi 2 = 1113.544$; $p < 0.001$), so the variables are interrelated and the data is suitable for explanatory factor analysis.

When the explanatory factor analysis results were examined, it was determined that the scale consists of a single factor and 4 items by its original structure. While determining the appropriate number of factors, factors with an eigenvalue greater than 1 and slope-slope graphs were taken into consideration. When the factor loads obtained as a result of the oplimum rotation were examined, it was seen that all items had a load of more than 0.50 and the total variance explanation rate of the single factor was 88.690%.

As a result of the explanatory factor analysis of the mobile applications usage scale used within the scope of the research. The resulting dimensions and reliability (Cronbach alpha) values are listed below.

When the assumptions were examined to make an explanatory factor analysis regarding the mobile applications usage scale, it was determined that the sample size was sufficient by finding the Kaiser-Meyer-Olkin measure, which represents the

Figure 2. Slope Plot to Determine the Number of Factors

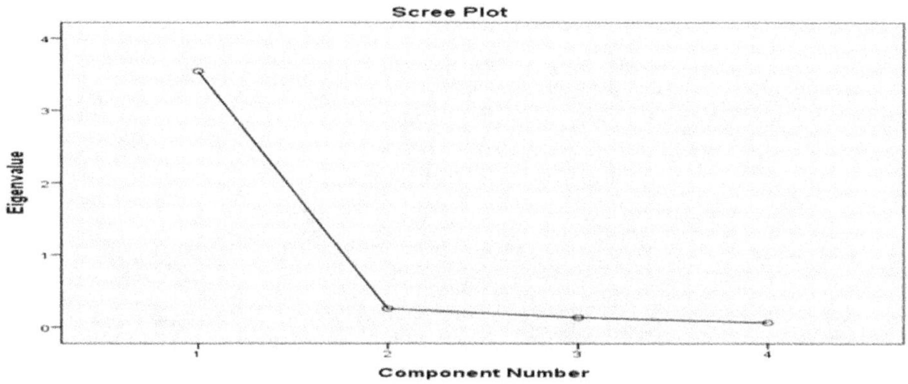

adequacy of the sample size, 0.769. In addition, according to Bartlett's sphericity test result, which is used to determine whether the correlation matrix for the variables is a unit matrix, it has been observed that the correlation matrix for the variables is

Table 5. Explanatory Factor Analysis

Scale / Items	Factor Loadings	Total Variance
	F1	
Mobile booking	.941	
Hotel Information (Hotel introduction, room information, activities, eating and drinking, meeting rooms, beauty, and spa, pools, hotel services)	.966	
Campaigns and offers	.849	
Guest relationships.	.944	
How to reach the hotel	.847	
Social media	.939	79.148
Photo gallery	.857	
Contact	.895	
Language option	.879	
Information about the destination	.923	
Other information and services	.745	
In-hotel use	.867	
Eigenvalues	9.498	
Variance Description Ratios (%)	79.148	
KMO = 0. 769; Bartlett Test of Sphericity = 8407,771, p<0.001		

Figure 3. Slope Plot to Determine the Number of Factors

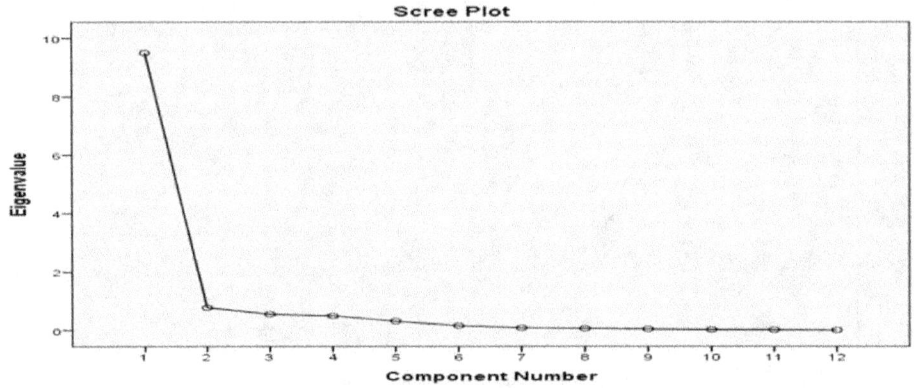

not a unit matrix ($\chi 2$ = 8407.771; p <0.001), so the variables are interrelated and the data is suitable for explanatory factor analysis.

When the explanatory factor analysis results were examined, it was determined that the scale consists of a single factor and 12 items in accordance with its original structure. While determining the appropriate number of factors, factors with an eigenvalue greater than 1 and slope-slope graphs were taken into consideration. When the factor loads obtained as a result of the oblimum rotation were examined, it was seen that all items had a load of more than 0.50 and the total variance explanation rate of the single factor was 79.148%.

Analyzes on the Relationship Between Organizational Innovation and Mobile Applications Usage

In the study, Pearson correlation analysis was applied to determine the effect of organizational innovation abilities of hotel managers' use of mobile applications, as the data on the relationships between variables showed normal distribution. The value of Pearson's correlation coefficient varies between +1.00 and -1.00, while the coefficient of +1 indicates a perfectly positive and -1 indicates a perfectly negative relationship; A coefficient of 0.00 indicates that there is no relationship. In this context, regardless of the sign of the level of the relationship between variables, if the Pearson correlation coefficient is below 0.30, it is defined as "low", a medium between 0.30-0.69, and "high" for values 0.70 and above (Çokluk et al. 2012: 52). Findings related to Pearson correlation analysis to determine the relationship between organizational innovation and mobile applications use of hotel managers are presented below.

Table 6. Correlation Analysis for the Relationship Between Organizational Innovation and Mobile Applications Usage

	X	Sd.	1	2	3
1.Organizational Innovation	3.40	0.93			
2. Use of Mobile Applications	3.57	0.78	0.865**		-

** p <0.001

According to the table, the correlation coefficient at the level of 0.001 significance in the relationship between the organizational innovation perceptions of hotel business managers and their perception of mobile applications; (0,70 <r <1) (r = 0,865) significant positive correlations were found at high power. In this case, it can be stated that a positive increase in the organizational innovation abilities of hotel businesses causes an increase in the use of mobile applications.

Table 7. Regression analysis results

Variables	Unstandardized		Standard	T	P
	B	S.H.	Beta		
Constant	1.08	0.12		26.01	0.00
Organizational Innovation	0.79	0.29	0.86	26.01	**0.00**

** p <0.001

As a result of the analysis, a simple regression analysis was conducted to examine the extent to which the organizational innovation capabilities of accommodation businesses determine the use of mobile applications. It is seen that simple regression analysis results are statistically significant (= 0.865; p<. 000). The regression equation for the simple linear relationship between variables is mobile applications usage = 1.093 + 0.697 (organizational innovation). The corrected R^2 value of the analysis results is 0.730. According to this value, it can be interpreted that 73% of the variance of mobile application usage of hotel enterprises depends on organizational innovation abilities.

The success of innovation policies in organizations is achieved through the successful use of human and material resources (Harrison, 2013). In this case, organizations need to develop their innovative abilities. In an environment where it is necessary to be innovative, organizations compete not only with their tangible assets but also with their intangible assets. In this sense, to measure the real values of businesses and to provide quality products or services; They should not ignore customer satisfaction and organizational development issues. However, in this case, sustainable competition can be mentioned (Büyük, 2010). Because, depending on the changes in their external environment, organizations can renew their working methods and methods and increase organizational performance with renewed practices and changes (Harrison, 2013).

CONCLUSION

The purpose of this study is to determine the effect of organizational innovation capabilities of hotel businesses on mobile applications. In line with this purpose, a questionnaire was applied to 225 managers working in the hotel establishments in the Cappadocia region. The majority of managers participating in the research; are male, graduate, and aged between 51 and over. In the study, the relationship between organizational innovation capabilities of hotel businesses and their use of mobile applications was revealed by Pearson correlation analysis. Simple regression analysis was applied to determine the effect of organizational innovation capabilities of hotel businesses on mobile applications.

The research aims to shed light on the use of mobile applications in the context of hotel businesses by determining the relationship between organizational innovation capabilities of hotel businesses and the use of mobile applications. First, the concept of organizational innovation was explained in the research, and then the use of mobile applications in hotel businesses was focused on. The focus here is on the use of mobile applications resulting from the impact of organizational innovation capabilities of hotel businesses. In addition, in the study, which is consistent with (Schumpeter's, 1934) 's Schumpeterian approach and Venkatesh et al. (2003) established a relationship with the Technology Acceptance and Use Unified Model. Then, the effects of organizational innovation capabilities of hotel businesses on the use of mobile applications were evaluated and the theoretical basis was revealed. As a result of the research, it has been verified that the organizational innovation capabilities of hotel businesses control the use of mobile applications. In this study conducted in the Cappadocia region, it was concluded that the organizational innovation capabilities of hotel enterprises affect the use of mobile applications. Therefore, the "H1: Organizational innovation capabilities of hotel businesses affect the use of mobile applications positively and significantly." hypothesis was accepted. These results show that hotel businesses' use of mobile applications varies depending on their organizational innovation capabilities. Considering the findings of the study, the conclusions are given below.

Theoretical Implications

In the literature; There is no empirical study on the relationship between the organizational innovation capability of hotel businesses and the use of mobile applications. Therefore, the study is important in terms of evaluating the effect of organizational innovation capabilities of hotel businesses on the use of mobile applications and it is predicted to contribute to the relevant literature. One of the theoretical contributions of the study is the results obtained as a result of correlation and regression analysis. In the study, it was determined that othe rganizational innovation capabilities of hotel businesses have a positive and significant effect on the use of mobile applications. Accordingly, as the organizational innovation decrease capabilities of hotel businesses increase or decrease, the use of mobile applications increases or decreases in that direction. A limited number of studies in the literature (Carvalho & Costa, 2011; Şanlıöz et al. 2013) show that there is a directly proportional relationship between organizational innovation and mobile application use. Hence the research results; supports the basic idea in the literature in terms of the relationship between the organizational innovation capabilities of hotel businesses and the use of mobile applications.

Practical Implications

The research was conducted on Turkey in the hotel business managers in the Cappadocia region, which has an important place in tourism. In terms of organizational innovation capabilities of the sector practitioners and managers of the research; It is thought that it will contribute to ensuring its sustainability, competitiveness and different marketing strategies. In the tourism sector where mobile applications are used the most (Brown and Chalmers 2003), the development and creation of the innovation ability of organizations ccontribute tothey're being ahead of their competitors (Essmann & Preez, 2009). Also, in the research, it was determined that the reservation system is the most common mobile application in hotel businesses. When we look at other studies, they stated that hotel businesses give more space to mobile reservation applications and offer mobile reservation opportunities to their guests (Wang et al., 2016; Anuar et al., 2014). In this context, hotel businesses should offer different preferences to their guests by using mobile applications more effectively. For example, the usage area of in-hotel mobile applications can be expanded or mobile applications can be used for guest relations. Because of the privatization of the tourism services provided in the hotel enterprises, the applications that will make the tourists feel special, will contribute to the increase in the service quality and will contribute to the increase of the prestige of the hotel business in the tourism sector when we look at the total benefit (Kemer, 2021).

Limitations and Future Research

The research was applied to the managers of 4 and 5-star hotel establishments in the Cappadocia region. However, data could not be collected from hotel businesses that were closed due to the restrictions during the pandemic process. In addition, no research has been found in the literature that examines the impact of organizational innovation capabilities of hotel businesses on mobile applications. Therefore, one of the limitations of the study is that the comparison and evaluation possibilities are limited. This research has been applied to hotel managers in the Cappadocia region. Therefore, different results can be obtained in different countries and regions. The results obtained can be compared by using different variables or working on different samples. In addition, this research can be evaluated as a prediction for future studies.

REFERENCES

Adukaite, A., Reimann, A.M., Marchiori, E., & Cantoni, L. (2014). Hotel mobile apps. the case of 4 and 5 Star hotels in Europian Germaan-speking countries. In Z. Xiang ve I. Tussyadiah (Ed.) *Information and Communication Technologies in Tourism*, 45-57.

Akgöz, E., Güral, R., & Gürsoy, Y. (2014). Yenilik kapsamında turistik ürün çeşitlendirmesi ve Kurban Bayramı örneği. *Selçuk Üniversitesi Sosyal Bilimler Enstitüsü Dergisi*, *31*, 1–12.

Anuar, J., Musa, M., & Khalid, K. (2014). Smartphone's application adoption benefits using mobile hotel reservation system (MHRS) among 3 to 5-star city hotels in Malaysia. *Procedia: Social and Behavioral Sciences*, *130*, 552–557. doi:10.1016/j.sbspro.2014.04.064

Atay, L., Yalçınkaya, P., & Bahar, F. (2019). İstanbul'daki akıllı otel uygulamalarının değerlendirilmesi. *Manas Sosyal Araştırmalar Dergisi*, *8*(1), 667–678.

Baloğlu, Ş., & Pekcan, Y. A. (2006). The website design and internet site marketing practices of upscale and luxury hotels in Turkey. *Tourism Management*, *27*(1), 171–176. doi:10.1016/j.tourman.2004.07.003

Brown, B., & Chalmers, M. (2003). Tourism and mobile technology. K. Kuutti ve E.H. Karsten (Ed.), *Proeceedings of the 8th European Conference on Computer Supported Cooperative Work*. Helsinki, Finland, 14-18 September. 10.1007/978-94-010-0068-0_18

Büyük, K. (2010). Stratejik Performans Yönetiminin Unsuru Olarak Örgüt Kültürünü Ölçümleme Üzerine Kavramsal Bir Çalışma, Eskişehir Osmangazi Üniversitesi. IBF Dergisi, *5*(2), 220–230.

Calantone, R. J., Cavusgil, T. S., & Zhaob, Y. (2002). Learning orientation, firm innovation capability, and firm performance. *Industrial Marketing Management, 31*(6), 515–524. doi:10.1016/S0019-8501(01)00203-6

Can, Ö. (2009). Tekstil kobilerinde inovasyon. *Tekstil Teknolojileri Elektronik Dergisi*, *3*(1), 57–63.

Carlsson, C., Hyvonen, K., Repo, P., & Walden, P. (2005). Asynchronous adoption patterns of mobile services. In *Proceedings of the 38th Hawaii International Conference on System Sciences*. IEEE Computer Society Press. 10.1109/HICSS.2005.106

Carvolha, L., & Costa, T. (2011). Tourism innovation – A literature review complemented by case study research. Internatıonal Conference on Tourism & Management Studies, 1, 23-33.

Çeliktaş, H. (2008). *İnovasyon yönetimi: Çukurova Bölgesinde faaliyet gösteren şirketlerde inovasyon uygulamalarının tespitine yönelik bir araştırma* [Yüksek Lisans Tezi]. Çukurova Üniversitesi Sosyal Bilimler Enstitüsü.

Charland, A., & Leroux, B. (2011). Mobile application development: Web vs. native. *Communications of the ACM*, *54*(5), 49–53. doi:10.1145/1941487.1941504

Clement, J. (2019). *Mobile Internet Usage Worldwide- Statistics & Facts*. https://www.statista.com/topics/779/mobile-internet/

Çokluk, Ö., Şekercioğlu, G., & Büyüköztürk, Ş. (2012). *Sosyal bilimler için çok değişkenli istatistik: SPSS ve LISREL uygulamaları*. Pegem Akademi.

Colombo, G. B., Chorley, M. J., Williams, M. J., Allen, S. M., & Whitaker, R. M. (2012). *You are where you eat: Foursquare checkins as indicators of human mobility and behaviour*. School of Computer Science & Informatics, Cardiff University.

Coşkun, S. (2013). *Stratejik rekabet üstünlüğü sağlama aracı olarak inovasyon stratejileri-Kocaeli otel işletmeleri üzerine bir araştırma*. Yüksek Lisans Tezi, Düzce Üniversitesi Sosyal Bilimler Enstitüsü Turizm ve Otel İşletmeciliği Anabilim Dalı, Düzce.

Demirkaya, H., & Zengin, R. (2014). Hizmet inovasyonu ve bir uygulama örneği. *Elektronik Mesleki Gelişim Ve Araştırmalar Dergisi*, *2*(1), 106–116.

Drucker, P. (1998). The discipline of innovation. *Harvard Business Review*, *76*(6), 54–66. PMID:10187245

Elçi, Ş. (2006). *İnovasyon: Kalkınmanın ve rekabetin anahtarı*. NOVA Basın Yayın.

Ercan, E., & Önal, A. (2007). *Mobil turist rehberlerine karşılaştırmalı bakış. Akademik Bilişim, IX*. Akademik Bilişim Konferansı Bildirileri, Dumlupınar Üniversitesi.

Essmann, H., & Preez, N.D. (2009). An innovation capability maturity model development and initial application. *International Journal Of Industrial And Manufacturing Engineering, 3*(5).

Gezici, B., Tarhan, A., & Chouseinoglou, O. (2018). Mobil uygulamaların evriminde karmaşıklık, boyut ve iç kalite gelişimi: Keşifsel bir çalışma. *Gazi Üniversitesi Mühendislik-Mimarlık Fakültesi Dergisi*, *34*(3), 18–22.

Harrison, D. (2013). Receptivit e e t Contrainte s d e L'innovatio n dan s L'administratio n Publique. *Telescope, 19*(2), 71-86. http://cerberus.enap.ca/Telescope/docs/Index/Vol_19_no_2/Telv19_no2_harris on.pdf

Henard, D. H., & Dacin, P. A. (2010). Reputation for product innovation: Its impact on consumers. *Journal of Product Innovation Management*, *27*(3), 321–335.

Horuz, A. (2012). *İnovasyon Nedir*. http://www.edebiarsiv.com/makale-arsivi/4256-inovasyon-nedir.html

İşlek, M. (2012). *Sosyal medyanın tüketici davranışlarına etkileri: Türkiye'deki sosyal medya kullanıcıları üzerine bir araştırma*. Karamanoğlu Mehmet Bey Üniversitesi, Sosyal Bilimler Enstitüsü Yüksek Lisans Tezi.

Kemer, E. (2021). Eğitim Seviyesinin Endüstri 4. 0 Farkındalığına Etkisi: Konaklama İşletmelerinde Bir Uygulama. *Türk Turizm Araştırmaları Dergisi, 5*(2), 1138-1149.

Kim, E., Lin, J., & Sung, Y. (2013). To App or Not to App: Engaging Consumers viaBranded Mobile Apps. *Journal of Interactive Advertising, 13*(1), 53-65. doi:10.1080/15252019.2013.782780

Kırlar Can, B., Yeşilyurt, H., Lale Sancaktar, C., & Koçak, N. (2017). Mobil çağda mobil uygulamalar: Türkiye'deki yerli otel zincirleri üzerine bir durum tespiti. *Journal of Yasar University*, *12*(45), 60–75.

Kırova, A. (2015). Critical and emerging discourses in multicultural education literature. In S. Guo & L. Wong (Eds.), *Revisiting Multiculturalism in Canada*. Transnational Migration and Education. SensePublishers. doi:10.1007/978-94-6300-208-0_15

Kwon, J. M., Bae, J., & Blum, S. C. (2013). Mobile applications in the hospitality industry. *Journal of Hospitality and Tourism Technology*, *4*(1), 81–92. doi:10.1108/17579881311302365

Lamberton, C., & Stephen, T. A. (2016). A Thematic Exploration of Digital, Social Media,and Mobile Marketing: Research Evolution from 2000 to 2015 and an Agendafor Future Inquiry. *Journal of Marketing*, *80*(6), 146–172. doi:10.1509/jm.15.0415

Landman, P. (2013). *How hotels can use QR codes for marketing and customer service.* http://www.tnooz.com/article/how-hotels-can-use-qr-codes-for-marketing-and-customerservice/#sthash.JFxJa6wB.dpuf

Lumpkin, G. T., & Dess, G.G. (1996). Clarifying the Achievement Orientations Construct and Linking it to Performance. Academy of Management Review, (21), 135-172.

Mickaiel, I. (2011). *Mobile the new black for travel.* http://www.zdnet.com.au/mobile-the-new-black-for-travel-339321469.htm

Öğüt, A. (2007). Stratejik insan kaynakları yönetimi bağlamında örgütlerdeki işgören motivasyonu süreci. *Selçuk Üniversitesi İktisadi ve İdari Bilimler Üniversitesi Dergisi*, *12*, 1–14.

Online Otel Rezervasyon Platformu. (2021). https://webrazzi.com/2020/02/11/otelz-2019/

Sabuncu, B. (2014). KOBİ'lerde yenilik ve engellerinin tespitine yönelik bir araştırma: Denizli örneği. *İşletme Araştırmaları Dergisi,* *6*(1), 103-112.

Şanlıöz, K., Dilek, E., & Koçak, N. (2015). Değişen dünya, dönüşen pazarlama: Türkiye turizm sektöründen öncü bir mobil uygulama örneği. Anatolia. *Turizm Araştırmaları Dergisi*, *24*(2), 250–260.

Schmookler, J. (1966). *Invention and economic growth.* Harvard University Press. doi:10.4159/harvard.9780674432833

Schumpeter, J. A. (1934). *The theory of economics development.* Oxford University Press.

Serçeoğlu, A. G. N. (2014). Yaratıcılık Ve Hizmet Odaklılık: Yiyecek İçecek İşletmelerinde Bir Uygulama. 9th Internatıonal Conference: New Perspectıves in Tourısm and Hospitality, 333-341.

Simonceska, D. L. (2012). The changes and innovation as a factor of competitiveness of thetourist offer (the case of Ohrid). *Procedia: Social and Behavioral Sciences*, *44*, 32–43. doi:10.1016/j.sbspro.2012.05.002

Smith, W. K., & Tushman, M. L. (2005). Managing strategic contradictions: A top management model for managing innovation streams. *Organization Science*, *16*(5), 522–536. doi:10.1287/orsc.1050.0134

Steinbock, D. (2005). *The mobile revolution: The making of worldwide mobile markets*. Kogan Page Limited.

Tabachnick, B. G., & Fidell, L. S. (2007). *Using multivariate statistics* (5th ed.). Allyn & Bacon/Pearson Education.

Tajeddini, K., & Trueman, M. (2008). Effect Of Customer Orientation And İnnovativeness On Business Performance: A Study Of Small-Sized Service Retailers. *International Journal of Entrepreneurship and Small Business*, *6*(2), 280–295. doi:10.1504/IJESB.2008.018633

Tether, B. S. (2005). Do service innovate (Differently)? Insights from the European innobarometer survey. *Industry and Innovation*, *12*(2), 153–184. doi:10.1080/13662710500087891

T.R. Ministry of Culture and Tourism. (2020). *Tourism statistics*. https://yigm.ktb.gov.tr/Eklenti/72701,turizmistatistikleri2020-1pdf.pdf?

Turizmde Bu Sabah. (2021). https://www.tourismtoday.net/

UNESCO. (2020). https //www.unesco.org.tr/Pages/125/122/UNESCO-D%C3%BCnya-Miras%C4%B1-List

UNESCO. (2021). *Reading in the mobile era: A study ofmobile reading in developing countries*. https://unesdoc.unesco.org/images/0022/002274/227436e.pdf

Üstel, İ., & Kabatepe, E. (2006). *Kobiler ve inovasyon*. http://www.turkab.org/dokumanlar/yayinlar/kobilerveinovaasyon.pdf

Venkatesh, V., Morris, M. G., Davis, G. B., & Davis, F. D. (2003). User acceptance of information technology: Toward a unified view. *Management Information Systems Quarterly*, *27*(3), 425–478. doi:10.2307/30036540

Verma, R., & Bashir, M. (2015). Business model innovation: Past, present and the future. *Indian Journal of Management*, *9*(1), 8–20.

Wang, D., Xiang, Z., Law, R., & Pui Ki, T. (2016). Assessing hotel-related smartphone apps using online reviews. *Journal of Hospitality Marketing & Management*, *25*(3), 291–313. doi:10.1080/19368623.2015.1012282

Wang, H. Y., & Wang, S. H. (2010). Predicting mobile hotel reservation adoption: Insight from a perceived value standpoint. *International Journal of Hospitality Management*, *29*(4), 598–698. doi:10.1016/j.ijhm.2009.11.001

Wijesekera, P., Baokar, A., Tsai, L., Reardon, J., Egelman, S., Wagner, D., & Beznosov, K. (2018). Dynamically regulating mobile application permissions. *IEEE Security and Privacy*, *16*(1), 64–71. doi:10.1109/MSP.2018.1331031

Zerenler, & Türker, & Kahin. (2007). Küresel teknoloji, araştırma geliştirme (Ar-Ge) ve yenilik ilişkisi. *Selçuk Üniversitesi Sosyal Bilimler Enstitüsü Dergisi*, *17*, 653–667.

Chapter 9
Employee Perception of the Effectiveness of Digitalized Performance Management Systems

Sneha Maindola
HNB Garhwal Central University, India

Surendra Kumar
HNB Garhwal Central University, India

ABSTRACT

Performance management is a valuable tool for any organization to achieve its strategic objectives and align its resources. It is identified to lead a productive workforce and improves employee engagement. However, due to the disruption of technology in the various dimensions of the environment, HRM systems have undergone many changes. Organizations have adapted to the technological outburst and synchronized their activity around it. Present times observe a heavy use of technology in the day-to-day HR functions. Performance management has also been hugely impacted by the manifestation of technology, where many organizations have adopted the use of technology for the same. The stance of the management on the use of technology for performance management is often deliberated upon; hence, the outlook of employees on the use of technology for performance management has been unclear. For this chapter, the authors consider the employees in the education sector and their perception of the effectiveness of the use of technology/software for performance management based on different parameters.

DOI: 10.4018/978-1-7998-9194-9.ch009

INTRODUCTION

Performance management (PM) is a tool used by Human Resource Management that enables them to manage and evaluate the performance of the employees and thus assist in the formulation of the strategies accordingly. On the other hand, Performance Management System (PMS) also aids the employees by communicating what is expected from them and eventually conveying how they are performing. Performance Management System also facilitates a decisive role to abet managerial decisions such as promotions, transfers, increments, rewards, training, and development & employee engagement. With so much to offer the role of PMS in any organization cannot be undermined therefore diligence is required in devising the most appropriate PMS for the organization, so that the information collected is not futile. Like many other service sector industries, the education sector is also highly performance-driven therefore the PMS associated with these organizations should be able to contribute the same. The education sector demands high performance not only in the way education is imparted but also in the research work propounded by the employee. The Performance Indicators (PI) for this sector also have to be pertinent as the performance cannot be evaluated merely by the business that is brought in. The education sector demands its employees to be high performers to promote their own standing/ranking in the industry. How good an institution is, is often determined by how well the academicians associated with the institution are acclaimed by the other academicians. Employees are expected to accomplish intellectual skills as well as institutional prestige and standing, both of which are critical to academic success and promotion (Benschop & Brouns, 2003). Research and literary work are imperative to ascertain the performance of the employees in this industry, for that these serve as a vital Performance Indicator for the employees associated with the education sector. An inappropriate Performance Management System can be a bane rather than a boon for the organization and can steer many problems pertaining to the employees of the organization (Biron et al., 2011).

It concurs that the use of technology helps to simplify and accelerate the associated process hence many industries have been witnessing the amalgam of different functions with technology. Likewise, the Human Resource functions have also observed the adaptation of technology in its many functions one of these being Performance Management (PM). Since Performance management is a highly crucial function that has its implication on various decisions subjected to the human resource of the organization it is only natural for it to be transformed in the age of technology. Although it is relatively clear as to what the organization wants but little is discussed about what the employees anticipate from the PMS. Hence, through this chapter, the authors aim to encapsulate the different elements that the employees seek in the PMS and also their perception towards the digitalization of the PMS.

BACKGROUND

Many a little makes a mickle is precisely what Performance management is about, where the performance of every individual in the organization is managed so that it contributes to the performance of the organization. In simple terms, Performance Management is the system the management deploys to analyze the performance of the employees based on the pre-determined standards or goals and comparing it to the actual performance. Performance Management according to (Armstrong 2000) is a systematic process for improving the performance of the organization through the improvement of the performance of individual and the team, by acting as a means to get a better result by considering & administering the organizations performance within the established structure of predefined goals and the proficiency required. Performance Management and Performance Management System are commonly used but when explored a considerable difference is established (Broadbent & Laughlin, 2009). Performance appraisals are the start of the Performance management activities, these also involve evaluation, goal-setting, training, and reward systems (Denisi & Murphy, 2017).

Feedback shared in a Performance Management System are grounded on the specific items not general and are built on the predefined standards (Amaratunga & Baldry, 2002)

It is observed a lot that feedback often reduces the performance rather than improving them, when the feedbacks are shared in the absence of predefined goals will have no significance outcome as the feedback shared will just pose as a shared information and its outcome will merely depend on how the receiver perceive the information (Latham et al., 2005).

Performance Measures and reporting lead to Performance Management that promotes motivation, better behaviour, and innovation (Plaček et al., 2020). Performance Indicators are essential for the organization since they reveal what is to be measured and the criteria the actual performance needs to satisfy (Flapper & Fortuin, 1996). Very few employees perceive that their organization's Performance Management system helps them improve their performance, and it is consistently one of the least popular topics in employee satisfaction surveys (Pulakos, 2009; (Gruman & Saks, 2011)

Formulating a Performance Management System and employing it is a very challenging process which may include obstacles such as the absence of support from the top management, flawed communication, unclear goals, and objectives, opinion that it utilizes more time, absence of uniformity among the other challenges (Managing employee performance, 2019; Agarwal, 2020). Higher academics feel (via a direct effect on their vitality level and an indirect effect on their stress levels through enhanced work experiences), the more they perceive the use of enabling performance management practices like better dialogue, connectivity, facilities, competence acknowledgment, and development of opportunities (Franco-Santos & Doherty, 2017).

Human Resource Management System is dedicated to automation and digitalization of the Human Resource functions hence they mainly serve the HR staff rather than the managers and the employees (Martin & Reddington, 2010).

(Kivistö et al., 2017) found that though the academicians value performance measurement their outlook does not correlate with the perception of high performance in research as well as teaching, additionally, they concluded that for academics high performance is perceived by the response of other academicians in place of financial incentives. (Kagaari et al., 2010) conclude in their study that the amalgamation of Information and Communication Technology (ICT) in Performance Management practices has a mediating effect on the managed performance.

(DiMaggio et al., 2001) deliberate on the fact that the growing use of technology in the organization may push the organizations towards the traditional methods of implementing control such as surveillance.

PERFORMANCE MANAGEMENT AND TECHNOLOGY

Over the years Performance Management has undergone many changes where several new methods and techniques have come into existence such as 360 Degree Feedback, Peer review, Management by Objectives, Balance Scorecard method, Personal Development Plans, TQM Technique, etc. Above all with the addition of technology, the whole process of Performance Management has been disrupted. Many generic and customizable software are available in the market catering to the specific need of the clients. Some of the well-known Performance Management software are HROne, Keka, HRMantra, etc. Many softwares are available which are solely used for performance management whereas many software packages are also available that assist in the different functional areas. The primary reason for using technology in any functional area is the fact that it simplifies the process by making the process easier and much faster. All this softwares are believed to be expediting the process. While Performance Management is a continuous process hence it requires continuous monitoring and analyzing. Therefore, the use of technology is going to save a lot of trouble. Traditionally Performance management also required a lot of paperwork which is curbed by the application of these softwares. It further helps in better record keeping and quicker access. The employees desire to access all the information with respect to their job and their performance hence the PMS should be able to deliver the same. A system where the necessary information cannot be accessed and there are barriers to conceal information will not be worthless as it will not be able to satisfy the needs of the employees.

However, many studies also indicate that the notation that Digitalization or the use of technology will only bring positive changes is also fallacious. Many studies have found that the PMS is not delivering what is expected out of it (Haines & St-Onge, 2012).

Only a few academics have proposed that, leaders and performance management systems digitalization, should demonstrate a higher output orientation and a bigger interest for personnel development to help employees meet the expected criterias (Curzi et al., 2019). (Lewis et al., 2005) The use of Information Communication Technology in the organization not only empowers its employees but at the same time enables the organization to exert centralized control thus the perfectionistic image created might be deceptive. Hence it can be inferred that the use of technology is pushing the organizations towards the traditional form of the management system.

WHAT THE MANAGEMENT SEEK FROM A PMS VS. WHAT AN EMPLOYEE SEEK

Performance Management Systems are devised to serve the need of not only the managers but also the employees. At the outset, it may appear that the Managers and the employees look for different outcomes from the PMS but they eventually lead to the same result. While both the managers and the employees anticipate the PMS to give a nudge to the actual performance however the intent for such expectation is quite different. The management seeks to accomplish the goals of the organization whereas the first instinct of the employee is the attainment or successful completion of the allotted task. Through the PMS the management intends to convey the goals established to the employees whereas the employees look forward to participating in the goal formulation process. When the employees have a say in goal setting it provides them with a sense of belongingness, increases the satisfaction level in employees, and promotes communication. PMS should also allow the managers to identify the low performers in the organization on the other hand the employees expect to identify where they are going wrong in delivering their performance. By identifying the low performance in the organization the management will have the required information to formulate the strategies required to implement improvement. Likewise, the employees will be aware of their shortcomings hence can work on improving them. Additionally, the PMS should also provide the necessary information to the management to take decisions such as increments, promotions, and evaluation of performance. For the employees, it should provide transparency, fair feedback and then should aid in the personal development of the employees.

Hence ideally a Performance Management System should take into consideration the requirements of both the management and the employees for it to be effective. Employee recognition is an exigence to strengthen the performance and adjust the behavior (Haines & St-Onge, 2012).

Performance Management has been considered as an instrument to support decisions such as career development, transfers & promotion, termination and retention, remuneration, however it also assists the employees to link their goals and objectives to those of the organization (Agarwal, 2020).

Figure 1.

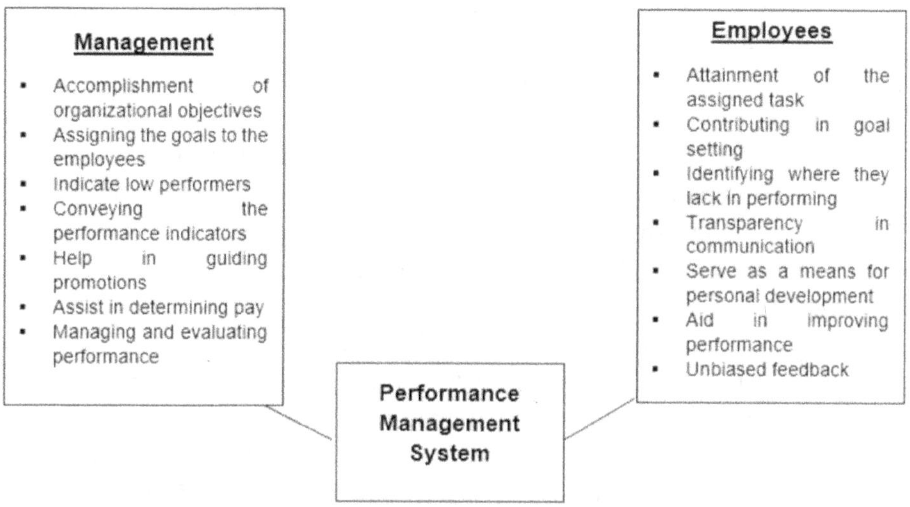

EMPLOYEES ON DIGITALIZED PERFORMANCE MANAGEMENT

The authors analyzed the effectiveness of digitalization of PMS as per the employees of the education sector based on seven criteria i.e. goal setting, transparency in communication, Honest feedback/reviews, Fairness, employee development, employee recognition, and elevate performance. The survey was conducted using five points Likert scale ranging from Strongly disagree to Strongly agree. The response was collected from 325 respondents consisting of the academic staff from the education sector, out of which 186 were male and 139 were female.

The finding of the study concluded that 14.15% of the population strongly agrees and 56.92% of the population agrees, 17.54% neither agreed nor disagreed whereas 6.77% disagreed and 4.62% strongly disagreed, that digitalization of the performance management system enables them to be a part of goal setting and determining the performance indicators. When considering Transparency in communication in digitalized PMS, 13.23% strongly agreed, 40.31% agreed, 28.31% neither agreed nor disagreed, 11.08% disagreed and 7.08% strongly disagreed; For honest feedback/ review in digitalized PMS the response included 16.62% strongly agreed, 31.38% agreed, 21.23% neither agreed nor disagreed, 28% disagreed and 2.77% strongly disagreed; For fairness in digitalized PMS, the responses were 20.92% strongly agreed, 41.85% agreed, 16.31% neither agreed nor disagreed, 12.92% disagreed and 8% strongly disagreed; Employee development in digitalized PMS obtained 14.15% strongly agreed, 37.85% agreed, 22.46% neither agreed nor disagreed, 19.69% disagreed and 5.85% strongly disagreed; Employee recognition induced 12.62% strongly agreed, 36% agreed, 25.23% neither agreed nor disagreed, 17.85% disagreed and 8.31% strongly disagreed; and elevate performance induced 9.85% strongly agreed, 29.23% agreed, 24.31% neither agreed nor disagreed, 21.85% disagreed and 14.77% strongly disagreed. From the results drawn it could be inferred that the majority of the population believes that they are involved in goal setting for the digitalized PMS and believe the process to be fair and transparent, the review received are satisfactory. Although the employee development, employee recognition, and elevation of performance were found to have a positive relationship with the perceived effectiveness of the digitalized performance management system but not as intense.

As for satisfaction derived from the digitalized PMS, the result indicates 36% strongly agreed, 33.23% agreed, 15.08% neither agreed nor disagreed, 11.69% disagreed and 4% strongly disagreed; signifying that at large the employees possess a positive attitude towards the digitalization of PMS and prefer it to the former system. The data analysis also pointed out that the employees who have higher experience were found to be more perceptive about the digitalization of PMS.

FUTURE RESEARCH DIRECTIONS

Since Performance Management is undeniably one of the most prominent functions of Human Resource Management which entails many other sub-functions it will be beneficial to study the effect of the Performance Management software and digital techniques on other functions of Performance Management such as Performance appraisal, employee engagement activities, etc. Moreover, there are numerous other elements of Performance Management whose implications can be studied in the future.

CONCLUSION

Performance Management Systems are required to serve not only the management but also the employees. However, despite undergoing many changes over the period of time it still possesses many shortfalls. Although with the amalgamation of technology it has been renewed and presented in a digitalized mode serving to many of the concerns raised time and again however many times it is observed to be serving the advantage of the Managers more than the employees by simplifying and speeding the whole process. Digitalization of PMS has aided in improved communication between the management and the employees, completion of the proceedings on times, better decision making, etc. yet more concentration is required to improve so that it can also enable the employees to be able to develop and feel that they are recognized for their performance, at the same time it should be able to assist in improving performance and concur better results. Performance Management System is very subjective in nature, the conjecture one fits all cannot be applied for it, however, customization of this software requires a lot of funds which might be an obstacle. The education sector also encompasses individuals from all walks of life hence the opinion fostered will not be unanimous. Performance Indicators used in the education sector should be appropriate for the said sector and should be the correct parameter for measuring the performance.

REFERENCES

Agarwal, A. (2020). Investigating design targets for effective performance management system: an application of balance scorecard using QFD. *Journal of Advances in Management Research.*

Amaratunga, D., & Baldry, D. (2002). *Moving from performance measurement to performance management.* Facilities. doi:10.1108/02632770210426701

Armstrong, M., & Baron, A. (2000). *Performance management.* Kogan Page Limited.

Benschop, Y., & Brouns, M. (2003). Crumbling ivory towers: Academic organizing and its gender effects. *Gender, Work and Organization, 10*(2), 194–212. doi:10.1111/1468-0432.t01-1-00011

Biron, M., Farndale, E., & Paauwe, J. (2011). Performance management effectiveness: Lessons from world-leading firms. *International Journal of Human Resource Management, 22*(06), 1294–1311. doi:10.1080/09585192.2011.559100

Broadbent, J., & Laughlin, R. (2009). Performance management systems: A conceptual model. *Management Accounting Research, 20*(4), 283–295. doi:10.1016/j.mar.2009.07.004

Curzi, Y., Fabbri, T., Scapolan, A. C., & Boscolo, S. (2019). Performance appraisal and innovative behavior in the digital era. *Frontiers in Psychology, 10*, 1659. doi:10.3389/fpsyg.2019.01659 PMID:31379682

DeNisi, A. S., & Murphy, K. R. (2017). Performance appraisal and performance management: 100 years of progress? *The Journal of Applied Psychology, 102*(3), 421–433. doi:10.1037/apl0000085 PMID:28125265

DiMaggio, P., Hargittai, E., Neuman, W. R., & Robinson, J. P. (2001). Social implications of the Internet. *Annual Review of Sociology, 27*(1), 307–336. doi:10.1146/annurev.soc.27.1.307

Flapper, S. D. P., Fortuin, L., & Stoop, P. P. (1996). Towards consistent performance management systems. *International Journal of Operations & Production Management.*

Franco-Santos, M., & Doherty, N. (2017). Performance management and well-being: A close look at the changing nature of the UK higher education workplace. *International Journal of Human Resource Management, 28*(16), 2319–2350. doi:10.1080/09585192.2017.1334148

Gruman, J. A., & Saks, A. M. (2011). Performance management and employee engagement. *Human Resource Management Review, 21*(2), 123–136. doi:10.1016/j.hrmr.2010.09.004

Haines, V. Y. III, & St-Onge, S. (2012). Performance management effectiveness: Practices or context? *International Journal of Human Resource Management, 23*(6), 1158–1175. doi:10.1080/09585192.2011.561230

Kagaari, J. R., Munene, J. C., & Ntayi, J. M. (2010). Performance management practices, information and communication technology (ICT) adoption and managed performance. *Quality Assurance in Education, 18*(2), 106–125. doi:10.1108/09684881011035330

Kivistö, J., Pekkola, E., & Lyytinen, A. (2017). The influence of performance-based management on teaching and research performance of Finnish senior academics. *Tertiary Education and Management, 23*(3), 260–275. doi:10.1080/13583883.2017.1328529

Latham, G. P., Almost, J., Mann, S., & Moore, C. (2005). New developments in performance management. *Organizational Dynamics*, *34*(1), 77–87. doi:10.1016/j.orgdyn.2004.11.001

Lewis, T., Marginson, S., & Snyder, I. (2005). The network university? Technology, culture and organisational complexity in contemporary higher education. *Higher Education Quarterly*, *59*(1), 56–75. doi:10.1111/j.1468-2273.2005.00281.x

Martin, G., & Reddington, M. (2010). Theorizing the links between e-HR and strategic HRM: A model, case illustration and reflections. *International Journal of Human Resource Management*, *21*(10), 1553–1574. doi:10.1080/09585192.2010.500483

Plaček, M., Nemec, J., Ochrana, F., Půček, M., Křápek, M., & Špaček, D. (2020). Do performance management schemes deliver results in the public sector? Observations from the Czech Republic. *Public Money & Management*, 1–10.

Pulakos, E. D. (2009). *Performance management: A new approach for driving business results*. John Wiley & Sons.

SHRM. (2019). *Managing employee performance*. Author.

KEY TERMS AND DEFINITIONS

Digitalization: The process of computerization of the process, which includes use of technology, internet, etc. It leads to reduced paperwork.

Elevated Performance: The stage where the performance exceeds the previous or the expected performance. The performance delivered is of higher quality.

Performance Indicators or Key Performance Indicators (PI/KPI): The criteria based on which the performance of the individual is measured.

Performance Management (PM): A tool to regulate the performance of the employees to achieve the overall objectives of the organization with respect to predefined goals and objectives and thus evaluate the performance of the individuals and provide feedback.

Performance Management System (PMS): The tools and techniques employed by the organization to appraise the performance of the employees. It is liable to communicate and allocate accountability and supervise the performance of the employees.

Transparency: Transparency refers to the degree of openness allowed to access the information to the employees.

Chapter 10
Digital Technologies and the Intangible Cultural Heritage of the Rural Destination

Aditya Ranjan
https://orcid.org/0000-0003-1304-5489
Jamia Millia Islamia, India

Priya Chaturvedi
Jiwaji University, India

ABSTRACT

Rural tourism continues to evolve toward an experience economy. Along with rural tourism activities, travelers often enjoy intangible heritage as part of their cultural tourism experience. Digital technologies could aid in the development of online preservation, learning tool, and a set of guidelines based on intangible cultural heritage to assist small rural businesses in designing and promoting sustainable tourist products. The digital revolution has the potential to foster mutual learning among tour operators, tourists, and host communities, in addition to boosting access to cultural material and making it publicly available. However, there is a lack of digital technology in creating a favorable environment to promote the inheritance and enhancement of the value of intangible cultural heritage through rural tourism development. Moreover, the digital optimization of intangible cultural heritage and rural tourism development needs special attention. The chapter provides insights on digitalizing intangible cultural heritage and rural tourism for sustainable destination development.

DOI: 10.4018/978-1-7998-9194-9.ch010

INTRODUCTION

Rural tourism continues to evolve toward an experience economy, and the visitor experience is increasingly becoming the focal focus of innovative tourism company activities (Loureiro, 2014). Occasionally combined with rural tourism, travellers often enjoy intangible heritage items as part of their cultural tourism experience (Soeroso & Susilo, 2014). Intangible cultural heritage is a significant and meaningful aspect of the tourist industry since it reflects the highest level of human cultural heritage (Zhang et al., 2018). Moreover, in addition to traditional intangible cultural heritage, there is a need for continual innovation and new products to meet tourist demand for new experiences and the evolution of rural destinations. However, the cultural heritage of a destination is at risk, especially when the vital cultural asset is not preserved because of rapid rural tourism development (Ma et al., 2021). Globalization and societal change are also posing risks to cultural heritage preservation, as these factors contribute to the present younger generation's apathy in learning about knowledge and their cultural heritage.

In the digital era, tourism growth towards heritage-based locations needs technical features, smart methods, and digital humanities support to deliver knowledge and experiences regarding cultural values and meanings (Roque & Forte, 2017). Digital technologies could aid in the development of online preservation, learning tool, and a set of guidelines based on intangible cultural heritage to assist small rural businesses in the design and promotion of sustainable tourist products. The digital revolution has the potential to foster mutual learning among tour operators, tourists, and host communities, in addition to boosting access to cultural material and making it publicly available. Furthermore, several examples demonstrate how creativity, particularly digital technology, might promote and transmit intangible cultural heritage to future generations. Host communities have used digital technologies for several objectives, including collecting the "essentials" of a type of performance, evaluating, and demonstrating relevant parts of the intangible cultural heritage, and building, modelling, and delivering tailored learning activities. Local governments have realized that the combination of ICH protection and tourism development is a harmonious way to protect and exploit local heritage (Zhang et al., 2018). However, there is a dearth in using digital technologies to create a favourable environment to promote the inheritance and enhancement of the value of intangible cultural heritage through rural tourism development. Moreover, the digital optimization of intangible cultural heritage and rural tourism development needs special attention. The chapter provides insights on digitalizing intangible cultural heritage and rural tourism for sustainable destination development. The chapter begins by explaining key concepts like rural tourism, cultural heritage, intangible cultural heritage, and the role of digital technologies at the rural destination. The chapter further explains how digital technologies help preserve the intangible cultural heritage and the challenges rural destinations face in implementing digital technology for preservation. Later, the authors have provided recommendations and suggestions to implement digital technologies for preservation of intangible cultural heritage of rural destination.

BACKGROUND

Everywhere globally, various destinations might elicit strong emotional responses among tourists (Giudici et al., 2013). However, rural destinations have an intangible quality that drives the imagination of many tourists. In rural communities with a wide range of traditions and practices, culture serves as an important conduit for the acquisition of knowledge and skills by both tourists and the locals and the accumulation of assets for local livelihoods (Ma et al., 2021). Since most rural destinations are isolated from the rest of the world, rural places have been able to retain their intangible cultural and natural treasures. Therefore rural destinations have the opportunity to develop a tourist offer that is based on real experiences, thanks to intangible cultural heritage that has its origins in the distant past (Giudici et al., 2013; Prohaska, 1995).

The modern tourist is known for regularly seeking new experiences (Giudici et al., 2013). More specifically, modern tourists are interested in learning about history, cultures, cooking habits, unique places that identify the countries they are visiting, and other factors that can make a vacation an emotionally and physically engaging experience (Grayson & Martinec, 2004). Visitors travelling to rural areas are drawn to the unique natural and cultural environments, allowing locals to engage in various tourism-related economic activities, such as tour guides, selling souvenirs, and managing homestays and farmhouses (Su et al., 2016).

RURAL TOURISM

Rural tourism is defined as a business endeavour in which rural host/s open their property or properties to paying guests/tourists who spend most of their time engaged in leisure activities on a farm, ranch, or countryside residence located in a predominantly rural environment (Fleischer & Pizam, 1997). It has emerged as a key driver of economic development and diversification in rural areas and a force for poverty reduction and local economic development (Hall, 2004; Ma et al., 2021). Rural tourism can widen livelihood channels and increase the value of household livelihood assets in both developed and developing countries (Mbaiwa, 2011; Qian et al., 2017). For example, as pointed out by Mbaiwa in (2011), rural tourism has changed traditional livelihood methods in the Okavango Delta, Botswana, such as hunting, farming, and livestock raising, into tourism activities, which has resulted in an improvement in the livelihood status of households as a whole.

Tourists visiting the countryside can participate in a variety of activities and attractions. Rural locations are thought to have much open space and moderate to low tourism development. It allows visitors to experience a rural and environmentally friendly natural setting environment (Nicolaides, 2020; Roberts, L. & Hall, 2001). Clean air, calm, ecologically friendly or organic and natural cuisine, proximity to nature, serene existence, awareness of rural lifestyle, and suitable living circumstances at home are important factors in rural tourism (Shaken et al., 2020). Rural tourism also provides a platform to the tourists for recreation, nature protection, involvement in traditional agricultural techniques, experiencing village/rural life, cultural place and activities, history, and heritage of locals (Nicolaides, 2020).

The researchers discovered that commodified cultural items, both in material and non-material forms, are the most important element of rural tourism development because they provide residents with the resources they need to run small businesses and create more jobs (Mitchell & Shannon, 2018). According to Horn & Tahi (2009), people's cultural knowledge allows them to offer distinctive tourism products, attract visitors, and reap economic rewards; local cultural patterns also influence company development by influencing how social networks operate. Samsudin & Maliki (2015) mentions that the cultural events and ceremonies (e.g., traditional dancing, singing, and cooking) conducted for tourists boost future generations' quality of life in rural Malaysia by enhancing tourists' lives. Even though households' excessive reliance on rural tourism may result in the extinction of certain traditional livelihood activities, rural tourism can bring economic benefits that enable them to maintain their way of life (Ma et al., 2021).

Rural Tourism and Cultural Heritage

Cultural legacy is a coordinated interaction including society, conventions, and values that can be traced back thousands of years (Giudici et al., 2013). Symbols, technologies, and things serve as tangible manifestations of underlying norms and values, and as such, they help form a symbiotic link between the tangible and ethereal worlds. "Culture" is defined as how people think, live, and engage in activities that are passed down from one generation to the next (Isa et al., 2018). Culture also refers to a way of doing things or being; it reflects a community's knowledge, laws, beliefs, morals, conventions, art, or any other capabilities necessary by humans in the community (Manaf, 2007; Matarasso, 2001). Hence, society's culture can be viewed as the ideas, values, and conventions that bind the people together, uniting the past, present, and future (Liew, 2005).

Heritage can be described as something significant that previous generations passed on to their children and that future generations will inherit (Isa et al., 2018). In other words, heritage is commonly defined as the essential components of the past and has been passed down to succeeding generations (Manaf & Ismail, 2010). Heritage is defined as information and competence that has been passed down through generations employing life and belief, and it is also sometimes referred to as the total memory of the community (Isa et al., 2018). Also, it is a valuable item owned by someone or a group of individuals tasked with keeping the item safe and secure. Further, one of the primary characteristics of a distinct and identifiable national identity is the inheritance of one's heritage (Petronela, 2016). Cultural heritage represents all civilizations' spiritual and intellectual wealth (Idris et al., 2016). Aside from representing a person's identity, it is an essential depiction of civilization and nation (Isa et al., 2018).

Rural tourism development is known to bring changes the quality of life in host or local communities. Researchers suggests that tourist-host relationships and tourism business development are two significant variables affecting host community quality of life (Mbaiwa, 2011). In rural communities with a wide range of traditional practices and culture serves as an important conduit for local farmers' acquisition of knowledge and skills (Daskon & McGregor, 2012). It also leads to the accumulation of assets for their livelihoods. Moreover, culture is the most important factor in the preservation of the natural environment (Samsudin & Maliki, 2015). A well-preserved culture is a useful resource for rural tourism development (Ma et al., 2021). Traditions such as ancient dwellings and farm tools made in the local style and intangible cultural elements such as traditional norms and values serve as unique tourist attractions that generate economic benefits while maintaining household livelihood activities (MacDonald & Jolliffe, 2003). Likeng village is one such example where the use of traditional Hui-style architecture and carving from the national intangible cultural property has significantly increased the attraction of tourists and the competitiveness of the hamlet, consequently raising the residents' living standards (Ma et al., 2021).

Rural tourism has evolved in reaction to post-modernist social norms and changes in tourist spending patterns, with traditional rural lives and customs emerging as the focal point of the rural tourism experience (Frochot, 2005). It is a focused exhibition of people's spiritual beliefs, aesthetic preferences, ethical relationships, and living practices that characterizes traditional culture in rural areas (Ma et al., 2021). The exploration and utilization of culture have emerged as critical features in developing rural tourism at a destination because local culture frequently acts as the source of a destination's charming and distinctive characteristics (Garau, 2015). It is necessary for tourists to consume rural material cultures, such as exquisite landscapes and architecture and farm life and food, to fully appreciate the location they are visiting, experience it, and comprehend it (Mitchell & Shannon, 2018). It is the most direct way to get a feel for what rural tourism is all about. According to Cheer et al. (2013), an additional cultural asset in the countryside that can provide travellers with authentic cultural experiences is rural institutional culture (including traditional festivals, folk activities, etiquette and traditions, and power systems, among other things). Visitors familiar with the rural spiritual culture (such as village morphology, the art of site selection, living practices, and oral arts) will be better able to recognize and understand the meanings associated with a community (Ma et al., 2021). The most profound degree of rural tourism is reached through the consumption of rural spiritual culture (MacDonald & Jolliffe, 2003). These types of rural cultures serve as essential resources for developing tourism in their respective regions (Ma et al., 2021).

Intangible cultural heritage

In human groups and communities, intangible cultural heritage is defined as the living culture of the community (Giudici et al., 2013). The term "Intangible Cultural Heritage" refers to a variety of traditional cultural expressions that people of all ethnic groups have passed down through generations and regarded as part of their cultural heritage, as well as the substance and locations associated with the traditional cultural expressions (Zhang et al., 2018). The Cultural Heritage Convention defines intangible cultural heritage as practices, representations, expressions, knowledge, skills, and the instruments, objects, artefacts, and cultural spaces associated with them that communities, groups, and, in some cases, individuals recognize as part of their cultural heritage (Isa et al., 2018). Intangible cultural heritage includes oral traditions and expressions, such as language; performing arts, social habits, rituals, and festivals; science and habits relating to nature and the world; traditional skills; and other forms of knowledge that cannot be easily quantified (UNESCO, 2003).

Intangible cultural heritage manifests two distinct characteristics: one is enduring and maintaining the core values in their unchanging nature, while the other is dynamic and changes in response to the historical and social context in which it is found (Giudici et al., 2013). Intangible cultural heritage also includes human acts or motions that may be seen, touched, perceived, inhaled, or heard when performed or exist, but also such heritage which could no longer be experienced when they are no longer performed or exist (Isa et al., 2018). Among its many characteristics are its dynamic nature, inherent fragility, and personal relationship with its creators and bearers, as well as the sense of self-identification felt by communities, groups, and people (Lenzerini, 2011). As a result of human connection with their environment, intangible cultural heritage refers to information and know-how that has been passed down from generation to generation (Giudici et al., 2013). Furthermore, communities and groups constantly recreate intangible cultural heritage according to their surroundings, interactions with nature, and history, providing a sense of identity and continuity and promoting respect for cultural diversity and human ingenuity (Isa et al., 2018).

Alternatively, the intangible cultural heritage can be considered a wider framework within which the physical or tangible cultural heritage takes shape and acquires importance (Giudici et al., 2013). As a result, intangible cultural heritage builds linkages with tangible cultural heritage, serving as a key to understanding and interpreting it. It is possible to view the intangible cultural heritage as a framework for the entire environment it interacts with, including both the social and natural environments (Giudici et al., 2013). Understanding intangible cultural legacy among diverse societies fosters mutual respect for how a community lives, thereby ensuring the future sustainability of intangible cultural heritage (Isa et al., 2018). The reason is that intangible cultural heritage can bridge these relationships with tangible heritage, and, as a result, it constitutes a framework that allows its interpretation (Giudici et al., 2013). The intangible cultural heritage, in this context, appears to serve as the interpretive key for the community and its surrounding environment. However, intangible cultural heritage is critical for preserving cultural variety in an era of increasing globalization.

Digital Technologies and Rural Destination

As a tool to encourage promotional activities, digital technologies can also promote better organization within the rural tourism supply chain, with all small enterprises interconnected in a network of micro-businesses (Inversini et al., 2020). Technology advancements continue to accelerate at an alarming rate, giving rise to digital society (Osin et al., 2021). Information has become a critical strategic resource for nations due to the rapid development of the modern era (Gao et al., 2021). On a worldwide scale, the use of information to foster economic development and improve urban and rural infrastructure is becoming more prevalent (Adamowicz, 2020). In this context, the word Information and Communications Technology (ICT) is defined broadly to include any digital information and communications technologies available to the public and to which they have access (Gan et al., 2018).

Digital technologies significantly impact national politics, economy, society, culture, and everyday life in many countries (Cheuk et al., 2018). Initially, internet marketing was focused on advertising and selling on the internet rather than leveraging the internet throughout the entire marketing process (Laxmi, 2016). However, due to the recent development in digital technologies focusing on integrating the internet into the overall marketing plan, this trend is changing. In rural destination marketing, the internet's influence is very new and is evolving rapidly (Laxmi, 2016). In addition to increasing tourist numbers, effective marketing of rural areas can result in visitors being more satisfied, and when they return to a particular location, they are more likely to recommend it to others (Murphy et al., 2007). Digital marketing has been recognized as a cost-effective and efficient technique of giving key information to target clients (Cheuk et al., 2018). Digital marketing thereby could minimize the physical hurdles of transmission of information to the intended consumer, a significant element of rural tourism (Cheuk et al., 2018).

Tourism is intended to be of significant economic and social value to rural communities, particularly to generate employment/income and much-needed restoration (Liu, 2006). Tourism resource optimization has evolved into a major component of tourism planning, integrating natural, human, and material resources to suit tourist needs and increase satisfaction levels through the three-dimensional depiction of genuine picturesque areas (Zhang et al., 2018). However, a transition has taken place in the rural economy, particularly among the young generation, from traditional or conventional systems to the digital economy or digital technologies (Osin et al., 2021). The advancement of technology increases at a breakneck pace, giving rise to the digital rural society. Moreover, digitalization would promote economic development, which is critical for rural communities (Gao et al., 2021). In addition, the use of digital technologies in homestays has provided the community with increased access to human capital in the form of increased opportunities for education, training in digital technologies, and the rejuvenation of skills training in cultural products, all of which have contributed to a more conscious use of digital technologies, particularly the internet (fixed-line and mobile) (Gan et al., 2018). Members of the community have had to learn how to use the numerous technology platforms necessary for the operation of homestay establishments (e.g., Booking, Agoda, Airbnb). Furthermore, digital technologies could help in establishing a powerful digital governance network at the rural destination. However, The historical context of the information technology revolution and the mix of generations are important considerations for any rural tourism destination (Osin et al., 2021).

A rural destination could make better use of resources by implementing digital and communication technologies. Rural communities could utilize digital technologies to preserve the intangible cultural heritage that ultimately serves as the destination's tourism product (Figure 1). Every day in the information era brings new developments in digital technologies such as the Internet, big data, the Internet of Things, cloud computing, artificial intelligence, and 5G, which are constantly evolving (Gao et al., 2021). Beyond communications, 5G implementation has the potential to promote the innovation and development of new businesses and services, as well as improve and speed up rural destination connectivity (Istanti, 2021). One distinguishing element of digital technologies is the widespread usage of chat applications, the most popular of which is WhatsApp, which almost everyone uses. It appears that such chat applications are the primary communication platform for

Figure 1. Role of digital technologies in sustaining the intangible cultural heritage of a rural destination

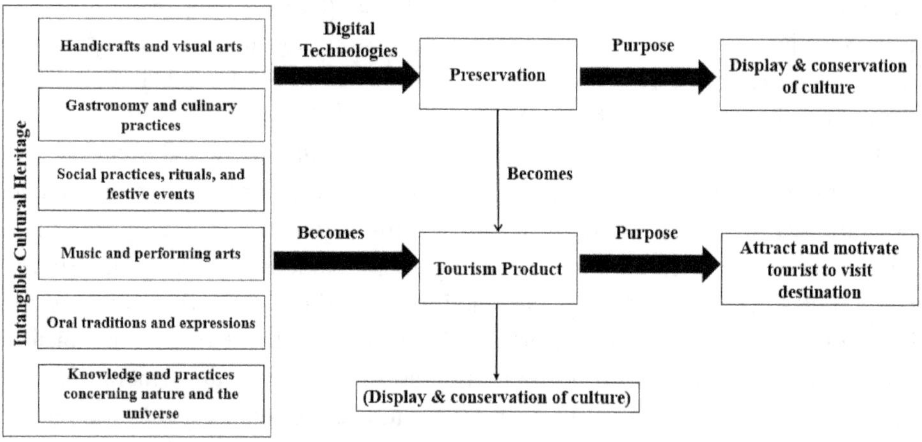

operations, logistics, and planning as well as some areas of communication with external parties and that they are supported by mobile and fixed-line broadband, as well as smartphones, according to the observations (Gan et al., 2018). Electronic messages floating on such chat applications can be considered a new medium of vernacular culture because certain aspects are intimately linked to intangible heritage and traditional communication.

Given that the young generation is extremely connected to technology, rural tourism stakeholders need to understand that technology is vital in determining how they travel. Because of the numerous sources of information available through social media platforms such as Facebook, YouTube, Instagram, and Telegram, these indications are well-represented (Osin et al., 2021). These technological advancements have, without question, had a huge impact on human needs and lifestyles (Entina et al., 2021). A better understanding of the young generation's travel behaviour, travel experiences, and life satisfaction on social media would aid in the clarification of the proposed theoretical linkages and the establishment of appealing rural tourism designations. Recent social media trends show that tourists are driven to visit authentic rural sites because they project an image of "being undiscovered and pristine." Expedia's survey is one of such examples where 52 percent of millennials evaluated experiencing authentic local culture as the "most essential" factor in their decision-making (Jyotsna & Maurya, 2019). Millennials and Gen Z are a generation that is adaptable and enjoys independence but not unbridled liberty (Osin et al., 2021). However, Generation Z is likely to have very different consumption habits from Millennials because they were born during a time when the economy was down (Entina et al., 2021). Understanding the link between travel preferences and life satisfaction can provide insight into improving existing services and policies to better support the young generation's well-being (Olsson et al., 2020).

Rural tourism strives to revitalize rural resources for local socio-economic benefits and environmental sustainability by involving and empowering local communities (Istanti, 2021). Community empowerment aims to increase tourism's competitiveness, which includes environmental support, policies, and conditions that foster it, as well as infrastructure and natural and cultural resources (Purnomo et al., 2020). Moreover, community empowerment promotes the economic capital that flows inside the social structure due to the character-building; as a result, it can be used as a foundation for pushing the economy towards the usefulness of the community's life (Ruastiti et al., 2020). In this way, communities thus save money and energy and improve the quality of services and lives (Gao et al., 2021). Increased competitiveness resulting from community empowerment is expected to improve rural tourism's sustainability, which in turn can benefit the rural community's welfare. Thus, it could be said that in order to improve tourism competitiveness, the community must be empowered to administer and provide excellent services that stimulate tourist satisfaction (Purnomo et al., 2020). Hence, it has become important for stakeholders that before a rural location is known on the tourism marketplace, travellers must be made aware of its presence and tourist potential before they visit (Cheuk et al., 2018).

ROLE OF DIGITAL TECHNOLOGIES IN PRESERVING INTANGIBLE CULTURAL HERITAGE

Preservation is defined as an action that protects cultural assets and historical artefacts (Isa et al., 2018). Preservation of intangible cultural heritage includes safeguarding oral traditions, performing arts, social practises, rituals, festive events, knowledge and traditions about nature and the universe, and knowledge and skills to manufacture traditional crafts. Cultural heritage preservation is important for four reasons: cultural memory, distance facilities, environmental variety, and economic benefits (Prompayuk & Chairattananon, 2016). The preservation of cultural heritage may conserve tangible stuff in physical form and can pass significant information and skills from previous generations to current and future generations. Hence it plays an important role in cultural memorials (Isa et al., 2018). Furthermore, cultural heritage preservation can help sustain interactions between humans, the environment, and community activities. The preservation of cultural heritage and the diversity of the environment as the local community's identity would keep local artefacts and artisans in line with the growth of a society. In terms of economic return, preservation can assist the community in two ways: saving money on new construction costs and becoming tourist attractions (Isa et al., 2018). However, due to its nonphysical nature, intangible cultural heritage is more restricted among the communities and hard to demonstrate in real life, which is a real challenge to preserve and prevent it from disappearing (Alivizatou-Barakou et al., 2017)

The rapid advancement of technology in recent years has demonstrated its importance in our daily lives, and this trend has contributed to an increase in the number of digital preservation activities in the historic domain (Isa et al., 2018). Digital technologies have evolved into the most remarkable platforms for cultural heritage preservation, communication, and social interaction. They have made it possible to compress enormous amounts of data into compact storage devices that could be preserved, stored and transported easily. While digital technologies are frequently seen as a threat to traditional expressions, they contribute significantly to preserving and transmitting intangible cultural heritage (Alivizatou-Barakou et al., 2017). One of the prominent reasons is that people who have a strong sense of their heritage or traditional cultures are more likely to accept technology and new ways of getting information and communicating without considering such adoption as a threat to their own cultures.

Digital preservation technologies are heavily used in the cultural heritage domain to preserve knowledge, manuscript collections, and objects (Prompayuk & Chairattananon, 2016). Digital preservation initiatives have been carried out in many settings, with the majority of them relying on digital technology and mixed media to conserve and promote the cultures of indigenous people (Papangelis et al., 2016). Audio-visual documentation and digital and multimedia materials from the fields of information and communication technology are extremely beneficial for capturing and gathering information about intangible heritage expressions (Alivizatou-Barakou et al., 2017). Interestingly, researchers and scholars have been using technologies such as photography and sound recording technology to record and preserve a wide range of intangible cultural heritage (such as cultural relics and archaeological discoveries) since the 1970s (Cozzani et al., 2017). The Digital Michelangelo project is one of such examples, which began in 1990 at Standard University in the United States and was later expanded to include other institutions, establishing the precedent for digital protection of cultural material (Zhang et al., 2018). Moreover, technologies such as 3D visualization and interaction technology further overcome the challenges in the preserving the intangible cultural heritage (Alivizatou-Barakou et al., 2017).

At the moment, digital protection of intangible cultural heritage resources in many countries is increasingly becoming a significant way of protecting intangible cultural heritage resources of the country (Zhang et al., 2018). In some countries, indigenous peoples and communities have made creative use of modern digital technologies to preserve intangible heritage on a local level. Traditional Music of the

World is an example of such a project that incorporates traditional music recordings and makes them available to a global audience to raise awareness of traditional music (Alivizatou-Barakou et al., 2017). Ethnomusicologists made the recordings in the field and subsequently duplicated them on vinyl and CD, along with relevant photographs. With the fast expansion of information technology worldwide, many governments, including the United Nations Educational, Scientific, and Cultural Organization (UNESCO), have fiercely pushed the digital protection of intangible cultural heritage (Severo & Venturini, 2016). Similarly, The EU-funded Cultural Capital Counts project focuses on intangible heritage resources such as living traditions, knowledge, and talents, more directly related to intangible heritage and local development (Alivizatou-Barakou et al., 2017). It aims to enable the positive development of six Central European regions by focusing on intangible heritage resources such as living traditions, knowledge, and talents.

Moreover, a large number of digital preservation projects are currently underway to prevent the extinction of indigenous cultural heritage. The semantic multimedia analysis, in particular, is used to map the performing arts (e.g. singing, dancing, etc.) and associated low-level features derived from the signal of the utilized sensors in order to capture significant aspects that identify the studied art (e.g. singing or dancing style) (Alivizatou-Barakou et al., 2017). Similarly, Singing voice synthesis (SVS) is a subset of text-to-speech (TTS) technology that acts as an effective tool in preserving oral traditions. SVS generates a synthetic interpretation of a song based on its text and musical score. For a long time, SVS has been a research subject, and each decade has seen a significant technological advancement (Alivizatou-Barakou et al., 2017). Similarly, game-like applications could also be a powerful tool for intangible cultural heritage transmission. Such applications follow a well-established trend in the technology-enhanced learning field that encourages the use of digital games to sustain learning and training in various educational fields, intending to empower constructive, experiential, self-regulated learning and increase user engagement and motivation (Alivizatou-Barakou et al., 2017).

Historically, cultural and nature-based experiences and preferences have been generally evaluated using discovered and stated preference methods (e.g., social surveys), which are frequently expensive and do not cover sufficient spatial and temporal space (Di Minin et al., 2015). Hence, conservationists are increasingly using digital technology and large-scale public data to monitor and manage nature's contributions to humanity to overcome these constraints (Richards & Friess, 2015). Moreover, the usage of social media data has gained particular attention under this "digital conservation" paradigm (Vaz et al., 2020). For example, content analysis of georeferenced photographs from social media platforms (e.g., Flickr and Instagram) can be used to infer aspects of nature appreciation (Oteros-Rozas et al., 2018), to track visitors' movements, or to identify visitor preferences in protected areas (Vaz et al., 2020).

Geographic Information Systems (GIS) and multisource remote sensing are useful tools for describing intangible culture and nature-based perceptions and preferences (Vaz et al., 2020). Combining georeferenced social media photographs with Earth observations can help us better grasp nature's cultural contributions to humanity. For example, Tenerelli et al. (2016) discovered social preferences for several cultural ecosystem services based on a set of GIS variables and Flickr photo series. Similarly, Van Berkel et al. in 2018 assessed landscape quality underlying cultural recreation using Panoramic photos and high-resolution Light Detection and Ranging (LiDAR); and Vaz et al. in 2019 used a combination of satellite images and LiDAR to assess landscape quality underlying cultural recreation. While mobile technologies have also made significant contributions to documenting intangible indigenous cultural heritage, their impact has been limited. It could be partly due to stakeholders focus on capturing heritage "snapshots" rather than engaging with those they are documenting over long periods, and it is also due to the constantly changing nature of such traditions (Papangelis et al., 2016). However, it could be difficult to create meaningful intangible cultural experiences in virtual worlds, especially when communicating the experiential qualities of the environment (Mitchenson, 2015). Likewise, meaningful and immersive interactions are lacking in today's digital cultural communications, characterized by an emphasis on quantity rather than quality in virtual spaces (Carrozzino et al., 2011).

CHALLENGES IN IMPLEMENTING DIGITAL TECHNOLOGIES IN RURAL DESTINATION

Currently, rural destination data collection, classification, processing, and analysis are theoretical and experimental (Gao et al., 2021). Due to the restrictions and complexity of gathering information about intangible cultural heritage, the digital theoretical and technical system of quick inheritance of rural destination information has certain challenges.

- **Rural information infrastructure construction is not yet perfect.**

The internet is essential to the promotion and development of digital technologies. However, information infrastructure is still lacking in rural destinations, especially distant ones (Gao et al., 2021). Moreover, the communication network signal in remote places is weak, and the optical fibre network is not entirely covered. So, expediting infrastructure construction is crucial to building digital rural destinations. Improving rural Internet infrastructure and speeding up the development of broadband, mobile, digital TV, and next-generation Internet would help rural areas digitally preserve the intangible cultural heritage of the rural destination.

- **Obstacles to rural data collection, transmission, and usage.**

Information and data on various areas are expanding in rural digital development. However, rural hardware restrictions and disparities in people's quality mean intangible heritage data collecting is non-standard and incomplete. Data transfer issues include bar segmentation, latency, and string modification. In the absence of a corresponding information exchange platform, all data transmission and sharing in rural construction is delayed (Gao et al., 2021). It further causes hindrance in intangible cultural heritage digital preservation and information sharing errors.

- **Inadequate technologies to capture emotional recognition.**

Cultural expressions allow us to predict, understand, and link emotions across cultures. These inclinations include an appraisal, action readiness, expression, instrumental behaviour, and regulatory mechanisms. One of the most critical concerns using digital technologies such as affecting computing (AC), brings forward the challenge of Emotion recognition (ER) (Alivizatou-Barakou et al., 2017). It is crucial to the attempt to integrate computers, and more broadly technology, with the ability to connect with humans by communicating signs that propose and display emotional intelligence-related attitudes.

- **Lack of talent and awareness of rural digitalization.**

Although agricultural and rural electronic digitalization is becoming more formalized, rural populations lack a thorough understanding of digital technology and economics (Gao et al., 2021). Local's understanding of digital rural development is weak. As a result of the wide economic disparity between villages and cities, villages lack digital technical personnel, contemporary rural data processing personnel, and information service personnel, which further pose a challenge to preserving intangible cultural heritage.

- **Inadequate technological support for rural destination data.**

Rural destination development is inextricably linked to digital technology, facilitated by big data, the Internet of Things (IoT), and cloud platforms. However, rural destinations face challenges in employing whole-process big data technology, including data collecting, data administration, data sharing, data analysis, data application, and data security, to extract meaningful information from vast data and apply it to rural development practice (Gao et al., 2021).

SUGGESTION AND RECOMMENDATION

The integration and diversification of tourism prospects that can result from linking rural tourism with cultural tourism can make the tourist destination as a whole a competitive destination (Garau, 2015). Indeed, rural areas lag behind urban areas and huge internet firms in developing and deploying digital technology. However, the application of robots and artificial intelligence technology, as well as big data analysis, economic sharing, social media, and other fast-growing technologies, might raise consumer interest in evaluating and utilizing rural tourism products offered by tourism players (Purnomo et al., 2020). EEG-based emotional recognition (ER) is an example of digital technologies that could be used to learn more about how intangible cultural hierarchies in different folklore cultures treat or ignore affective aspects and study rare singers and their audience (Alivizatou-Barakou et al., 2017). It would allow people to identify the affective space of such folklore cultures. Similarly, motion capture can be used for precise documentation of hand and finger movement throughout the creation process in the case of craftsmanship and pottery (Alivizatou-Barakou et al., 2017).

Rural intangible cultural heritage data production and exploitation should be included in the national strategy for information development at the national level. It is critical to accelerate the digital transformation of the rural tourism industrial chain and promote digital technology's penetration at rural destinations throughout the industrial chain (Gao et al., 2021). Instead of just relying on documenting intangible cultural heritage at rural destinations, the integration of technology could result in a novel approach to intangible heritage preservation (Alivizatou-Barakou et al., 2017). It is necessary to develop a three-phase strategy of preservation, promotion, and growth for digital preservation projects of the intangible cultural heritage of indigenous cultures to achieve the goals. The strategy includes 1) documentation, 2) translation into technology, and 3) a set of guidelines for the development of digital technologies (Papangelis et al., 2016). The documentation phase would include creating materials and documenting tangible and intangible cultures significant to the represented rural communities. The translation phase involves exploring the modes of expression of intangible cultural heritage concerning the technology and the rural destination's habit. The third phase is including indigenous peoples in the co-creation process of technology based on their lives, practises, ways of living, thinking, and traditions. Such a preservation process of intangible cultural heritage could be accomplished through comprehensive ethnography and various direct and indirect knowledge acquisition strategies at rural destinations (Papangelis et al., 2016).

Although technology cannot replace human connection, there is a tremendous opportunity to establish activities that chronicle and preserve knowledge about rare songs, dances, compositions, and craftsmanship while also ensuring the transmission of this knowledge to future generations (Alivizatou-Barakou et al., 2017). Additionally, digital technologies create a new and easily accessible arena for preserving key aspects of intangible cultural legacy and e-communication, allowing rural communities to communicate, engage in discourse and debate, and contribute to their cultural traditions. The digital record and translation of culture and traditions within their specific environment would entail the fabrication of materials and the documentation of the tangible and intangible culture that is significant to the communities. Moreover, to overcome the existing rural talent deficit, there is a need to create a talent engine for rural rejuvenation, actively introduce foreign talent while fostering local talent (Gao et al., 2021), and help preserve the intangible cultural heritage of the rural destination.

CONCLUSION

Cultural resources are property, as is natural, physical, financial, human, and social capital for community groups (for example, traditional knowledge, skills and customs, building systems, beliefs systems, and societal structures) (Ma et al., 2021). Rural tourism can help local inhabitants and improve the sustainable livelihoods of households. Moreover, rural and cultural tourism could be linked for creating a more competitive tourist destination (Garau, 2015). Rural tourism destinations and enterprises can use digital technologies to establish a sort of "virtual size" in which even minuscule businesses can market their offerings, get bookings, and eventually manage the value chain of their business (Gan et al., 2018).

Knowledge of intangible cultural heritage needs to be digitalized to preserve the information and skills of intangible cultural heritage in a long-term and systematic manner (Isa et al., 2018). Protecting and transferring intangible cultural heritage through digital technologies has shown to be a beneficial and economically viable solution (Mitchenson, 2015). However, it is critical to guarantee that such heritage is passed down to future generations. It is important to stimulate the weak links of rural information infrastructure to promote intangible cultural heritage digital building at rural destinations. Such digital buildings could be constructed based on better overall planning and improved policies and procedures (Gao et al., 2021). It is possible to further tap into the enormous potential of informatization in rural revitalization by developing digital rural construction. Such digital transformation is conducive to driving the modernization of rural areas with digital guidance and preservation of intangible cultural heritage.

On the other hand, it is not easy to develop digital rural construction without first establishing a solid foundation of intangible cultural heritage in rural revitalization. For future generations, cultural legacy must be conserved and protected. It is important to maintain a community's heritage since it reflects the identity of that community (Isa et al., 2018). Additionally, intangible cultural heritage is an important subject that requires protection in addition to tangible cultural heritage. When it comes to preserving this priceless heritage in the age of digital technology, digital preservation is one of the most effective approaches (Isa et al., 2018). By fostering a digital-electronic and online culture that disseminates offline legacies, digital technologies have the potential to transform the intangible cultural heritage of rural destinations in both a formal and informal manner.

However, digital technologies frequently center on and revolve around tangible heritage in modern heritage settings. Due to budget constraints, intangible parts of history are sometimes overlooked (Mitchenson, 2015). Traditions and rituals that were prominent throughout past generations are now at risk of disappearing if the ageing population can no longer pass on their teachings. A great deal of concern exists over digitizing intangible cultural heritage using digital media and mobile technologies. However, problems remain regarding how intangible cultural heritage content should be presented and which media and technology are most suited to conserve it for future generations. Because of a lack of digital preservation of intangible cultural heritage, more efforts must be made to preserve the heritage from fading and becoming extinct. Moreover, another concern is whether the technology would replace human interaction to transmit intangible cultural heritage. As the world becomes more reliant on digital resources, rural tourism stakeholders have a chance to establish a platform that facilitates the transmission of traditional knowledge and skills while addressing the concerns mentioned above.

REFERENCES

Adamowicz, M. (2020). *The "Smart Village" as a Way to Achieve Sustainable Development in Rural Areas of Poland.* Academic Press.

Alivizatou-Barakou, M., Kitsikidis, A., Tsalakanidou, F., Dimitropoulos, K., Giannis, C., Nikolopoulos, S., Al Kork, S., Denby, B., Buchman, L., Adda-Decker, M., Pillot-Loiseau, C., Tillmane, J., Dupont, S., Picart, B., Pozzi, F., Ott, M., Erdal, Y., Charisis, V., Hadjidimitriou, S., . . . Grammalidis, N. (2017). Intangible Cultural Heritage and New Technologies: Challenges and Opportunities for Cultural Preservation and Development. In Mixed Reality and Gamification for Cultural Heritage (pp. 129–158). Springer International Publishing. doi:10.1007/978-3-319-49607-8_5

Carrozzino, M., Scucces, A., Leonardi, R., Evangelista, C., & Bergamasco, M. (2011). Virtually preserving the intangible heritage of artistic handicraft. *Journal of Cultural Heritage*, *12*(1), 82–87. doi:10.1016/j.culher.2010.10.002

Cheer, J. M., Reeves, K. J., & Laing, J. H. (2013). Tourism and traditional culture: Land diving in vanuatu. *Annals ofTourism Research*, *43*(xx), 435–455. doi:10.1016/j.annals.2013.06.005

Cheuk, S., Atang, A., Chiun, L. M., & Ramayah, T. (2018). Barriers to digital marketing adoption at remote rural tourism destinations in Sarawak: An exploratory study. *IACSIT International Journal of Engineering and Technology*, *7*(2), 86–90. doi:10.14419/ijet.v7i2.29.13135

Cozzani, G., Pozzi, F., Dagnino, F., Katos, A., & Katsouli, E. (2017). Innovative technologies for intangible cultural heritage education and preservation: The case of i-Treasures. *Personal and Ubiquitous Computing*, *21*(2), 253–265. doi:10.100700779-016-0991-z

Daskon, C., & McGregor, A. (2012). Cultural Capital and Sustainable Livelihoods in Sri Lanka's Rural Villages: Towards Culturally Aware Development. *The Journal of Development Studies*, *48*(4), 549–563. doi:10.1080/00220388.2011.604413

Di Minin, E., Tenkanen, H., & Toivonen, T. (2015). Prospects and challenges for social media data in conservation science. *Frontiers in Environmental Science*, *3*(SEP), 1–6. doi:10.3389/fenvs.2015.00063

Entina, T., Karabulatova, I., Kormishova, A., Ekaterinovskaya, M., & Troyanskaya, M. (2021). Tourism industry management in the global transformation: Meeting the needs of generation z. *Polish Journal of Management Studies*, *23*(2), 130–148. doi:10.17512/pjms.2021.23.2.08

Fleischer, A., & Pizam, A. (1997). Rural tourism in Israel. *Tourism Management*, *18*(6), 367–372. doi:10.1016/S0261-5177(97)00034-4

Frochot, I. (2005). A benefit segmentation of tourists in rural areas: A Scottish perspective. *Tourism Management*, *26*(3), 335–346. doi:10.1016/j.tourman.2003.11.016

Gan, S. W., Inversini, A., & Rega, I. (2018). Tourism, Development and Digital Technologies: Insights from Malaysian Homestays. In Information and Communication Technologies in Tourism 2018 (Vol. 1, pp. 52–63). Springer International Publishing. doi:10.1007/978-3-319-72923-7_5

Gao, X., Guo, X., & Lo, T. (2021). Digital infrastructure - A potential method for rural revitalization through digitization of rural information. *Projections - Proceedings of the 26th International Conference of the Association for Computer-Aided Architectural Design Research in Asia, CAADRIA 2021, 2*, 699–708.

Garau, C. (2015). Perspectives on cultural and sustainable rural tourism in a smart region: The case study of Marmilla in Sardinia (Italy). *Sustainability (Switzerland)*, *7*(6), 6412–6434. doi:10.3390u7066412

Giudici, E., Melis, C., Dessì, S., & Francine Pollnow Galvao Ramos, B. (2013). Is intangible cultural heritage able to promote sustainability in tourism? *International Journal of Quality and Service Sciences*, *5*(1), 101–114. doi:10.1108/17566691311316275

Grayson, K., & Martinec, R. (2004). Consumer perceptions of iconicity and indexicality and their influence on assessments of authentic market offerings. *The Journal of Consumer Research*, *31*(2), 296–312. doi:10.1086/422109

Hall, D. (2004). Rural tourism development in southeastern Europe: Transition and the search for sustainability. *International Journal of Tourism Research*, *6*(3), 165–176. doi:10.1002/jtr.482

Horn, C., & Tahi, B. (2009). Some Cultural and Historical Factors Influencing Rural Maori Tourism Development In New Zealand. *Journal of Rural and Community Development*, *4*(1), 84–101.

Idris, M. Z., Mustaffa, N. B., & Yusoff, S. O. S. (2016). Preservation of Intangible Cultural Heritage Using Advance Digital Technology: Issues and Challenges. *Harmonia: Journal of Arts Research and Education*, *16*(1), 1. doi:10.15294/harmonia.v16i1.6353

Inversini, A., Rega, I., & Gan, S. W. (2020). E-Tourism as a Tool for Socio-economic Development. Handbook of E-Tourism, 1–16.

Isa, W. M. W., Zin, N. A. M., Rosdi, F., & Sarim, H. M. (2018). Digital preservation of intangible cultural heritage. *Indonesian Journal of Electrical Engineering and Computer Science, 12*(3), 1373–1379. doi:10.11591/ijeecs.v12.i3.pp1373-1379

Istanti, L. N. (2021). *Rural Tourism Perspectives on Digital Innovation: Small Enterprises in Indonesia*. Academic Press.

Jyotsna, J. H., & Maurya, U. K. (2019). Experiencing the real village–a netnographic examination of perceived authenticity in rural tourism consumption. *Asia Pacific Journal of Tourism Research, 24*(8), 750–762. doi:10.1080/10941665.2019.1630455

Laxmi, K. C. (2016). *Role of E-Marketing in Rural Tourism: A Case Study of Travel Agency of Kathmandu District* (Thesis). Faculty of Humanities and Social Sciences Department of Rural Development, Tribhuvan University.

Lenzerini, F. (2011). Intangible cultural heritage: The living culture of peoples. *European Journal of International Law, 22*(1), 101–120. doi:10.1093/ejil/chr006

Liew, C. L. (2005). Online cultural heritage exhibitions: A survey of information retrieval features. *Program, 39*(1), 4–24. doi:10.1108/00330330510578778

Liu, A. (2006). Tourism in rural areas: Kedah, Malaysia. *Tourism Management, 27*(5), 878–889. doi:10.1016/j.tourman.2005.05.007

Loureiro, S. M. C. (2014). The role of the rural tourism experience economy in place attachment and behavioral intentions. *International Journal of Hospitality Management, 40*, 1–9. doi:10.1016/j.ijhm.2014.02.010

Ma, X., Wang, R., Dai, M., & Ou, Y. (2021). The influence of culture on the sustainable livelihoods of households in rural tourism destinations. *Journal of Sustainable Tourism, 29*(8), 1235–1252. doi:10.1080/09669582.2020.1826497

MacDonald, R., & Jolliffe, L. (2003). Cultural rural tourism: Evidence from Canada. *Annals of Tourism Research, 30*(2), 307–322. doi:10.1016/S0160-7383(02)00061-0

Manaf, Z. A. (2007). The state of digitisation initiatives by cultural institutions in Malaysia: An exploratory survey. *Library Review, 56*(1), 45–60. doi:10.1108/00242530710722014

Manaf, Z. A., & Ismail, A. (2010). Malaysian cultural heritage at risk?: A case study of digitisation projects. *Library Review, 59*(2), 107–116. doi:10.1108/00242531011023862

Matarasso, F. (2001). *Recognising Culture: A series of briefing papers on culture and development*. Canadian Heritage.

Mbaiwa, J. E. (2011). Changes on traditional livelihood activities and lifestyles caused by tourism development in the Okavango Delta, Botswana. In Tourism Management (Vol. 32, Issue 5, pp. 1050–1060). doi:10.1016/j.tourman.2010.09.002

Mitchell, C. J. A., & Shannon, M. (2018). Exploring cultural heritage tourism in rural Newfoundland through the lens of the evolutionary economic geographer. *Journal of Rural Studies, 59*(May), 21–34. doi:10.1016/j.jrurstud.2017.12.020

Mitchenson, D. (2015). Safeguarding Intangible Cultural Heritage by Creating Meaningful Transmission Experiences. *International Journal of Heritage in the Digital Era*, *4*(1), 57–70. doi:10.1260/2047-4970.4.1.57

Murphy, L., Moscardo, G., & Benckendorff, P. (2007). Using brand personality to differentiate regional tourism destinations. *Journal of Travel Research*, *46*(1), 5–14. doi:10.1177/0047287507302371

Nicolaides, A. (2020). Sustainable ethical tourism (SET) and rural community involvement. *African Journal of Hospitality, Tourism and Leisure*, *9*(1), 1–16.

Olsson, L. E., Friman, M., Lättman, K., & Fujii, S. (2020). Travel and life satisfaction - From Gen Z to the silent generation. *Journal of Transport and Health, 18*(November). doi:10.1016/j.jth.2020.100894

Osin, R. F., Purwaningsih, N. K., & Anggayana, I. W. A. (2021). The Model of Development Tourism Village Through the Involvement of Millennial Generation in Bali. *International Journal of Multicultural and Multireligious Understanding*, 300–306.

Oteros-Rozas, E., Martín-López, B., Fagerholm, N., Bieling, C., & Plieninger, T. (2018). Using social media photos to explore the relation between cultural ecosystem services and landscape features across five European sites. *Ecological Indicators*, *94*, 74–86. doi:10.1016/j.ecolind.2017.02.009

Papangelis, K., Chamberlain, A., & Liang, H.-N. (2016). New directions for preserving intangible cultural heritage through the use of mobile technologies. *Proceedings of the 18th International Conference on Human-Computer Interaction with Mobile Devices and Services Adjunct*, 964–967. 10.1145/2957265.2962643

Petronela, T. (2016). The Importance of the Intangible Cultural Heritage in the Economy. *Procedia Economics and Finance, 39*(November), 731–736. doi:10.1016/S2212-5671(16)30271-4

Prohaska, S. S. (1995). Trends in cultural heritage tourism. In M. V. Conlin & T. Baum (Eds.), *Island tourism: management principles and practice* (pp. 33–52). Wiley.

Prompayuk, S., & Chairattananon, P. (2016). Preservation of Cultural Heritage Community: Cases of Thailand and Developed Countries. *Procedia: Social and Behavioral Sciences, 234*, 239–243. doi:10.1016/j.sbspro.2016.10.239

Purnomo, S., Rahayu, E. S., Riani, A. L., Suminah, S., & Udin, U. (2020). Empowerment model for sustainable tourism village in an emerging country. *Journal of Asian Finance. Economics and Business*, *7*(2), 261–270. doi:10.13106/jafeb.2020.vol7.no2.261

Qian, C., Sasaki, N., Jourdain, D., Kim, S. M., & Shivakoti, P. G. (2017). Local livelihood under different governances of tourism development in China – A case study of Huangshan mountain area. *Tourism Management*, *61*, 221–233. doi:10.1016/j.tourman.2017.01.006

Richards, D. R., & Friess, D. A. (2015). A rapid indicator of cultural ecosystem service usage at a fine spatial scale: Content analysis of social media photographs. *Ecological Indicators*, *53*, 187–195. doi:10.1016/j.ecolind.2015.01.034

Roberts, L., & Hall, D. (Eds.). (2001). *Rural tourism and recreation: Principles to practice*. CABI. doi:10.1079/9780851995403.0000

Roque, M. I., & Forte, M. J. (2017). Digital Strategies to a Local Cultural Tourism Development: Project e-Carnide. *International Journal of Cultural and Digital Tourism*, *x*(x), 365–383. doi:10.1007/978-3-319-47732-9_24

Ruastiti, N. M., Sudirga, I. K., & Yudarta, I. G. (2020). Model of innovative wayang wong for millenial generation to meet 4.0 industrial revolution era in Bali. *Journal of Environmental Treatment Techniques*, *8*(3), 999–1004.

Samsudin, P. Y., & Maliki, N. Z. (2015). Preserving Cultural Landscape in Homestay Programme Towards Sustainable Tourism: Brief Critical Review Concept. *Procedia: Social and Behavioral Sciences*, *170*, 433–441. doi:10.1016/j.sbspro.2015.01.004

Severo, M., & Venturini, T. (2016). Intangible cultural heritage webs: Comparing national networks with digital methods. *New Media & Society*, *18*(8), 1616–1635. doi:10.1177/1461444814567981

Shaken, A., Mika, M., & Plokhikh, R. V. (2020). Exploring the social interest in agritourism among the urban population of Kazakhstan. *Miscellanea Geographica*, *24*(1), 16–23. doi:10.2478/mgrsd-2019-0026

Soeroso, A., & Susilo, Y. S. (2014). Traditional Indonesian Gastronomy As a Cultural Tourism Attraction. *Journal of Applied Economics in Developing Countries*, *1*(1), 45–49.

Su, M. M., Wall, G., & Xu, K. (2016). Heritage tourism and livelihood sustainability of a resettled rural community: Mount Sanqingshan World Heritage Site, China. *Journal of Sustainable Tourism*, *24*(5), 735–757. doi:10.1080/09669582.2015.1085868

Tenerelli, P., Demšar, U., & Luque, S. (2016). Crowdsourcing indicators for cultural ecosystem services: A geographically weighted approach for mountain landscapes. *Ecological Indicators*, *64*, 237–248. doi:10.1016/j.ecolind.2015.12.042

UNESCO. (2003). *Intangible Heritage - 2003 Convention*. https://ich.unesco.org/en/intangible-heritage-domains-00052

Van Berkel, D. B., Tabrizian, P., Dorning, M. A., Smart, L., Newcomb, D., Mehaffey, M., Neale, A., & Meentemeyer, R. K. (2018). Quantifying the visual-sensory landscape qualities that contribute to cultural ecosystem services using social media and LiDAR. *Ecosystem Services*, *31*, 326–335. doi:10.1016/j.ecoser.2018.03.022 PMID:30148061

Vaz, A. S., Gonçalves, J. F., Pereira, P., Santarém, F., Vicente, J. R., & Honrado, J. P. (2019). Earth observation and social media: Evaluating the spatiotemporal contribution of non-native trees to cultural ecosystem services. *Remote Sensing of Environment*, *230*(April), 111193. doi:10.1016/j.rse.2019.05.012

Vaz, A. S., Moreno-Llorca, R. A., Gonçalves, J. F., Vicente, J. R., Méndez, P. F., Revilla, E., Santamaria, L., Bonet-García, F. J., Honrado, J. P., & Alcaraz-Segura, D. (2020). Digital conservation in biosphere reserves: Earth observations, social media, and nature's cultural contributions to people. *Conservation Letters*, *13*(3), 1–9. doi:10.1111/conl.12704

Zhang, Y., Han, M., & Chen, W. (2018). The strategy of digital scenic area planning from the perspective of intangible cultural heritage protection. *Eurasip Journal on Image and Video Processing, 2018*(1). doi:10.1186/s13640-018-0366-7

Chapter 11
Mobile Technology:
Simplifying Tourism Business Operations and Facilitating Tourists

Pramendra Singh
Amity University, Noida, India

ABSTRACT

The tourism industry is very dynamic, and tourism businesses have witnessed drastic change in their operations since the inception and growth of technology. Mobile technology is one of the emerging segments that is facilitating tourism businesses on a large scale. It saves time, effort, money, and also provides ease, convenience, and comfort. Mobile technology has enhanced tourism business operations and helps the tourism businesses in guided tours, navigation, reservation, payment, information search, content creation, product development, getting feedback, digital marketing, etc. Mobile technology has also facilitated tourists for different purposes. It has made travelling convenient, easy, and safe for tourists. Adoption of mobile technology is bound to grow in the future for tourism businesses as well as for more tourists. The present study investigates the role of mobile technology for tourists and for various tourism-related business organizations. With the help of review of literature, the study aims to highlight its importance.

INTRODUCTION

The advent and large-scale use of the internet has made the world globalized in real sense. And the smartphones with internet have brought revolution in all the area, be it education, business, personal use or for anything else as well. According to some

DOI: 10.4018/978-1-7998-9194-9.ch011

recent studies, approximately half of the world population has access to internet and smart phones. India is one of the top users of smart phones with every part of the country has now good internet connectivity and affordability of its usage. With the efforts of government, competition among service providers & mobile manufacturers the mobile user base has drastically increased in recent times across all geographical and economic groups (Tenhunen, 2008). Mobile technology has three main elements which are software, hardware & internet.

As the current era is led by the technology, it has penetrated in all areas of human involvement and participation. Within the domain of technology, mobile technology has seen tremendous growth because of applicability, affordability, mobility & connectivity. The technology also gets transformed implying the potential changes based on how users interact with the technology and use it (Tussyadiah, 2015). Mobile technology has changed our sensing of individuality, our interactions with all other people & organizations, mobility, and participation in business and other areas (Cowley, 2010). Smartphones or mobiles are playing very important role in our day-to-day life and has become a part of it. We perform many operations with the help of these mobile phones, and they have made our lives much more easier and simpler.

Adoption and applicability of mobile technology has become one of the most widely undertaken subjects for many researchers (Law, Chan & Wang, 2018). As a result of these widely undertaken research, mobile technology has achieved tremendous growth and development. Different forms of business organizations including tourism have adopted mobile technology to accrue its multifarious benefits. The use of mobile devices in travel context is significantly correlated with the use of mobile technology in in daily lives (Wang, Park & Fesenmaier, 2016). As tourists are by nature mobile, they need mobile technology in order do away with time and space constraints (Nunes & Mayer, 2014). Mobile technology has immense potential in tourism because of mobile nature of the tourists and the need of the tourists related to stay connected virtually, seeking travel information, entertainment, and other fulfilment of their needs (Dickinson, Hibbert & Filimonau, 2016).

For tourism activities, tourists require many kinds of information for various purposes. Mobile technology gives tourists the access to real time information anytime and anywhere according to their convenience and helps in their learning (Martin & Ertzberger, 2013). The tourism information system characteristics include – internal search, mobile search, advanced collaboration, search via editorial communications etc. (Ho, Lin, Yuan & Chen, 2016).

Lee and Mills (2010) have highlighted the important role of mobile technology in tourism as -

"By perfectly meeting customers' information needs about products and services prior to purchase, the tourism industry is benefiting from mobile technology in satisfying customer expectations, in improving convenience, and in decreasing costs" (p.94).

All the stakeholders in tourism industry are so much benefitted from mobile technology that different tools and applications for dedicated services have been made available for them. The various travel related applications from a value chain perspective have applicability for navigation, social, safety, information & entertainment (Kennedy-Eden & Gretzel, 2012). The mobile technology has enormous potential to be implemented and used for the all-round development of tourism and facilitation of tourism stakeholders.

TOURISM FACILITATION THROUGH MOBILE TECHNOLOGY

As technology transformed, it brought many changes in devices and equipment used for making the processes simple and easy. One of the greatest achievements of technology was to do away with its nature of being stationary. Making devices compact and easy to carry was another milestone in ensuring its wider reach. This mobility of devices was also supported by necessary softwares and applications. Tourism industry made significant gains due to the advancement in mobile technology. The ease of use has significant impact on extrinsic and intrinsic motivations of usefulness and enjoyment which in turn impact usage intention (Kim, Kim & Kim, 2016). Advancement in mobile technology provide enormous and suitable information to tourists to take right decisions regarding their tour and it also benefits the tourism businesses to make accurate predictions for the demand and effectively respond to them (Kim & Kim, 2017).

Wang, Xiang and Fesenmaier (2014) have stated the use of mobile technology as –

"The use of the smartphone also enhances the pluralization of tourists and the role of subjectivity by enabling tourists to be involved in many creative occasions through smartphone applications such as video making, photo editing, and painting, and the process of creation evokes self-identities that are hidden by monotonous routines in everyday living. Further, the communication of pictures or videos through online social network applications enables tourists to reflect on and construct the meanings of their experience from different perspectives while they are experiencing the tourist moments" (pp. 24-25).

Law, Chan and Wang (2018) have explained the multiple usage of mobile technology as in tourism by the tourists as –

Pre-trip – For information search

During trip – For adjusting itineraries in contingency situations, exploring destination, service consumption, perform task, manage time, communication, social media engagement, entertainment, safety, travel assistance,

Post trip – For sharing experiences, providing feedback, providing their updates, storing – retrieving memories.

Mobile technology is used in all sectors of service industry like tourism, hospitality, airlines for information search, guided tours, audio guides, navigation, reservation, payment, writing reviews, online community development, interaction with various stakeholders, content creation and sharing etc. Mobile technology provides many values added services in tourism industry like easy & timely access to the information, immediate purchase opportunity, beaming money, buddy finding, updating the virtual presence (Siau, Lim & Shen, 2001). It facilitates the tourists for different services on different occasions before, during and after their tours. Tourists visit the destinations for different purposes, most significant being their learning which contributes much in their satisfaction with the destination.

Availability of well trained and experienced guides who could deliver it to the utmost level of professionalism and knowledge are hard to find at many tourist destinations. Mobile technology proves to be vital in those areas with correct, detailed, and updated guidance. Mobile guides enabled through mobile technology helps tourists in spatial and contextual understanding of the destination and activities for the tourists by providing them real time information, routing, services etc. (Tussyadiah & Fesenmaier, 2007). Electronic guidebooks & maps are popular application area for mobile technology, comparison of information, locating nearby amenities etc. are simplified by mobile technology (Brown & Chalmers, 2003). Not only the understanding of the destination but also locating the attractions, eateries, accommodation, and other amenities at unknown destinations is well assisted by mobile technology.

MOBILE TECHNOLOGY & TOURISM PRODUCT DEVELOPMENT

Products of business organizations augur their fate deciding survival, excellence, or doomsday. Business products prove to be the lifeline of the organizations on which all other business activities are dependent. Business products decide mode and type of distribution channel, marketing strategies & consumption and ultimately decides the future of the business organizations. Tourism products are also created keeping in mind many factors like seasonality, tourist segmentation, destination attributes and other service required.

Creating, distributing, marketing, and promoting tourism products have been now easy than earlier for the tourism business organizations. Making the product information accessible to tourist helps businesses as tourist can decide on taking decision about the product which is well facilitated by mobile technology (Lee & Mills, 2010). New information and communication technology tools have empowered the tourism suppliers and destinations to improve their efficiency and communication strategies. Travellers are socially connected not only before or after the trip but during the trip as well, all because of mobile technology.

The mobile technology has also renewed the distribution system as well as the orientation of marketing efforts (Condratov, 2013). Advances in mobile technology creates innovative experiences for the tourists, fosters business growth and makes the distribution system more efficient & effective and brings in the concept of smart tourism (Kim & Kim, 2017). Mobile tourism also helps in bringing to fruition the applicability of smart tourism. What makes tourism smart is real time information sharing and consuming services by equipping tourists & businesses with modern gazettes.

Zhang, Zhang and Shi (2020) describe how with the help of mobile technology a unique and appealing tourism product could be drawn. With the pervasive utilization and rapid development of information technology in all areas, it has also brought new innovations and creative programs. It thus helps in developing new experiences of diversified, creative and augmented tourism products. This kind of creativity through information technology connects past with present and has also become a driving force for new experiences. GIFs were created from the static paintings of King Yongzheng from the palace of Forbidden city in China. Narrative elements were also added to the paintings with the help of Virtual reality (VR) and mobile technology. The growing adoptability and use of mobile devices make it convenient to use.

The present-day tourist is not the traditional one who goes for mass tourism rather looks for niche area. For developing the cultural, creative and other types of tourism product, the mobile technology is one of the most frequently used method. The information about niche form of tourism, destination, pricing, amenities everything is created, marketed and booked easily through mobile technology.

ENABLING COMMERCE THROUGH MOBILE TECHNOLOGY (M-COMMERCE)

Technology has made it easy for many to start and run businesses but at the same time doing business in cut-throat competition is equally challenging & rewarding. Reaching out to wider customer base and serve them efficiently could be made possible with the help of advanced technology. Mobile commerce (m-commerce) has further paved the way for simplification of the business processes including transactions and selling. All businesses including those of tourism businesses are readily adopting m-commerce as a means of economic facilitator. Liang et al. (2007) have explained m-commerce as the new age e-commerce which is carried out by mobile devices such as mobiles or other personal digital assistant for direct and indirect transactions.

The ease of mobility and portability of mobile devices make the use of m-commerce convenient for the businesses and customers. M-commerce has many benefits and applicability in all areas of businesses. Siau, Lim and Shen (2001) have described the features of m-commerce as – Ubiquity, Personalization, Flexibility and Dissemination. It can facilitate the businesses by being flexible, present at many nodes simultaneously, providing customized or personalized services individually to the customers and disseminate the information of its usefulness. They have further described m-commerce as –

"Promising unlimited information, entertainment, and commerce, mobile commerce gives users the ability to access the Internet from any location at any time, the capability to pinpoint an individual mobile terminal user's location, the functionality to access information at the point of need, and a need-based data/ information update capability. Mobile commerce has features not available to traditional" (p.4).

Mobile commerce not only provides the benefits of web, but also unique services enabled by technology. The tourism industry gets benefited by its use in expanding the customer base, enhancing revenue streams and reducing the operating cost (Kim, Park & Morrison, 2008). Mobile commerce provides flexibility to tourism service providers in a highly volatile market by enabling them to update the promotional message more quickly than printed ones, enabling to reduce the time lag between framing & implementing policy decisions and quickly processing the payments (Lee & Mills, 2010). All the sectors and businesses within tourism industry are inclined and eager to use m-commerce for their businesses to harness maximum benefits of the advanced technology. Most of the multinational chain hotels use web based and mobile technologies for customer handling, online services and payments (Gulbahar & Yildirim, 2015).

Not only the businesses but other stakeholders including the customers have also adopted the new technology m-commerce. Customers now also prefer not to carry cash and deal with m-commerce, which is convenient, safe and rewarding. Many new businesses have popped up to facilitate the mobile payment and offer rewards in doing transactions with them. Tourists also use mobile wallet (m-wallet) for its easiness and advantage of use (Lew et. al, 2020). M-commerce is coming up with renewed convenience, multi-location access, less time taking and reward giving features.

ADOPTION OF MOBILE TECHNOLOGY IN TOURISM

Time demands transformation in business processes and distribution system as per the changing needs of the tourists and competitive business environment. Technology contributes a lot in bridging the gap between demand and service delivery with disseminating its benefits to concerned stakeholders. Tourists need services at fast pace with ease and comfort. Mobile technology helps the tourists in achieving these objectives before, during and after their tours.

When tourists look for accomplishing travel related tasks, they tend to adopt the mobile technology because of the utility and convenience provided by it. The modern utility of mobile technology also helps in building trust when people are searching about the information and suggestions online (Magano & Cunha, 2020). Tourists especially the frequent travellers are more inclined towards adoption of mobile technology enabled services therefore the tourism and hospitality service providers should provide mobile technology enabled services and environment in order to convert would-be customers into retained repeat guests (Kim, Park & Morrison, 2008).

Law, Chan and Wang (2018), on the basis of their study found five major factors which impact the consumers' intention towards adoption of mobile technologies in tourism which are Utilitarian, Hedonic, Dispositional, Behavioural, Environmental factors.

Utilitarian – Utility & convenience of mobile technology; Personalization; Easy to use

Hedonic – Consumers' travel preferences & image of a specific destination; Emotional attachment; For social acceptance & interaction

Dispositional – On the basis of own personal traits; Trust & Privacy concern; Therefore, popular in younger generation

Behavioural – Consumer behaviour, e.g. High spenders, frequent travellers, continuous mobile usage

Environmental – Service Environment like encouragement by service providers to consumers to use mobile technology in order to consume their services, booking, payment etc.

Kamboj and Joshi, 2020 have asserted two set of factors that may determine the use of mobile technology enabled apps by the tourists which may impact behavioural aspects in direct and indirect ways. Firstly, those factors which may impact in directly impact behavioural outcomes are as aesthetic scope, device portability or convenience. Secondly, those which may impact behavioural aspects in indirect way are as social loneliness, perceived value, hedonism, habit, innovation & convenience.

Liang et al. (2007) said, adopting mobile technology may benefit the organizations in two ways. First it facilitates communication between organization, employees and customers. Secondly it improves business processes by providing improved data access pattern. Both of these functions enhance organizational profitability and productivity.

Mobile technology has reached far and wide in all domains and industries throughout the world. Tourism industry has utilized mobile technology optimally for its growth and development. The perceived value of mobile technology for tourists, businesses and other stakeholders has gone through different stages and witnessed acceptance and adoption with changing paradigm. Perceived usefulness and perceived ease of use have influence on adoption of mobile technology which is further influenced by attitude of the tourists (Nizar & Rehmat, 2018). Ease of use of mobile technology is most important, real time and correct information gathering through mobile technology is also important which impact the perceived value of mobile technology for the tourists (Chang, 2017).

Perception and perceived value of tourists affect the satisfaction of tourists with mobile technology, thus developing positive attitude towards perception and perceived value is important (Lee & Mills, 2010). If optimism and innovation are there, the tourists are likely to see the perceived benefits of mobile technology and if insecurity and discomfort are there then the tourists are less likely to use new technology (Jarrar, Awobamise & Sellos, 2020). Therefore, efforts should be made so that tourists and businesses have positive perception toward the mobile technology. And it could be achieved by addressing the needs and concerns of tourism stakeholder. Swift action, less time taking process, convenience to use, mobility with other benefits may prove to act as catalyst for developing positive perception towards mobile technology and result in its adoption on large scale.

CONCLUSION

Mobile technology has made it easier for everyone from all walks of life to get the things done in minimal time with great convenience. Service industry specifically tourism industry has benefitted a lot because of advancement in mobile technology. It has benefitted all the stakeholders in tourism industry, be it tourists, service providers, intermediaries or organizations. It facilitates tourists during their travel planning process, during travel and after their tour for multiple functions like information search, decision making, selecting right choices, collecting and storing memories, finding the service providers at the destination, signage etc. It is also helpful for service providers in promoting their businesses, reaching to their current & prospective customers and retaining them as loyal customers. It also benefits other stakeholders in simplifying their processes and prolonging their existence.

Internet has contributed much in the growth and development of mobile technology. In past it has gone through different stages and continues to do so. Much research has been done by the scientists in further advancing the scope and applicability of mobile technology in all areas including the tourism industry. The process of advancing is still going on to accommodate the changing needs and requirements of all concerned stakeholders. But one thing is sure that mobile technology has been at forefront in serving the tourism industry and will continue to do so.

REFERENCES

Brown, B., & Chalmers, M. (2003). Tourism and mobile technology. In *Proceedings - Eighth European conference on computer-supported cooperative work*. Kluwer Academic Publishers. 10.1007/978-94-010-0068-0_18

Chang, P. (2017). The Importance Performance Analysis of Taiwan Tourism Mobile Marketing. *Journal of Tourism Management Research*, *4*(1), 12–16. doi:10.18488/journal.31.2017.41.12.16

Condratov, I. (2013). E-Tourism: Concept And Evolution. *Ecoforum, 2*(1). www.internetworldstats.com

Dickinson, J. E., Hibbert, J. F., & Filimonau, V. (2016). Mobile technology and the tourist experience: (Dis)connection at the campsite. *Tourism Management*, *57*, 193–201. doi:10.1016/j.tourman.2016.06.005

Evans-Cowley, J. (2010). Planning in the real-time city: The future of mobile technology. Journal of Planning Literature, 25(2), 136–149. doi:10.1177/0885412210394100

Gulbahar, M. O., & Yildirim, F. (2015). Marketing Efforts Related to Social Media Channels and Mobile Application Usage in Tourism: Case Study in Istanbul. *Procedia: Social and Behavioral Sciences*, *195*, 453–462. doi:10.1016/j.sbspro.2015.06.489

Ho, C. I., Lin, Y. C., Yuan, Y. L., & Chen, M. C. (2016). Pre-trip tourism information search by smartphones and use of alternative information channels: A conceptual model. *Cogent Social Sciences*, *2*(1), 1136100. Advance online publication. doi:10.1080/23311886.2015.1136100

Jarrar, Y., Awobamise, A. O., & Sellos, P. S. (2020). Technological readiness index (TRI) and the intention to use smartphone apps for tourism: A focus on indubai mobile tourism app. *International Journal of Data and Network Science*, *4*(3), 297–304. doi:10.5267/j.ijdns.2020.6.003

Kamboj, S., & Joshi, R. (2021). Examining the factors influencing smartphone apps use at tourism destinations: A UTAUT model perspective. *International Journal of Tourism Cities*, *7*(1), 135–157. doi:10.1108/IJTC-05-2020-0094

Kennedy-Eden, H., & Gretzel, U. (2012). *A taxonomy of mobile applications in tourism. Research Online*. University of Wollongong. https://ro.uow.edu.au/commpapers/2510

Kim, D., & Kim, S. (2017). The role of mobile technology in tourism: Patents, articles, news, and mobile tour app reviews. *Sustainability (Switzerland)*, *9*(11), 2082. Advance online publication. doi:10.3390u9112082

Kim, D. Y., Park, J., & Morrison, A. M. (2008). A model of traveller acceptance of mobile technology. *International Journal of Tourism Research*, *10*(5), 393–407. doi:10.1002/jtr.669

Kim, M. J., Kim, W. G., Kim, J. M., & Kim, C. (2016). Does knowledge matter to seniors' usage of mobile devices? Focusing on motivation and attachment. *International Journal of Contemporary Hospitality Management*, *28*(8), 1702–1727. doi:10.1108/IJCHM-01-2015-0031

Law, R., Chan, I. C. C., & Wang, L. (2018). A comprehensive review of mobile technology use in hospitality and tourism. *Journal of Hospitality Marketing & Management*, *27*(6), 626–648. doi:10.1080/19368623.2018.1423251

Lee, J., & Mills, J. E. (2007). Exploring Tourist Satisfaction with Mobile Technology. In *Information and Communication Technologies in Tourism 2007* (pp. 141–152). Springer Vienna. doi:10.1007/978-3-211-69566-1_14

Lew, S., Tan, G. W. H., Loh, X. M., Hew, J. J., & Ooi, K. B. (2020). The disruptive mobile wallet in the hospitality industry: An extended mobile technology acceptance model. *Technology in Society*, *63*, 101430. Advance online publication. doi:10.1016/j.techsoc.2020.101430 PMID:33071395

Liang, T. P., Huang, C. W., Yeh, Y. H., & Lin, B. (2007). Adoption of mobile technology in business: A fit-viability model. *Industrial Management & Data Systems*, *107*(8), 1154–1169. doi:10.1108/02635570710822796

Martin, F., & Ertzberger, J. (2013). Here and now mobile learning: An experimental study on the use of mobile technology. *Computers & Education, 68*, 76–85. doi:10.1016/j.compedu.2013.04.021

Meiliana, I., Irmanti, D., Hidayat, M. R., Amalina, N. V., & Suryani, D. (2017). Mobile Smart Travelling Application for Indonesia Tourism. *Procedia Computer Science, 116*, 556–563. doi:10.1016/j.procs.2017.10.059

Nizar, N. N. M., & Rahmat, M. K. (2018). Examining the Museum Visitors Use of Mobile Technology Through Technology Acceptance Model (TAM). *Journal of Tourism, Hospitality and Environment Management, 3*(11). www.jthem.com

Nunes, M. D. O., & Mayer, M. (2014). Mobile technology, games and nature areas: The tourist perspective In. *Tourism & Management Studies, 10*(1). https://pt.foursquare.com/

Sarisakal, M. N., & Aydin, M. A. (2005). Mobile commerce. *Istanbul University -. Journal of Electrical and Electronics Engineering (Oradea), 5*(1), 1249–1254. doi:10.4018/jdm.2001070101

Sirpa, T. (2008). Mobile technology in the village. *Journal of the Royal Anthropological Institute, 14*(3), 515–534. doi:10.1111/j.1467-9655.2008.00515.x

Tussyadiah, I. P. (2015). Personal Technology and Tourism Experiences. In *ESCONTOUR 2015 Tourism Research Perspectives* (pp. 1-10). Academic Press.

Tussydiah, I., & Fesenmaier, D. (2007). *Interpreting Tourist Experiences from First-Person Stories: A Foundation for Mobile Guides*. https://aisel.aisnet.org/ecis2007http://aisel.aisnet.org/ecis2007/104

Wang, D., & Fesenmaier, D. R. (2016). *Mobile Technology, Everyday Experience and Travel*. https://scholarworks.umass.edu/ttra/2012/Oral/28

Wang, D., Xiang, Z., & Fesenmaier, D. R. (2014). Adapting to the mobile world: A model of smartphone use. *Annals of Tourism Research, 48*, 11–26. doi:10.1016/j.annals.2014.04.008

Zhang, L., Zhang, C., & Shi, M. (2020). Applying Mobile Technology for Developing Cultural and Creative Products in Tourism: A Case Study on the Forbidden City. *Proceedings - Companion of the 2020 IEEE 20th International Conference on Software Quality, Reliability, and Security, QRS-C 2020*, 542–549. 10.1109/QRS-C51114.2020.00095

Zulmira, M., Amorim, B., & Cunha, N. (2020). *Digital marketing impact on tourism in Portugal: a quantitative study*. https://www.researchgate.net/publication/338655966

Chapter 12
Sustainability in the Gig Economy:
An Indian Perspective

Deepika Dhingra
https://orcid.org/0000-0001-5967-8834
Bennett University, India

Shruti Ashok
Bennett University, India

Nidhi Sinha
Bennett University, India

Mugdha S. Kulkarni
https://orcid.org/0000-0001-5443-0725
Symbiosis Center for Information Technology, Symbiosis International University (Deemed), India

ABSTRACT

A gig economy is a free market structure in which temporary positions are widespread, and organizations employ independent workers for short-term commitments.The gig economy is fragmented and spans a wide diversity of workers such as independent contributors, freelancers, self-employed, and part-time workers. This chapter deliberates on the major factors that influence the gig economy from a multi-stakeholder perspective (e.g., employers/organizations, gig workers, customers, and economy). The study explores the various common factors such as globalization, digitalization, technological change, financial pressures, and emerging competition including other factors about different stakeholders who are influencing the gig economy, thereby propelling the entry of the next generation of workers in this system. Pandemic due to covid-19 has made survival even harder for gig workers. The chapter also discusses the challenges from different aspects of all stakeholders with due consideration of Industry 4.0 in detail.

DOI: 10.4018/978-1-7998-9194-9.ch012

INTRODUCTION

21st Century is marked by digital revolution, center of which is the giant economy alongside artificial intelligence and algorithms. The labor pool of the 21st century is characterized by the cooperation between man and technology, the result of which is a high degree of wellness for all nations. It is to be noted that, what unites us globally is the economy, not politics or governments, and the gig economy anticipates the potential impact of industrialization and the beneficial potential it might bring. With rapid technological advancements such as artificial intelligence, the development of robotics, and the resulting automation, great transformation can be observed in the country's job market. Full-time and tenure-based employment are being considered lucrative as more people acquire multiple streams of income from various jobs while also shifting between different industries throughout their working life.

An economy based on performing tasks and projects, increasingly through digital platforms, and replacing regular full-time employment is defined as a gig economy (Wood et al, 2019). In other words, it can be defined as a system where the workforce primarily works on short-term contracts and engages in freelance assignments. Gig economy is characterised with flexible industry dynamics such as temporary, freelance jobs, connecting clients and service providers through an online platform. Arrangements where short-term contracts, independent jobs, and freelance assignments are commonplace, and organizations intend to hire independent employees predominantly on contracts and freelancers instead of full-time workers constitute a gig economy. Freelancers or more broadly, gig workers, use this form of employment willingly due to lack of full-time job offers. The challenges that this revolutionary advancement towards gig economy can be transformed into opportunities, but it requires creativity and a correct mindset of the human capital to maximize the benefits of the revolution and minimize potential threats.

The idea of work is transforming future employment and business along the same lines. Advancement in technology with the international supply chain has also reformed the system of manufacturing, retail, service, and workforce. Remote online working jobs are easily accessible to workforce of developing countries. Infact, the traditional working model has changed to on demand working which is managed through apps and runs on demand and supply. In India, cab drivers, online beauty, carpentry, cleaning, transport are some of the services that can be availed on demand. (Chaudhary, Mitra, & CeMIS, 2019, November). Example Swiggy,Zo mato,Dunzo,Urbanclap,Ola,uber,Dunzo.

The growth of online media platforms has given rise to the phenomenon of the gig economy. A new monetary model that holds various of forms of short-term service is propagating across all corners of the world, becoming a day in day out need changing the employment market. The new gig economy has adapted to new measures creating opportunities for alternative employment. (Banik & Padalkar, 2021)

Covid-19 pandemic has transformed the trade function as numerous businesses have taken the advantage of the digital mode rather than relying on cash. According to the ASSOCHAM, Gig economy in India is expected to rise to US$455 billion with 17% increase in CAGR by the year 2024.

At present, India has approximately15 million freelance jobs in software, human resource, and designing plans. India's workforce is rising by ~4 million every year. As most youth prefer gig contracts, it is expected that the market of jobs for freelancers and gig workers will be greatly impacted in short term. Start ups in IT, data science machine learning domains are looking to hire freelancer's on hourly basis giving strength to the tech industry.

BACKGROUND OF GIG ECONOMY

The gig economy can be equated to Industrial Revolution of contemporary times. A few years ago, the on-demand or "gig" system was an innovative and modern arrangement that facilitates all stakeholders such as companies, workers, and consumers with convenience, independence, and flexibility. Working patterns are changing and people are choosing to walk out of conventional permanent jobs to work independently on a project-by-project basis for various companies driven by technology. At one point in time, often freelancing was thought of for creative work such as content developers, web designers, graphic designers, and contracting was associated with IT-related jobs. But now, roles from diverse fields such as Healthcare, Accounting, and Finance comprising of senior-level executive positions, are marking their prominent presence in the Gig Economy. Infact, it is almost passé to discuss the growing importance of the Gig Economy as it has infiltrated almost every major industry and its disadvantages have also been observed. The emergence of digital talent platforms and programs that cater to freelance professionals has further catalyzed this growth. Millions of individuals across the globe do work that is paid by gig – rather than a full-time job. Yet, several organizations are still trying to catch up to this ballooning occurrence and are seriously underprepared for this rapidly approaching high-churning workforce scenario. It is projected that part-time employees will surpass 40% (as per report by Intuit 2020: Twenty trends that will shape the next decade) by 2020. Companies, founders, and activists are enthusiastic to figure out how to build a sustainable economic system for these workers.

Freelancing has been advocated and presented to workers in the light of freedom, autonomy, and enhanced work-life balance. Entrepreneurs often find the gig world alluring and irresistible allowing them to set their own schedule, dress code, working when they want, and having the discretion to decide their potential income. Though, this may be a choice; often there is no fixed-contract employment available and even though gig income can surpass the minimum threshold of wages, frequently it does not. Unfortunately, in a gig economy, it's easier said than done.

Companies also enjoy various benefits from working with gig workers by having a fluid workforce, global accessibility to rich talent, cost-cutting, and improved productivity (Aloisi, 2015). It enables organizations to react more intensely to inconsistent demand. The company needs to pay only for the work when they need. Organizations don't feel burdened with the disbursements of payroll, employee benefits, insurance, vacations, and sick leave. But according to Howson "If a business is not sustainable while allowing basic rights to its workers, like minimum wages and sick leave, it's not a very good business."

Significance of the Gig Economy

Over a period, labor market has transformed from regular employment to "gig economy", where large numbers of individuals work on temporary positions or part-time. As gig economy is cost-effective and efficient, more industries are keen to embrace it. Its industry dynamics are a function of flexible, temporary and freelance jobs bridging the gap between clients and service providers. Gig economy is scattered and spread across widely with personnel such as freelancers, self-employed, part-time workers and independent contributors in sectors comprising insurance, finance, retail, IT, media, healthcare, property management and education.

Gig system challenges the conventional economy of permanent employees who hardly ever change positions and focus on a lifetime career (Balaram, 2017). This new economy is getting popular rapidly. It helps to improve work-life balance by providing opportunities to individuals to take up assignments that align with their interests and career objectives, offer diversity of work, and facilitate flexibility and capability to earn from multiple sources. Adaptability towards new work and flexible régimes is the need of the moment and makes it beneficial for stakeholders like consumers, businesses, and workers.

The gig staffing model allows a company to plug skill gaps by hiring experts and professionals on an impermanent basis. The talent pool comprising of specialized external experts with high skillsets are appointed to drive critical enterprise initiatives and projects. This phenomenon applies to all sectors of the economy- from artificial intelligence and machine learning as the highest-paid sector, to finance and insurance industry followed by agriculture, mining, manufacturing, and transport and logistics. Gig economy embraces most of the sectors and has worked on all kind of skill sets according to their qualifications and level of competence. In a research report published by BCG, more than 30% of the participants downsized by employers claimed that the development of the gig economy provided them the opportunity to find employment again and to learn new skills.

Globalization of Gig Economy

Depending on the industry, the workers in gig economy are being termed as remote, virtual, or contingent workers, independent contractors, freelancers or consultants. Irrespective of the title, this pool of professionals comprises consultants and highly skilled specialists encompassing all industries. Big establishments are hiring them evermore to supplement their regular employees.

Organizations have acknowledged the benefits of gig workers (Connelly, 2021), including quick access to a rich talent pool across the world that can be engaged without the troublesome recruitment and onboarding process for demanding projects that are often conducted outside of standard business processes. According to the Oxford University researchers, in the years 2016-2017 the outsourced talent-based projects by the largest global organizations, grew by as much as 26%.

Though the Gig Economy comprises participants from every age group, primarily it comprises two age groups. The first group of people belongs to the age bracket of 55-64 who display high predisposition and propensity towards flexibility. It is expected that they will constitute 15% of the global workforce by 2025. The satisfaction rate is high for gig workers in their 40s, 50s, and early 60s. The second group belongs to the millennials who manifest their professional freedom due to lack of alternate options. The gig economy is not restricted to developed economies, but it is going global. According to a study conducted by Morgan Stanley, as much as 35% of the US working population (over 55 million people) may be involved in part-time work, which can reach up to 50% in the world's largest economy by 2027. In United Kingdom, Germany and France, the growth rate will exceed the average employment growth rate. The gig worker's numbers doubled in the years 2000-2014 in the European Union, and they were the fastest-growing group of employees. Either workers treat freelance as the main source of their income or work for extra money in both developed and developing countries. Figure 1 shows the percentage of gig workers across major nations.

Perceived Benefits to Various Stakeholders

Experts are of the view that the number of people working in the gig economy will grow manifold, as it not only facilitates independent contractual work but also provides flexibility of place of operation as workers do not necessarily need to report at their official workplaces. From an organization's perspective, such a set up empowers it with greater choice from a wider talent pool and provides available

Figure 1. Gig Work as the source of income in different countries 2018 (%)
(Sources: BCG, Future of Work 2018)

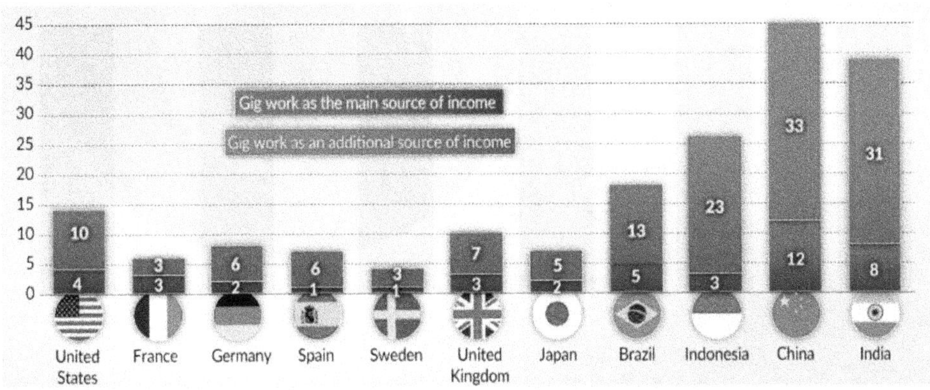

workforce when companies do not have the financial resources to hire regular and full-time workers.

A report by BMO Wealth Management on its employees suggests that millennials have distinctive viewpoints and motives to work in the gig economy environment. They were more motivated to be employed as gig work gives them an additional source of income. Around (58%) of those surveyed found flexible working a better opportunity. Fig: 2 represents the survey conducted by BMO Wealth Management displaying the topmost reasons for emergence of the gig economy:

In a study, McKinsey (2016) estimations are that 20-30% of the workers in developed economies are already involved in freelance work. According to another recent study by MasterCard, it is expected that half of the US population will be engaged in gig work by 2028, and financial institutions catering to this demography

Figure 2. BMO Wealth Management Survey

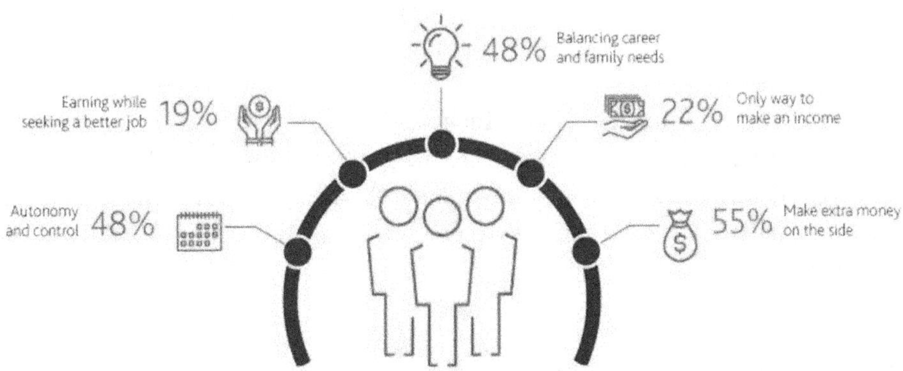

Figure 3. A study by SAP Fieldglass and Oxford Economics

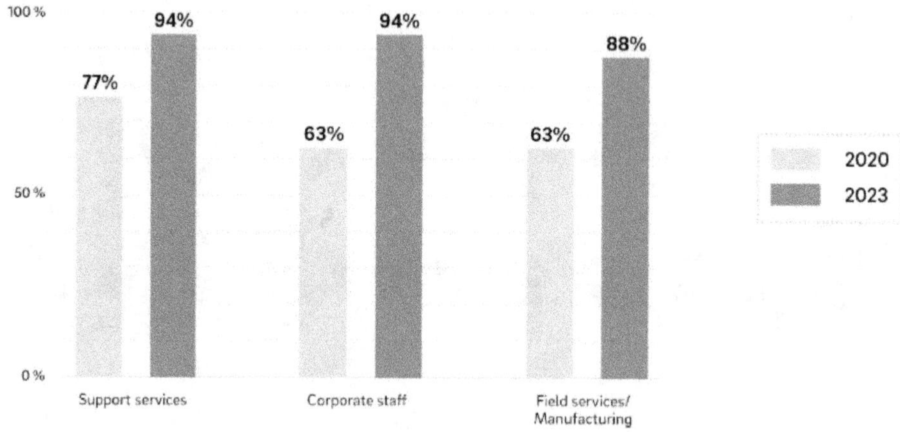

could tap a massive monetization opportunity. In 2018, digital and online gig work created $204 billion in customer volume and it is projected to increase to $455 billion by 2023. The key finding in a study by SAP Fieldglass and Oxford Economics determines that there is a high demand for gig workers. The survey found that 38% of managers have already appointed freelancers through online platforms and the requirement is set to become even higher in several organizations. The study predicts substantial growth in demand in the next few years which is shown in figure 3 below.

Perceived Benefits of Gig Economy

Factors that have motivated organizations to embrace the gig economy are mentioned below:

- **Globalization:** Due to increased accessibility, both physical and virtual, workers today are traveling and working across continents. Companies are also able to scout for the best global talent in regions where they may not have their footprints.
- **Artificial Intelligence and Machine learning enabled technology** has made a huge impact on globalizing the gig economy. Highly competent and experienced experts, who do not want to be tied to a particular organization permanently, can be hired on project basis through technology-driven platforms.

- **Reduced Overhead Cost**: Owing to the flexibility of gig workers., companies are not obligated to shell out all privileges and perks to them. This results in significant cost savings for corporates thus adding to their bottom-line.
- **Adaptability to Unpredictability: Adoption of gig economy facilitates b**usinesses to save significant time on lengthy and burdensome recruitment and onboarding processes. This makes them more agile and more responsive to the unpredictability of the market. This enables companies to create a team of experts from diverse fields to work on short-term projects (Harpur, 2020).
- **Boost to the Economy**: Gig economy provides impetus to a growing economy. The diversification of the gig economy has helped to create jobs, utilized untapped time and resources, offered additional income & driven economic growth.

On the other side, for the last few decades, professionals have followed trends such as switching jobs frequently or undertaking multiple assignments. Factors mentioned below have motivated employees to embrace the gig economy:

- **Avenue to earn extra bucks:** To make extra money, even regular employees have become part of the gig economy and re providing their services to other companies.
- **Freedom of choice:** Working in a gig economy gives you the freedom to decide where, when, which task would give paramount flexibility and share options to choose from.
- **Alternative source of Income**: Individuals who do not have regular jobs and lack other income alternatives opt for freelancing in gig culture to meet their basic needs. For many, it is not just a matter of choice and flexibility, but a compulsion.
- **Multitasking**: Working in a gig economy provides multiple working options to workers, enabling millennials to try something else apart from their regular monotonous jobs.
- **Opportunity for retrenched workers:** People downsized by the employers also opt for freelancing. They work as freelancers while looking for another opportunity or if they want make freelancing a regular source of income.

Sustainability

Gig economy redefines work culture that gives freedom to choose working hours that suit the workers. Entrepreneurs find the allure of the gig economy irresistible. Gig economy has envisaged a world where one sets one's own calendar, govern one's own dress code, and operates when -- and only when -- one wants. One's income potential, presumably, is restricted only by one's drive. Also, as one's entrepreneurial company expands, one does not need to get burdened with the cost of payroll insurance, employee benefits, sick leave, and vacations. Entrepreneurs pay only for the work they need. Even though gig economy appears like a win-win situation for all stakeholders, questions still arise on its sustainability. Proponents of gig economy are hopeful that due to increase in the quantum of work in remote areas, many new sectors are poised for growth in demand of gig workforce. Though, opponents argue that different social structures across nations alter the suitability and need of gig workforce. The emerging trends and challenges posed by Gig economy are complex and contagious (Randstad, 2016). Its threat to financial stability globally is one of the main reasons that world's multilateral establishments such as United Nations, World Bank, International Monetary Fund, International Labor Organization, and many governments have started focusing on the unemployment problem. In essence, some shortcomings that present real challenges and sustainability issues related to the gig economy must be debated.

Challenges for the Organization

- In a survey conducted by (Deloitte 2016) on freelance economies, one of the main challenges that emerged in an organization is that 'Freelance workers are impervious to corporate culture'. Owing to the temporary nature of job, workers often fail to align with the organization's culture. Freelancers do not care to absorb organization's culture knowing their predefined and capped tenure.
- Compilation of economic data becomes challenging when a gig job is not directly comparable to a full-time job. This aspect coupled with the slow growth rate of wages, particularly for low-skilled workers, widens earnings disparity, leading to wider implications on the global economy.
- Freelancers have predefined tenure with the company they are working for, there are high chances for them not being disloyal to the company or leak or share confidential information or data to competitors.
- In absence of any specific measures or parameters to the assigned work, it becomes difficult to determine the contribution of gig workers to the company they are working for.
- The current gig model adopted by several organizations consequentially gets them high worker turnover very often and can impact the services of the company too (Schroeder, 2021). For increased stability, organizations must invest in workers to help slow down the continuous churning of employees and improve its services. "There are two kinds of business models: squeeze

the employee, or invest in them," Hatton says. "Both models yield almost the same profits; it's just that the second is focused on the long-term objectives."

- The fluid nature of the gig economy can erode long-term associations of employers, vendors, clients, and workers. This can eradicate all paybacks of familiarity with clients and employers, customary practice, and long-term trust. It can demotivate investments in relationship-specific assets, as no party will have a motivation to invest substantially in a relationship that is not going to last for a reasonable amount of time.

Challenges for Workers in Gig Economy

Nobody can negate the benefits attached to being involved in the gig economy. But along with these benefits, there can be various challenges and drawbacks concerning the generation of workers working in this arrangement. For whatever reason workers choose to engage with a gig environment, it can also present financial and other downsides.

- Many organizations are appointing Gig workers as substitute for their full-time employees (Smith et al, 2021). In this arrangement, organizations do not offer many perks and benefits to gig workers that permanent or regular employees tend to enjoy such as Sick pay, paid vacations, pharmacies, tourism - the list goes on.
- Flexibility in a gig economy often comes with the rider that workers must always be available for projects or assignments, irrespective of their other requirements, and are always under pressure to search for the next gig assignment.
- There are chances that bigger firms outsource the most hazardous jobs to gig workers who may not have appropriate regulatory training, and smaller firms may exempt regulatory safeguards to workers making gig economy unsustainable or undesirable.
- Conventional jobs offer a lot of protection and perks, but gig culture offers less social protection and perks, and gig workers do not get any benefit (Wood, 2019). They need to manage and buy health insurance, plan for their retirement, and use their car and fuel.
- Most of the gig jobs may bring loneliness as workers miss office culture, colleagues, and boss. Many times, people regret those complaints from the old days. However, due to the development of technology and the culture of co-working spaces coming up, these issues are not hard to solve.
- Freedom in gig culture requires a lot of discipline and workers need to be very resilient. Everyone is not well-matched for this independence. Some

Figure 4. Represents the state of gig workers in the US

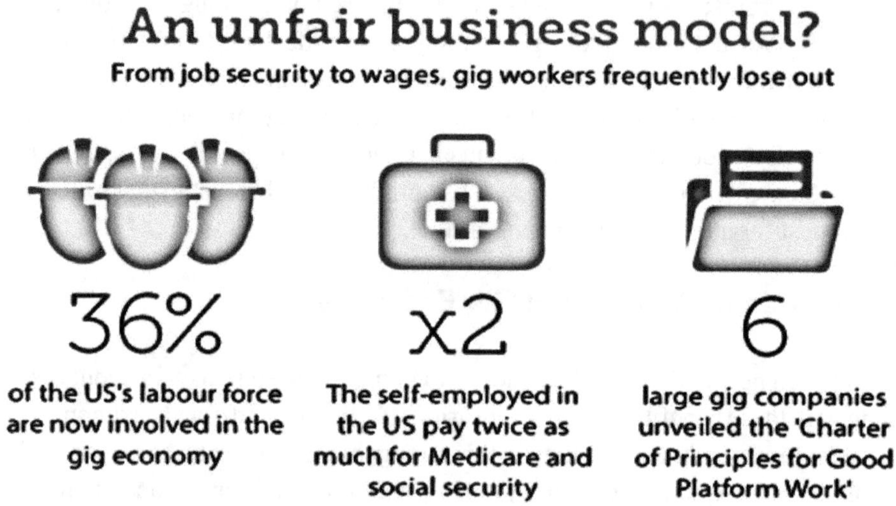

people only work efficiently when things are more structured, and someone sets the guidelines.

- For some workers, flexibility in the gig system can disturb their daily life activities, sleeping patterns, and work-life balance. Due to the pandemic, competitiveness in the gig market has increased.
- Adaptability to new culture and technology is very much required. Gig companies challenge established businesses and compel them to adapt and develop various new technologies. In some cases, big companies have swapped long-standing industries and their workforce.
- The volatility of income is the next big issue in this work arrangement. Unlike regular employees, gig workers do not have any fixed paycheck and they earn according to work done.

Imperatives for Building a Gig Economy

Gig economy has now permeated nearly every major industry — and its adverse externalities have become undeniably apparent. In the preceding year alone, whether it was new headline-grabbing regulations or new disclosures from the high-profile IPOs of Uber and Lyft, the issue of unbalanced labor treatment for gig workers has risen to the forefront of public debate. Now, more activists, founders and companies are dedicated to figuring out how to create a more just and sustainable economic system for gig workers. For sustainable growth of the organization in the gig economy, an organization must consider the practical approaches mentioned below to pass on its culture and values to Gig workers.

- **Organizations need quality workers.** Quality employees are always required even if they are gig workers, organizations get what they pay for.
- **Quality workers need benefits & compensation.** A quality employee cannot last without sufficient earnings and the social safety net normally provided by companies for an emergency. Their need for compensation and benefits are not different from regular permanent workers.
- **Gig economy is here to stay (at least for a while) and supports competitive business models.** As employers are increasingly using consultants and independent contractors to stay competitive in the industry, companies also need to compete for better qualified independent human resources.
- **Employers benefit from a business model that supports freelance workers.** If the employer doesn't support independent workers, they will not be able to give their best to the company and will not stay as several other organizations are hiring freelance employees. Organizations offering benefits and perks are likely to retain and attract quality independent workers.
- **Sustainability to support and protect.** It is not complicated to support part-time employees. They not only need help to make a living wage but also need to fulfil their safety needs. Offering insurance protection to temporary workers helps corporate Key Performance Indicators (KPIs) and benefits companies and their employees.
- Even for short-term positions, 'Screening for Culture' should be a significant part of interviews and hiring. Hiring professionals should discuss culture and opportunities to improve the same while recruiting and onboarding.
- Organizations should empower staff to make Culture-Driven decisions and motivate workers by recognizing and rewarding them. If there is an environment where the workers truly contribute, executives do not need control. They know and do what needs to be done.
- The leaders of the organization should tell stories to communicate the values of the organization and motivate team members to become storytellers too.

Executives in the organization should narrate and exemplify the organization's cultural impact on the community. For part-timers, a stint with the organizations can be temporary, but the communities are often persistent.

Figure 5. Source- AppJobs

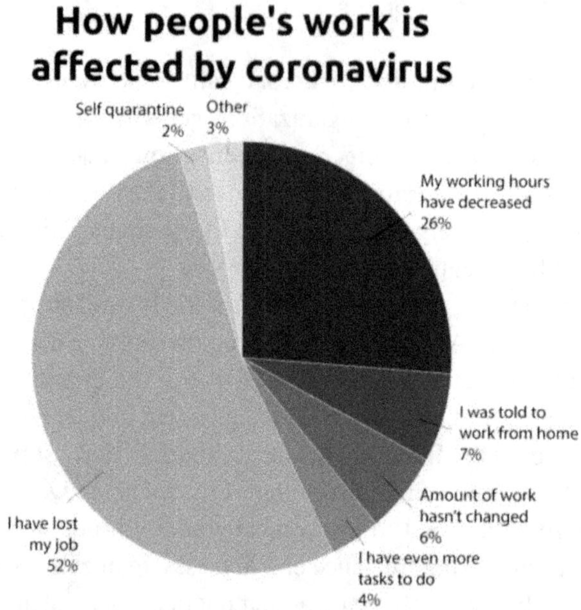

GIG ECONOMY IN COVID-19 TIMES

The COVID-19 pandemic has underlined many of the long-term struggles gig employees faced in the absence of safety nets. In a survey conducted amongst the gig workers, around 70% of those surveyed shared that they were not satisfied with the support system their organizations had provided through the pandemic. Most of them sought minimum level of security to fall back upon in case of an emergency.

According to a survey conducted by AppJobs – an online platform, Gig workers have been brutally affected and are amongst the hardest hit economically by the COVID19 crises. It is observed that more than half of them have lost their jobs, more than a quarter has seen cut down in their working hours due to decreased demand and many of them have quit gig jobs due to their safety concerns. There is no source or protection of income. Around 70% have no income, and only 23% are left with some savings.

However, in these extremely uncertain times, inclination towards gig economy is expected to strengthen and grow rather than shrink. The early signs of development in this direction can be observed already and we can assume this trend to catch up. Therefore, tapping into the gig economy appears to be an absolute requirement.

FUTURE OF GIG ECONOMY AND INDUSTRY 4.0

Due to the advent of Industry 4.0 characterized by rapid technological advancements such as artificial intelligence, development of robotics and automation, the job market is also undergoing tremendous change. With an increasing demand for flexible and autonomous work both from workers and employers, gig economy is expected to soar. The rise of digital talent platforms has multiplied the prominence of gig economy manifold, with a view to address imbalances in the labor market and support future jobs.

With the changing needs and demand of the industry, companies are now expected to be compatible with a fluid workforce, have access to hyper-specialised talent, reduce costs while aiming to enhance productivity. The emerging technologies of Industry 4.0 have made flexible working arrangements imperative for many workers and has provided businesses with multiple opportunities to build a dynamic and diverse team. All of this means that offering flexible working arrangements is integral to business success in Industry 4.0. At present, Hays figures show that a third of professionals identified flexible work as being critical for remaining employed, this number is projected to grow soon. Millennial workers, who will soon comprise most of the workforce, increasingly see flexible work as a given. Younger workers are more open to the idea of shifting from one contract or project to another as well as sharing and collaborating online.

CONCLUSION

As this radical transformation of work called the "gig economy" continues to sweep through our economy, red flags are being raised about its sustainability. Irrespective of age or the reasons for working in this system, there are both positives and negatives aspects attached to it. Having the chance to manage your time and schedule, the gig industry offers work-life balance, the flexibility to work within your expertise and placing your life first and work next is certainly empowering. If you have the discipline, you can get full-time work in the gig industry. On the other hand, working on your terms may attract financial challenges including varying working hours, no fixed and regular salary checks, and no benefits provided by companies like health insurance cover or retirement/pension plan. The governing authorities need to adjust to this new trend and guarantee social security to gig employees. Hatton says, "Time will tell, but I suspect overall it will have an aggravating impact on disparity because marginalized workers will be pushed disproportionately into this line of work and shall struggle to make ends meet."

As for whether the gig economy is or not for you? This industry does not suit everyone: only to those who are resilient and disciplined. Or for those who use it as a side job to make some extra money as they grow a career in their area of interest, or someone living without any long-term planning. One needs to assess his/her profile and area of expertise and decide whether s/he is a good fit for part-time or full-time employment and which market she/he is looking for. There is no rush to take the decision, rest assured: the gig economy is here to stay.

Due to various kind of work and insufficient data, it is difficult to quantify the impacts of the gig economy, however, the gig economy shows no signs of slowing down and the forecasts are that it will continue to grow and rise. There is unanimity that the gig economy will not sustain in its current form for long and need some fundamental changes as big corporations are already struggling to turn.

REFERENCES

Wood, Graham, Lehdonvirta, & Hjorth. (2019). Good gig, bad gig: Autonomy and algorithmic control in the global gig economy. *Work, Employment and Society*, *33*(1), 56–75. PMID:30886460

Allen, J. (2018). Understanding the impact of e-commerce on lastmile light goods vehicle activity in urban areas: The case of London. *Transportation Research Part D: Transport and Environment*.

Aloisi, A. (2015). Commoditized workers: Case study research on labor law issues arising from a set of on-demand/gig economy platforms. *Comp. Lab. L. & Pol'y J.*, *37*, 653.

Balaram, B., Warden, J., & Wallace-Stephens, F. (2017). *Good Gigs: A fairer future for the UK's gig economy*. RSA.

Bates, O., & Friday, A. (2018). Intangible commodities with free delivery: Minding the limit in digitally mediated e-commerce and workforce injustice. In *Proceedings of the 2018 Workshop on Computing within Limits*. ACM. 10.1145/3232617.3232622

Bates, O., Friday, A., Allen, J., Cherrett, T., McLeod, F., Bektas, T., Nguyen, T., Piecyk, M., Piotrowska, M., Wise, S., & Davies, N. (n.d.). *Transforming last-mile logistics: Opportunities for more*. Academic Press.

BMO Global Asset Management. (2017). *Gig Economy*. Retrieved from https://bmogamviewpoints.com/wp-content/uploads/2018/07/The-gig-economy_Wealth-Institute_Final.pdf

Connelly, C. E., Fieseler, C., Černe, M., Giessner, S. R., & Wong, S. I. (2021). Working in the digitized economy: HRM theory & practice. *Human Resource Management Review*, *31*(1), 100762. Advance online publication. doi:10.1016/j.hrmr.2020.100762

De Stefano, V. (2014). The rise of the just-in-time workforce: On demand work, crowd work, and labor protection in the gig economy. *Comp. Lab. L. & Pol'y J., 37.*

Friedman, G. (n.d.). Workers without employers: shadow corporations and the rise of the gig economy. Review of Keynesian Economics, 2, 2.

Gall, G. (2020). Emerging forms of worker collectivism among the precariat: When will capital's 'gig' be up? *Capital and Class*, *44*(4), 485–492. doi:10.1177/0309816820906344

Harpur, P., & Blanck, P. (2020). Gig workers with disabilities: Opportunities, challenges, and regulatory response. *Journal of Occupational Rehabilitation*, *30*(4), 511–520. doi:10.100710926-020-09937-4 PMID:33146784

Healy, J., Nicholson, D., & Pekarek, A. (2017). Should we take the gig economy seriously? *Labour & Industry: A Journal of the Social and Economic Relations of Work, 27*(3), 232-248.

Woodcock, J., & Graham, M. (2019). The gig economy: A critical introduction. *Polity.*

Manyika, J., Lund, S., Bughin, J., Robinson, K., Mischke, J., & Mahajan, D. (2016). Independent work: Choice, necessity, and the gig economy. *McKinsey Global Institute*, *2016*, 1–16.

McKinsey. (2016). *Gig Economy.* https://www.mckinsey.com/~/media/mckinsey/featured%20insights/employment%20and%20growth/independent%20work%20choice%20necessity%20and%20the%20gig%20economy/independent-work-choice-necessity-and-the-gig-economy-executive-summary.ashx

Prassl, J. (2018). *Humans as a service: The promise and perils of work in the gig economy.* Oxford University Press. doi:10.1093/oso/9780198797012.001.0001

Randstad. (2016). https://www.randstadusa.com/about/news/randstad-us-study-projects-massive-shift-to-agile-employment-and-staffing-model-in-the-next-decade/sustainable deliveries

Schroeder, A. N., Bricka, T. M., & Whitaker, J. H. (2021). Work design in a digitized gig economy. *Human Resource Management Review*, *31*(1), 100692. Advance online publication. doi:10.1016/j.hrmr.2019.100692

Smith, B., Goods, C., Barratt, T., & Veen, A. (2021). Consumer 'appetite' for workers' rights in the Australian 'gig' economy. *Journal of Choice Modelling*, *38*, 100254. Advance online publication. doi:10.1016/j.jocm.2020.100254

Wood, A. J., Graham, M., Lehdonvirta, V., & Hjorth, I. (2019). Good gig, bad gig: Autonomy and algorithmic control in the global gig economy. *Work, Employment and Society*, *33*(1), 56–75. doi:10.1177/0950017018785616 PMID:30886460

Compilation of References

Accenture. (2012). *Getting Personal with Digital Mastering the digital revolution in the lodging industry*. Available at: https://www.cas-ag.eu/us-en/Documents/PDF/Accenture-Getting-Personal-Lodging-Master-Digital.pdf

Adamowicz, M. (2020). *The "Smart Village " as a Way to Achieve Sustainable Development in Rural Areas of Poland.* Academic Press.

Adeyinka-Ojo, S., & Abdullah, S. K. (2019). Disruptive Digital Innovation and Sharing Economy in Hospitality and Tourism Destination. *IOP Conference Series. Materials Science and Engineering*, *495*(012006), 1–7. doi:10.1088/1757-899X/495/1/012006

Adner, R. (2002). When are technologies disruptive? A demand-based view of the emergence of competition. *Strategic Management Journal*, *23*(8), 667–688. doi:10.1002mj.246

Adukaite, A., Reimann, A.M., Marchiori, E., & Cantoni, L. (2014). Hotel mobile apps. the case of 4 and 5 Star hotels in Europian Germaan-speking countries. In Z. Xiang ve I. Tussyadiah (Ed.) *Information and Communication Technologies in Tourism*, 45-57.

Agarwal, A. (2020). Investigating design targets for effective performance management system: an application of balance scorecard using QFD. *Journal of Advances in Management Research.*

Ahmad, S. Z. (2014). Entrepreneurship in the small and medium-sized hotel sector. *Current Issues in Tourism*, *18*(4), 328–349. doi:10.1080/13683500.2014.934211

Akama, J. S., & Kieti, D. M. (2003). Measuring tourist satisfaction with Kenya's wildlife safaari: A case study of Tsavo West National Park. *Tourism Management*, *24*(1), 73–81. doi:10.1016/S0261-5177(02)00044-4

Akgöz, E., Güral, R., & Gürsoy, Y. (2014). Yenilik kapsamında turistik ürün çeşitlendirmesi ve Kurban Bayramı örneği. *Selçuk Üniversitesi Sosyal Bilimler Enstitüsü Dergisi*, *31*, 1–12.

Alegre, J., & Garau, J. (2010). Tourist satisfaction and dissatisfaction. *Annals of Tourism Research*, *37*(1), 52–73. doi:10.1016/j.annals.2009.07.001

Alivizatou-Barakou, M., Kitsikidis, A., Tsalakanidou, F., Dimitropoulos, K., Giannis, C., Nikolopoulos, S., Al Kork, S., Denby, B., Buchman, L., Adda-Decker, M., Pillot-Loiseau, C., Tillmane, J., Dupont, S., Picart, B., Pozzi, F., Ott, M., Erdal, Y., Charisis, V., Hadjidimitriou, S., . . . Grammalidis, N. (2017). Intangible Cultural Heritage and New Technologies: Challenges and Opportunities for Cultural Preservation and Development. In Mixed Reality and Gamification for Cultural Heritage (pp. 129–158). Springer International Publishing. doi:10.1007/978-3-319-49607-8_5

Alkhaleefah, A. (2018). What to do to improve the international saudi innovation Rank/Score. *International Journal of Mechanical Engineering and Technology*, *9*(3), 435–442.

Allen, J. (2018). Understanding the impact of e-commerce on lastmile light goods vehicle activity in urban areas: The case of London. *Transportation Research Part D: Transport and Environment.*

Aloisi, A. (2015). Commoditized workers: Case study research on labor law issues arising from a set of on-demand/gig economy platforms. *Comp. Lab. L. & Pol'y J.*, *37*, 653.

Amaratunga, D., & Baldry, D. (2002). *Moving from performance measurement to performance management.* Facilities. doi:10.1108/02632770210426701

Anand, A. (2007). E-*Satisfaction: A Comprehensive Framework.* International Marketing Conference on Marketing and SocietyIMK.

Anderson, R. E., & Srinivasan, S. S. (2003). E-satisfaction and e-loyalty: A contingency framework. *Psychology and Marketing*, *20*(2), 123–138. doi:10.1002/mar.10063

Anuar, J., Musa, M., & Khalid, K. (2014). Smartphone's application adoption benefits using mobile hotel reservation system (MHRS) among 3 to 5-star city hotels in Malaysia. *Procedia: Social and Behavioral Sciences*, *130*, 552–557. doi:10.1016/j.sbspro.2014.04.064

Armstrong, M., & Baron, A. (2000). *Performance management.* Kogan Page Limited.

Arvanitis, L. G., Ramachandran, B., Brackett, D. P., Abd, R. E., Hesham, A., & Du, X. (2000). Multiresource inventories incorporating GIS, GPS and database management systems: A conceptual model. *Computers and Electronics in Agriculture*, *28*(2), 89–100. doi:10.1016/S0168-1699(00)00124-1

Atay, L., Yalçınkaya, P., & Bahar, F. (2019). İstanbul'daki akıllı otel uygulamalarının değerlendirilmesi. *Manas Sosyal Araştırmalar Dergisi*, *8*(1), 667–678.

Avaya. (2011). *The Impact of Guest Experience on Hotel Revenues How the right technology can result in higher profitability.* Available at: https://www.avaya.com/usa/documents/impactguestexperienceshotelrevs.pdf

Aydin, E., Polat, A., & Ergene, L. T. (2016, November). Vector control of DFIG in wind power applications. In *2016 IEEE International Conference on Renewable Energy Research and Applications (ICRERA)* (pp. 478-483). IEEE. 10.1109/ICRERA.2016.7884383

Azila, J. (2014). *Factors Affecting Customers' Experience in Local Fast Food Restaurant.* 2nd World Conference on Islamic Thought and Civilization, Perak, Malaysia.

Balaram, B., Warden, J., & Wallace-Stephens, F. (2017). *Good Gigs: A fairer future for the UK's gig economy*. RSA.

Baloğlu, Ş., & Pekcan, Y. A. (2006). The website design and internet site marketing practices of upscale and luxury hotels in Turkey. *Tourism Management, 27*(1), 171–176. doi:10.1016/j.tourman.2004.07.003

Baltagi, B. H., Egger, P. H., & Kesina, M. (2016). Bayesian Spatial Bivariate Panel Probit Estimation', Spatial Econometrics: Qualitative and Limited Dependent Variables (Advances in Econometrics, Volume 37). Emerald Group Publishing Limited.

Bangladesh Bureau of Educational Information and Statistics (BANBEIS). (2020). *Bangladesh education statistics book*. Author.

Barrows, S. (2015). *Six Ways to Create a Memorable Customer Experience*. Available at: https://www.entrepreneur.com/article/206760

Bates, O., Friday, A., Allen, J., Cherrett, T., McLeod, F., Bektas, T., Nguyen, T., Piecyk, M., Piotrowska, M., Wise, S., & Davies, N. (n.d.). *Transforming last-mile logistics: Opportunities for more*. Academic Press.

Bates, O., & Friday, A. (2018). Intangible commodities with free delivery: Minding the limit in digitally mediated e-commerce and workforce injustice. In *Proceedings of the 2018 Workshop on Computing within Limits*. ACM. 10.1145/3232617.3232622

Beesley, L. G., & Davidson, M. (2013). A critical analysis of skilled labor supply and demand in the Australian hospitality industry. *Journal of Quality Assurance in Hospitality & Tourism, 14*(3), 264–280. doi:10.1080/1528008X.2013.802552

Benschop, Y., & Brouns, M. (2003). Crumbling ivory towers: Academic organizing and its gender effects. *Gender, Work and Organization, 10*(2), 194–212. doi:10.1111/1468-0432.t01-1-00011

Biancolino, C. A., Maccari, E. A., & Pereira, M. F. (2013). Innovation as a tool for generating value in the IT services sector. *Review of Business Management, 15*(48), 410–426. doi:10.7819/rbgn.v15i48.1367

Biron, M., Farndale, E., & Paauwe, J. (2011). Performance management effectiveness: Lessons from world-leading firms. *International Journal of Human Resource Management, 22*(06), 1294–1311. doi:10.1080/09585192.2011.559100

Bloomberg, J. (2018). Digitization, digitalization, and digital transformation: confuse them at your peril. *Forbes*.

BMO Global Asset Management. (2017). *Gig Economy*. Retrieved from https://bmogamviewpoints.com/wp-content/uploads/2018/07/The-gig-economy_Wealth-Institute_Final.pdf

Bousquet, J., Bedbrook, A., Czarlewski, W., Onorato, G. L., Arnavielhe, S., Laune, D., ... Morais-Almeida, M. (2019). Guidance to 2018 good practice: ARIA digitally-enabled, integrated, person-centred care for rhinitis and asthma. *Clinical and Translational Allergy*, *9*(1), 1–19.

Bowen, D., & Clark, J. (2002). Reflections on tourist satisfaction research: Past, present and future. *Journal of Vacation Marketing*, *8*(4), 297–308. doi:10.1177/135676670200800401

Bower, J. L., & Christensen, C. M. (1995). Disruptive technologies: Catching the wave. *Harvard Business Review*, *73*(1), 43–53.

Brewer, P. (2008). *Current and Future Technology Use in the Hospitality Industry*. Available at: https://www.ahla.com/uploadedFiles/AHLA/Members_Only/Property_and_Corporate/Property_-_Publications/Current%20and%20Future%20Technology.pdf

Broadbent, J., & Laughlin, R. (2009). Performance management systems: A conceptual model. *Management Accounting Research*, *20*(4), 283–295. doi:10.1016/j.mar.2009.07.004

Brown, B., & Chalmers, M. (2003). Tourism and mobile technology. K. Kuutti ve E.H. Karsten (Ed.), *Proeceedings of the 8th European Conference on Computer Supported Cooperative Work*. Helsinki, Finland, 14-18 September. 10.1007/978-94-010-0068-0_18

Brunner-Sperdin, A., & Peters, M. (2004). Importance and measurement of entrepreneurial quality and processes in tourism. *Journal of Quality Assurance in Hospitality & Tourism*, *5*(1), 73–90. doi:10.1300/J162v05n01_06

Buhalis, D., & Foerste, M. (2015). SoCoMo marketing for travel and tourism: Empowering co-creation of value. *Journal of Destination Marketing & Management*, *4*(3), 151–161. doi:10.1016/j.jdmm.2015.04.001

Burke, R. R. (2002). Technology and the customer interface: What consumers want in the physical and virtual store. *Journal of the Academy of Marketing Science*, *30*(4), 411–432. doi:10.1177/009207002236914

Büyük, K. (2010). Stratejik Performans Yönetiminin Unsuru Olarak Örgüt Kültürünü Ölçümleme Üzerine Kavramsal Bir Çalışma, Eskişehir Osmangazi Üniversitesi. IBF Dergisi, *5*(2), 220–230.

Calantone, R. J., Cavusgil, T. S., & Zhaob, Y. (2002). Learning orientation, firm innovation capability, and firm performance. *Industrial Marketing Management*, *31*(6), 515–524. doi:10.1016/S0019-8501(01)00203-6

Can, Ö. (2009). Tekstil kobilerinde inovasyon. *Tekstil Teknolojileri Elektronik Dergisi*, *3*(1), 57–63.

Canonica, G. W., Antó i Boqué, J. M., Mullol i Miret, J., & Valero Santiago, A.MASK study group. (2019). Guidance to 2018 good practice: ARIA digitally enabled, integrated, person-centred care for rhinitis and asthma. *Clinical and Translational Allergy*, *9*, •••.

Cantú-Ortiz, F. J., Sánchez, N. G., Garrido, L., Terashima-Marin, H., & Brena, R. F. (2020). An artificial intelligence educational strategy for the digital transformation. *International Journal on Interactive Design and Manufacturing*, 1-15.

Car, T. (2012). *Mobile marketing and advertising strategies in tourism and hospitality industry*. Faculty of Tourism and Hospitality Management Opatija, University of Rijeka.

Carlsson, C., Hyvonen, K., Repo, P., & Walden, P. (2005). Asynchronous adoption patterns of mobile services. In *Proceedings of the 38th Hawaii International Conference on System Sciences*. IEEE Computer Society Press. 10.1109/HICSS.2005.106

Carrozzino, M., Scucces, A., Leonardi, R., Evangelista, C., & Bergamasco, M. (2011). Virtually preserving the intangible heritage of artistic handicraft. *Journal of Cultural Heritage*, *12*(1), 82–87. doi:10.1016/j.culher.2010.10.002

Carvolha, L., & Costa, T. (2011). Tourism innovation – A literature review complemented by case study research. Internatıonal Conference on Tourism & Management Studies, 1, 23-33.

Castagna, F., Centobelli, P., Cerchione, R., Esposito, E., Oropallo, E., & Passaro, R. (2020). Customer Knowledge Management in SMEs Facing Digital Transformation. *Sustainability*, *12*(9), 3899. doi:10.3390u12093899

Çeliktaş, H. (2008). *İnovasyon yönetimi: Çukurova Bölgesinde faaliyet gösteren şirketlerde inovasyon uygulamalarının tespitine yönelik bir araştırma* [Yüksek Lisans Tezi]. Çukurova Üniversitesi Sosyal Bilimler Enstitüsü.

Chandler, A. D. (1990). *Strategy and structure: Chapters in the history of the industrial enterprise* (Vol. 120). MIT Press.

Chang, P. (2017). The Importance Performance Analysis of Taiwan Tourism Mobile Marketing. *Journal of Tourism Management Research*, *4*(1), 12–16. doi:10.18488/journal.31.2017.41.12.16

Charitou, C., & Markides, C. (2003). Responses to Disruptive Strategic Innovation. *Sloan Management Review*, *44*(2), 55–63.

Charland, A., & Leroux, B. (2011). Mobile application development: Web vs. native. *Communications of the ACM*, *54*(5), 49–53. doi:10.1145/1941487.1941504

Chaudhuri, S. (2016). Geographic Information Portals: Maldives Tourism Perspective. *6th Int'l Conference on Advances in Engineering Sciences and Applied Mathematics*.

Cheer, J. M., Reeves, K. J., & Laing, J. H. (2013). Tourism and traditional culture: Land diving in vanuatu. *Annals of Tourism Research*, *43*(xx), 435–455. doi:10.1016/j.annals.2013.06.005

Cheuk, S., Atang, A., Chiun, L. M., & Ramayah, T. (2018). Barriers to digital marketing adoption at remote rural tourism destinations in Sarawak: An exploratory study. *IACSIT International Journal of Engineering and Technology*, *7*(2), 86–90. doi:10.14419/ijet.v7i2.29.13135

Cho, Y., & Agrusa, J. (2006). Assessing use acceptance & satisfaction toward online travel agencies. *Journal of Information Technology and Tourism*, *8*(3/4), 179–195. doi:10.3727/109830506778690795

Christensen, C. M. (1997). *The innovator's dilemma: When new technologies cause great firms to fail*. Harvard Business School Press.

Christensen, C. M. (2006). The ongoing process of building a theory of disruption. *Journal of Product Innovation Management, 23*(1), 39–55. doi:10.1111/j.1540-5885.2005.00180.x

Christensen, C. M., McDonald, R., Altman, E. J., & Palmer, J. E. (2018). Disruptive Innovation: An Intellectual History and Directions for Future Research. *Journal of Management Studies, 55*(7), 1043–1078. doi:10.1111/joms.12349

Christensen, C. M., & Raynor, M. (2003). *The innovator's solution: creating and sustaining successful growth*. Harvard Business Review Press.

Christensen, C. M., Raynor, M., & McDonald, R. (2015). What is disruptive innovation? *Harvard Business Review, 93*(12), 44–53. PMID:17183796

Clement, J. (2019). *Mobile Internet Usage Worldwide- Statistics & Facts*. https://www.statista.com/topics/779/mobile-internet/

Cohen, L. (2007). *Research methods in education* (6th ed.). Routledge. doi:10.4324/9780203029053

Çokluk, Ö., Şekercioğlu, G., & Büyüköztürk, Ş. (2012). *Sosyal bilimler için çok değişkenli istatistik: SPSS ve LISREL uygulamaları*. Pegem Akademi.

Collins, H. (2011). *Creative Research: The Theory and Practice of Research for the Creative Industries*. AVA Publications.

Colombo, G. B., Chorley, M. J., Williams, M. J., Allen, S. M., & Whitaker, R. M. (2012). *You are where you eat: Foursquare checkins as indicators of human mobility and behaviour*. School of Computer Science & Informatics, Cardiff University.

Condratov, I. (2013). E-Tourism: Concept And Evolution. *Ecoforum, 2*(1). www.internetworldstats.com

Confente, I. (2015). Twenty-five years of word-of-mouth studies: A critical review of tourism research. *International Journal of Tourism Research, 17*(6), 613–624. doi:10.1002/jtr.2029

Connelly, C. E., Fieseler, C., Černe, M., Giessner, S. R., & Wong, S. I. (2021). Working in the digitized economy: HRM theory & practice. *Human Resource Management Review, 31*(1), 100762. Advance online publication. doi:10.1016/j.hrmr.2020.100762

Connolly, D. J., Olsen, M. D., & Moore, R. G. (1998). The Internet as a distribution channel. *The Cornell Hotel and Restaurant Administration Quarterly, 39*(4), 42–54. doi:10.1177/001088049803900408

Cooper, D. R., & Schindler, P. S. (2006). *Business Research Method* (9th ed.). McGraw-Hill Irwin.

Correani, A., De Massis, A., Frattini, F., Petruzzelli, A. M., & Natalicchio, A. (2020). Implementing a digital strategy: Learning from the experience of three digital transformation projects. *California Management Review, 62*(4), 37–56. doi:10.1177/0008125620934864

Coşkun, S. (2013). *Stratejik rekabet üstünlüğü sağlama aracı olarak inovasyon stratejileri-Kocaeli otel işletmeleri üzerine bir araştırma.* Yüksek Lisans Tezi, Düzce Üniversitesi Sosyal Bilimler Enstitüsü Turizm ve Otel İşletmeciliği Anabilim Dalı, Düzce.

Coutinho, R., Joao, L., Simao, A., & Antunes, C. H. (2011). GIS-based multicriteria spatial decision support system for planning urban infrastructures. *Decision Support Systems, 51*(3), 720–726. doi:10.1016/j.dss.2011.02.010

Cozzani, G., Pozzi, F., Dagnino, F., Katos, A., & Katsouli, E. (2017). Innovative technologies for intangible cultural heritage education and preservation: The case of i-Treasures. *Personal and Ubiquitous Computing, 21*(2), 253–265. doi:10.100700779-016-0991-z

Crespo, N. F., & Crespo, C. F. (2016). Global innovation index: Moving beyond the absolute value of ranking with a fuzzy-set analysis. *Journal of Business Research, 69*(11), 5265–5271. doi:10.1016/j.jbusres.2016.04.123

Creswell, J. W. (2009). *Research design: Qualitative, quantitative, and mixed methods approaches* (3rd ed.). Sage.

Creswell, J. W. (2012). *Qualitative inquiry and research design: Choosing among five traditions* (3rd ed.). Sage.

Creswell, J. W., & Clark, P. V. L. (2007). *Designing and conducting mixed methods research.* Sage.

Crowther, D., & Lancaster, G. (2008). *Research Methods: A Concise Introduction to Research in Management and Business Consultancy.* Butterworth-Heinemann.

Curzi, Y., Fabbri, T., Scapolan, A. C., & Boscolo, S. (2019). Performance appraisal and innovative behavior in the digital era. *Frontiers in Psychology, 10*, 1659. doi:10.3389/fpsyg.2019.01659 PMID:31379682

Danneels, E. (2004). Disruptive technology reconsidered: A critique and research agenda. *Journal of Product Innovation Management, 21*(4), 246–258. doi:10.1111/j.0737-6782.2004.00076.x

Dash, A., & Kuddus, K. (2020) Leveraging the benefits of ICT usage in teaching of English language and literature. In Smart intelligent computing and applications, vol 160. Smart innovation, systems and technologies. Springer.

Daskon, C., & McGregor, A. (2012). Cultural Capital and Sustainable Livelihoods in Sri Lanka's Rural Villages: Towards Culturally Aware Development. *The Journal of Development Studies, 48*(4), 549–563. doi:10.1080/00220388.2011.604413

De Longueville, B. (2010). Community-based geoportals: The next generation? Concepts and methods for the geospatial Web 2.0. *Computers, Environment and Urban Systems, 34*(4), 299–308. doi:10.1016/j.compenvurbsys.2010.04.004

De Stefano, V. (2014). The rise of the just-in-time workforce: On demand work, crowd work, and labor protection in the gig economy. *Comp. Lab. L. & Pol'y J., 37.*

Demirkaya, H., & Zengin, R. (2014). Hizmet inovasyonu ve bir uygulama örneği. *Elektronik Mesleki Gelişim Ve Araştırmalar Dergisi*, *2*(1), 106–116.

DeNisi, A. S., & Murphy, K. R. (2017). Performance appraisal and performance management: 100 years of progress? *The Journal of Applied Psychology*, *102*(3), 421–433. doi:10.1037/apl0000085 PMID:28125265

Di Minin, E., Tenkanen, H., & Toivonen, T. (2015). Prospects and challenges for social media data in conservation science. *Frontiers in Environmental Science*, *3*(SEP), 1–6. doi:10.3389/fenvs.2015.00063

Dibiase, D., & Kidwai, K. (2010). Wasted on the young? comparing the performance and attitudes of younger and older US adults in an online class on geographic information: JGHE annual lecture. *Journal of Geography in Higher Education*, *34*(3), 299–326. doi:10.1080/03098265.2010.490906

Dickinson, J. E., Hibbert, J. F., & Filimonau, V. (2016). Mobile technology and the tourist experience: (Dis)connection at the campsite. *Tourism Management*, *57*, 193–201. doi:10.1016/j.tourman.2016.06.005

DiMaggio, P., Hargittai, E., Neuman, W. R., & Robinson, J. P. (2001). Social implications of the Internet. *Annual Review of Sociology*, *27*(1), 307–336. doi:10.1146/annurev.soc.27.1.307

Disruption Drives the Hospitality Industry to Innovation. (2020). Retrieved from https://www.hotelbusiness.com/disruption-drives-the-hospitality-industry-to-innovation

Divisekera, S., & Nguyen, V. K. (2018). Determinants of innovation in tourism evidence from Australia. *Tourism Management, 67*, 157–167. Retrieved from https://www.researchgate.net/publication/323931154_Determinants_of_Innovation_in_tourism_Evidence_from_Australia

Dominici, G., & Rosa, G., (2010). Customer Satisfaction in the Hotel Industry: A Case Study from Sicily. *International Journal of Marketing Studies, 10*(2).

Drucker, P. (1998). The discipline of innovation. *Harvard Business Review*, *76*(6), 54–66. PMID:10187245

Drummond, W. J., & French, S. P. (2008). The future of GIS in planning: Converging technologies and diverging interests. *Journal of the American Planning Association*, *74*(2), 161–174. doi:10.1080/01944360801982146

Duarte, M. P., & Carvalho, F. M. (2020). *Portugal in the Global Innovation Index: A panel data analysis* (No. 0144). Gabinete de Estratégia e Estudos, Ministério da Economia.

Duhaney. (2005). Technology and Higher Education: Challenges in the Halls of Academe. Academic Press.

Dutta, S., Kumar Chauhan, R., & Chauhan, K. (2017). Factors affecting customer satisfaction of online travel agencies in India. *Tourism and Hospitality Management*, *23*(2), 267–277. doi:10.20867/thm.23.2.3

Dzhandzhugazova, E.A. (2015). Innovative marketing mix of hotels: Seven sensual notes of hospitality. *Russian Regions: Looking Into the Future, 3,* 17–27.

Dzhandzhugazovaa, E. A., Ekaterina, A., Blinovaa, E. A., Orlovaa, L. N., & Romanovaa, M. M. (2016). Innovations in Hospitality Industry. *International Journal of Environmental and Science Education, 11*(17), 10387–10400.

Elçi, Ş. (2006). *İnovasyon: Kalkınmanın ve rekabetin anahtarı.* NOVA Basın Yayın.

Emrich, C. T., Cutter, S. L., & Weschler, P. J. (2011). GIS and emergency management. The SAGE handbook of GIS and society, 321-343. doi:10.4135/9781446201046.n17

Entina, T., Karabulatova, I., Kormishova, A., Ekaterinovskaya, M., & Troyanskaya, M. (2021). Tourism industry management in the global transformation: Meeting the needs of generation z. *Polish Journal of Management Studies, 23*(2), 130–148. doi:10.17512/pjms.2021.23.2.08

Ercan, E., & Önal, A. (2007). *Mobil turist rehberlerine karşılaştırmalı bakış. Akademik Bilişim, IX.* Akademik Bilişim Konferansı Bildirileri, Dumlupınar Üniversitesi.

Escobar, A. E. S., & Parra, W. C. (2011). Matriz de Inteligência Hotelera - MIH: Una propuesta para el mejoramiento de la calidad em la prestación del servicio hotelero. *Pensamiento Y Gestión, 31,* 211–246.

Essmann, H., & Preez, N.D. (2009). An innovation capability maturity model development and initial application. *International Journal Of Industrial And Manufacturing Engineering, 3*(5).

Europa. (2014). *Classification Of Hotel Establishments Within The EU.* Available at: https://ec.europa.eu/consumers/ecc/docs/hotel_establishment_classification_EU_en.pdf

Evanschitzky, H., Iyer, G. R., Hesse, J., & Ahlert, D. (2004). E-satisfaction: A re-examination. *Journal of Retailing, 80*(3), 239–247. doi:10.1016/j.jretai.2004.08.002

Evans-Cowley, J. (2010). Planning in the real-time city: The future of mobile technology. Journal of Planning Literature, 25(2), 136–149. doi:10.1177/0885412210394100

Faghih, N., & Sazegar, M. (2019). A Taxonomy of Country Performance Based on GDP and Innovation Indicators for the Group of Twenty (G20). In *Globalization and Development* (pp. 163–200). Springer. doi:10.1007/978-3-030-14370-1_7

Fischer, M., Imgrund, F., Janiesch, C., & Winkelmann, A. (2020). Strategy archetypes for digital transformation: Defining meta objectives using business process management. *Information & Management, 57*(5), 103262. doi:10.1016/j.im.2019.103262

Flapper, S. D. P., Fortuin, L., & Stoop, P. P. (1996). Towards consistent performance management systems. *International Journal of Operations & Production Management.*

Fleischer, A., & Pizam, A. (1997). Rural tourism in Israel. *Tourism Management, 18*(6), 367–372. doi:10.1016/S0261-5177(97)00034-4

Flint, D. J., Blocker, C. P., & Boutin, P. J. Jr. (2011). Customer value anticipation, customer satisfaction and loyalty: An empirical examination. *Industrial Marketing Management, 40*(2), 219–230. doi:10.1016/j.indmarman.2010.06.034

Ford, R. C. (2012). *Managing Quality Service in Hospitality: How Organizations Achieve Excellence in the Guest Experience*. Delmar, Cengage Learning.

Fornell, C., Rust, R. T., & Dekimpe, M. G. (2010). The Effect of Customer Satisfaction on Consumer Spending Growth. *JMR, Journal of Marketing Research, 47*(1), 28–35. doi:10.1509/jmkr.47.1.28

Fraj, E., Matute, J., & Melero, I. (2015). Environmental strategies and organizational competitiveness in the hotel industry: The role of learning and innovation as determinants of environmental success. *Tourism Management, 46*(6), 30–42. doi:10.1016/j.tourman.2014.05.009

Franco-Santos, M., & Doherty, N. (2017). Performance management and well-being: A close look at the changing nature of the UK higher education workplace. *International Journal of Human Resource Management, 28*(16), 2319–2350. doi:10.1080/09585192.2017.1334148

Frennert, S. (2018). Lost in digitalization? Municipality employment of welfare technologies. *Disability and Rehabilitation. Assistive Technology*. PMID:30264649

Friedman, G. (n.d.). Workers without employers: shadow corporations and the rise of the gig economy. Review of Keynesian Economics, 2, 2.

Frochot, I. (2005). A benefit segmentation of tourists in rural areas: A Scottish perspective. *Tourism Management, 26*(3), 335–346. doi:10.1016/j.tourman.2003.11.016

Gaile-sarkane, E., & Andersone, I. (2011). Modeling of Consumer Behavior for Business Sophistication. *The 15th World Multi-Conference on*. https://www.iiis.org/CDs2011/CD2011SCI/SCI_2011/PapersPdf/SA275VH.pdf

Gall, G. (2020). Emerging forms of worker collectivism among the precariat: When will capital's 'gig' be up? *Capital and Class, 44*(4), 485–492. doi:10.1177/0309816820906344

Gan, S. W., Inversini, A., & Rega, I. (2018). Tourism, Development and Digital Technologies: Insights from Malaysian Homestays. In Information and Communication Technologies in Tourism 2018 (Vol. 1, pp. 52–63). Springer International Publishing. doi:10.1007/978-3-319-72923-7_5

Ganapati, S. (2011). Uses of public participation geographic information systems applications in e-government. *Public Administration Review, 71*(3), 425–434. doi:10.1111/j.1540-6210.2011.02226.x

Gandolfo, D., & Rosa, G., (2010). Customer Satisfaction in the Hotel Industry: A Case Study from Sicily. *International Journal of Marketing Studies, 2*(2).

Gao, X., Guo, X., & Lo, T. (2021). Digital infrastructure - A potential method for rural revitalization through digitization of rural information. *Projections - Proceedings of the 26th International Conference of the Association for Computer-Aided Architectural Design Research in Asia, CAADRIA 2021, 2*, 699–708.

Garau, C. (2015). Perspectives on cultural and sustainable rural tourism in a smart region: The case study of Marmilla in Sardinia (Italy). *Sustainability (Switzerland), 7*(6), 6412–6434. doi:10.3390u7066412

Garrido-Baserba, M., Corominas, L., Cortés, U., Rosso, D., & Poch, M. (2020). The fourth-revolution in the water sector encounters the digital revolution. *Environmental Science & Technology, 54*(8), 4698–4705. doi:10.1021/acs.est.9b04251 PMID:32154710

Gemini, E., & Alpkan, L. (2015). An Application of Disruptive Innovation Theory to Create a Competitive Strategy in Turkish Air Transportation Industry. *Procedia: Social and Behavioral Sciences, 207*, 797–806. doi:10.1016/j.sbspro.2015.10.169

Gezici, B., Tarhan, A., & Chouseinoglou, O. (2018). Mobil uygulamaların evriminde karmaşıklık, boyut ve iç kalite gelişimi: Keşifsel bir çalışma. *Gazi Üniversitesi Mühendislik-Mimarlık Fakültesi Dergisi, 34*(3), 18–22.

Ghobakhloo, M. (2020). Determinants of information and digital technology implementation for smart manufacturing. *International Journal of Production Research, 58*(8), 2384–2405. doi :10.1080/00207543.2019.1630775

Giudici, E., Melis, C., Dessì, S., & Francine Pollnow Galvao Ramos, B. (2013). Is intangible cultural heritage able to promote sustainability in tourism? *International Journal of Quality and Service Sciences, 5*(1), 101–114. doi:10.1108/17566691311316275

Giuffrida, N., Le, P., Inturri, G., & Ignaccolo, M. (2019). Mapping with stakeholders: An overview of public participatory GIS and VGI in transport decision-making. *ISPRS International Journal of Geo-Information, 8*(4), 198. doi:10.3390/ijgi8040198

Gomez, M. I., McLaughlin, E. W., & Wittink, D. R. (2004). Customer satisfaction and retail sales performance: An empirical investigation. *Journal of Retailing, 80*(4), 265–278. doi:10.1016/j.jretai.2004.10.003

Goodchild, M. F. (2007). Citizens as voluntary sensors: Spatial data infrastructure in the world of Web 2.0. *International Journal of Spatial Data Infrastructures Research, 2*(2), 24–32.

Govindarajan, V., & Kopalle, P. K. (2006). The usefulness of measuring disruptiveness of innovations ex post in making ex ante predictions. *Journal of Product Innovation Management, 23*(1), 12–18. doi:10.1111/j.1540-5885.2005.00176.x

Grameen Bank Shikka Barta. (2009). *Five highest scholars' faces from the children of GB members in 2009*. Grameen Bank.

Grameen Bank. (2004). *Opening Speech by Muhammed Yunus, 30th Zonal Manager Conference*. Dhaka: Grameen Bank.

Grameen Bank. (2005). Opening Speech by Muhammed Yunus, *30th Zonal Manager Conference*. Dhaka: Grameen Bank

Grameen Shakka Bartta. (2014). *Talented children stories*. Grameen Bank.

Grameen Shikka Bartta. (2008). *Proud mothers from the borrowers of GB*. Department Administration, Grameen Bank.

Grameen Shikka Bartta. (2014). *Grameen Bank talented Scholars*. Department Administration, Grameen Bank.

Grameen Shikka, . (2006). *Grammen Shikka Activities*. Grameen Shikka.

Grameen Shikka, . (2019). *Arsenic mitigation program in Bangladesh*. Grameen Shikka.

Grayson, K., & Martinec, R. (2004). Consumer perceptions of iconicity and indexicality and their influence on assessments of authentic market offerings. *The Journal of Consumer Research*, *31*(2), 296–312. doi:10.1086/422109

Gruman, J. A., & Saks, A. M. (2011). Performance management and employee engagement. *Human Resource Management Review*, *21*(2), 123–136. doi:10.1016/j.hrmr.2010.09.004

Guan, H., & Yin, M. (2007). Empirical study of user satisfaction of travel website information resources-take C-trip as an example. *Journal of Beijing International Studies University*, *151*(11), 64-68.

Gulbahar, M. O., & Yildirim, F. (2015). Marketing Efforts Related to Social Media Channels and Mobile Application Usage in Tourism: Case Study in Istanbul. *Procedia: Social and Behavioral Sciences*, *195*, 453–462. doi:10.1016/j.sbspro.2015.06.489

Gupta, A., & Dogra, N. (2017). Tourist adoption of mapping apps: A UTAUT2 perspective of smart travellers. *Tourism and Hospitality Management*, *23*(2), 145–161. doi:10.20867/thm.23.2.6

Haber, S., & Lerner, M. (1998). Correlates of Tourist Satisfaction. *Annals of Tourism Research*, *25*(4), 197–201.

Hague & Logan. (2009). *Informal Learning and Non-Formal Education for Development*. Academic Press.

Haines, V. Y. III, & St-Onge, S. (2012). Performance management effectiveness: Practices or context? *International Journal of Human Resource Management*, *23*(6), 1158–1175. doi:10.1080/09585192.2011.561230

Haklay, M., Basiouka, S., Antoniou, V., & Ather, A. (2010). How many volunteers does it take to map an area well? The validity of Linus' law to volunteered geographic information. *The Cartographic Journal*, *47*(4), 315-322.

Hall, D. (2004). Rural tourism development in southeastern Europe: Transition and the search for sustainability. *International Journal of Tourism Research*, *6*(3), 165–176. doi:10.1002/jtr.482

Hanelt, A., Bohnsack, R., Marz, D., & Antunes, C. (2020). A systematic review of the literature on digital transformation: Insights and implications for strategy and organizational change. *Journal of Management Studies*.

Harmer, J. (2011). *Budget hotel market has grown by 35% during the recession*. Available at: https://www.thecaterer.com/articles/337431/budget-hotel-market-has-grown-by-35-during-the-recession

Harpur, P., & Blanck, P. (2020). Gig workers with disabilities: Opportunities, challenges, and regulatory response. *Journal of Occupational Rehabilitation*, *30*(4), 511–520. doi:10.100710926-020-09937-4 PMID:33146784

Harrison, D. (2013). Receptivit e e t Contrainte s d e L'innovatio n dan s L'administratio n Publique. *Telescope*, *19*(2), 71-86. http://cerberus.enap.ca/Telescope/docs/Index/Vol_19_no_2/Telv19_no2_harris on.pdf

Hasibović, A. Ć., & Tanović, A. (2019, May). PRINCE2 vs Scrum in digital business transformation. In *2019 42nd International Convention on Information and Communication Technology, Electronics and Microelectronics (MIPRO)* (pp. 1514-1518). IEEE. 10.23919/MIPRO.2019.8756716

Haslett, J. R. (1990). Geographic information systems. A new approach to habitat definition and the study of distributions. *Trends in Ecology & Evolution*, *5*(7), 214–218. doi:10.1016/0169-5347(90)90134-Y PMID:21232358

Hathaivaseawong, N., Mohamad, O., & Ramayah, T. (2004). *Acquisition of Marketing Knowledge in Thai International Joint Venture Firms*. Preliminary research. https://ramayah.com/journalarticlespdf/acquisitionofmarketing.pdf

Healy, J., Nicholson, D., & Pekarek, A. (2017). Should we take the gig economy seriously? *Labour & Industry: A Journal of the Social and Economic Relations of Work*, *27*(3), 232-248.

Henard, D. H., & Dacin, P. A. (2010). Reputation for product innovation: Its impact on consumers. *Journal of Product Innovation Management*, *27*(3), 321–335.

Hill & Rivera. (2001). How Is the Liver Primed or Sensitized for Alcoholic Liver Disease? Academic Press.

Hjalager, A. M. (2010). A review of innovation research in tourism. *Tourism Management*, *31*(1), 1–12.

Ho, C. I., Lin, Y. C., Yuan, Y. L., & Chen, M. C. (2016). Pre-trip tourism information search by smartphones and use of alternative information channels: A conceptual model. *Cogent Social Sciences*, *2*(1), 1136100. Advance online publication. doi:10.1080/23311886.2015.1136100

Ho, C., & Lee, Y. (2007). The development of an E-Travel Service Quality Scale. *Tourism Management*, *28*(6), 434–1449. doi:10.1016/j.tourman.2006.12.002

Hongxiu, L., Yong, L., & Reima, S. (2009). *Measurement of e-service quality: an empirical study on online travel service*. 17th European Conference on Information Systems (ECIS, 2009), Verona.

Horn, C., & Tahi, B. (2009). Some Cultural and Historical Factors Influencing Rural Maori Tourism Development In New Zealand. *Journal of Rural and Community Development*, *4*(1), 84–101.

Horuz, A. (2012). *İnovasyon Nedir*. http://www.edebiarsiv.com/makale-arsivi/4256-inovasyon-nedir.html

Hotelivate report: Disruptions that will redefine hospitality in a post-pandemic world. (n.d.). Retrieved from https://www.hotelierindia.com/business/10909-hotelivate-report-disruptions-that-will-redefine-hospitality-in-a-post-pandemic-world

Hudson, S., & Hudson, L. (2013). *Customer Service for Hospitality and Tourism*. Good Fellow Publishers Limited.

Hudson, S., & Hudson, L. (2011). *Customer Service for Hospitality and Tourism*. Goodfellow Publishers Limited.

Huffcut, A. I. (2010). From science to practice: Seven principles for conducting employment interviews. *Applied H.R.M. Research*, *12*, 121–136.

Idris, M. Z., Mustaffa, N. B., & Yusoff, S. O. S. (2016). Preservation of Intangible Cultural Heritage Using Advance Digital Technology: Issues and Challenges. *Harmonia: Journal of Arts Research and Education*, *16*(1), 1. doi:10.15294/harmonia.v16i1.6353

Iliachenko, E. Y. (2006 b). *Customer needs with Tourism websites: Tourism Consumer requirements for Electronic Service Quality (E-SQ) Characteristics of Tourism websites, Department of Business Administration and social Science*. Lulea University.

Ilyenkova, S. D., & Kuznetsov, V. I. (2009). *Innovation Management*. Eurasian Open Institute.

Insights, E. H. L. Retrieved from https://hospitalityinsights.ehl.edu/leading-through-disruption-hospitality

International Finance Corporation. (n.d.). Retrieved from https://www.ifc.org/wps/wcm/connect/537b9b66-a35c-40cf-bed8-6f618c4f63d8/202009-COVID-19-Impact-Disruptive-Tech-EM.pdf

Inversini, A., Rega, I., & Gan, S. W. (2020). E-Tourism as a Tool for Socio-economic Development. Handbook of E-Tourism, 1–16.

Irvine, W., & Anderson, A. (2008). ICT (information communication technology), peripherality and smaller hospitality businesses in Scotland. *International Journal of Entrepreneurial Behaviour & Research*, *14*(4), 200–218. doi:10.1108/13552550810887381

Isa, W. M. W., Zin, N. A. M., Rosdi, F., & Sarim, H. M. (2018). Digital preservation of intangible cultural heritage. *Indonesian Journal of Electrical Engineering and Computer Science*, *12*(3), 1373–1379. doi:10.11591/ijeecs.v12.i3.pp1373-1379

İşlek, M. (2012). *Sosyal medyanın tüketici davranışlarına etkileri: Türkiye'deki sosyal medya kullanıcıları üzerine bir araştırma*. Karamanoğlu Mehmet Bey Üniversitesi, Sosyal Bilimler Enstitüsü Yüksek Lisans Tezi.

Istanti, L. N. (2021). *Rural Tourism Perspectives on Digital Innovation: Small Enterprises in Indonesia*. Academic Press.

Jarrar, Y., Awobamise, A. O., & Sellos, P. S. (2020). Technological readiness index (TRI) and the intention to use smartphone apps for tourism: A focus on indubai mobile tourism app. *International Journal of Data and Network Science*, *4*(3), 297–304. doi:10.5267/j.ijdns.2020.6.003

Jen-Her Wua, B., & Shu-Ching Wanga, C. (2009). What drives mobile commerce?: An empirical evaluation of the revised technology acceptance model. *Information & Management*, *42*(5), •••.

Jeong, C. W., Chung, J. Y., Joo, C. S., & Lee, J. (2006). Tourism guided information system for location-based services. *Asia-Pacific Web Conference*, 749-755. 10.1007/11610496_101

Jin-zhao, W., & Jing, W. (2009). Issues, Challenges, and Trends, that Facing Hospitality Industry. *Management Science and Engineering*, *3*(4), 53–58.

Joshi, B. P. (2018). Disruptive Innovation in Hospitality Human Resource. *Journal of Tourism and Hospitality Education*, *8*(48), 1–29. doi:10.3126/jthe.v8i0.20010

Jovanovic, V. (2016). The application of GIS and its components in tourism. *Yugoslav Journal of Operations Research*, (18), 2016.

Jüttner, U., Schaffner, D., Windler, K., & Maklan, S. (2013). Customer service experiences: Developing and applying a sequential incident laddering technique. *European Journal of Marketing*, *47*(5/6), 738–769. doi:10.1108/03090561311306769

Jyotsna, J. H., & Maurya, U. K. (2019). Experiencing the real village–a netnographic examination of perceived authenticity in rural tourism consumption. *Asia Pacific Journal of Tourism Research*, *24*(8), 750–762. doi:10.1080/10941665.2019.1630455

Kagaari, J. R., Munene, J. C., & Ntayi, J. M. (2010). Performance management practices, information and communication technology (ICT) adoption and managed performance. *Quality Assurance in Education*, *18*(2), 106–125. doi:10.1108/09684881011035330

Kallmuenzer, A. (2018). Exploring drives of innovation in hospitality family firms. *International Journal of Contemporary Hospitality Management*, *30*(3), 1978–1995. doi:10.1108/IJCHM-04-2017-0242

Kallmuenzer, A., & Peters, M. (2018). Innovativeness and control mechanisms in tourism and hospitality family firms: A comparative study. *International Journal of Hospitality Management*, *70*, 66–74. doi:10.1016/j.ijhm.2017.10.022

Kamboj, S., & Joshi, R. (2021). Examining the factors influencing smartphone apps use at tourism destinations: A UTAUT model perspective. *International Journal of Tourism Cities*, *7*(1), 135–157. doi:10.1108/IJTC-05-2020-0094

Kandampully, J., Bilgihan, A., & Zhang, T. C. (2016). Developing a people-technology hybrids model to unleash innovation and creativity: The new hospitality frontier. *Journal of Hospitality and Tourism Management, 29*, 154–164. doi:10.1016/j.jhtm.2016.07.003

Kar, A., & Singh, S. (1997). Remote sensing data products and visual interpretation tools for land resources and grazing land studies. *Silvipastoral Systems in Arid and Semi-Arid Ecosystems, 87.*

Kardes, & … . (2015). *Consumer Behavior* (2nd ed.). Cengage Learning.

Karthikeyan, N., & Balamurgan, T. (2012). Mobile Marketing: Examining the impact of Interest, Individual attention, Problem faced and consumer's attitude on intention to purchase. *Interdisciplinary Journal of Contemporary Research in Business, 3*(6).

Kasriel, A. D. (2016). *Top 10 global consumer trends for 2015*. Euromonitor International.

Kawamoto, C. T., & Spers, R. G. (2019). A Systematic Review of the Debate and the Researchers of Disruptive Innovation. *Journal of Technology Management & Innovation, 14*(1), 73–82. doi:10.4067/S0718-27242019000100073

Keller, A., & Hüsig, S. (2009). Ex ante identification of disruptive innovations in the software industry applied to web applications: The case of Microsoft's vs. Google's office applications. *Technological Forecasting and Social Change, 76*(8), 1044–1054. doi:10.1016/j.techfore.2009.03.005

Kemer, E. (2021). Eğitim Seviyesinin Endüstri 4. 0 Farkındalığına Etkisi: Konaklama İşletmelerinde Bir Uygulama. *Türk Turizm Araştırmaları Dergisi, 5*(2), 1138-1149.

Kennedy-Eden, H., & Gretzel, U. (2012). *A taxonomy of mobile applications in tourism. Research Online*. University of Wollongong. https://ro.uow.edu.au/commpapers/2510

Kessler, A., Pachucki, C., Stummer, K., Mair, M., & Binder, P. (2015). Types of organizational innovativeness and success in Austrian hotels. *International Journal of Contemporary Hospitality Management, 27*(7), 1707–1727. doi:10.1108/IJCHM-03-2014-0150

Khan, S. (2016). *Leadership in the digital age: A study on the effects of digitalisation on top management leadership*. Academic Press.

Khan, I., Garg, R. J., & Rahman, Z. (2015). Customer Service Experience in Hotel Operations: An Empirical Analysis. *Procedia: Social and Behavioral Sciences, 189*, 266–274. doi:10.1016/j.sbspro.2015.03.222

Khan, M., Hasan, M., & Clement, C. K. (2012). Barriers to the introduction of ICT into education in developing countries: The example of Bangladesh. *Online Submission, 5*(2), 61–80.

Kim, E., Lin, J., & Sung, Y. (2013). To App or Not to App: Engaging Consumers viaBranded Mobile Apps. *Journal of Interactive Advertising, 13*(1), 53-65. doi:10.1080/15252019.2013.782780

Kima, S. (2014). Mobile Technology: An Exploratory Study of Hotel Managers. *International Journal of Hospitality & Tourism Administration, 15*(4), 417–446. doi:10.1080/15256480.2014.961795

Kim, D. Y., Park, J., & Morrison, A. M. (2008). A model of traveller acceptance of mobile technology. *International Journal of Tourism Research, 10*(5), 393–407. doi:10.1002/jtr.669

Kim, D., & Kim, S. (2017). The role of mobile technology in tourism: Patents, articles, news, and mobile tour app reviews. *Sustainability (Switzerland), 9*(11), 2082. Advance online publication. doi:10.3390u9112082

Kim, M. J., Kim, W. G., Kim, J. M., & Kim, C. (2016). Does knowledge matter to seniors' usage of mobile devices? Focusing on motivation and attachment. *International Journal of Contemporary Hospitality Management, 28*(8), 1702–1727. doi:10.1108/IJCHM-01-2015-0031

Kim, W. G., & Lee, H. Y. (2005). Comparison of web service quality between online travel agencies and online travel suppliers. *Journal of Travel & Tourism Marketing, 17*(2-3), 105–116. doi:10.1300/J073v17n02_09

Kim, W. G., Ma, X., & Kim, D. J. (2006). Determinants of Chinese hotel customers' e-satisfaction and purchase intentions. *Tourism Management, 27*(5), 890–900. doi:10.1016/j.tourman.2005.05.010 PMID:32287716

Kirikkaleli, D., & Ozun, A. (2019, February). Innovation capacity, business sophistication and macroeconomic stability: Empirical evidence from OECD countries. *Journal of Business Economics and and Management, 252*(2), 351–367. doi:10.3846/jbem.2019.9602

Kırlar Can, B., Yeşilyurt, H., Lale Sancaktar, C., & Koçak, N. (2017). Mobil çağda mobil uygulamalar: Türkiye'deki yerli otel zincirleri üzerine bir durum tespiti. *Journal of Yasar University, 12*(45), 60–75.

Kırova, A. (2015). Critical and emerging discourses in multicultural education literature. In S. Guo & L. Wong (Eds.), *Revisiting Multiculturalism in Canada*. Transnational Migration and Education. SensePublishers. doi:10.1007/978-94-6300-208-0_15

Kivistö, J., Pekkola, E., & Lyytinen, A. (2017). The influence of performance-based management on teaching and research performance of Finnish senior academics. *Tertiary Education and Management, 23*(3), 260–275. doi:10.1080/13583883.2017.1328529

Korachi, Z., & Bounabat, B. (2020). *Towards a Frame of Reference for Smart City Strategy Development and Governance*. Academic Press.

Kotler, P. (2010). *Marketing for Hospitality and Tourism* (5th ed.). Pearson.

Kotler, P., & Keller, L. K. (2012). *Marketing Management (14th ed.)*. Pearson Education Limited.

Koutroumanis, D.A. (2011). Technology's Effect on Hotels and Restaurants: Building a Strategic Competitive Advantage. *Journal of Applied Business and Economics, 12*(1).

Kozak, M., & Rimmington, M. (2000). Tourist satisfaction with Mallorca, Spain, as an off-season holiday destination. *Journal of Travel Research*, *38*(3), 260–269. doi:10.1177/004728750003800308

Kuddus, K. (2013). Role of mass media and technology in fostering English language acquisition. *Proceedings of the UGC national seminar on English language acquisition development and environment*, 107-116.

Kumar, S., & Zahn, C. (2010). Mobile communications: Evolution and impact on business operations. *Technovation*, *23*(6), 515–520. doi:10.1016/S0166-4972(02)00120-7

Kursunluoglu, D. E. (2011). Customer Service Effects on Customer Satisfaction and Customer Loyalty: A Field Research in Shopping Centers in Izmir City – Turkey. *International Journal of Business and Social Science*, *2*(17).

Kwan, M. P. (2000). Interactive geovisualization of activity-travel patterns using three-dimensional geographical information systems: a methodological exploration with a large data set. *Transportation Research Part C: Emerging Technologies*, *8*(1 - 6), 185-203.

Kwon, J. M., Bae, J., & Blum, S. C. (2013). Mobile applications in the hospitality industry. *Journal of Hospitality and Tourism Technology*, *4*(1), 81–92. doi:10.1108/17579881311302365

Lamberton, C., & Stephen, T. A. (2016). A Thematic Exploration of Digital, Social Media,and Mobile Marketing: Research Evolution from 2000 to 2015 and an Agendafor Future Inquiry. *Journal of Marketing*, *80*(6), 146–172. doi:10.1509/jm.15.0415

Landman, P. (2013). *How hotels can use QR codes for marketing and customer service*. http://www.tnooz.com/article/how-hotels-can-use-qr-codes-for-marketing-and-customerservice/#sthash.JFxJa6wB.dpuf

Lankshear, C., & Knobel, M. (Eds.). (2008). *Digital literacies: Concepts, policies and practices* (Vol. 30). Peter Lang.

Larsson, Z. Y., Di Gangi, P. M., & Teigland, R. (2019). Sharing my way to success: A case study on developing entrepreneurial ventures using social capital in an OSS community. *Information and Organization*, *29*(1), 23–40. doi:10.1016/j.infoandorg.2018.12.001

Latham, G. P., Almost, J., Mann, S., & Moore, C. (2005). New developments in performance management. *Organizational Dynamics*, *34*(1), 77–87. doi:10.1016/j.orgdyn.2004.11.001

Law, R., Chan, I. C. C., & Wang, L. (2018). A comprehensive review of mobile technology use in hospitality and tourism. *Journal of Hospitality Marketing & Management*, *27*(6), 626–648. doi:10.1080/19368623.2018.1423251

Law, R., & Leung, R. (2000). A study of airline's online reservation service on the Internet. *Journal of Travel Research*, *39*(2), 202–211. doi:10.1177/004728750003900210

Law, R., Leung, R., & Buhalis, D. (2009). Information technology application in hospitality and tourism: A review of publication from 2005-2007. *Journal of Travel & Tourism Marketing*, *26*(5-6), 599–623. doi:10.1080/10548400903163160

Laxmi, K. C. (2016). *Role of E-Marketing in Rural Tourism: A Case Study of Travel Agency of Kathmandu District* (Thesis). Faculty of Humanities and Social Sciences Department of Rural Development, Tribhuvan University.

Lee, J., & Mills, J. E. (2007). Exploring Tourist Satisfaction with Mobile Technology. In *Information and Communication Technologies in Tourism 2007* (pp. 141–152). Springer Vienna. doi:10.1007/978-3-211-69566-1_14

Lemke, D.F. (2009). *What makes a great customer experience?* Available at: http://www.som.cranfield.ac.uk/som/dinamic-content/media/Yvonne/What%20makes%20a%20great%20customer%20experience%20with%20front%20.pdf

Lenzerini, F. (2011). Intangible cultural heritage: The living culture of peoples. *European Journal of International Law*, *22*(1), 101–120. doi:10.1093/ejil/chr006

Leung, L. (2015). Validity, reliability, and generalizability in qualitative research. *Journal of Family Medicine and Primary Care*, *4*(3), 324. doi:10.4103/2249-4863.161306 PMID:26288766

Lewis, T., Marginson, S., & Snyder, I. (2005). The network university? Technology, culture and organisational complexity in contemporary higher education. *Higher Education Quarterly*, *59*(1), 56–75. doi:10.1111/j.1468-2273.2005.00281.x

Lew, S., Tan, G. W. H., Loh, X. M., Hew, J. J., & Ooi, K. B. (2020). The disruptive mobile wallet in the hospitality industry: An extended mobile technology acceptance model. *Technology in Society*, *63*, 101430. Advance online publication. doi:10.1016/j.techsoc.2020.101430 PMID:33071395

Liang, T.-P., Huang, C.-W., Yeh, Y.-H., & Lin, B. (2007). Adoption of mobile technology in business: A fit-viability model. *Industrial Management & Data Systems*, *107*(8), 1154–1169. doi:10.1108/02635570710822796

Liew, C. L. (2005). Online cultural heritage exhibitions: A survey of information retrieval features. *Program*, *39*(1), 4–24. doi:10.1108/00330330510578778

Li, M., & Hsu, C. H. C. (2016). A review of employee innovative behavior in services. *International Journal of Contemporary Hospitality Management*, *28*(12), 2820–2841. doi:10.1108/IJCHM-04-2015-0214

Limani, Y., Hajrizi, E., Stapleton, L., & Retkoceri, M. (2019). Digital Transformation Readiness in Higher Education Institutions (HEI): The Case of Kosovo. *IFAC-PapersOnLine*, *52*(25), 52–57. doi:10.1016/j.ifacol.2019.12.445

Liu, A. (2006). Tourism in rural areas: Kedah, Malaysia. *Tourism Management*, *27*(5), 878–889. doi:10.1016/j.tourman.2005.05.007

Loureiro, S. M. C. (2014). The role of the rural tourism experience economy in place attachment and behavioral intentions. *International Journal of Hospitality Management*, *40*, 1–9. doi:10.1016/j.ijhm.2014.02.010

Lu, I. Y., & Tseng, C. J. (2010). A study of service innovation activities of tourist hotels in Taiwan. *The International Journal of Organizational Innovation*, *3*(1), 156–172.

Lumpkin, G. T., & Dess, G.G. (1996). Clarifying the Achievement Orientations Construct and Linking it to Performance. Academy of Management Review, (21), 135-172.

MacDonald, R., & Jolliffe, L. (2003). Cultural rural tourism: Evidence from Canada. *Annals of Tourism Research*, *30*(2), 307–322. doi:10.1016/S0160-7383(02)00061-0

Mahiny, S. A., & Clarke, K. C. (2012). Guiding SLEUTH land-use/land-cover change modeling using multicriteria evaluation: Towards dynamic sustainable land-use planning. *Environment and Planning. B, Planning & Design*, *39*(5), 925–944. doi:10.1068/b37092

Manaf, Z. A. (2007). The state of digitisation initiatives by cultural institutions in Malaysia: An exploratory survey. *Library Review*, *56*(1), 45–60. doi:10.1108/00242530710722014

Manaf, Z. A., & Ismail, A. (2010). Malaysian cultural heritage at risk?: A case study of digitisation projects. *Library Review*, *59*(2), 107–116. doi:10.1108/00242531011023862

Manyika, J., Lund, S., Bughin, J., Robinson, K., Mischke, J., & Mahajan, D. (2016). Independent work: Choice, necessity, and the gig economy. *McKinsey Global Institute*, *2016*, 1–16.

Markides, C. (2006). Disruptive innovation in need of better theory. *Journal of Product Innovation Management*, *23*(1), 19–25. doi:10.1111/j.1540-5885.2005.00177.x

Martin, F., & Ertzberger, J. (2013). Here and now mobile learning: An experimental study on the use of mobile technology. *Computers & Education*, *68*, 76–85. doi:10.1016/j.compedu.2013.04.021

Martin, G., & Reddington, M. (2010). Theorizing the links between e-HR and strategic HRM: A model, case illustration and reflections. *International Journal of Human Resource Management*, *21*(10), 1553–1574. doi:10.1080/09585192.2010.500483

Masoomeh, M., Tahayori, H., & Sadeghian, A. (2013). Drivers of customer satisfaction in online tourism-the case of uropean countries. *Middle East Journal of Scientific Research*, *13*(9), 1172–1179.

Matarasso, F. (2001). *Recognising Culture: A series of briefing papers on culture and development*. Canadian Heritage.

Matt, C., Hess, T., & Benlian, A. (2015). Digital transformation strategies. *Business & Information Systems Engineering*, *57*(5), 339–343. doi:10.100712599-015-0401-5

Matzler, K., Waiguny, M., Toschkov, A., & Mooradian, T. A. (2006). Usability, emotions, and customer satisfaction in online travel booking. In Information and Communication Technologies in Tourism (pp. 135-146). Springer-Wien. doi:10.1007/3-211-32710-X_21

Ma, X., Wang, R., Dai, M., & Ou, Y. (2021). The influence of culture on the sustainable livelihoods of households in rural tourism destinations. *Journal of Sustainable Tourism*, *29*(8), 1235–1252. doi:10.1080/09669582.2020.1826497

Mbaiwa, J. E. (2011). Changes on traditional livelihood activities and lifestyles caused by tourism development in the Okavango Delta, Botswana. In Tourism Management (Vol. 32, Issue 5, pp. 1050–1060). doi:10.1016/j.tourman.2010.09.002

McKinsey. (2016). *Gig Economy*. https://www.mckinsey.com/~/media/mckinsey/featured%20insights/employment%20and%20growth/independent%20work%20choice%20necessity%20and%20the%20gig%20economy/independent-work-choice-necessity-and-the-gig-economy-executive-summary.ashx

McNiff, J., & Whitehead, J. (2002). *Action research: Principles and practice* (2nd ed.). Routledge Falmer. doi:10.4324/9780203199961

Meiliana, I., Irmanti, D., Hidayat, M. R., Amalina, N. V., & Suryani, D. (2017). Mobile Smart Travelling Application for Indonesia Tourism. *Procedia Computer Science*, *116*, 556–563. doi:10.1016/j.procs.2017.10.059

Meira, J. V. S., Anjos, S. J. G. D., & Falaster, C. D. (2018). Innovation and performance in the hotel industry. *Journal of Quality Assurance in Hospitality & Tourism*, *20*(2), 185–205. doi:10.1080/1528008X.2018.1512936

Melhem, S. B., Zeffane, R., & Albaity, M. (2018). Determinants of employees' innovative behavior. *International Journal of Contemporary Hospitality Management*, *30*(3), 1601–1620. doi:10.1108/IJCHM-02-2017-0079

Merriam, S. B. (1998). *Qualitative research and case study applications in education*. Jossey-Bass Publishers.

Mesas-Carrascosa, F. J., de Castro, A. I., Torres-Sánchez, J., Triviño-Tarradas, P., Jiménez-Brenes, F. M., García-Ferrer, A., & López-Granados, F. (2020). Classification of 3D point clouds using color vegetation indices for precision viticulture and digitizing applications. *Remote Sensing*, *12*(2), 317. doi:10.3390/rs12020317

Mickaiel, I. (2011). *Mobile the new black for travel*. http://www.zdnet.com.au/mobile-the-new-black-for-travel-339321469.htm

Mills, J. E., & Morrison, A. M. (2004). Measuring customer satisfaction with online travel. In *Information and Communication Technologies in Tourism* (pp. 11–28). Springer-Wien.

Mintzberg, H. (1979). Patterns in strategy formation. *International Studies of Management & Organization*, *9*(3), 67–86. doi:10.1080/00208825.1979.11656272

Mitchell, C. J. A., & Shannon, M. (2018). Exploring cultural heritage tourism in rural Newfoundland through the lens of the evolutionary economic geographer. *Journal of Rural Studies*, *59*(May), 21–34. doi:10.1016/j.jrurstud.2017.12.020

Mitchenson, D. (2015). Safeguarding Intangible Cultural Heritage by Creating Meaningful Transmission Experiences. *International Journal of Heritage in the Digital Era*, *4*(1), 57–70. doi:10.1260/2047-4970.4.1.57

Mittal, V., & Frennea, C. (2010). *Customer Satisfaction: A Strategic Review and Guidelines for Managers*. Marketing Science Institute: MSI Fast Forward (10-701).

Mobasser & Muhammed. (2010). Higher Education in Bangladesh: Status, Issues and Prospects. Academic Press.

Mohammed, E. M., Wafik, G. M., Abdel Jalil, S. G., & El Hasan, Y. A. (2016). The Effects of E-Service Quality Dimensions on Tourist's Satisfaction. *International Journal of Hospitality and Tourism Systems*, (9), 1221.

Motiur. (2019). *Pulsed flow-through cultivation of Margaritifera: Effects of water source and food quantity on the survival and growth*. Academic Press.

Moyo, S. (2000). *Land reform under structural adjustment in Zimbabwe: land use change in the Mashonaland provinces*. Nordic Africa Institute.

Murname, R. J., & Willett, J. B. (2011). *Methods matter: Improving causal inference in educational and social science research*. Oxford University Press.

Murphy, L., Moscardo, G., & Benckendorff, P. (2007). Using brand personality to differentiate regional tourism destinations. *Journal of Travel Research*, *46*(1), 5–14. doi:10.1177/0047287507302371

Mussa, A., & Suryabhagavan, K. (2019). *Solid waste dumping site selection using GIS-based multi-criteria spatial modeling: a case study in Logia town, Afar region*. Geology, Ecology, and Landscapes.

Mutanov, G., Mamykova, Z., Kopnova, O., & Bolatkhan, M. (2020). Applied research of data management in the education system for decision-making on the example of Al-Farabi Kazakh National University. In *E3S Web of Conferences* (Vol. 159, p. 09003). EDP Sciences. doi:10.1051/e3sconf/202015909003

Möhlmann, M. (2015). Collaborative consumption: Determinants of satisfaction and the likelihood of using a sharing economy option again. *Journal of Consumer Behaviour*, *14*(3), 193–207. doi:10.1002/cb.1512

Nair, H., Staat, H. J., Tran, T., van Houselt, A., Prosperetti, A., Lohse, D., & Sun, C. (2014). The Leidenfrost temperature increase for impacting droplets on carbon-nanofiber surfaces. *Soft Matter*, *10*(13), 2102–2109. doi:10.1039/C3SM52326H PMID:24651906

Naveed, M. (2012). Customer Relationship Management In Hospitality. *Journal of Good Governance And Sustainable Development*, *1*(1), 40–47.

Neuhofer, B., Buhalis, D., & Ladkin, A. (2014). A typology of technology-enhanced tourism experiences. *International Journal of Tourism Research*, *16*(4), 340–350. doi:10.1002/jtr.1958

Nicolaides, A. (2020). Sustainable ethical tourism (SET) and rural community involvement. *African Journal of Hospitality, Tourism and Leisure*, *9*(1), 1–16.

Nielsen, R. (2010). Customer satisfaction: The customer experience through the customer's eyes. *Total Quality Management & Business Excellence*, *21*(11), 1229–1230. doi:10.1080/14783360903332361

Nizar, N. N. M., & Rahmat, M. K. (2018). Examining the Museum Visitors Use of Mobile Technology Through Technology Acceptance Model (TAM). *Journal of Tourism, Hospitality and Environment Management*, *3*(11). www.jthem.com

Nowak, J. (2006). *Public Access to Remotely Accessible Spatial Information. Geographic Information Systems Conference and Exhibition*. GIS Odyssey.

Nunes, M. D. O., & Mayer, M. (2014). Mobile technology, games and nature areas: The tourist perspective In. *Tourism & Management Studies*, *10*(1). https://pt.foursquare.com/

O'Connor, P. (2004). A Review of Research on Information Technology in the Hospitality Industry. *International Journal of Hospitality Management*, *23*(5).

OECD. (2016). *Energy and Air Pollution: World Energy Outlook Special Report 2016*. OECD.

Öğüt, A. (2007). Stratejik insan kaynakları yönetimi bağlamında örgütlerdeki işgören motivasyonu süreci. *Selçuk Üniversitesi İktisadi ve İdari Bilimler Üniversitesi Dergisi*, *12*, 1–14.

Oh, H., Fiore, A. M., & Jeoung, M. (2007). Measuring experience economy concepts: Tourism applications. *Journal of Travel Research*, *46*(2), 119–132. doi:10.1177/0047287507304039

Oliver, R. L. (1980). A cognitive model of the antecedents and consequences of satisfaction decisions. *JMR, Journal of Marketing Research*, *17*(4), 460–469. doi:10.1177/002224378001700405

Olsson, L. E., Friman, M., Lättman, K., & Fujii, S. (2020). Travel and life satisfaction - From Gen Z to the silent generation. *Journal of Transport and Health*, *18*(November). doi:10.1016/j.jth.2020.100894

Omid, G., Samereh, P., Thomas, B., & Bakhtiar, F. (2019). Mapping potential nature-based tourism areas by applying GIS-decision making systems in East Azerbaijan Province, Iran. *Journal of Ecotourism*, *18*(3), 1–23.

Online Otel Rezervasyon Platformu. (2021). https://webrazzi.com/2020/02/11/otelz-2019/

Oparanma, O. (2009). Strategies for Managing Hospitality in a Turbulent Environment: Nigerian Experience. *International Journal of Management and Innovation*, *1*(1), 24–37.

Osin, R. F., Purwaningsih, N. K., & Anggayana, I. W. A. (2021). The Model of Development Tourism Village Through the Involvement of Millennial Generation in Bali. *International Journal of Multicultural and Multireligious Understanding*, 300–306.

Oteros-Rozas, E., Martín-López, B., Fagerholm, N., Bieling, C., & Plieninger, T. (2018). Using social media photos to explore the relation between cultural ecosystem services and landscape features across five European sites. *Ecological Indicators*, *94*, 74–86. doi:10.1016/j.ecolind.2017.02.009

Ottenbacher, M. C. (2007). Innovation Management in the Hospitality Industry: Different Strategies for Achieving Success. *Journal of Hospitality & Tourism Research (Washington, D.C.)*, *31*(4), 431–454. doi:10.1177/1096348007302352

Papangelis, K., Chamberlain, A., & Liang, H.-N. (2016). New directions for preserving intangible cultural heritage through the use of mobile technologies. *Proceedings of the 18th International Conference on Human-Computer Interaction with Mobile Devices and Services Adjunct*, 964–967. 10.1145/2957265.2962643

Parasuraman, A., Zeithaml, V. A., & Malhotra, A. (2005). ES-QUAL: A multiple- item scale for assessing electronic service quality. *Journal of Service Research*, *7*(3), 213–233. doi:10.1177/1094670504271156

Patton, M. (2002). *Qualitative research and evaluation methods* (3rd ed.). Sage Publications.

Peòalba-Aguirrezabalaga, C., & Ritala, P. (2021). Putting marketing knowledge to use: Marketing-specific relational capital and product/service innovation performance. *Journal of Business*. https://www.emerald.com/insight/content/doi/10.1108/JBIM-07-2020-0369/full/html

Petronela, T. (2016). The Importance of the Intangible Cultural Heritage in the Economy. *Procedia Economics and Finance, 39*(November), 731–736. doi:10.1016/S2212-5671(16)30271-4

Peuquet, D. J., & Duan, N. (1995). An event-based spatiotemporal data model (ESTDM) for temporal analysis of geographical data. *International Journal of Geographical Information Systems*, *9*(1), 7–24. doi:10.1080/02693799508902022

Phiri, D., Simwanda, M., Salekin, S., Nyirenda, V. R., Murayama, Y., & Ranagalage, M. (2020). Sentinel-2 data for land cover/use mapping: A review. *Remote Sensing*, *12*(14), 2291. doi:10.3390/rs12142291

Piccoli, G., Anglada, L. D., & Watson, R. T. (2004). Using information technology to improve customer service: Evaluating the impact of strategic opportunities. *Journal of Quality Assurance in Hospitality & Tourism, 5*(1), 3–26.

Piccoli, G. (2008). Information technology in hotel management: A framework for evaluating the sustainability of IT-dependent competitive advantage. *Cornell Hospitality Quarterly*, *49*(3), 282–296. doi:10.1177/1938965508320722

Pierret, F. (2011). *About hotel classification systems*. Available at: https://ec.europa.eu/consumers/ecc/docs/hotel_establishment_classification_EU_en.pdf

Plaček, M., Nemec, J., Ochrana, F., Půček, M., Křápek, M., & Špaček, D. (2020). Do performance management schemes deliver results in the public sector? Observations from the Czech Republic. *Public Money & Management*, 1–10.

Pradhan, B., Lee, S., & Buchroithner, M. F. (2009). Use of geospatial data and fuzzy algebraic operators to landslide-hazard mapping. *Applied Geomatics*, *1*(1), 3–15. doi:10.100712518-009-0001-5

Prassl, J. (2018). *Humans as a service: The promise and perils of work in the gig economy*. Oxford University Press. doi:10.1093/oso/9780198797012.001.0001

Prebensen, N. K. (2004). *Tourist Satisfaction with a Destination: Antecedents and Consequences. Finmark College*. Department of Hospitality and Tourism.

Prebensen, N. K. (2007). Exploring tourists' images of a distant destination. *Tourism Management, 28*(3), 747–756. doi:10.1016/j.tourman.2006.05.005

Prohaska, S. S. (1995). Trends in cultural heritage tourism. In M. V. Conlin & T. Baum (Eds.), *Island tourism: management principles and practice* (pp. 33–52). Wiley.

Prompayuk, S., & Chairattananon, P. (2016). Preservation of Cultural Heritage Community: Cases of Thailand and Developed Countries. *Procedia: Social and Behavioral Sciences, 234*, 239–243. doi:10.1016/j.sbspro.2016.10.239

Pulakos, E. D. (2009). *Performance management: A new approach for driving business results*. John Wiley & Sons.

Purnomo, S., Rahayu, E. S., Riani, A. L., Suminah, S., & Udin, U. (2020). Empowerment model for sustainable tourism village in an emerging country. *Journal of Asian Finance. Economics and Business, 7*(2), 261–270. doi:10.13106/jafeb.2020.vol7.no2.261

Qian, C., Sasaki, N., Jourdain, D., Kim, S. M., & Shivakoti, P. G. (2017). Local livelihood under different governances of tourism development in China – A case study of Huangshan mountain area. *Tourism Management, 61*, 221–233. doi:10.1016/j.tourman.2017.01.006

Ramphal, R. (2014). Service and quality and quality service: Satisfying customers in the hospitality industry. *African Journal of Hospitality, Tourism and Leisure, 3*(2).

Randstad. (2016). https://www.randstadusa.com/about/news/randstad-us-study-projects-massive-shift-to-agile-employment-and-staffing-model-in-the-next-decade/sustainable deliveries

Reis, D. A., de Moura, F. R., & de Aragao Gomes, I. M. (2019, May). The Linkage between Intellectual Property and Innovation in the Global Innovation Ecosystem. In *European Conference on Intangibles and Intellectual Capital* (pp. 218-XIII). Academic Conferences International Limited.

Report, G. A. (2005). *Grameen Bank scholarship program*. Grameen Bank.

Richards, D. R., & Friess, D. A. (2015). A rapid indicator of cultural ecosystem service usage at a fine spatial scale: Content analysis of social media photographs. *Ecological Indicators, 53*, 187–195. doi:10.1016/j.ecolind.2015.01.034

Rimbau-Gilabert, E., & Ficapal-Cusı, P. (2008). The power of technology for learning. Academic Press.

Rimbau-Gilabert. (2014). Article. *E-learning in Economics and Business, 11*(2).

Río-Rama, M. C., Álvarez-García, J., & Coca-Pérez, J. L. (2017). Práticas de qualidade, responsabilidade social corporativa e o critério "resultados na sociedade" do modelo EFQM. *Revista Brasileira de Gestão de Negócios*, *19*(64), 307–328. doi:10.7819/rbgn.v0i0.3026

Roberts, L., & Hall, D. (Eds.). (2001). *Rural tourism and recreation: Principles to practice*. CABI. doi:10.1079/9780851995403.0000

Roche, S. (2016). Geographic information science II: Less space, more places in smart cities. *Progress in Human Geography*, *40*(4), 565–573. doi:10.1177/0309132515586296

Roque, M. I., & Forte, M. J. (2017). Digital Strategies to a Local Cultural Tourism Development: Project e-Carnide. *International Journal of Cultural and Digital Tourism*, *x*(x), 365–383. doi:10.1007/978-3-319-47732-9_24

Ruastiti, N. M., Sudirga, I. K., & Yudarta, I. G. (2020). Model of innovative wayang wong for millenial generation to meet 4.0 industrial revolution era in Bali. *Journal of Environmental Treatment Techniques*, *8*(3), 999–1004.

Ryu, K. (2011). The influence of the quality of physical environment, food, and service on restaurant image, customer satisfaction, and behavioral intentions. *International Journal of Contemporary Hospitality Management*, *24*(2), 200–223. doi:10.1108/09596111211206141

Saarbrücken. (2016). *Transition from Nonformal to Formal Education in Bangladesh: An Exploration of the Challenges Student Face*. LAMBERT Academic Publishing.

Sabuncu, B. (2014). KOBİ'lerde yenilik ve engellerinin tespitine yönelik bir araştırma: Denizli örneği. *İşletme Araştırmaları Dergisi, 6*(1), 103-112.

Salas-Velasco, M. (2018). Production efficiency measurement and its determinants across OECD countries: The role of business sophistication and innovation. *Economic Analysis and Policy*. https://www.sciencedirect.com/science/article/pii/S0313592616302417

Samsudin, P. Y., & Maliki, N. Z. (2015). Preserving Cultural Landscape in Homestay Programme Towards Sustainable Tourism: Brief Critical Review Concept. *Procedia: Social and Behavioral Sciences*, *170*, 433–441. doi:10.1016/j.sbspro.2015.01.004

Şanlıöz, K., Dilek, E., & Koçak, N. (2015). Değişen dünya, dönüşen pazarlama: Türkiye turizm sektöründen öncü bir mobil uygulama örneği. Anatolia. *Turizm Araştırmaları Dergisi*, *24*(2), 250–260.

Sarisakal, M. N., & Aydin, M. A. (2005). Mobile commerce. *Istanbul University -. Journal of Electrical and Electronics Engineering (Oradea)*, *5*(1), 1249–1254. doi:10.4018/jdm.2001070101

Saunders, M. (2007). *Research methods for business students* (4th ed.). London: Financial Times Prentice Hall.

Saunders. (2009). *Research Methods for Business Students*. Financial Times.

Schmidthuber, L., Maresch, D., & Ginner, M. (2020). Disruptive technologies and abundance in the service sector-toward a refined technology acceptance model. *Technological Forecasting and.* https://www.sciencedirect.com/science/article/pii/S0040162517308430

Schmookler, J. (1966). *Invention and economic growth.* Harvard University Press. doi:10.4159/harvard.9780674432833

Schroeder, A. N., Bricka, T. M., & Whitaker, J. H. (2021). Work design in a digitized gig economy. *Human Resource Management Review, 31*(1), 100692. Advance online publication. doi:10.1016/j.hrmr.2019.100692

Schumpeter, J. (1985). *A teoria do desenvolvimento econômico.* Nova Cultural.

Schumpeter, J. A. (1934). *The theory of economics development.* Oxford University Press.

Scott, N., Laws, E., & Boksberger, P. (2009). The marketing of hospitality and leisure experiences. *Journal of Hospitality Marketing & Management, 18*(2-3), 99–110. doi:10.1080/19368620802590126

Sekaran, U., & Bougie, R. (2010). *Research Methods for Business: A Skill Building Approach* (5th ed.). John Wiley and Sons.

Serçeoğlu, A. G. N. (2014). Yaratıcılık Ve Hizmet Odaklılık: Yiyecek İçecek İşletmelerinde Bir Uygulama. 9th Internatıonal Conference: New Perspectıves in Tourısm and Hospitality, 333-341.

Severo, M., & Venturini, T. (2016). Intangible cultural heritage webs: Comparing national networks with digital methods. *New Media & Society, 18*(8), 1616–1635. doi:10.1177/1461444814567981

Shaken, A., Mika, M., & Plokhikh, R. V. (2020). Exploring the social interest in agritourism among the urban population of Kazakhstan. *Miscellanea Geographica, 24*(1), 16–23. doi:10.2478/mgrsd-2019-0026

Sharma, G., & Baoku, L. (2013). Customer satisfaction in web 2.0 and information technology development. *Information Technology & People, 26*(4), 347–367. doi:10.1108/ITP-12-2012-0157

SHRM. (2019). *Managing employee performance.* Author.

Sigala, M. (2009). Geoportals and Geocollaborative Portals: Functionality and Impacts on Travellers' Trip Panning and Decision Making Processes. *International CHRIE Conference-Refereed Track, 28.*

Sigala, M. (2010). *The Role of Customers in Sustainable Supply Chain Management in Tourism.* Academic Press.

Sigala, M., & Marinidis, D. (2012). Web map services in tourism: A framework exploring the organisational transformations and implications on business operations and models. *International Journal of Business Information Systems, 9*(4), 415–434. doi:10.1504/IJBIS.2012.046293

Simonceska, D. L. (2012). The changes and innovation as a factor of competitiveness of thetourist offer (the case of Ohrid). *Procedia: Social and Behavioral Sciences*, *44*, 32–43. doi:10.1016/j.sbspro.2012.05.002

Sinclair, M., & Sinclair, C. (2009). Improving hotel efficiency through integration of service and project management cultures. *International Journal of Hospitality & Tourism Administration*, *10*(4), 344–360. doi:10.1080/15256480903337155

Singh, M., Mukherjee, S., & Mukherjee, M. (2021). Recent Development in Geospatial Platform and its significance in Tourism Planning. *ICIEM*, 40-45.

Singh, P. (2015). *Role of geographical information systems in tourism decision making process: a review.* Academic Press.

Sipe, L. J. (2016). How do senior managers influence experience innovation? Insights from a hospitality marketplace. *International Journal of Hospitality Management*, *54*(0), 75–83. doi:10.1016/j.ijhm.2016.01.009

Sirpa, T. (2008). Mobile technology in the village. *Journal of the Royal Anthropological Institute*, *14*(3), 515–534. doi:10.1111/j.1467-9655.2008.00515.x

Smith, B., Goods, C., Barratt, T., & Veen, A. (2021). Consumer 'appetite' for workers' rights in the Australian 'gig' economy. *Journal of Choice Modelling*, *38*, 100254. Advance online publication. doi:10.1016/j.jocm.2020.100254

Smith, W. K., & Tushman, M. L. (2005). Managing strategic contradictions: A top management model for managing innovation streams. *Organization Science*, *16*(5), 522–536. doi:10.1287/orsc.1050.0134

Soeroso, A., & Susilo, Y. S. (2014). Traditional Indonesian Gastronomy As a Cultural Tourism Attraction. *Journal of Applied Economics in Developing Countries*, *1*(1), 45–49.

Sohn, S. Y., Kim, D. H., & Jeon, S. Y. (2016). Re-evaluation of global innovation index based on a structural equation model. *Technology Analysis & Strategic*. https://www.tandfonline.com/doi/abs/10.1080/09537325.2015.1104412

Sohn, S. Y., Kim, D. H., & Yoon, J. H. (2016). Technology credit scoring model with fuzzy logistic regression. *Applied Soft Computing*, *43*, 150–158. doi:10.1016/j.asoc.2016.02.025

Solis, B. (2011). *Engage! The Complete Guide for Brands and Businesses to Build, Cultivate, and Measure Success in the New Web*. John Wiley & Sons.

Sparks, B. A., & Browning, V. (2010). Complaining in cyberspace: The motives and forms of hotel guests' complaints online. *Journal of Hospitality Marketing & Management*, *19*(7), 797–818. doi:10.1080/19368623.2010.508010

Steinbock, D. (2005). *The mobile revolution: The making of worldwide mobile markets*. Kogan Page Limited.

Su, M. M., Wall, G., & Xu, K. (2016). Heritage tourism and livelihood sustainability of a resettled rural community: Mount Sanqingshan World Heritage Site, China. *Journal of Sustainable Tourism*, *24*(5), 735–757. doi:10.1080/09669582.2015.1085868

Swaid, S. I., & Wigand, R. T. (2009). Measuring the quality of e-service: Scale development and initial validation. *Journal of Electronic Commerce Research*, *10*(1), 13–28.

Szymanski, D. M., & Hise, R. T. (2000). E- satisfaction: An initial examination. *Journal of Retailing*, *76*(3), 309–322. doi:10.1016/S0022-4359(00)00035-X

T.R. Ministry of Culture and Tourism. (2020). *Tourism statistics*. https://yigm.ktb.gov.tr/Eklenti/72701,turizmistatistikleri2020-1pdf.pdf?

Tabachnick, B. G., & Fidell, L. S. (2007). *Using multivariate statistics* (5th ed.). Allyn & Bacon/ Pearson Education.

Tait, M. G. (2005). *Implementing geoportals: Applications of distributed GIS*. Academic Press.

Tajeddini, K., & Trueman, M. (2008). Effect Of Customer Orientation And İnnovativeness On Business Performance: A Study Of Small-Sized Service Retailers. *International Journal of Entrepreneurship and Small Business*, *6*(2), 280–295. doi:10.1504/IJESB.2008.018633

Talpur, A., & Zhang, Y. (2018). A Study of Tourist Sequential Activity Pattern through Location Based Social Network (LBSN). *2018 International Conference on Orange Technologies (ICOT)*, 1-8. 10.1109/ICOT.2018.8705895

Tekic, Z., & Koroteev, D. (2019). From disruptively digital to proudly analog: A holistic typology of digital transformation strategies. *Business Horizons*, *62*(6), 683–693. doi:10.1016/j.bushor.2019.07.002

Tenerelli, P., Demšar, U., & Luque, S. (2016). Crowdsourcing indicators for cultural ecosystem services: A geographically weighted approach for mountain landscapes. *Ecological Indicators*, *64*, 237–248. doi:10.1016/j.ecolind.2015.12.042

Tether, B. S. (2005). Do service innovate (Differently)? Insights from the European innobarometer survey. *Industry and Innovation*, *12*(2), 153–184. doi:10.1080/13662710500087891

Thakkar, M. (2010). *Mobile-based technology for monitoring & evaluation*. Available at: https://www.theclearinitiative.org/mobile-based-tech.pdf

Tigu, G., Iorgulescu, M.-C., & Ravar, A. S. (2013). The impact of creativity and innovation in the hospitality industry on customers. *Journal of Tourism Challenges and Trends*, *6*(1), 9–34.

Timothy, D. J., & Tosun, C. (2003). Arguments for community participation in the tourism development process. *Journal of Tourism Studies*, *14*(2), 2–15.

Tourism and GIS: Mapping and Promoting Places. (2019, October). Retrieved June 14, 2021, from https://www.vmap.rocks/blog-detail/tourism-and-gis-mapping-and-promoting-places

Travelodge. (2011). *The UK budget hotel sector has grown by 35% during the recession*. Available at: http://www.melvingoldconsulting.com/2011%20Budget%20sector%20report%20press%20release.pdf

Trubnikov, D. (2017). Analysing the Impact of Regulation on Disruptive Innovations: The Case of Wireless Technology. *Journal of Industry, Competition and Trade*, *17*(4), 399–420. doi:10.100710842-016-0243-y

Turizmde Bu Sabah. (2021). https://www.tourismtoday.net/

Tussyadiah, I. P. (2015). Personal Technology and Tourism Experiences. In *ESCONTOUR 2015 Tourism Research Perspectives* (pp. 1-10). Academic Press.

Tussydiah, I., & Fesenmaier, D. (2007). *Interpreting Tourist Experiences from First-Person Stories: A Foundation for Mobile Guides*. https://aisel.aisnet.org/ecis2007http://aisel.aisnet.org/ecis2007/104

UNESCO. (2003). *Intangible Heritage - 2003 Convention*. https://ich.unesco.org/en/intangible-heritage-domains-00052

UNESCO. (2020). https //www.unesco.org.tr/Pages/125/122/UNESCO-D%C3%BCnya-Miras%C4%B1-List

UNESCO. (2021). *Reading in the mobile era: A study of mobile reading in developing countries*. https://unesdoc.unesco.org/images/0022/002274/227436e.pdf

Üstel, İ., & Kabatepe, E. (2006). *Kobiler ve inovasyon*. http://www.turkab.org/dokumanlar/yayinlar/kobilerveinovaasyon.pdf

Van Berkel, D. B., Tabrizian, P., Dorning, M. A., Smart, L., Newcomb, D., Mehaffey, M., Neale, A., & Meentemeyer, R. K. (2018). Quantifying the visual-sensory landscape qualities that contribute to cultural ecosystem services using social media and LiDAR. *Ecosystem Services*, *31*, 326–335. doi:10.1016/j.ecoser.2018.03.022 PMID:30148061

Vaz, A. S., Gonçalves, J. F., Pereira, P., Santarém, F., Vicente, J. R., & Honrado, J. P. (2019). Earth observation and social media: Evaluating the spatiotemporal contribution of non-native trees to cultural ecosystem services. *Remote Sensing of Environment*, *230*(April), 111193. doi:10.1016/j.rse.2019.05.012

Vaz, A. S., Moreno-Llorca, R. A., Gonçalves, J. F., Vicente, J. R., Méndez, P. F., Revilla, E., Santamaria, L., Bonet-García, F. J., Honrado, J. P., & Alcaraz-Segura, D. (2020). Digital conservation in biosphere reserves: Earth observations, social media, and nature's cultural contributions to people. *Conservation Letters*, *13*(3), 1–9. doi:10.1111/conl.12704

Venkatesh, V., Morris, M. G., Davis, G. B., & Davis, F. D. (2003). User acceptance of information technology: Toward a unified view. *Management Information Systems Quarterly*, *27*(3), 425–478. doi:10.2307/30036540

Verma, R., & Bashir, M. (2015). Business model innovation: Past, present and the future. *Indian Journal of Management, 9*(1), 8–20.

Viglia, G., Pera, R., & Bigné, E. (2018). The determinants of stakeholder engagement in digital platforms. *Journal of Business Research, 89*(C), 404–410. doi:10.1016/j.jbusres.2017.12.029

Viglia, G., Werthner, H., & Buhalis, D. (2016). Disruptive innovations. *Information Technology & Tourism, 16*(4), 327–329. doi:10.100740558-016-0072-1

Vijayadurai, J. (2008). Service Quality, Customer Satisfaction and Behavioural Intention in Hotel Industry. *Journal of Marketing Communications, 3*(3), 14–26.

Vrooman, J. C. (2009). *Rules of relief: Institutions of social security, and their impact.* Academic Press.

Wahid, A. N. M. (1999). The Grameen Bank and women in Bangladesh. *Challenge, 42*(5).

Wamba, S. F. (2008). Exploring the impact of RFID technology and the EPC network on mobile B2B eCommerce: A case study in the retail industry. *International Journal of Production Economics, 112*(2).

Wang, D., & Fesenmaier, D. R. (2016). *Mobile Technology, Everyday Experience and Travel.* https://scholarworks.umass.edu/ttra/2012/Oral/28

Wang, D., Xiang, Z., & Fesenmaier, D. R. (2014). Adapting to the mobile world: A model of smartphone use. *Annals of Tourism Research, 48*, 11–26. doi:10.1016/j.annals.2014.04.008

Wang, D., Xiang, Z., Law, R., & Pui Ki, T. (2016). Assessing hotel-related smartphone apps using online reviews. *Journal of Hospitality Marketing & Management, 25*(3), 291–313. doi:10.1080/19368623.2015.1012282

Wang, F., & Yuan, H. (2010). Challenges of the sensor web for disaster management. *International Journal of Digital Earth, 3*(3), 260–279. doi:10.1080/17538947.2010.484510

Wang, H. Y., & Wang, S. H. (2010). Predicting mobile hotel reservation adoption: Insight from a perceived value standpoint. *International Journal of Hospitality Management, 29*(4), 598–698. doi:10.1016/j.ijhm.2009.11.001

Wang, H., Feng, J., Zhang, H., & Li, X. (2020). The effect of digital transformation strategy on performance. *International Journal of Conflict Management, 31*(3), 441–462. doi:10.1108/IJCMA-09-2019-0166

Wang, X., Zhang, J., Gu, C., & Zhen, F. (2009). Examining antecedents and consequences of tourist satisfaction: A structural modeling approach. *Tsinghua Science and Technology, 14*(3), 397–406. doi:10.1016/S1007-0214(09)70057-4

Wang, Y. Q. (2014). MeteoInfo: GIS software for meteorological data visualization and analysis. *Meteorological Applications, 21*(2), 360–368. doi:10.1002/met.1345

Warnock, C. (2015). *How mobile technology impacts both guest experience and hotel operations.* Available at: http://www.hotel-industry.co.uk/2015/04/how-mobile-technology-impacts-both-guest-experience-and-hotel-operations/

Weber, N., Murphy, H., Schegg, R., & Murphy, J. (2005). An Investigation of Satisfaction and Loyalty in the Virtual Hospitality Environment. In A. Frew (Ed.), *Information and Communication Technologies in Tourism* (pp. 452–461). Springer Verlag.

Wijesekera, P., Baokar, A., Tsai, L., Reardon, J., Egelman, S., Wagner, D., & Beznosov, K. (2018). Dynamically regulating mobile application permissions. *IEEE Security and Privacy, 16*(1), 64–71. doi:10.1109/MSP.2018.1331031

Williams, W., & Elmore, R. F. (Eds.). (2014). *Social Program Implementation: Quantitative Studies in Social Relations.* Academic Press.

Wood, Graham, Lehdonvirta, & Hjorth. (2019). Good gig, bad gig: Autonomy and algorithmic control in the global gig economy. *Work, Employment and Society, 33*(1), 56–75. PMID:30886460

Wood, A. J., Graham, M., Lehdonvirta, V., & Hjorth, I. (2019). Good gig, bad gig: Autonomy and algorithmic control in the global gig economy. *Work, Employment and Society, 33*(1), 56–75. doi:10.1177/0950017018785616 PMID:30886460

Woodcock, J., & Graham, M. (2019). The gig economy: A critical introduction. *Polity.*

Wooldridge, J. M. (2016). *Introductory econometrics: A modern approach.* Nelson Education.

Yu, D., & Hang, C. C. (2009). A reflective review of disruptive innovation theory. *International Journal of Management Reviews, 12*(4), 435–452. doi:10.1111/j.1468-2370.2009.00272.x

Yu, H., & Hang, C. C. (2011). Creating technology candidates for disruptive innovation: Generally applicable R&D strategies. *Technovation, 31*(8), 401–410. doi:10.1016/j.technovation.2011.02.006

Zaitseva, N. A. (2013). *Management in service industry: tourism and hospitality.* Academia Publishing House.

Zehrer, A., Muskat, B., & Muskat, M. (2015). Enablers of corporate innovation in tourism. In H. Pechlaner & E. Innerhofer (Eds.), *Competence-based innovation in hospitality and tourism.* Gower Publishing.

Zeithaml, V. A., Parasuraman, A., & Malhotra, A. (2002). Service quality delivery through web sites: A critical review of extent knowledge. *Journal of the Academy of Marketing Science, 30*(4), 362–375. doi:10.1177/009207002236911

Zerenler, & Türker, & Kahin. (2007). Küresel teknoloji, araştırma geliştirme (Ar-Ge) ve yenilik ilişkisi. *Selçuk Üniversitesi Sosyal Bilimler Enstitüsü Dergisi, 17*, 653–667.

Zervas. (2017). Formal and informal education during the rise of Greek nationalism. Academic Press.

Zhang, L., Zhang, C., & Shi, M. (2020). Applying Mobile Technology for Developing Cultural and Creative Products in Tourism: A Case Study on the Forbidden City. *Proceedings - Companion of the 2020 IEEE 20th International Conference on Software Quality, Reliability, and Security, QRS-C 2020*, 542–549. 10.1109/QRS-C51114.2020.00095

Zhang, Y., Han, M., & Chen, W. (2018). The strategy of digital scenic area planning from the perspective of intangible cultural heritage protection. *Eurasip Journal on Image and Video Processing, 2018*(1). doi:10.1186/s13640-018-0366-7

Zhou, K. Z., & Li, C. B. (2012). How knowledge affects radical innovation: Knowledge base, market knowledge acquisition, and internal knowledge sharing. *Strategic Management Journal*. Retrieved from https://onlinelibrary.wiley.com/doi/abs/10.1002/smj.1959

Zhou, K. Z., Yim, C. K. B., & Tse, D. K. (2005). The Effects of Strategic Orientations on Technology- and Market-Based Breakthrough Innovations. *Journal of Marketing*, *69*(2), 42–60. doi:10.1509/jmkg.69.2.42.60756

Zulmira, M., Amorim, B., & Cunha, N. (2020). *Digital marketing impact on tourism in Portugal: a quantitative study*. https://www.researchgate.net/publication/338655966

About the Contributors

Shruti Ashok is an academician, researcher & finance professional with a Ph.D. in Finance from (FMS) Faculty of Management Studies, Delhi University and B. Com (Hons) From SRCC, Delhi University, with over 14 years of experience across academia and corporate. Skilled in equity valuation, corporate finance, financial statement analysis and Portfolio management. Currently working with Bennett University as an Assistant Professor in Finance. Also held visiting faculty engagements with Bombay Stock Exchange and NMIMS, Mumbai. Industry engagements include working in banks like HSBC Dubai, Citibank, HDFC Bank and State Bank of India over a 3 year period, spanning various domains like relationship banking, wealth management (both front end and backend) and operations. Has published research papers in ABDC listed journals, Scopus indexed journals, national and international refereed journals and presented research work at conferences organised by IITs, IIMs and FMS in the area of reverse mortgage, capital markets and corporate Finance. Research areas of interest including banking, corporate finance, distress prediction, corporate restructuring, and financial analysis. Look forward to collaborating and publishing with academicians in these areas.

Priya Chaturvedi, with about 2+ years of teaching experience, is a Senior Research Fellow working on Intangible Cultural Heritage. She has written a chapter for an edited book and has presented ideas at various national and international conferences. She has also contributed manuscripts on various terms in the upcoming Encyclopedia of Tourism Management and Marketing. She has taught various tourism-related subjects in bachelor and master programmes.

Rajdeep Deb is currently working as an Assistant Professor at the Department of Tourism & Hospitality Management, Mizoram University. He has a teaching experience of around 13 years and also published articles and research papers in journals.

S. K. Gupta, PhD, a Professor in Tourism in Centre for Mountain Tourism and Hospitality Studies, HNB Garhwal University (A Central University), Srinagar Garhwal, Uttarakhand, India, is committed in imparting knowledge through research and innovation in the field of Tourism and Hospitality since last 27 years. His expertise in areas of tourism planning, Travel Trade, Community based Tourism promotion and technological innovation in tourism and hospitality industry are widely acclaimed. He is currently holding the responsibility of Director, Centre for Mountain Tourism and Hospitality Studies, Dean, School of Management, and Director, Career Counseling and Placement Cell, HNB Garhwal University. He is also the Coordinator, European Union Erasmus+ programme for Inter-institutional collaboration between Dimitrie Cantemir University, Romania and HNBG University. He is the member of different academic bodies and expert committee of different universities. He has completed many national research projects to deal with regional issues of tourism promotion. Prof. Gupta has delivered guest lecturer in many international and national universities. He has published Eight books both as author and editor, several research papers in national and international journals and edited books and has also prepared study materials for distance learning programs of various universities and MOOCs. He has guided fourteen doctoral research scholars to his credit. He has participated in a number of national and international conferences in India and abroad and has organized several national and international conferences. He is Editor of "Journal of Tourism" (JoT), an international journal and Associate Editor of, "Ecoforum Journal" and "Revista de Turism- Studi si Cercetari in turism", International Journals, from Romania and member of Editorial Board of European Journal of Management Issues. He was President, Northern Region of Indian Tourism and Hospitality Congress in the year 2013-2014 and currently member of National Executive of Indian Tourism and Hospitality Congress and also member of RSA,United Kingdom.

Ebru Kemer graduated from Akdeniz University School of Tourism Management, Department of Hospitality Management (2010). She received his master's degree from Niğde University Production Management and Marketing branch (2013) and her Ph.D. degree from Nevşehir Hacı Bektaş Veli University Tourism Management (2017). Her main fields of work are Tourism and Gastronomy.

Mugdha Kulkarni is M. Com MBA(finance) and PhD in Accounting. Her Expertise lies in Financial Analysis, Financial Modelling. She has published in the area of block chain technology and TOE, TAM, Fintech, stock market analysis.

Pankaj Kumar is presently working as an Assistant Professor at the Department of Tourism & Hospitality Management, Mizoram University. He has a teaching experience of around 8 years and also published articles and research papers in journals and edited books.

Sudipta Mukherjee is a faculty of Jamia Millia Islamia, Delhi and visiting lecturer of IIHS. With more than 20 years of experience in the field of aviation, tourism and hospitality, he served Airline as GM, and other premiere tourism organizations like Malaysian Airlines, SOTC, American Express etc. As an educationalist, he has served Amity University and Lovely Professional University as HOD. He is an enthusiastic entrepreneur who is currently positioned as CEO of HAATS, Holidayers Academy of Aviation and Tourism Studies, Delhi and Director of Sofine Holidays and Events Pvt Ltd (B2B), and Wahtrip, logistics management & DMC of Goa. He also owns another company named Geomaticx Scientific Technology Services Pvt. Ltd which deals with GIS and remote sensing. In the research line, he has published more than ten articles in reputed national and internal journals. Contributing to the academics, two books have been authored by him, and few more book chapters have been published in different edited books. Recently he has contributed to 2 edited books on tourism and hospitality that have been endorsed by The Tourism Minister of India. He is a doctorate in Tourism Management from the University of Burdwan.

Aditya Ranjan is a Senior Research Fellow, a scholarship awarded by the University Grants Commission, and pursuing a Ph.D. in the Department of Tourism and Hospitality Management, Jamia Millia Islamia. He has a research interest in Rurality, Rural Tourism, Destination marketing. He has published research papers and has presented ideas at various national and international conferences. He has edited a book titled "Rurality, Ruralism and Rural tourism: Challenges and Coping Strategies" and has written chapters for different edited books. He has also contributed manuscripts on various terms in the upcoming Encyclopedia of Tourism Management and Marketing. His advisory work involves helping students, researchers, and stakeholders answer difficult tourism questions, specifically rural tourism. Previously, he taught various tourism-related courses as Assistant Professor at the University Institute of Tourism and Hospitality Management, Chandigarh University.

Ricardo Gouveia Rodrigues is an Assistant Professor at the University of Beira Interior, Portugal. He holds a PhD in Business and completed the European Doctoral Programme in Entrepreneurship and Small Business in the University Autònoma de Barcelona, Spain, and Växjö University (now Linnæus University), Sweden. He is currently a researcher and the director of NECE-UBI – Research Centre for Business Sciences. His main research interests are Entrepreneurial Marketing, Entrepreneurial Intention, Entrepreneurship Education, and Social Marketing. Still, he is also interested in studying the impact of marketing efforts on topics such as physical activity and children and teen behaviour. He has published more than 80 papers in international journals and chapters in international books. He has participated in several national research projects, namely implementing a pilot programme of Entrepreneurship

Education in secondary schools and its impact assessment. He has coordinated an international research project on the impact of Entrepreneurship Education. He is the director of the Doctoral Programme in Marketing and Strategy. The Doctoral Programme is jointly held by the Universities of Minho, Aveiro and Beira Interior, and is associated with NECE - Research Centre for Business Sciences, graded with Very Good by the FCT; NIPE - Research Centre in Economic and Business Policies, graded with Very Good by the FCT; and GOVCOPP - Research Unit on Governance, Competitiveness and Public Policies, graded with Very Good by the FCT.

Nidhi Sinha has more than 16 years of rich experience in teaching, research, and training. She is Assistant Professor of Marketing and Communication in School of Management at Bennett University. She specializes in the areas of Brand Management, Marketing communication, Internet and Digital Marketing and Social media marketing. Her current research focuses on branding in the digital domains, use of online and social media in today's world of marketing. As an educator she aims to inspire, empower, and encourage students to produce authentic, innovative and socially conscious research outcomes in the domain of marketing. To her credit she has several research papers in the various refereed International and National Journals and has presented research papers at diverse National and International forums. She has also been awarded with diverse prestigious Best Paper awards for her work. Prior to joining Bennett University, she has worked for 11 years with Jaypee Institute of Information Technology, Noida and also with Corporates like Educomp Solutions, BPCL and Subsidiaries of Mahindra Group at managerial levels.

Index

H

I

K

M

O

P

R

S

T

U

V

W

www.ingramcontent.com/pod-product-compliance
Lightning Source LLC
LaVergne TN
LVHW061540290926
849162LV00004B/855